FASHION

FROM CONCEPT TO CONSUMER

FASHION

FROM CONCEPT TO CONSUMER

Ninth Edition

Gini Stephens Frings

UPPER SADDLE RIVER, NEW JERSEY
COLUMBUS, OHIO

Library of Congress Cataloging-in-Publication Data

Frings, Gini Stephens.
  Fashion : from concept to consumer / Gini Stephens Frings. — 9th ed.
     p. cm.
  ISBN 0-13-159033-2
  1. Fashion. 2. Clothing trade. 3. Fashion merchandising. I. Title.
  TT518.F74 2008
  687—dc22   2007014923

Editor in Chief: Vernon R. Anthony

Acquisitions Editor: Jill Jones-Renger

Production Editors: Janice Stangel, Alexandrina Benedicto Wolf

Production Coordination: Linda Zuk, WordCraft, LLC

Design Coordinator: Miguel Ortiz

Cover Designer: Wanda España, Wee Design Group

Cover Images (left to right): 1. Courtesy of Andrew Gn, Paris; 2. and 3. Courtesy of Badgley Mischka, New York, photos by Dan Lecca; 4. Courtesy of Oscar de la Renta, New York, photo by Dan Lecca; 5. Courtesy of Giorgio Armani Spa; 6. Courtesy of Giorgio Armani Spa, Milan, Italy; 7. Courtesy of Prada, Milan; 8. Courtesy of Elie Saab and Denta & Christina

Production Manager: Patricia A. Tonneman

Director of Marketing: David Gesell

Marketing Manager: Jimmy Stephens

Marketing Coordinator: Alicia Dysert

This book was set in Giovanni Book by Carlisle Publishers Services. It was printed and bound by R.R. Donnelley & Sons Company. The cover was printed by Phoenix Color Corp.

Pearson Prentice Hall™ is a trademark of Pearson Education, Inc.
Pearson® is a registered trademark of Pearson plc
Prentice Hall® is a registered trademark of Pearson Education, Inc.

Pearson Education Ltd.   Pearson Education Australia Pty. Limited
Pearson Education Singapore Pte. Ltd.   Pearson Education North Asia Ltd.
Pearson Education Canada, Ltd.   Pearson Educación de Mexico, S.A. de C.V.
Pearson Education—Japan   Pearson Education Malaysia Pte. Ltd.

10 9 8 7 6 5 4 3 2 1

ISBN-13: 978-0-13-159033-5

ISBN-10:   0-13-159033-2

Contents

2 | Consumer Demand and Fashion Marketing — **39**

■ PART TWO
The Raw Materials of Fashion

■ PART THREE
Fashion Manufacturing and Marketing

8 | International Fashion 183

9 | Product and Design Development — 213

12 | Wholesale Marketing and Distribution   311

■ PART FOUR
Fashion Retailing

13 | Retailing 351

Preface

The purpose of this book is to tell the entire story of how the fashion business works, in sequential order from concept to consumer. The fashion business is a series of buying supplies, creating and developing a new product, and marketing the product. The fashion business includes all the processes involved with producing raw materials, apparel, and accessories, as well as the retail stores that sell fashion merchandise to the public. It is important for executives in the fashion industry to understand how all of these processes interrelate.

Fashion designers and merchandisers work with textile producers to develop fabrics that they need for their apparel and accessories. Manufacturers must know how to create garments and accessories that sell on the retail level. Retail fashion buyers should understand how garments and accessories are designed so that they can be creative merchandisers and make wise buying decisions. They may also have to develop products and source production themselves for private-label merchandise. The entire marketing chain has become interconnected.

PART ONE concentrates on fashion fundamentals: information needed by everyone in the fashion business. Chapter 1 traces the development of fashion and the fashion industry as a background to understanding today's business. Chapter 2 shows how consumer demand affects fashion marketing. Chapter 3 explains fashion change and consumer acceptance. Chapter 4 covers market research, fashion analysis, and design resources.

PART TWO covers the development, production, and marketing of raw materials, including textiles, trimmings, leather, and fur—the supplies needed for fashion manufacturing.

PART THREE discusses international fashion centers and traces the fashion manufacturing process from design and merchandising development through production and marketing to retailers.

PART FOUR covers retailing: types of retail organizations, merchandising (the buying and selling process), and marketing.

Each chapter contains a career focus, chapter objectives, review questions, terminology, and projects to aid in understanding the subject matter. The appendix contains information on career guidelines, and the book ends with a glossary of fashion terminology.

Just as the fashion industry has changed dramatically over the last 20 years, each edition of *Fashion: From Concept to Consumer* changes with it. As the industry has become more marketing oriented, so has this book. As the industry has seen a tremendous growth in men's wear and accessories, this book has much more information on both. As computer technology has changed how fashion is produced and distributed, the book describes applications in every area. As production has moved offshore, this book has introduced new information on global sourcing. *Fashion* explains the changes in relationships between levels of the industry: how some textile companies are producing full-garment packages, and how manufacturers have become retailers and retailers have become manufacturers. *Fashion: From Concept to Consumer* describes how these major changes have affected every aspect of the fashion business.

This book tells the complete story of the fashion business and is a valuable tool for any introductory course in fashion: Introduction to Fashion Design, Introduction to the Fashion Industry or Manufacturing, Introduction to Fashion Merchandising or Retailing, or Introduction to the Fashion Business. There is also important information on trend research; textile marketing; apparel manufacturing; accessory design, production and marketing; and advertising and promotion. This is a text for specialists as well as those who are taking only a single course in fashion. In fact, it will interest anyone who wants to know more about fashion and the fashion business.

Acknowledgments

I wish to thank the many friends and business associates who took time to answer questions, make suggestions, and donate photographs during the revision of this book. I am particularly indebted to the following persons and companies:

- Giorgio Armani, Prada, Dior, Louis Vuitton, Lanvin, Elie Saab, Pucci, Andrew Gn, and Jonathan Saunders.

- Vera Wang, Ralph Lauren, Oscar de la Renta, Ralph Rucci, Badgley Mischka, Carmen Marc Valvo, Tuleh, and Jessica McClintock.

- Bergdorf Goodman, Neiman Marcus, Harvey Nichols, Fenwick of London, Huntsman of Savile Row, Prêt-à-Porter Paris, Council of Fashion Designers of America and Dan Lecca, Fur Fashion Council of Canada, and the Dallas Mart.

To the reviewers, who provided helpful suggestions and comments, I offer my heartfelt thanks: Gregory Arend, Nassau Community College and Fashion Institute of Technology; Cherie Bodenstab, Fashion Institute of Design and Merchandising; Andrew Burnstine, American Intercontinental University; Barbara Dyer, University of North Carolina, Greensboro; Janet Gregg, Fullerton College; Chelsey Jackson, International Academy of Design and Technology, Chicago; David I. Netherton, Old Dominion University; Zoya Nudelman; Sally Shapiro, Laboratory Institute of Merchandising; Patricia T. Stealey, Shepherd University; and Nelly Tejeda, Keiser College.

Most of all, I offer my love and thanks to my husband Philipp for his support.

FASHION

FROM CONCEPT TO CONSUMER

A CASCADE OF PINK CHIFFON RUFFLES BY ANDREW GN *(COURTESY OF ANDREW GN, PARIS)*

PART ONE

The Fundamentals of Fashion

Part I provides students with the fundamental knowledge that they need to understand the workings of the fashion industry. Reading these chapters before reading any other parts of the book is essential.

- **CHAPTER 1** traces the *development* of fashion and the fashion industry as a background to understanding changes in the industry today.

- **CHAPTER 2** concerns the importance of the *consumer* and the essentials of *fashion marketing*, which are the very basis of the fashion business.

- **CHAPTER 3** explains the principles of *fashion change* and theories of consumer acceptance.

- **CHAPTER 4** covers the market and design *research* necessary for product development.

OSCAR DE LA RENTA INTERPRETS NINETEENTH-
CENTURY FASHION WITH A NEW TWIST, A BLUE SILK
GOWN THAT IS SHORT IN THE FRONT TO REVEAL
MATCHING LEGGINGS! *(COURTESY OF
OSCAR DE LA RENTA, PHOTO BY DAN LECCA)*

FASHION DEVELOPMENT

1

Career Focus

Fashion executives at every level of the industry need to understand how the fashion business developed as a basis for their education. Lessons in history help them to make decisions for today and for the future. It is also interesting to see how ideas from the past are often reinterpreted for today's fashion.

To preserve this information for us, some fashion professionals work as costume curators for museums or in the archives department of a fashion company.

CHAPTER OBJECTIVES

After reading this chapter, you should be able to:

1. List the major changes in American lifestyles since the Industrial Revolution and how they have influenced fashion
2. Explain how fashion has reflected the social, cultural, political, economic, and technological changes since the Industrial Revolution
3. Outline and discuss major changes in the fashion industry
4. Name the major designers of the past 100 years

More than just a designer's whim, fashion is a reflection of the social, political, economic, and artistic forces of any given time. The changing styles that evolve from these forces tell of historical events as poignantly as textbooks, journals, or periodicals. Dressing room mirrors throughout the ages have reflected the trends in how people think, live, and love.

We will examine some of the major influences on fashion in history as a background to understanding contemporary fashion and anticipating future change. Chapter 1 traces the development of the fashion industry in Europe and America from the seventeenth century to the present, emphasizing the last 100 years. It briefly discusses how fashion innovators, together with society, technology, economics, and politics, change fashion.

Fashion, as we known it, is relatively new. In ancient and medieval times, clothing styles remained practically unchanged for a century at a time. Fashion change began to accelerate during the Renaissance, as Western civilization discovered different cultures, customs, and costumes. As new fabrics and ideas became available, people craved more new things. The pace of fashion change has continued to increase.

France, the Center of Fashion

France's dominance over international fashion began in the early eighteenth century.

Fashion Dictated by Royalty

Until the Industrial Revolution, people belonged to one of two main classes: the wealthy landowners or the poor laborers and farmers.

Because wealth was concentrated in the landowning class, these people were the only ones who could afford to wear fashionable clothes. Royalty, at the top of both the social and economic ladders, set fashion trends, whereas other members of the aristocracy followed their example to gain approval.

At the turn of the eighteenth century, members of King Louis XIV's court became the arbiters of taste, making Paris the fashion capital of Europe. The textile industry grew in Lyon and other

French cities, supplying the court with silk fabrics, ribbons, and laces. Dressmakers and tailors, sponsored by the wealthy, developed their skills to a high level using these beautiful materials.

Hand Sewing by Dressmakers and Tailors

The elaborate detail and intricate tailoring and dressmaking at that time required an enormous amount of painstaking hand labor. All clothes were not only handmade but also *custom made*. Each garment was made to fit the customer's exact measurements. Dresses and suits were individually sewn by dressmakers or tailors to their employers' specifications. The identities of personal dressmakers were secrets guarded by the wealthy. No one wanted to share the talents of clever dressmakers for fear of losing them. Rose Bertin (Ber-tan'), dressmaker to Queen Marie Antoinette, was known only because she was made the official court minister of fashion.

Poor people wore cast-off clothing from the rich or made their own clothing. The very elaborate peasant clothing for special occasions was passed from one generation to another and became the traditional *folk costume*, different in every region. The contrast between the plight of the poor and the extravagancies of the court during the eighteenth century was one cause of the French Revolution, which began in 1789. In response to a general revulsion against excess, fashion changed from elaborately decorated costumes to simpler garments.

Growth of the Couture

France became the center of fashion because of the patronage of the royal court and the development of the silk industry there. In France, the art of dressmaking was known as *couture* (koo-tour'). A male designer was a *couturier* (koo-tu-ree-ay'); his female counterpart was a *couturière* (koo-tu-ree-air').

Charles Worth is considered the father of the couture because he was the first successful independent designer. Born in England, he came to Paris at age 20 in 1846 (the same year that Elias Howe

■ WORTH GOWN TYPICAL OF THE SECOND EMPIRE PERIOD IN FRANCE, 1852–1860. *(COURTESY OF THE UNION FRANÇAISE DES ARTS DU COSTUME)*

patented his sewing machine). Worth attracted prominent women as clients, culminating in Empress Eugénie, wife of Emperor Napoleon III.

Some couturiers became business forces as well as creative ones, directing salons staffed with seamstresses and tailors. Other couture houses followed Worth, including Paquin, Cheruit, Doucet, Redfern, the Callot sisters, and Jeanne Lanvin. The couture became a bridge between the class-structured fashion of the past and the democratized fashion of today.

From these beginnings, an international market for Parisian high fashion grew. In 1868, the couturiers of Paris formed a trade association. Other European capitals followed the leadership of Paris; Vienna became the next in importance. Couturiers were the major influence on fashion design for more than 100 years, setting style trends for all of Europe, as well as the rest of the Western world.

Fashion dolls, dressed in miniature versions of couture gowns, were sent from France as a convenient means of publicizing fashion. Orders from wealthy women were mailed back to Paris, where the gowns were made to fit the customers' requirements. Some of these dolls made their way to the United States. Most people could not afford couture clothes but managed to copy them to some degree.

Effects of the Industrial Revolution on Fashion

The Industrial Revolution marked the beginning of technological advances in textile and apparel production.

Growth of the Textile Industry

Colonial America had virtually no textile or fashion industry. Most materials were imported from abroad: silks from Italy, France, India, and China; and woolens, calicoes, and cashmeres from Britain.

The modern textile industry, which enabled more fabrics to be produced in less time, began in England with John Kay's development of the flying shuttle in 1733, James Hargreaves' invention of the spinning jenny in 1764, Richard Arkwright's water frame in 1769, and Edmund Cartwright's power loom in 1785. To protect its industry, England passed strict laws preventing textile machines, parts, blueprints, tools, and even the mechanics and inventors themselves from leaving the country. However, Samuel Slater memorized every detail of Arkwright's water frame and other machinery and secretly left England. Within two years of his arrival in New England, he had a new mill built and in operation. Textile mills began to produce cloth in America, and New England became America's first textile center.

In 1814, Francis Cabot Lowell of Boston developed the power loom. His factory was the first to have a vertical operation: complete textile production from raw cotton fiber to finished cloth by one company. By 1847, more Americans worked in textiles than in any other industry.

After the Civil War, the American textile industry began to relocate to the South, the source of cotton. Southern states provided other incentives, such as cheaper labor. Eventually, the South became the center of textile production in the United States.

Growth of the Middle Class

Great economic, social, and fashion changes throughout the Western world accompanied the Industrial Revolution in the late eighteenth century. Burgeoning trade and industry in turn created a middle class with money to spend on the luxuries of life, including better clothing. Money gave the new middle class power, not only in business and society, but also to influence fashion trends. Fashion became a status symbol, a visual means to show off wealth.

Establishment of the Business Suit

Until 1800, men's and women's fashions had equal amounts of decoration. In Louis XIV's time, men's dress was at least as elaborate as women's. As the middle class grew, businessmen wanted to establish an image of respectability and dependability. At that point, "men's garb descended from brilliant finery . . . into bleak conformity." Men adopted the conservative, dignified business suit with long trousers, jacket, vest, shirt, and necktie—"a permanent noose, you might say."[1] Men's business attire remained basically conservative with very few changes.

Men's clothing was also custom made. The finest tailor shops—such as Henry Poole and Company, established in 1843—were on Savile Row in London, which became the international center of men's fashion.

Some ready-made men's clothing was made by hand in France in the late 1700s. In America, some enterprising tailors made the first ready-to-wear suits for sailors so that they would have clothes to wear when they came on land. At first, tailors cut the fabrics, bundled the pieces, and sent them out to homes to be sewn by hand, known as the *cottage industry process*. The tailors also became retailers, with factory shops located in seaport cities, such as New Bedford, Boston, New York, and Philadelphia.

In 1818 in New York, Henry Brooks started the men's clothier business that became Brooks Brothers. Because of his determination to make and deal only in merchandise of the best quality, Brooks helped to advance ready-made clothing. There, Abraham Lincoln bought an overcoat for his second inauguration.[2]

Mass Production of Clothing

THE FIRST SINGER SEWING MACHINE, 1851. *(COURTESY OF THE SINGER COMPANY)*

The mass production of clothing led to accessible fashion for everyone.

Invention of the Sewing Machine

The democratization of fashion began with the invention of the sewing machine, which turned a handicraft into an industry. The sewing machine made the mass production of clothing possible. In 1829, a French tailor named Thimmonier patented a wooden chain-stitch sewing machine, but all existing models were destroyed by rioting tailors who feared for their jobs. Walter Hunt, an American, developed a sewing machine in 1832 but failed to patent it. Thus, the man who is usually credited with its invention is Elias Howe, who patented his in 1846. All of Howe's machines were run by hand.

In 1859, Isaac Singer, whose name has become a household word because of his mass production of the sewing machine, developed the foot treadle, an improvement that left the hands free to guide the fabric, and mass-produced these machines. Singer spent $1 million a year on sales promotion and, by 1867, was producing a thousand machines per day (electrically powered models were not available until 1921).[3] To save time and to keep control over production, entrepreneurs brought workers and machinery together in factories. This caused many people in search of work to move to the cities where the factories were located.

EMPLOYEES OUTSIDE THE LEVI STRAUSS COMPANY HEADQUARTERS IN SAN FRANCISCO ABOUT 1873. *(COURTESY OF LEVI STRAUSS & COMPANY)*

In 1853, after the Gold Rush attracted thousands of men to California in search of gold, a 20-year-old Bavarian immigrant by the name of Levi Strauss opened a dry goods store in San Francisco. In 1873, he began to manufacture long-wearing pants with riveted pockets, using a tough cotton fabric called *serge de Nimes* (loomed in Nimes, France), later shortened to *denim*. They are an item of wearing apparel that has remained basically the same for nearly 150 years!

Another early use for sewing machines was to make Civil War uniforms. The Union army recorded the chest and height measurements of over a million soldiers to come up with the first standardization of sizes. After the war, sewing machines and uniform sizing promoted the mass production of everyday men's wear.

Women's Fashion Reflects Social Changes

Fashion conveyed the rigid differences between the roles of the sexes. Men wore trousers, which became a symbol of dominance, while women wore constraining garments characteristic of their restricted lifestyles and obedience to their husbands and fathers. Women did not have the right

11

to own anything except their wardrobes, which is one reason women became so interested in clothes.[4]

Aside from the small number of wealthy women who bought couture, most women had about three basic garments in their wardrobes. Fashionable one-piece fitted dresses were impossible to mass-produce because each dress had to be custom made to fit at least three sets of measurements. Even after the invention of the sewing machine, only hoop skirts and cloaks could be manufactured for women.

A YOUNG WOMAN DRESSED IN THE GIBSON GIRL STYLE. *(COURTESY OF THE NATIONAL ARCHIVES, WASHINGTON, D.C.)*

Mass Production of Women's Separates

The introduction of separate blouses and skirts in the 1880s made it possible to manufacture ready-to-wear clothes for women. A blouse could be made to fit the shoulder and bust measurements, the skirt to fit the hips. Waistlines and hemlines were easily adjusted, and blouses were simply tucked in. This innovation made it possible for the working- or middle-class woman to add variety to her wardrobe simply by mixing separates. The cost of a new ready-made blouse was a mere fraction of the cost of a custom-tailored dress.

Charles Dana Gibson, a popular illustrator in the 1890s, created drawings of young women wearing the new blouses and skirts. His *Gibson Girl* sketches were the personification of the ideal young middle-class American woman and gave style to the basic high-neck, puffed-sleeve blouse and long-skirt look. The Gibson Girl look paved the way for the simplified, functional dress that typifies American fashion.

Children's Fashion

The wealthy were the only ones who had money to spend on fashionable children's clothes; members of the middle and working classes made their children's clothes at home. Babies and toddlers, both girls and boys, wore dresses. As they grew older, children were supposed to act like adults, and they were dressed in miniature versions of adult apparel, usually cut-down remakes of their parents' old clothes. Mothers were particularly grateful for the advent of patterns for children's clothes because, previously, home-sewn garments had been cut and fitted by trial and error.

Paper patterns, inspired by French fashions, were made available to American home sewers in 1850 by Ellen and William Demorest.[5] Demorest Patterns, followed by Butterick and McCall's, fostered fashion consciousness at all levels of society. Women on small budgets were especially happy to have patterns to make the clothes that they could never afford to buy.

Retailing During the Nineteenth Century

Modern retailing had its roots in the nineteenth century when affordable fashion was first made available to the general public.

Fairs and bazaars were the predecessors of the retail store. The traveling merchant brought clothes to these markets. Expensive goods were shown only to selected wealthy customers. Prices were not marked on the merchandise, so buyer and seller usually bargained.

As large numbers of people settled in towns, the first general stores were established to cater to the desire for wider assortments of merchandise. Also, artisans sold their handmade goods in their own shops. These shops were grouped together by trade and regulated by guilds.

The Industrial Revolution triggered a self-supporting manufacturing and retailing cycle. As more goods were produced, there were more products to sell. This increased business activity and gave the growing middle class more money to spend, which created a demand for more products. This growing demand for the variety of goods being produced was the basis for the growth of retailing. Retail stores grew up in the cities, close to production and population centers. As more people clustered in cities to work, stores opened in areas convenient to shoppers.

Two types of stores finally emerged to bring fashion to the public: the specialty store and the department store. Traditional handicraft stores evolved into *specialty stores*, and general stores developed into *department stores*, which carried a wide variety of merchandise. Shopping in department stores became a popular activity, like going to an exhibition. For the first time, people of all incomes could at least enjoy browsing and looking at beautiful things.

The First Department Stores

In 1826, Samuel Lord and George Washington Taylor formed a partnership to open the first Lord and Taylor store in New York City. Jordan Marsh and Company, opening in Boston, claimed they could sell, cut, sew, trim, and furnish a dress in half a day.[6] Edward Filene opened a comparable department store in Boston, as did John Wanamaker in Philadelphia, Joseph Hudson in Detroit, Morris Rich in Atlanta, and R. H. Macy in New York. Their stores grew to a prominence that lasted 150 years.

A SKETCH OF MARSHALL FIELD'S STATE STREET STORE IN 1879. *(COURTESY OF MARSHALL FIELD)*

Harrod's of London, established by Henry Harrod in 1849, began as a small grocery store. By 1880, it had 100 employees and became the largest department store in Europe. Liberty of London opened its retail store in 1875 and produced its own prints as early as 1878. In France, department stores such as the Bon Marché and Printemps opened in the nineteenth century.

The nineteenth century also saw the beginning of customer service, a major contribution to American retailing. In Chicago, Marshall Field once admonished a store clerk who was arguing with a customer, "Give the lady what she wants." "The customer is always right" has been a principle of American retailing ever since.

Early Mail-Order Merchandising

In the 1800s, nearly three-quarters of the American population lived in rural areas, usually served by only a few general stores with a limited selection. The extension of the railroads to the West Coast and the inauguration of free rural mail delivery enabled merchants to start reaching these potential consumers with mail-order services.

While working for a wholesaling firm, traveling to country stores by horse and buggy, Aaron Montgomery Ward conceived the idea of selling directly to country people by mail. He opened his business in 1872 with a one-page list of items that cost one dollar each. People could later order goods through a distributed catalog, and the store would ship the merchandise cash on delivery (COD). The idea was slow to catch on because people were suspicious of a strange name. However, in 1875, Ward announced the startling policy of "satisfaction guaranteed or your money back." Contrasting with the former retailing principle of *caveat emptor* (Latin for "buyer beware"), this policy set off a boom in Ward's business.

In 1886, a Chicago jewelry company erroneously shipped some watches to a jeweler in Richard Sears' hometown in Minnesota. Sears offered to resell them for the jeweler, thereby creating his own watch business. Alvah Roebuck answered Sears' ad for a watchmaker and became his business partner. In 1893, the firm name was changed to Sears, Roebuck and Company. From a modest beginning, they expanded by 1895 to a 507-page catalog including clothing and household goods, often referred to as the "dream book" or "wish book." The mail-order business did more to bring a variety of up-to-date merchandise to rural consumers than any other form of retailing.

Changes Caused by Communications, Leisure, and Industry

Communications, leisure activities, labor conditions, and industrial technology have a continuing effect on fashion.

The desire for fashionable clothing was fostered by its increased availability, as well as by new communications media, such as the mail service, magazines, newspapers, telephones, automobiles, and later airplane travel, radio, motion pictures, television, and computers.

The First Fashion Magazines

During the 1800s, fashion magazines began to be published in France and England. Eighteen fashion magazines were being published in New York and Philadelphia in the late 1800s.[7] Two American magazines that began in the nineteenth century are still published today: *Harper's*

Bazaar commenced publication in both New York and Paris in 1867, and *Vogue* started in New York in 1894.

These publications spread the latest fashion ideas from Paris by means of sketches and descriptions. Dressmakers in other countries copied the styles as best they could with available fabrics. As more women became aware of fashion styles through magazines and other forms of mass communication, their desire to wear these fashions increased. The faster a style was adopted by the public, the greater was the demand for more new looks.

Growth of Leisure Activities

The popularity of sports such as tennis and bicycling created a need for functional sportswear. As early as 1851, Amelia Jenks Bloomer had tried to introduce pants for women. However, they were not accepted until the bicycling craze of the 1890s. Bloomers, full in the leg and gathered at the ankle, were also worn under bathing dresses. Finally, after 1900, swimwear was pared down enough that people could actually swim.

Pants became an acceptable part of the horse-riding habit for women around the turn of the century, when women discovered that riding sidesaddle in a skirt "often caused one to dismount before the ride was over."[8] As women became more and more involved in sports, pants gave them the mobility for a more active life. However, it was not until the 1920s that pants became fashionable as well as functional for women.

Conditions in the Garment Industry

New York Becomes the Center of the U.S. Fashion Industry

The influx of European immigrants to New York helped to establish that city as the center of the industry in the latter part of the century. The immigrants, used to hardship and willing to work for low wages, provided the skilled labor the industry needed to grow. By 1900, the American women's clothing industry consisted of 2701 establishments.[9] They produced mostly cloaks and suits, with some shirtwaists (blouses) and underwear.

Unionization

As more workers crowded into the industry, working conditions became appalling. Tenement workrooms were known as *sweatshops* because of the excessively long hours required of laborers in unsanitary surroundings for extremely low wages.

WOMEN WORKING IN A LEVI STRAUSS FACTORY. *(COURTESY OF LEVI STRAUSS & COMPANY)*

In 1900, cloak makers, mostly immigrants living in cities in the northern United States, met to discuss working conditions. The result was the formation of the International Ladies' Garment Workers' Union, which tried to protect its members against unfair employers. At first, the union was not very popular, but it did make progress with strikes against the shirtwaist industry in 1909 and the cloak industry in 1910. The men's clothing workers' union, which became the Amalgamated Clothing Workers of America in 1914, also had a successful strike in 1910 against Hart, Schaffner & Marx in Chicago. It brought working hours *down* to 54 hours per week!

"On March 25, 1911, the nation was stunned by the horror of the Triangle Shirtwaist Company fire in New York City."[10] The factory's main exit door had been bolted, and the lone fire escape was a death trap that ended in midair. The 146 deaths, mostly of girls, aroused Americans' indignation against the plight of the sweatshop workers. Finally, action was taken on demands for regular hours, minimum wages, paid vacations, sick benefits, and better working conditions. Increased labor costs naturally added to the inevitable simplification of fashion.

Effects of World War I on the Status of Women and Fashion

World War I put women in the workforce and gave them new rights and practical clothing.

Women in the Workforce

The status of women has hinged firmly on their participation in the working world. Before 1900, very few women worked outside the home. Without a prominent place in business, women had no authority and no rights. At the turn of the century, women began to work in factories, offices, and retail stores. The need for the convenience of ready-made clothing made the apparel industry grow and made ready-to-wear clothing even more acceptable.

COCO CHANEL
(COURTESY OF CHANEL, PARIS, PHOTOGRAPHED BY HATAMI)

In 1914, World War I began in Europe, and the United States entered in 1917. World War I greatly promoted women's rights, because it enabled European and American women to replace men in previously all-male jobs. The functional working clothes worn by these women had a great impact on fashion. "Now that women work," *Vogue* reported in 1918, "working clothes have acquired a new social status and a new chic."[11]

A trend toward masculinity in women's fashion emerged: decorative details disappeared in favor of a tailored look that imitated businessmen's suits. Corsets were discarded and the curved hourglass silhouette was replaced by the tube. Hemlines rose and skirts widened to permit freedom of movement. No one wanted or had time for complicated dressing. This change coincided with the need to simplify clothing construction because of rising labor costs and resulted in the democratization of fashion. Fashion reflected women's growing independence and, in 1920, women finally won the right to vote in the United States.

Important Trendsetting Designers

While mass production was growing in the American fashion industry, the French couture still concentrated on fashion leadership among the wealthy. Paris was a cultural meeting ground for designers, artists, and writers. The exchange of their ideas created the exceptional atmosphere needed for fashion innovation.

Often one or a few designers became *trendsetters*; they dominated the field because they were able to capture the spirit of their times and translate it into highly accepted fashion. American retailers bought French fashions for their wealthy customers and often worked with American manufacturers to have them copied or adapted for the American market.

Paul Poiret (Pwah-ray'), whose tubular dresses liberated women from corsets, was the first Paris couturier of this century to become a trendsetter.

Gabrielle Chanel (Sha-nelle'), also known as Coco, was at the forefront of French fashion after World War I. Chanel popularized the "Garçon" (gar-sohn') or boyish style with sweaters and jersey dresses and was the first designer to make high-fashion pants for women.

Jean Patou (Gsahn Pa-Too) created the famous "Flapper" look in 1925 by accentuating the hipline, strengthening a straight silhouette, and making shorter skirts with uneven hemlines. He confirmed that the young, independent woman was the new ideal.

The ready-to-wear apparel industry began to prosper when designers such as Poiret, Vionnet, and Chanel simplified styles and thereby construction. Couture styles were then copied by mass producers for consumers at every price level. Because individual fitting was not so important to their straight silhouettes, the mass production of dresses became practical. As early as the 1920s, designers such as Lucien Lelong in France and Hattie Carnegie in America were adding ready-to-wear lines to their made-to-order collections. Although custom-made clothing remained important, fashionable ready-to-wear was firmly established by the 1920s.

■ JEAN PATOU AND HIS AMERICAN MODELS ARRIVING AT LE HAVRE IN 1924. *(COURTESY OF THE NATIONAL ARCHIVES, WASHINGTON, D.C.)*

Retail Expansion in the Early Twentieth Century

The needs of the growing middle class stimulated both apparel manufacturing and retailing.

Specialty Stores for Quality Fashion

In the early twentieth century, specialty stores emerged with new retailing approaches and offered their customers high-fashion merchandise. Bergdorf Goodman and Saks Fifth Avenue in New York City and Neiman Marcus in Dallas concentrated solely on the finest fashion and customer service. By the 1930s, the first women presidents of major retail firms had been installed: Dorothy Shaver at Lord and Taylor and Hortense Odlam at Bonwit Teller. Shaver gave American fashion a boost by mentioning American designers in store ads.

The Expansion of Chain Stores

While great retailing establishments were growing in the big cities, chain stores selling lower-priced merchandise were taking hold elsewhere. James Cash Penney was such an industrious employee at a small Wyoming store that the owners offered him a partnership in their new store in 1902. Called the Golden Rule Store in honor of their belief in high business standards, it proved an immediate success, in part because of Penney's door-to-door advertising campaign. In 1907, the original partners sold their shares to Penney; the store's name was officially changed to J. C. Penney in 1912. When the chain-store concept caught on in the 1920s, Penney opened stores in all parts of the United States. Chain stores became a national phenomenon.

The Advent of Suburban Retail Centers

As more and more people moved to the suburbs and owned cars, personal mobility increased, creating a revolution in retailing. Finding that its mail-order business was dropping off, Sears & Roebuck opened stores not in the city centers, but rather near the highways that led to the growing suburbs, where they could offer free parking. It was also the beginning of suburban shopping centers such as the Country Club Plaza in Kansas City, which opened in 1922.

Effects of the Depression on Fashion

The experience of the Great Depression of the 1930s still causes manufacturers and retailers to worry at the sign of a recession.

Bursting of the Credit Bubble

In the 1920s, so much credit was extended that eventually there was not enough money to back it up. In the stock market, a person needed to put up only 10 percent of the price to buy stock; when the price rose, the shares could be sold at a profit. So it went until September 3, 1929, when the stock market started a steep decline. In less than a month, the market value of all stocks dropped $30 billion. Unemployment rose from 1.5 million to 12.8 million, and business profits fell from $10.3 billion to a net loss of $2 billion. Nearly half of the nation's banks had to close. Industrial production fell to half of what it had been, and many companies went bankrupt. More than one-third of the ready-to-wear manufacturers went out of business. The slump set off a chain reaction that soon put the whole world into a depression. The American economy did not entirely recover until World War II escalated production.

Hollywood's Influence on Fashion

Americans tried to take their minds off the Depression at the movies. Because people in pre-television days commonly visited the local movie theater once or twice a week, American films brought fashion to every woman. Every young woman wanted to look like her favorite film star. Katharine Hepburn and Marlene Dietrich made slacks popular for women; Clark Gable popularized the sport shirt for men. The 1930s were the most glamorous years in film history, a paradoxical contrast with the deprivations of real life.

Gilbert Adrian emerged as the leading Hollywood designer. He was the first American designer to influence fashion throughout the world. Macy's sold half a million copies of one dress he designed for Joan Crawford to wear in *Letty Lynton* in 1932.[12]

■ FILM STAR JOAN CRAWFORD GLANCES ADMIRINGLY AT ADRIAN, HOLLYWOOD TRENDSETTING DESIGNER OF THE 1930S. *(COURTESY OF THE JOSEPH SIMMS COLLECTION)*

Paris's Influence on International Fashion

The influence of Parisian couture designers on international fashion remained.

Elsa Schiaparelli (Ska-pa-rell'-ee) was the trendsetter of European fashion in the 1930s. Schiaparelli moved the center of interest to the shoulders, which she began to widen, accentuating them by pleats, padding, or braid, a silhouette that remained popular through World War II.

James Mainbocher (Main-bow-shay') was the first American designer to be successful in Europe. When King Edward VIII of England abdicated his throne to marry the divorced American Wallis Simpson, Mainbocher designed the wedding dress, which became the most copied dress of the 1930s. Scandals and fashion remain intertwined to this day!

Effect of World War II on Fashion

America was cut off from Europe during World War II.

During World War II, the French couture banded together under the leadership of Lucien Lelong, then president of the Paris Couture Syndicale, during the German occupation. Under great restrictions and privation—practically no fabrics to work with, no trimmings, no press coverage, no heat, and little food—most designers barely managed to stay in business. Some were forced to close. Of course, under these circumstances, little was achieved.

America's Isolation from Paris Fashion

Isolated from Paris fashion leadership during the war, Americans had to find their own style direction. The lack of imports from France was actually a boon to the development of American talent. In 1940, *Vogue* reported on the New York collection openings. With Mainbocher as an example of success, other American designers such as Claire McCardell, Hattie Carnegie, and Vera Maxwell gained recognition.

Claire McCardell, considered the top American designer of this time, was credited with originating the "American Look" in practical separates, inspired by the work clothes of farmers, railroad engineers, soldiers, and sportsmen.

American designers became especially skilled at and known for their sportswear, reflecting the more casual American lifestyle, which would eventually influence the rest of the world. Sportswear, with its simpler construction, also suited mass production.

Fashion remained relatively stable during the war years. The U.S. government's wartime regulations restricted the use of fabric and hardware. Functional clothes became a necessity as women doing war work wore uniforms or work clothes. Women's suits were heavily influenced by miltary uniforms. The result was a masculine silhouette for the women who now shouldered the responsibilities at home.

CLAIRE MCCARDELL SKETCHING IN A MUSEUM. *(COURTESY OF THE NATIONAL ARCHIVES, WASHINGTON, D.C.)*

Reactionary Postwar Fashion

The postwar era brought about a suburban lifestyle and an accent on family life.

In the postwar search for domestic tranquility, American families wanted to escape the deteriorating cities and find a healthy environment in which to raise their children. For many, this meant a move to the suburbs. The informal suburban lifestyle brought about the popularity

DIOR'S "NEW LOOK." *(COURTESY OF CHRISTIAN DIOR)*

of casual sportswear by American designers, new wash-and-wear manufactured fabrics such as nylon, and more convenient shopping centers.

French Fashion Direction

Women were so happy to see men home after the war that most reverted completely to stereotypical feminine roles, leaving jobs open for the returning men. Fashion catered to their feminine ideal. Paris recaptured fashion dominance, almost to the point of dictatorship in Dior's case.

Christian Dior (Chris-tee-ahn' Dee-or') showed his first collection in 1947 and was an instant success. In a reaction against the wartime silhouette, women adopted his "New Look," with longer, fuller skirts; smooth, rounded, sloping shoulders; and tiny fitted waists. Within a few seasons, Dior's name became a household word, and he was doing as much business as the rest of the French couture combined.[13]

Christobal Balenciaga (Bah-lehn'-see-ah'-gah), a Spaniard who worked in Paris, was regarded as the master of tailors. When American stores purchased rights to manufacture *line-for-line* copies, Balenciaga's designs were always the most popular.

American Fashion Innovators

Although Parisian designers set international trends, Americans also enjoyed continued success at home because of the exposure given to them during the war. These women's wear designers included Bonnie Cashin, Oleg Cassini, Ann Fogarty, James Galanos, Charles James, Anne Klein, Norman Norell, Mollie Parnis, Fernando Sarmi, Adele Simpson, Jacques Tiffeau, Pauline Trigere, Sydney Wragge, and Ben Zuckerman.

Movie star Audrey Hepburn and Jacqueline Kennedy, wife of the president, set a new ideal of beauty. They established an impeccable look predicated on simplicity that was universally imitated. Jackie practically made a uniform of her two-piece jewel-necked A-line dresses and pillbox hats.

Until the 1950s, the average man's wardrobe had only a few dark suits, white shirts, somber neckties, overcoat, raincoat, and hat. For the first time, designers such as Don Loper and John Weitz developed coordinated sportswear for men.

Some American designers custom-made fashion for the wealthy, but most built their reputation on what Americans did best, ready-to-wear, especially sportswear. The French may have been the high-fashion innovators, but Americans developed and excelled at producing fashion looks for everyone.

The late 1940s and 1950s also saw the the biggest increase of births ever, called the postwar baby boom. As these children became teenagers, industry catered to this newly emerging market. Records, cosmetics, magazines, and *junior* fashions were created.

The Youth-Directed 1960s

The postwar baby boom had an increasing effect on fashion change. Breaking with convention, young designers created fashions for their own age group.

By 1965, 50 percent of the U.S. population was under the age of 25. Sheer numbers brought increased buying power and encouraged a youth-oriented market. Reminiscent of the 1920s, young people's tastes were to dominate the fashion scene through the 1970s.

London Emerges as a Leader in Youthful Fashion

During the 1960s, Mary Quant and other young British designers such as Zandra Rhodes and Jean Muir set international fashion trends. They were influenced by a group of British youth called the Mods, who put together odd separates and old clothes from flea markets to create individual looks. Miniskirts, which rose above the knee, tights (the first panty hose), and unusual fabrics such as vinyl were characteristic of the "Mod" look.

In the United States, young designers, such as Betsey Johnson, also created youthful fashions. Even the couture designers in Paris, such as André Courrèges, followed the lead of these young designers. This was the first evidence of a reverse in the traditional fashion-adoption process. The popularity of the youthful look made all women want to look young.

Revival of Men's Fashion

The English Mod Look affected men's wear as well as women's. Carnaby Street tailors made an attempt to return color and fashion to men's clothing. The initial impact of Carnaby Street did not last, but the general interest in men's fashion did. Men became more concerned with their roles outside work and with leisure dressing. French and Italian designers also became important in men's wear.

Pierre Cardin (Car-dahn') signed his first contract for men's shirts and ties in 1959 and opened his men's ready-to-wear department in 1961. Dior, Saint Laurent, and other women's designers followed his example. The 1960s brought the first designer clothes for men and the first fashion changes since the introduction of the business suit.

Fashion Business Evolution

In the 1960s, the nature of the fashion business began to change. Although some designers such as Pierre Cardin were able to make new successes, the youthful direction in fashion caused financial setbacks for the French couture designers. The 1960s saw the last of elegant fashion for 20 years.

In the United States, the growing population and economy changed the structure of fashion companies. Small, family-owned fashion businesses began to disappear. Some merged or were purchased by large, multiproduct corporations. Others, spurred by the flourishing economy, raised money for expansion by selling stocks, to become publicly owned. Public investment gave apparel companies the needed capital to grow and meet rising textile supplier minimums and growing retail distribution.

Boutiques Set Retailing Trends

British shops such as Mary Quant's Bazaar set a new trend in retailing. The French term *boutique* was adopted by Western countries as these small shops gained popularity. Traditional retailing in department and large specialty stores had competition from small boutiques. Following the trend, Yves Saint Laurent opened his Rive Gauche (Reev Gōsh) boutiques around the world. Henri Bendel's in New York introduced an atmosphere of many boutiques within one store. This idea brought freshness and excitement to retailing.

Antifashion of the Late 1960s and 1970s

Antifashion became the style statement from the late 1960s into the 1970s.

The tumultuous late 1960s—a time of the Vietnam War, assassinations, riots, and civil strife—made people turn away from showy displays of frivolity. In suburban America, the polyester pantsuit became almost a uniform. It even became stylish to look poor. Workmen's Levis became an antifashion statement, and the popularity of denim remains today. Some young people, bored with the lack of excitement in retail merchandise, wore vintage clothing purchased at thrift stores.

The Ethnic Look

Society's dropouts, the "hippies," made their antifashion statement in tattered jeans, long hair, beads, and old clothes. In their desire to emulate the simple life, they combined their old clothes to simulate ethnic or native American costume.

Eventually, the "Ethnic Look" widened to include traditional folk costumes from practically every country. Black people developed pride in their heritage, sporting Afro hairdos and the dashiki, traditional African garb. The resumption of diplomatic relations with China in 1972 created widespread interest in the Chinese people and their traditional costume. Designers incorporated the ethnic idea of layering and combining separates into their collections.

Yves Saint Laurent (Eve Sahn'Law-rahn') of Paris emerged as the fashion star of the 1970s because he was able to interpret ethnic and other street looks into high fashion. At that time, he was best known for his blazers, city pants, and ethnic looks. The epitome of reverse fashion adoption was Saint Laurent's "Elegant Peasant" collection of 1975: ethnic looks done in silks with high price tags.

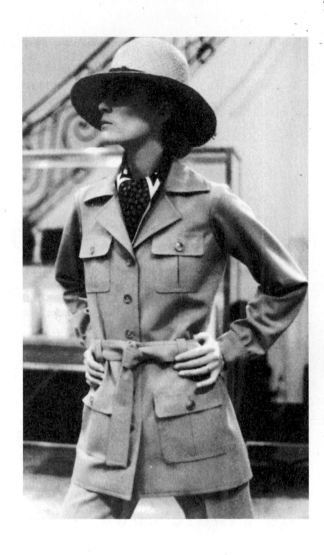

1970S TRENDSETTING
DESIGNER YVES
SAINT LAURENT.
*(COURTESY OF
YVES SAINT LAURENT)*

Physical Fitness as Fashion

In the 1970s, sports and exercise, such as jogging, became generally popular. Fashion was not lost in the race, and soon everyone had a jogging suit, even people who did not run. By the 1980s, active sportswear was a firmly established fashion category. Designers and manufacturers created clothing for every sport. A newly developed elastic fiber, spandex, was used to give garments the stretch needed for movement.

The denim look culminated in "designer jeans" by Calvin Klein and Gloria Vanderbilt. The sexy "Me and My Calvins" advertisements were the most noteworthy example of the growing role of advertising in the fashion business. In the late 1970s, there was a wave of conservative leisure dressing, featuring khaki shorts, penny loafers, polo shirts, button-down shirts, and blazers, called the "Preppy Look."

The Women's Movement

The 1970s witnessed women at work striving for an equal place with men in the business world. Women were trying to make it up the corporate ladder rather than the social one. To fit into a man's world, they adopted the conservative business suit (with skirt) to give themselves a visual business-like credibility. "Dressing for success" became the byword for those who wanted to get ahead. In a somewhat misguided attempt at quality consciousness, *status dressing* became important. The label of the garment became more important than the design. Calvin Klein, Halston, Geoffrey Beene, Ralph Lauren, and Mary McFadden became important designer names. Rolex watches, Gucci shoes, and Louis Vuitton bags became the status accessories.

The Acquisitive 1980s

Overspending and overborrowing in the 1980s caused many of the problems that the fashion business still faces today.

During the 1980s, a trend toward aquisition was manifested in the workplace as well as in fashion. Large manufacturers and retailers got larger by gobbling up small firms. The general public also was primarily interested in climbing the corporate ladder and acquiring money. Many aging baby boomers went back to college to further their careers. More than 60 percent of women ages 18 to 54 worked outside the home, and increasing numbers of them rose to executive-level positions. Their new status was exhibited by the "power suit," a structured but elegant look that dominated fashion.

Globalization

During the 1980s, fashion evolved into a global phenomenon. Both American and European manufacturers and retailers greatly increased imports of textiles, apparel, and accessories.

Giorgio Armani, of Milan, Italy, became the trendsetter of the 1980s because his immaculate tailored look so perfectly suited the career woman. His fashion empire included Emporio Armani and many licenses. Italy became a major international fashion capital; Missoni knits, Armani suits, and Krizia sportswear were in great demand worldwide.

Japan emerged briefly as an important fashion center in the early 1980s led by Kenzo Takada and then Issey Miyake. Japanese designers showed their collections in Paris and influenced world fashion with their oversized silhouettes, wrapping, and layering. In 1981, the eyes of the world were on England, where Prince Charles wed Lady Diana Spencer. Copies of her wedding gown were in London shop windows eight hours after the wedding! In France, Karl Lagerfeld's elegance and Christian Lacroix's flamboyant silhouettes and colors helped to rejuvenate the French couture. The 1980s also saw the beginning of international recognition of American designers, led by Calvin Klein. This prompted other American fashion companies to consider exporting.

■ 1980S INTERNATIONAL TRENDSETTING DESIGNER GIORGIO ARMANI. *(COURTESY OF GIORGIO ARMANI SPA)*

Domestic Industry Trends

Textiles and Apparel
Textile and apparel manufacturers, faced with increased competition from imports, especially from Asia, began using electronic data interchange (EDI) to foster cooperation between textile and apparel producers and retailers to react quickly to trends and cut out wasted time in distribution (see Chapter 12).

Growth of Designer and Brand Names
In the mood of acquisitions, well-known designers and brands became even more pervasive by diversifying their product lines. This was often accomplished by *licensing*, a royalty or percentage paid for the use of a designer or brand name, supported by tremendous amounts of advertising. The growth of the Ralph Lauren, Liz Claiborne, and Nike brands, for instance, was astounding (see Chapter 12).

Retailing Trends
Retailing went through an optimistic period, which unfortunately caused overexpansion. The United States became an *overstored* (industry jargon for too many stores) nation besieged with buyouts and takeovers. Mail-order retailing grew, attracting busy career women who preferred to shop by catalog. Nordstrom, a Seattle-based retailer, built a national reputation for customer service that set a standard for other stores to follow (see Chapters 13 and 14).

The Value-Oriented 1990s

In the last decade of the century, Americans
had to readjust to a less indulgent
way of life.

Recession

The biggest impact of the early 1990s was an international recession beginning in the United States
and the United Kingdom and finally reaching Japan and continental Europe. This had far-reaching
consequences for the fashion industry.

Value Orientation   Consumers, facing job layoffs caused by the poor economy
in the early 1990s, became value oriented. In 1991, more than half of all apparel sold in the
United States was bought on sale.[14] Discount and off-price stores such as Wal-Mart enjoyed
success in spite of the recession because their low prices appealed to consumers. Retailers tried
to win back customers with various new strategies, including value, customer service, and
private-label collections.

Retailing   Retail overexpansion in the 1980s, which resulted in overwhelming competition, combined with careful consumer spending, forced bankruptcies and store closures in the
1990s. Many long-established retailers, such as I. Magnin, Abraham & Straus, and John Wanamaker,
closed or were taken over by large retail groups. Macy's, faced with bankruptcy, was taken over by
Federated Stores, but retained its name.

Manufacturing   Naturally, textile and apparel manufacturers were affected by the
recession as there were fewer retailers to sell to, and imports continued to climb. Textile and apparel
producers joined retailers to debate the pros and cons of the North American Free Trade Agreement
(see Chapter 2). Textile producers hoped that manufacturers would be able to use U.S. textiles if
garments were produced in Mexico instead of Asia.

Information Age   Because of growing imports, there was a shift away from
manufacturing to focus on marketing and information. Both strategies were fostered by the
great advances made by computer technology in all phases of the fashion industry. As discussed
in Chapter 2, the 1990s introduced us to electronic industry partnerships, computer-aided
design, high-tech manufacturing, cable TV and computer shopping, infomercials, and the
Internet.

Fashion Direction

In the early 1990s, the recession in the United States was reflected in the "Grunge Look," an antifashion statement. Internationally, Parisian designer Karl Lagerfeld increased his influence and became the foremost international trendsetter with four major collections: Chanel, Lagerfeld, Fendi, and Chloe. His designs had an impact on many market segments and price ranges, especially with the "conservative chic" look. By the mid-1990s, Tom Ford, the American design director of Gucci, and Mariuccia Prada, both in Italy, also became global trendsetters with their sleek, minimalist fashions.

The men's wear market grew tremendously during the 1990s. Relaxed corporate dress codes allowed men to wear casual clothing to work, and the men's sportswear market, in turn, thrived. Men's wear designers, first Giorgio Armani and then Tommy Hilfiger, Tom Ford (for Gucci), and Richard Tyler, were so successful that they started women's collections.

■ 1990S INTERNATIONAL
TRENDSETTING DESIGNER
KARL LAGERFELD.
*(COURTESY OF KARL
LAGERFELD)*

The Twenty-First Century

Tumultuous times have an influence on fashion.

The First Decade

Fashion has become a global phenomenon with a very similar international product base. What consumers are wearing in Southern California is very similar to what consumers are wearing in London, Tokyo, or Buenos Aires. Part of this is due to the same retail stores opening around the world. Competition is tougher than ever.

Film and music celebrities have become very important in fashion promotion. Their photos grace the covers of fashion magazines, and they are given or loaned gowns to wear to award ceremonies. Some have even started their own fashion companies. However, although fashion has increasing prominence in popular culture, Americans are buying fewer clothes. Now fashion includes iPods, cell phones, and cameras as accessories.

Manufacturing   In an effort to keep prices down, manufacturers and retailers increased imports to 90 percent of apparel sold in the United States. The United States, Canada, and Europe continue to lose their manufacturing base as production in Asia grows, especially in China. China has built a reputation for quality manufacturing at low prices. Chinese designers are also developing global businesses.

Retail Trends   In an overstored nation, store consolidations and mergers were inevitable. Many retailers have closed underproducing stores to increase profits. Other retail companies, such as the Neiman Marcus Group, have been sold. In an effort to have a national presence, Federated Stores acquired May Department Stores and converted many of those stores to Macy's. The loss of Marshall Field's, Strawbridge's, Hecht's, and other regional stores, however, was disappointing to consumers. This merger leaves the department store field quite narrow, resulting in more sameness in the malls and less competition between department stores. In addition, the Sears–Kmart merger created a giant discount retail corporation. Luxury retailers, discount retailers, and warehouse clubs led the industry, indicating that shoppers were willing to splurge while also looking for bargains.

Fashion Direction   At the onset of the first decade of the new century, color and sexy, more-is-more styling dominated fashion. By mid-decade, more sophisticated and classic styles, and more subtle colors, came back into vogue. Many companies added new brands to try to attract additional customers, and a new generation of designers became successful.

SUMMARY

THIS CHAPTER BRIEFLY COVERED THE GROWTH OF THE FASHION INDUSTRY. TECHNOLOGICAL ADVANCES, ESPECIALLY THE INVENTION OF THE SEWING MACHINE, CHANGED CLOTHING PRODUCTION FROM CUSTOM-MADE TO READY-TO-WEAR. THE INDUSTRIAL REVOLUTION ALSO NOURISHED THE GROWTH OF A LARGE MIDDLE CLASS, WHICH DEMANDED AND COULD AFFORD FASHION AT EVERY PRICE LEVEL. AS A RESULT, FASHION BECAME AVAILABLE TO EVERYONE, INSTEAD OF JUST THE WEALTHY FEW.

FASHION HAS ALSO BEEN INFLUENCED BY THE CHANGING STATUS OF WOMEN AND BY THE CHANGING ROLES OF BOTH SEXES. FASHION LEADERSHIP ORIGINATED WITH AND WAS MAINTAINED BY THE FRENCH, EXCEPT DURING WORLD WAR II AND IN THE 1960S AND 1970S. THE 1980S WERE THE BEGINNING OF CORPORATE GROWTH THROUGH MERGERS AND ACQUISITIONS. FIERCE COMPETITION AND OVERSTORING CAUSED MANY BANKRUPTCIES OF FORMER LEADING COMPANIES AT ALL LEVELS OF THE INDUSTRY. COMPETITION ALSO DROVE MANUFACTURERS AND RETAILERS TO SEEK CHEAPER LABOR ABROAD. THESE IMPORTS COST MANY DOMESTIC TEXTILE AND APPAREL WORKERS THEIR JOBS, AND COMPANY CLOSURES FORCED THE INDUSTRY TO STREAMLINE PRODUCTION. THE INFORMATION AGE AND GLOBALIZATION BROUGHT RENEWAL AND THE FASHION INDUSTRY INTO THE TWENTY-FIRST CENTURY.

Terms and Concepts

Briefly define and discuss the following terms and concepts:

1. France, the fashion center
2. Royalty as trendsetters
3. Couture
4. Charles Worth
5. Business suit
6. Isaac Singer
7. Levi Strauss
8. Gibson Girl
9. Department stores
10. Specialty stores
11. Richard Sears
12. Coco Chanel
13. Gilbert Adrian
14. "The New Look"
15. Claire McCardell
16. Postwar baby boom
17. Mary Quant
18. Mod fashion
19. Antifashion
20. Ethnic look
21. Active sportswear
22. Globalization
23. Power suit
24. Giorgio Armani
25. Karl Lagerfeld

Questions for Review

1. How did the growth of a middle class affect fashion in the eighteenth and nineteenth centuries?
2. What factors made Paris the center of world fashion?
3. How did the American textile industry get its start?
4. Give two examples of how fashion reflects social or political history.
5. Discuss the growth of mass production in the United States and the technical developments that made it possible.
6. What are the origins of specialty and department stores?
7. How did retail development and expansion in the nineteenth and twentieth centuries reflect social changes?
8. How did the growth of a garment industry encourage the growth of unionism?
9. How did the change in women's status influence fashion in the twentieth century?

Projects for Additional Learning

1. Trace the fashions of one of the designers listed in the Historical Chart of Influential Designers by consulting newspapers and magazines from the period in which he or she was best known. Trace the evolution of the designer's styles with sketches or photocopies. Discuss the characteristics that made his or her designs unique. How did the designs reflect lifestyles?
2. If possible, visit an historic costume collection at a museum and examine costumes from each decade since the turn of the twentieth century to compare design details.
3. Start a small costume collection with your class. Canvass your family, friends, and neighbors for attic donations, or shop at flea markets and thrift shops. Keep a record of all items as to donor and approximate year made. Examine them for construction methods and design details. These clothes will not only be fun to wear, but can be used as inspiration for future design projects.
4. Visit a local sewing machine dealer. Ask the dealer to trace the technical advances in machines as far back as he or she can remember. The dealer may have old catalogs or old machines that you can examine. Discuss the advantages of the old and the new models.

Notes

1 Phyllis Feldkamp, "Men's Fashion, 1750–1975," *New York Times Magazine*, September 14, 1975, p. 66.
2 "Bicentennial of American Textiles," *American Fabrics and Fashions*, no. 106 (Winter-Spring 1976), p. 12.
3 Ishbel Ross, *Crusades and Crinolines* (New York: Harper & Row, 1963), p. 12.
4 Ibid., p. 99.
5 Ibid., p. 20.
6 Ibid., p. 116.
7 Ibid., p. 220.

8 "Women's Pants," *L'Officiel USA*, Spring 1977, p. 109.

9 Florence S. Richards, *The Ready to Wear Industry 1900–1950* (New York: Fairchild Publications, 1951), p. 8.

10 *Signature of 450,000* (New York: International Ladies' Garment Workers' Union, 1965), p. 24.

11 Quoted by Helen Brockman, *The Theory of Fashion Design* (New York: Wiley, 1965), p. 69.

12 Ernestine Carter, *The Changing World of Fashion* (London: Weidenfeld & Nicolson, 1977), p. 70.

13 Charlotte Calasibetta, *Fairchild's Dictionary of Fashion* (New York: Fairchild Publications, 1975), p. 561.

14 Ira Schneiderman, "A Look at the Future," *Women's Wear Daily*, August 1992, p. 15.

HISTORICAL CHART OF INFLUENTIAL DESIGNERS

Years Most Influential	Designers and International Fashion Directions
1774–1793	Rose Bertin: dressmaker to Marie Antoinette
1790–1815	Hippolyte le Roy: dressmaker for the court of Napoleon, creator of the classic revival Empire style
1860s	Charles Worth (b. England): father of modern couture for women
	London's Savile Row tailors set standards for men's tailoring
Late 1800s	Redfern, Cheruit, Doucet, Paquin
Early 1900s	Madame Gerber (house of Callot Sisters), Jeanne Lanvin
1909–1911	Paul Poiret: his tunics freed women from corsets
1912–1915	Charlotte Premet
Post-World War I	Madelaine Vionnet: first to do bias cut
1916–1921	Coco Chanel: known for the Boyish Look and for using jersey
1922–1929	Jean Patou: known for the Flapper Look
1930–1935	Elsa Schiaparelli (b. Italy): "hard chic" and unconventional styling
1936–1938	Mainbocher (b. United States) and Molyneux (b. Ireland): understatement and broadening shoulders
	Gilbert Adrian: Hollywood glamour copied in ready-to-wear
1940–1945	Claire McCardell (American): known for American Look of practical sportswear
	The war years made communication with Europe impossible and made Americans begin to appreciate their own designers
1947–1957	Christian Dior: with his New Look, Paris fashion leadership is regained
	American sportswear for men appears
1950–1960	Balenciaga, Givenchy, Saint Laurent, Andre Courrèges, Pierre Cardin (France) Pucci (Italy)
1960s	Mary Quant: English designers have international influence. Beginning of young designers creating for young people
	Miniskirts and Mod Look
	Pierre Cardin builds empire for men's and women's fashion
1968–1975	Confusion in fashion direction; Paris influence is waning
	Ethnic influence; street fashion
	American jeans become international fashion
1970s	International exchange of fashion
	Major influence from French prêt-à-porter: Saint Laurent, Kenzo (b. Japan), Rykiel, Lagerfeld (b. Germany)
	Italian designers important: Armani, Missoni, Krizia (Mandelli), Ferragamo shoes, Gucci handbags
	Geoffrey Beene, Halston, Calvin Klein, Mary McFadden important in American fashion
1980s	Global outlook; acquisition
	Japanese have international influence
	Rise of internationally known, moderately priced sportswear by manufacturers such as Liz Claiborne, Esprit, and Benetton
	Armani (Italy) sets the fashion tone for professional women
	Lagerfeld and Lacroix rejuvenate the French couture
	American fashion designers begin exporting
1990s	Recession followed by value orientation; grunge look
	Karl Lagerfeld is major international trendsetter with five collections
	Gucci and Prada of Italy are trendsetters; minimalist look
	John Galliano at Dior; Alistair McQueen at Givenchy; outrageous couture
	American designers known worldwide
	Growth of men's designer sportswear; Tommy Hilfiger
2000+	Return of enthusiasm for fashion yet casual clothes prevalent
	Multiple trendsetters
	Growth of E-commerce for fashion retailing
	Global expansion and global sourcing
	Continuing acquisitions and consolidations; manufacturing and retailing giants

FLOWING SILK CHIFFON WITH A CONTRAST MIDRIFF,
RUFFLES, AND FLOWER TRIM BY ELIE SAAB.
(COURTESY OF ELIE SAAB AND DENTE & CRISTINA)

2

CONSUMER DEMAND AND FASHION MARKETING

Career Focus

Fashion executives, including product managers, merchandisers, designers, buyers, and all the people involved in marketing, continually learn about new developments in consumer demand, economics, world trade, and technology. All product development, production, and marketing decisions are based on this information.

CHAPTER OBJECTIVES

After reading this chapter, you should be able to:

1. Understand fashion marketing and the fashion marketing chain

2. Know the technical, economic, and global influences on fashion marketing

3. Be aware of the importance of the consumer on fashion marketing and how demographic and psychographic studies help the industry to determine target markets

Fashion marketing is the entire process of researching, planning, promoting, and distributing the raw materials, apparel, and accessories that consumers want to buy. It involves everyone in the fashion industry and occurs throughout the entire channel of distribution. Marketing is the power behind the product development, production, distribution, retailing, and promotion of fibers, fabrics, leathers, furs, trimmings, apparel, and accessories.

Fashion marketing begins and ends with the consumer. This chapter first discusses the effect of consumer demand on marketing. It begins with a survey of consumer groups and demographic and psychographic trends, and explains how these help to define target markets. The chapter goes on to discuss economic, global, and technological influences on the fashion industry and ends with a discussion of the marketing chain.

Consumer Demand

Consumers, people who buy and use merchandise, are the primary influence on marketing.

The history of the fashion industry in America is the story of a growing economy, based on manufacturing, that consumed more than it could produce. As competition increased, however, the consumer had more choice of products to the point of oversaturation. Consumers now have the income to influence fashion marketing by their buying decisions. In addition to better and cheaper products, consumers also demand constant availability, convenience, and a pleasant shopping experience. As a result, consumers' demands have shifted the industry from a production to a marketing orientation.

With this change in marketing philosophy, the industry now endeavors to find out what consumers will want to buy through research and then tries to develop the products to answer these needs. Fashion industry executives continually learn about consumer behavior to get clues as to what products consumers might need or want to buy in the future. They hire professional marketing firms to analyze lifestyles and buying behaviors. Professional analysts have developed sophisticated marketing research methods (see Chapter 4) to determine consumer wants and needs. In turn, manufacturers and retailers have emphasized product development to answer these needs.

Fashion producers and retailers also spend large amounts of money on increased advertising and other marketing activities to *create* consumer demand. The ultimate achievement of advertising is to establish the identity of a particular brand name or store so solidly that consumers will seek it out, that it will become a "destination brand." Consumers are bombarded with million-dollar advertising campaigns (see Chapters 12 and 15). However, there is a limit to which marketing can win acceptance for a fashion. If the public is not ready for a product or is tired of it, no amount of advertising or publicity can gain or hold its acceptance.

Consumer Groups

Fashion executives try to satisfy the wants and needs of particular consumer groups or market segments.

Consumers are not one homogeneous mass. Traditionally, society was divided by income classes. The wealthiest were the most fashionable, because only they could afford to buy expensive clothes. Those traditional class systems have broken down. Almost all clothing is mass-produced, and almost everyone can enjoy fashion on some price level.

The fashion industry has reached a consumer saturation point. In general, the U.S. population is spending less on apparel, along with food and entertainment, as they spend more on housing, health care, transportation, home furnishings and equipment, education, electronics, beauty, and fitness. Analysts believe that apparel purchases, as a percentage of spending, will continue to decline. In addition, busy schedules and multiple responsibilities limit the amount of time people have free to shop.

Demographic Trends

Market research companies, manufacturers, and retailers try to understand consumer needs by studying information about society. Market researchers do sophisticated demographic and

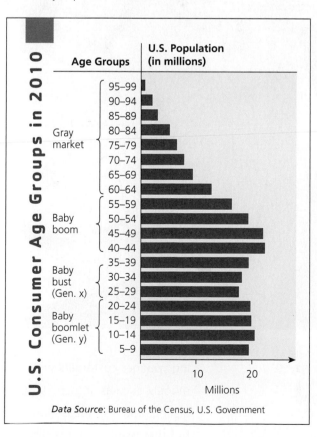

U.S. Consumer Age Groups in 2010

Age Groups		U.S. Population (in millions)
Gray market	95–99	
	90–94	
	85–89	
	80–84	
	75–79	
	70–74	
	65–69	
	60–64	
Baby boom	55–59	
	50–54	
	45–49	
	40–44	
Baby bust (Gen. x)	35–39	
	30–34	
	25–29	
Baby boomlet (Gen. y)	20–24	
	15–19	
	10–14	
	5–9	

10   20

Millions

Data Source: Bureau of the Census, U.S. Government

psychographic studies to classify the population into consumer groups or *market segments*, based on age, lifestyle, living area, educational and ethnic backgrounds, and so on. *Demographics* are statistical studies of measurable population characteristics such as birthrate, age distribution, and income. Demographic studies demonstrate that the American population is aging and diversifying.

The Gray Market   Americans born before 1945 are the most neglected by designers, retailers, and the media. In fact, the 60- to 75-year-old group is the second fastest growing age segment. People in this age group tend to feel 10 to 15 years younger than their actual age, but they have been marketed to as if they were 10 to 15 years older. Studies show that mature people have money to spend and enjoy new products as much as anyone and tend to dress up more often than younger people. Primarily, this age group prefers shopping for apparel and accessories by catalog, via the Internet, or at department stores. By 2010, one-third of the population will be over age 50, indicating that in the future marketers will need to cater to a more conservative value-, function-, comfort-, and quality-oriented customer.

The Postwar Baby Boom   *Baby boomers*, the age group caused by the increase in the birthrate between 1946 and 1964, are still the largest generation and the primary demographic spending group in the United States to influence the apparel market. These women shop a wide variety of retail venues from luxury specialty stores to discounters. Women 45 to 62 spend more on clothing per capita than any other age group.[1] Yet this group is also generally ignored by the fashion industry. Joan Kaner, former fashion director at Neiman Marcus, said, "The 45-and-up customer is not being represented, or even addressed, in most fashion advertising and editorial."[2]

EILEEN FISHER AD SHOWING THREE CONSUMER GROUPS OF WOMEN. *(COURTESY OF EILEEN FISHER, INC.)*

Fashion advertisers have stereotypical ideas about the style sensibilities of people over 40 and are also afraid of alienating younger customers with multigenerational ads. However, a few advertisers are using older models, such as Sharon Stone for Badgley Mischka and Madonna for H&M. Baby boomers have distinct and firm ideas about what they want. They expect more service, comfort, and quality, but they want the same fashion as young people with appropriate length and fit.

The Baby Busters (Generation X)   The generation born between 1965 and 1979 is referred to as the *baby busters*, because this age bracket is much smaller than the one preceding it. Now in their 30s and early 40s, they have become career- and family-oriented, and their spending patterns reflect these interests, with more spending on housing, home goods, transportation, and education.

The Baby Boomlet (Generation Y)   Fashion marketing's most sought after consumer group is referred to as the *baby boomlet* or *generation Y* (also called the *millennial generation* or the *Net generation*), the children of the baby boomers, created by the rise in the birthrate that began in 1980. They are a racially diverse group with a global, sports, computer, and entertainment orientation that will affect their buying decisions in the future. Advertising, television shows, movies, Web sites, and magazines are created specifically for this market. This demographic group is fashion hungry and has a passion for buying clothes, but usually cannot afford to spend as much as baby boomers. The contemporary and young men's market is already strong as a result of people in this age group reaching their 20s, while teens spend heavily on junior fashions. Young people tend to prefer specialty apparel chains and small boutiques.

By 2010, the nation will be rather polarized, with the postwar boomers over 50 years of age and the millennial generation under 30. Some companies, such as the Gap and Eileen Fisher, are responding with multigenerational advertising campaigns.

Ethnic Diversity   Another important demographic trend is the ethnic diversity of the U.S. population. The Immigration and Naturalization Service projects that legal immigration exceeds 700,000 per year. The Census Bureau has determined that the black, Hispanic, Asian, and Native American segments of the population will all grow much faster than the white majority. People of different cultural backgrounds look for different things in a fashion purchase. They have various cultural perceptions and partialities regarding styling, color, pattern, fabrics, fit, quality, and value. With a multicultural society, retailers and manufacturers try to cater to these various market segments.

Psychographic or Lifestyle Trends

People can share the same demographic characteristics and still be very different from each other. Whatever the age group, market researchers try to pinpoint delineations of lifestyles, called *psychographics*. These studies use psychological, sociological, and anthropological factors to further separate consumers based on the differences in their lifestyles. Manufacturers and retailers often turn to psychographics to further segment and analyze consumer groups and their fashion preferences.

Independent Women

Today, more than 75 percent of the female population aged 20 to 60 are employed. More than 22 million women live alone or head single-women households. These circumstances have empowered women to make more purchasing decisions. For these women, who divide their days between the demands of home and career, time becomes a critical issue. Busy working women tend to shop less often and favor convenient, one-stop shopping, which has aided the growth of certain catalogs, Web sites, and superstores. However, like the majority of the population, they have more important claims on their paychecks than apparel and accessories.

Larger Sizes

Another phenomenon influencing the fashion industry is the increasing number of people wearing larger sizes. As the population ages, people are getting heavier. Approximately 68 percent of all Americans are overweight. At Haggar, core sizes for its pants used to be sizes 32 to 40; now the core sizes go up to 44. As a result, retail stores are devoting more square footage to large-size apparel.

Other Psychographic Trends

The key to appealing to apparel shoppers is to merchandise according to consumer lifestyles—by relating to where shoppers work, as well as to their family demands, recreational activities, and cultural interests. Observers generally believe that the following are also important psychographic or lifestyle trends:

- **Community**—People are looking for a connection to the community; for the first time in more than 40 years, cities are gaining in population.
- **Renewed interest in family life**—People spend more money on the home and family activities than on fashion.
- **Cocooning**—Many people try to insulate themselves from the fears of terrorism, war, and crime by staying home as much as possible, shopping less, or shopping by catalog or on the Internet. At home they feel a sense of comfort and protection from an increasingly insecure and hostile world.
- **Work at home**—The number of people who work at home is expected to increase dramatically.
- **Increased at-home use of computers**—People are more likely to shop on the Internet.
- **Comfort**—People want relaxed and casual dressing at home and at work and activewear for exercise.
- **Value of time**—People are willing to trade money for free time, which makes shopping by catalog or the Internet appealing.
- **Stress**—Overwhelmed consumers have busy schedules and are overwhelmed with too much choice of merchandise; they prefer to limit shopping to a few favorite stores, catalogs, or Web sites.

Target Marketing

Textile and apparel producers and retailers use demographic and psychographic information in an effort to understand the buying habits and preferences of each market segment. They also use direct customer contact in stores, informal interviews, surveys, consumer focus groups, and point-of-sale data analysis to define their *target market*, the group of consumers they want to reach. They try to be very specific to find even smaller potential *market niches* within larger markets. Ideally, appropriate consumer goods are then created for each of these groups of people to satisfy their wants and needs.

Database Marketing (Datamining)
Fashion merchants gather data about consumers to strengthen marketing strategies. Through their purchases, consumers unwittingly give manufacturers and retailers information about their shopping habits, size and color preferences, lifestyle, age, income, and address, which are recorded and stored in computers. Many retailers now issue their own store credit cards or cobranded cards (in partnership with a bank or a major credit card) to build more elaborate marketing databases.

This information is combined with answers to surveys and other sources, such as sweepstake entries, coupon request forms, and public records, and categorized into *databases*, consumer taste profiles for all consumer groups (see Market Research, Chapter 4). A retailer might evaluate credit card purchases by maternity customers, for example, and send these shoppers direct-mail advertising on baby goods nine months later.

Mapping Merchants translate sales data and purchasing patterns into geographic maps, visual representations of their markets. Breaking out sales by customer zip codes vividly illustrates primary and secondary markets for each store location and helps management to understand traffic flow and sales potential.

Merchants use consumer profiles from databases to:

- Learn about their customers
- Find new customers
- Establish a target market
- Find or create new products to suit their target customers
- Help to find new ways to advertise to these markets
- Keep them focused on their customers

Manufacturers and retailers in touch with the needs of their target customers are the ones who succeed in an increasingly competitive marketplace. However, in spite of sophisticated research methods, fashion companies still have a problem understanding changing demographics and creating fashion products that their customers will want to buy.

The Impact of Economics on Consumer Demand

Consumer spending, the state of the economy, the international money market, and labor costs have an effect on fashion marketing.

Consumer Spending

The amount of money that consumers spend on fashion and other goods depends on their income. Income, as it affects spending, is measured in three ways: personal income, disposable income, and discretionary income.

Personal income is the gross amount of income from all sources, such as wages and salaries, interest, and dividends.

Disposable income is personal income minus taxes. This amount determines a person's purchasing power.

Discretionary income is income left over after food, lodging, and other necessities have been paid for. This money is available to be spent or saved at will. The increase in discretionary income enjoyed by most people in our society means that more people are able to buy fashion. Young people spend the highest proportion of their income on clothes.

Purchasing Power

Purchasing power is related to the economic situation. Although incomes in the Western world have risen in recent years, so have prices. Thus, income is meaningful only in relation to the amount of goods and services that it can buy, or its *purchasing power*. Credit, productivity, inflation, recession, and international currency values affect purchasing power.

Credit The growth of consumer credit and the proliferation of credit cards have greatly extended consumer purchasing power. More and more retailers are offering their own credit cards to obtain consumer information for their databases. Now, there is too much easy credit available, which has resulted in a huge increase in personal bankruptcies, with losses to both retailers and banks.

Fashion companies, too, need credit to be able to operate through seasonal peaks and valleys and to finance their businesses through the long lead times required for buying supplies long before the finished product is paid for. The accumulation of too much corporate debt is one of the factors that has led to many manufacturer and retailer bankruptcies and closings during the past 30 years.

Corporate Ownership Fashion manufacturers and retailers were traditionally privately owned companies. Now, most of these companies have grown into corporations or have been purchased by other corporations. There has been a steady barrage of mergers and acquisitions, resulting in giant "corporate groups" such as Liz Claiborne, Jones Apparel Group, and LVMH. In addition, many of these corporations sell stock to the public to gain broader access to funding. Their initial public offerings (IPOs) and the impressive performance of certain stocks have gained attention from the press. Bottom lines, instead of hemlines, often dominate the fashion news. These publicly held corporations now have an added responsibility to their shareholders. They are pressured to build sales and profits, increase cost efficiency, and sink millions into advertising to build their brand image (see Chapters 8, 12, and 13 for more information).

Labor Costs As people receive higher salaries and live better, the cost of making products increases. Rising domestic labor costs have caused most manufacturers to search for cheaper sources of labor in Asia, Mexico, the Caribbean Basin, and elsewhere.

Inflation In an inflationary period such as the United States experienced in the 1980s, people earn more money each year, but higher prices and higher taxes result in little or no real increase in purchasing power.

Recession A recession, such as we experienced in 2002–2003, is a cycle beginning with a decrease in spending. Many companies are forced to cut back production, which results in unemployment and a drop in the gross national product (GNP). Unemployment furthers the cycle of reduced spending.

■ RISING DOMESTIC LABOR COSTS HAVE CAUSED U.S. AND EUROPEAN MANUFACTURERS TO SEEK CHEAPER LABOR IN ASIA, RESULTING IN A HUGE INCREASE IN IMPORTS. *(COURTESY OF LIZ CLAIBORNE)*

When the economic situation is unstable, the fashion picture is also unstable. Not only is money in short supply, but people seem to be confused about what they really want. In an economic upswing, colors are basically cheerful and happy, but they have a grayed palette when the economy is in trouble. Also, people are likely to buy conservatively or buy merchandise that they believe to be of lasting value in a recession, but they are more willing to pay for fashion in prosperous times.

Foreign Exchange Market   When the dollar is strong against other currencies, American consumers are able to buy foreign-made merchandise more cheaply. At the same time, American industry is hurt, because imported merchandise competes with domestic goods and exports become too expensive for other countries to buy.

On the other hand, when the dollar is weak (loses value relative to other currencies), foreign countries can buy American goods more cheaply. This situation encourages American fashion manufacturers to export and is good for business. In this case, however, imported goods are more expensive for Americans to buy.

The Euro   In 1999, the euro became the official common currency of 11 of the 15 members of the European Union (EU). The use of a single currency boosts European industries' ability to compete in world markets, especially against the dollar and yen, and makes trade easier by eliminating exchange rate fluctuations within Europe.

The Impact of Global Trade on Marketing

Fierce competition from imports and a saturated domestic market have led to a new global viewpoint in marketing on all levels of the industry.

A major trend in fashion marketing is globalization. World trade in apparel and accessories is growing despite high tariffs and drastic currency fluctuations. Many countries may be involved in the production of a single garment. For example, a garment could be designed in New York, made in China with fabric from Korea, and then distributed to retail stores all over the world. Retailers, too, are expanding globally. Stores as diverse as Christian Dior (French), H&M (Hennes & Mauritz, Swedish), Zara (Spanish), and the Gap (American) have opened stores worldwide.

Imports

Imports are goods that are brought in from a foreign country to sell here. The people or firms that import goods are usually manufacturers that produce apparel in another country, and wholesalers and retailers acting as *importers*. Retailers want to give their customers the best quality products at the lowest prices. Therefore, ever-increasing amounts of textiles, apparel, and accessories are being imported into the United States and the European Union (EU) because of the availability of cheaper labor in low-wage countries. U.S. and European manufacturers compete with labor rates of 69 cents per hour in parts of China and 60 cents or less in India.[3]

Imported Fashion Merchandise

Traditionally, imports were fashion merchandise designed and produced by foreign designers and manufacturers and purchased by domestic retailers at international markets. The United States has long imported fashion from Paris, woolens from the British Isles, sweaters from Scandinavia, and leather goods from Italy. Currently, the European Economic Community, followed by the United States, is the largest importer and consumer of apparel in the world.

Sourcing Cheaper Fabrics and Production
Manufacturers *source* (search the world for) the best fabrics available at low cost to make into garments. U.S. textile and apparel imports increased from $10 billion in 1982 to $96 billion in 2006.[4] This corresponds to the enormous growth of the textile industries of China, Korea, Taiwan, and India. One reason for this is that U.S. manufacturers contracting production overseas tend to use fabrics from the region where production is done, thereby taking sales away from U.S. domestic textile producers (see Chapter 6). As a result, after the North American Free Trade Agreement (NAFTA) was passed in 1994, U.S. textile producers encouraged apparel production in Mexico and the Caribbean Basin, where U.S. textiles can be used, but this production is now limited to basics.

Today less than 10 percent of apparel sold in the United States is made here. Most manufacturers buy fabrics, patternmaking services, and production (cutting and sewing) from a contractor in a

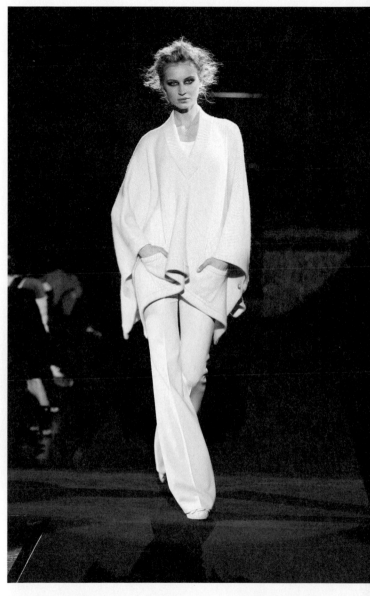

KNITWEAR BY GIANFRANCO FERRÉ. THE COVETED "MADE IN ITALY" LABEL IS DISAPPEARING AS ITALIAN MANUFACTURERS SEEK CHEAPER PRODUCTION IN EASTERN EUROPE AND ASIA. *(COURTESY OF GIANFRANCO FERRÉ)*

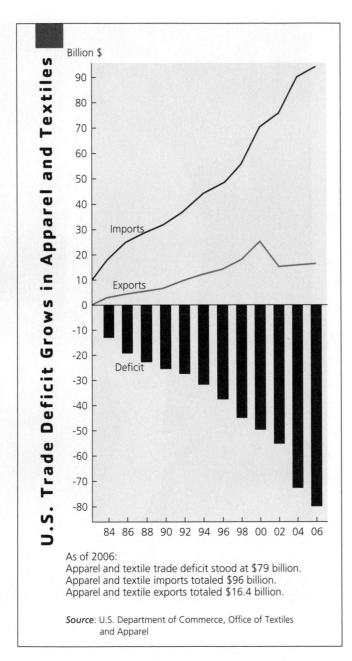

U.S. Trade Deficit Grows in Apparel and Textiles

Billion $

As of 2006:
Apparel and textile trade deficit stood at $79 billion.
Apparel and textile imports totaled $96 billion.
Apparel and textile exports totaled $16.4 billion.

Source: U.S. Department of Commerce, Office of Textiles and Apparel

foreign country where labor is cheaper (see Chapter 10), especially China. The intense collaboration between the Chinese government and its textile and apparel sectors enables China to underprice its competitors. Government support takes the form of currency undervaluation, subsidized shipping costs, export tax rebates, and direct subsidization. Unless limited in some way, Chinese apparel exports will continue to grow, and China will eventually supply most of our apparel. The huge increase in imports in recent years has stimulated a great deal of controversy. The controversy revolves around two key points: the balance of trade and the loss of jobs at home.

Balance of Trade

The *balance of trade* is the difference in value between a country's exports and its imports. Ideally, the two figures should be about equal. Lately, however, the United States has been importing much more than it exports, sending American dollars abroad to pay for these goods and creating a huge *trade deficit*. Many people believe that we should import fewer goods to balance trade. Others think that the consumer should be given the best merchandise at the best price, regardless of the balance of trade.

Labor versus Free Trade

There has been an enormous increase of imported fabric and apparel and accessory production. Labor unions have complained that overseas production has stolen thousands of domestic jobs in textile and apparel production. The American textile industry has lost more than 900,000 jobs, and thousands of plants have closed since 1980. The United States has lost its manufacturing base.

On the other hand, proponents of *free trade* (trade without restrictions), such as importers and retailers, believe that, in the long run, world trade should be based on specialization; each nation would contribute to the world market what it produces best at the most reasonable cost. In this way, consumers would obtain the most value for their money.

Import Tariffs or Duties   *Duties* or *tariffs* are customs charges imposed on imports in an attempt to protect domestic industry. Duties vary according to the type of garment, the fiber content, and whether the fabric is woven or knitted. However, the United States is considering eliminating them.

Harmonized Tariff Schedule   The Harmonized Tariff Schedule (HTS) is an international system of product classification used since 1988 for international customs clearance and the collection of data on imports and exports. Formerly, every country had its own system of naming or numbering imports and exports. Now a system of six-digit codes allows participating countries to classify traded goods on a common basis.

World Trade Organization

The World Trade Organization (WTO), which governs worldwide trade, is located in Geneva. The organization has 149 member countries, which together account for over 90 percent of world merchandise trade. Its basic objectives are to achieve the expansion and progressive liberalization of world trade. Additional functions of the WTO are to set rules governing trade behavior, set environmental and labor standards, protect intellectual property, resolve disputes between members, and serve as a forum for trade negotiations. It was hoped that negotiations would help to alleviate poverty in poor countries with an increase of global commerce. However, the last meeting, called the Doha Round because it began in Doha, Qatar, in 2001, ended in deadlock in 2006.

The Agreement on Textiles and Clothing   The Agreement on Textiles and Clothing (ATC) was negotiated under the auspices of the WTO. It provided for the 2005 quota removal from all apparel and textile imports for its 145 member countries.

Quota Elimination

Many governments regulate imports by means of *quotas* that control the quantity of imported merchandise. Quotas are negotiated between two trading countries and are allocated for a 12-month period. Until now, a manufacturer or importer

A MEETING OF THE WORLD TRADE ORGANIZATION IN GENEVA, SWITZERLAND. *(PHOTO BY TANIA TANG, COURTESY OF THE WTO)*

had to be sure that quotas were high enough to allow the merchandise in question to be produced in that country. Quotas involved a nightmare of complexities and middlemen. Governments allocated quotas to companies who paid for them. Countries were limited on what and how much they could export. However, in 2005, the international quota system was officially eliminated, except for countries that are not members of the World Trade Organization, although some special temporary limits on China still exist.

The end of the quota system on textiles and apparel will bring major economic changes to many parts of the world. It poses a great opportunity for China, but many other developing countries that rely on apparel exports for economic growth may lose their business to China. China's high unemployment and migration from rural areas to the cities will provide even more people willing to work for low wages. The National Textile Association (NTA) wants the U.S. government to impose safeguard measures, such as higher tariffs and duties, if China dominates world textile and apparel trade.

North American Free Trade Agreement

Trade agreements, most often created for foreign policy and national security reasons, continue to change the world trade flow. In 1994, the North American Free Trade Agreement (NAFTA) created a *free market* (devoid of import duties), including 560 million people in Canada, the United States, and Mexico. The agreement promotes economic growth through the expansion of trade and investment opportunities within the free trade area. Canada and Mexico are the largest trading partners of the United States, and, in turn, the United States accounts for more than two-thirds of their total trade.

NAFTA gives U.S. textile firms the opportunity to ship their fabric to Mexican contractors to be made into garments, usually basics such as underwear or jeans. Manufacturers and retailers that have garments produced in Mexico are able to receive shipments much more quickly than shipments from Asia. Likewise, a Central American Free Trade Agreement has been enacted. The United States has also negotiated trade agreements with Australia, Chile, Israel, Jordan, Morocco, Singapore, and Sub-Saharan Africa. It is also working on a Free Trade Agreement of the Americas (FTAA) encompassing 34 Western Hemisphere nations, as well as free trade agreements with Bangladesh, Indonesia, Vietnam, South Africa, South Korea, Thailand, Bahrain, Oman, Egypt, and the United Arab Emirates.

Exports

Because the U.S. market is no longer growing, and to help to balance imports, there is an increasing trend for American manufacturers to try to sell their merchandise to foreign retailers either through direct export or licensing arrangements. The recent low exchange rate of the U.S. dollar against the euro makes exporting a promising proposition. However, manufacturers have to pay import and export duties.

An increasing number of American manufacturers are exhibiting at industry trade shows in France, Switzerland, Germany, Italy, the United Kingdom, and Japan. U.S. manufacturers that are already exporting include Liz Claiborne, Donna Karan, and Levi Strauss. So far, the United States has had the most success exporting to Canada, Mexico, and Japan.

The fastest growing economies in the world are those in Southeast Asia, Eastern Europe, and Latin America. India and the Middle East are also growing. At its current growth rate, China will have the largest economy in the world in 2025. No longer will these countries be simply a place to source goods, but they will also be attractive new markets because of their growing middle classes.

The Impact of Technology on Marketing

Changes in technology, for communications, information gathering, textile development, and apparel production, have a great effect on the marketing of fashion.

Communications

The development of modern communications has had a huge impact on the fashion industry. Communications that formerly took days or weeks happen instantly. A variety of communication systems provide fashion business executives and consumers alike with up-to-the-minute fashion information. Accurate, timely, and useful communications are critical to the success of fashion companies.

Business Communications Fashion industry executives use the latest technology to make communications easier. They have to assess the viability of the myriad of new communication options.

- **Computers**—Fashion industry executives are able to communicate with their offices from anywhere in the world on their laptop computers via satellite.
- **Intranet**—Industry executives may use electronic mail (E-mail) on a closed Intranet network system to share information internally, both among departments and with branch offices and

stores. These private systems allow people to share information without worrying about data security.

- **Internet**—Executives also use E-mail via the Internet to communicate worldwide with their associates. Manufacturers can communicate with their suppliers and production facilities worldwide and exchange digital design and pattern images.

- **Video**—Videoconferencing provides communications and visuals on products, trends, floor presentations, selling techniques, and electronic staff meetings, acting as a *virtual boardroom*. Videoconferencing is used between manufacturers and factories, manufacturers and retailers, management and sales representatives, and among chain stores of a retail organization. It is especially helpful when travel is impossible due to terrorists or war.

- **Fax**—A facsimile (fax) machine can send a fashion sketch or list of specifications around the world in seconds.

Communication with Consumers

The Internet, fax machines, and television bring fashion from around the world into our homes instantly.

- **Television**—Television is a vehicle for home shopping, infomercials, and direct-response commercials.

- **Telephone**—The 800 number revolutionized telephone ordering. Now, fiber-optic cables carry digital signals to facilitate interactive shopping.

- **Web sites**—Many manufacturers and retailers have created Web sites to advertise their brands and to give information to consumers. Even small companies can afford to advertise globally.

- **E-commerce**—The Internet opens up global markets. Forecasters predict strong growth for fashion sales on the Internet as more consumers go online and more retailers develop "shops" in cyberspace.

ON CAMERA AT QVC CABLE SHOPPING NETWORK. *(PHOTO BY GINI STEPHENS FRINGS)*

Information Technology

Manufacturers and retailers also use computer technology to collect information, or *data*, to help them to make accurate marketing decisions.

- **Databases**—As discussed earlier in the chapter, retailers use information gathered from their customers to help them to determine target markets and customer preferences and to develop marketing activities and directional selling relevant to that market.

- **Research**—Manufacturers and retailers use the Internet to do research to help them to make important merchandising decisions. The Internet can provide fashion industry members with global information on suppliers, fashion services, directories, and libraries (see Chapter 4).

Information Systems

Each manufacturer and retailer works with computer experts to develop software programs and systems based on its company's needs. These systems bring order out of chaos by keeping track of and controlling planning, production, inventory, sales, and distribution, and they allow companies to collaborate with factories and supply-chain partners around the world.

- In product development, designers and merchandisers rely on consumer statistics and sales data to track trends. Customer relation management (CRM) systems keep track of customer preferences and purchasing patterns.
- Product data management (PDM) and product lifecycle management (PLM) systems coordinate each step of the design process from initial concept through production, including keeping track of resources for fabrics and trims, specifications, work-in-progress, and inventory.
- In production, goods are given *universal product codes* (UPC) that identify style, color, size, price, and fabrication.
- Radio frequency identification (RFID) tags, embedded in fabric with a computer chip, keep track of inventory so that everyone knows what is on order, in work, or in inventory at all times.

Electronic Data Interchange

In an attempt to reduce waiting time in ordering and distribution, textile producers, apparel manufacturers, and retailers use *electronic data interchange (EDI)*, the exchange of business data between two parties by means of computers. Inventory information is fed through the EDI pipeline from textile producers to manufacturers and retailers.

Automatic Replenishment   Agreements between suppliers and retailers allow the manufacturer to ship goods to stores automatically when inventory levels are low. Coded information immediately informs the retail buyer to replenish stock, the apparel manufacturer in turn to issue new cuts, and the fabric producer to send more fabric to the apparel manufacturer.

Value Chain Initiative (VCI)   Standardized codes and linkage systems have been developed throughout the industry. A consortium of approximately 90 leading software, hardware, transportation, and logistics companies has developed a set of international standards for sharing information among retailers, manufacturers, and suppliers. VCI covers nearly all aspects of the supply chain, including distribution management, electronic data interchange, import and export transportation, inventory control, and warehouse management.

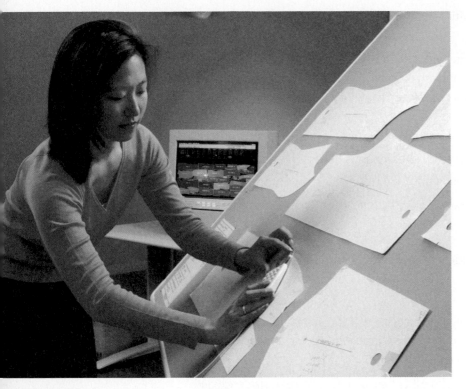

Textile and Apparel Production Technology

Modern technology makes fashion production more efficient. Computer-aided yarn spinning, fabric design, weaving, knitting, dyeing, and finishing allow our domestic textile industry to compete with imports.

Technological research has made it possible to develop nanotechnology, which controls the structure of matter at the molecular level, to create fibers with multifunctional properties as well as finishes that change fabric characteristics (see Chapter 5). Color-technology software has been developed to speed collaboration on color choices and matching between designers and fabric producers. Manufacturers are even experimenting with conductive fibers to build electronics into clothing.

The development of modern production machinery, such as power sewing machines and cutting tools, has streamlined the process of manufacturing. Modern cutting techniques include the use of computers, water jets, and laser beams. Computer technology has revolutionized manufacturing with computer-aided design (CAD), patternmaking, grading, cutting, unit and modular production systems, pressing, and distribution systems (see Chapter 10). Today's power machines can run faster than a car engine, sewing more than 5000 stitches per minute. Specialized machines make seamless activewear. Engineers are linking all phases of production from design to delivery.

The Marketing Chain

The marketing chain is the flow of product development, production, and distribution from concept to consumer.

The traditional chain of marketing—textiles to apparel manufacturers to retailers to consumers—is no longer clearly divided. The old relationships between suppliers and retailers are disappearing.

Traditional Marketing Chain

This textbook follows the sequential order of the traditional marketing chain. Formerly, each level of the industry was clearly separated. The textile industry developed and produced fibers, yarns, and fabrics and sold them to their customers, the apparel and accessory manufacturers. The manufacturers designed and produced the apparel and accessories and sold them to the retailers. The retailers sold it all to consumers. All levels did their own marketing activities, such as advertising, sometimes in cooperation with each other. Today, the old divisions have broken down.

Vertical Integration

Many companies are combining fabric production and apparel manufacturing, or manufacturing and retailing, a strategy called *vertical integration*. A completely vertical company produces fabrics, manufactures clothing, and sells the finished apparel in its own stores. Cutting out distribution costs (from manufacturer to retailer) increases profits and keeps prices down for the consumer. Vertical companies also like having total control of the supply, production, and marketing chain.

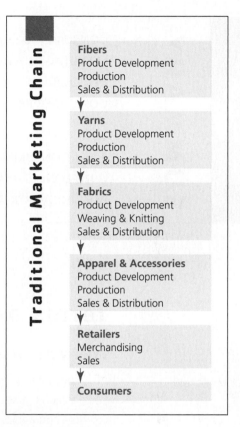

Traditional Marketing Chain

Fibers
Product Development
Production
Sales & Distribution

Yarns
Product Development
Production
Sales & Distribution

Fabrics
Product Development
Weaving & Knitting
Sales & Distribution

Apparel & Accessories
Product Development
Production
Sales & Distribution

Retailers
Merchandising
Sales

Consumers

Full Package Manufacturing

With today's focus on global production, most American and European manufacturers and retailers design their own fashion, but buy "full garment packages" from contractors in Asia and elsewhere. They source (find the best production available at the cheapest price) contract production to suppliers who can handle everything from buying piece goods to booking space on ships (see Chapter 10).

Manufacturer–Retailer Alliances

Fierce competition has forced manufacturers and retailers to work together to achieve quick and cost-effective *seamless distribution*. They form informal partnerships or alliances to integrate the marketing chain (see Chapter 12). Retailers discuss their needs with their manufacturer-partner; they work on product development together and plan production and shipping timetables together. For this arrangement to work, manufacturers and retailers must have complete trust in each other and open communications. In addition, many retailers have become manufacturers themselves.

SUMMARY

CONSUMER DEMAND HAS CAUSED THE FASHION INDUSTRY TO CONVERT FROM A MANUFACTURING TO A MARKETING FOCUS. MANUFACTURERS AND RETAILERS STUDY DEMOGRAPHIC AND PSYCHOGRAPHIC TRENDS AND DATABASES TO LEARN ABOUT CONSUMER PREFERENCES AND DEFINE TARGET MARKETS.

ECONOMICS, GLOBAL TRADE, AND MODERN TECHNOLOGY HAVE A GREAT IMPACT ON BOTH CONSUMERS AND FASHION MARKETING. THE TRADITIONAL MARKETING CHAIN IS NO LONGER MADE UP OF TOTALLY SEPARATE LEVELS. FASHION COMPANIES ARE EXPANDING VERTICALLY OR FORMING ALLIANCES TO STRENGTHEN THE CHAIN.

Terms and Concepts

Briefly define and discuss the following terms and concepts:

1. Consumer demand
2. Fashion marketing
3. Psychographics
4. Demographics
5. Market segments
6. Disposable income
7. Discretionary income
8. Automatic replenishment
9. Imports
10. Balance of trade
11. Tariffs
12. Quota elimination
13. World Trade Organization
14. NAFTA
15. Full garment manufacturing
16. Marketing chain
17. FTAA

Questions for Review

1. Why has the fashion industry shifted from a manufacturing to a marketing orientation?
2. What impact do demographics and psychographics have on fashion marketing?
3. What factors influence consumer spending?
4. What effect do fashion imports have on prices and jobs?
5. How does a retailer define its target market?
6. How are customer profiles compiled?
7. How does a retailer use databases?
8. Discuss global influences on the fashion industry.
9. Describe merchandise information systems.
10. How does technology influence fashion marketing?
11. What are the benefits of automatic replenishment?
12. How has the traditional market chain broken down?

Projects for Additional Learning

1. Analyze fashion styles today. Is there one trend that you believe is the result of a social, economic, or technological influence? Briefly explain the reasons for your choice.

2. Prepare a survey addressed to women over 50. Make up at least 10 questions regarding age, income, and clothing preferences and needs. Ask if these women are finding the kinds of clothes they want at the price they want to pay. Ask where they shop. Distribute at least 50 of these surveys to women at supermarkets. Ask for a mailed reply or completion of the survey in person. Compile the answers into a report. This would be a terrific class project as you canvass a larger group of women.

3. Interview a store executive at a local department store or chain store unit. Ask if this store is part of a vertical organization or if it has formed alliances with manufacturers. Who are their major suppliers? Write a report on your findings.

Notes

1. "Redefining Fashion for 50+," Advertising Supplement, *Women's Wear Daily*, March 1, 2002, p. 1.

2. Joan Kaner, former fashion director, Neiman Marcus, as quoted by Valerie Seckler, "Boomers: Buried Treasure," *Women's Wear Daily*, May 15, 2002, p. 8.

3. David Link, textile economist, E-mail correspondence, February 2003.

4. U.S. Department of Commerce, Textiles and Apparel Division, 2006.

NEW COLLECTIONS HERALD FASHION CHANGE
BUYERS AND THE PRESS AT THE OSCAR DE LA
RENTA SHOW AT 7TH ON SIXTH, MERCEDES
BENZ FASHION WEEK, IN NEW YORK CITY.
(COURTESY OF OSCAR DE LA RENTA.
PHOTO BY DAN LECCA.)

FASHION CHANGE AND CONSUMER ACCEPTANCE

Career Focus

Designers, merchandisers, and marketers at every level of the industry must be aware of fashion change, cycles, and consumer acceptance and how these concepts will affect product development and marketing. They also have to be aware of all the categories of apparel, particularly in their specialty area.

CHAPTER OBJECTIVES

After reading this chapter, you should be able to:

1. Discuss the dimensions of fashion
2. Identify the phases and lengths of fashion cycles and how they relate to consumer acceptance
3. Explain fashion adoption theories in relation to consumer acceptance
4. Describe buyer motivation
5. Demonstrate knowledge of clothing size and price ranges, style categories, and clothing classifications in women's wear, men's wear, and children's wear

Consumers' wants and needs create a cycle of consumer demand, industry catering to that demand, and, finally, consumer acceptance with the purchase of merchandise in the retail market. The first part of this chapter discusses fashion acceptance and rejection, a cycle that creates fashion change. The middle of the chapter covers consumers' connection to fashion cycles, how cycles relate to fashion adoption, and what factors motivate consumers to buy fashion. Last, all the categories of women's wear, men's wear, and children's wear are described. To set the stage, the chapter begins with terms associated with fashion acceptance.

Fashion Terms

All fashion executives use the following terms daily to discuss various aspects of fashion.

Fashion

Fashion is the style or styles most popular at a given time. The term implies four components: style, change, acceptance, and taste.

Style   *Style* is any particular characteristic or look in apparel or accessories. The term *style* can be interpreted three ways:

- Designers interpret fashion ideas into new styles and offer them to the public. The manufacturer assigns a *style number* to each new design in each collection, which is used to identify it throughout production, marketing, and retailing.

- Designs that have the same characteristics are referred to as a style, such as a blazer-style jacket, an empire-style dress, or an envelope-style handbag. A style may come and go in fashion, but that specific style always remains that style, whether it is in fashion or not. For example, the polo-shirt style will not always be in fashion, yet it will always have variations of the same styling and details, which make it a polo shirt.

- A person can have "style" by wearing fashionable clothes particularly suited to him or her, or a designer may become known for a certain "style" or look.

- A "stylist" is a fashion consultant who helps edit a designer's collection, selects flattering clothes for celebrities to wear, and/or puts fashion looks together with accessories for fashion photographers or a magazine.

Change   What makes fashion interesting is that it is always changing. Designer Karl Lagerfeld said, "What I like about fashion is change. Change means also that what we do today might be worthless tomorrow, but we have to accept that because we are in fashion. There's nothing safe forever in fashion . . . fashion is a train that waits for nobody. Get on it, or it's gone."[1] Vera Wang tells her assistants, "If you're afraid of change, you're in the wrong business."[2]

Many people criticize the fickleness of fashion, saying that fashion changes only to stimulate buying. And it is true that if fashion never changed, the public would not buy apparel and accessories so often. However, fashion is one way for consumers to visually express their relationship to current events and to life itself.

Fashion changes because

- It reflects changes in people's lifestyles and current events.
- People's needs change.
- People get bored with what they have.

As a result of modern communications, the public is quickly made aware of the existence of new styles. Thus, one of the greatest impacts on fashion is the acceleration of change. Consumers are aware of new styles before they reach the stores.

Because fashion is a product of change, a *sense of timing* (the ability to understand the speed of acceptance and change) is an important asset for anyone involved with product development or marketing in the fashion industry. Designers have to decide *when* their customers will be ready to accept a particular style. Italian designer Valentino remarked, "Timing is the key to a successful idea."[3]

■ STYLE #103 FROM THE ANDREW GN FALL WOMEN'S COLLECTION. *(COURTESY OF ANDREW GN, PARIS)*

Acceptance   Acceptance implies that consumers must buy and wear a style to make it a fashion. Karl Lagerfeld remarked, "There's no fashion if nobody buys it."[4] It is then up to the public to decide whether these styles will become fashion. Acceptance, that is, purchases by a large number of people, makes a style into fashion. The degree of acceptance also provides clues to fashion trends for coming seasons (see Chapter 4).

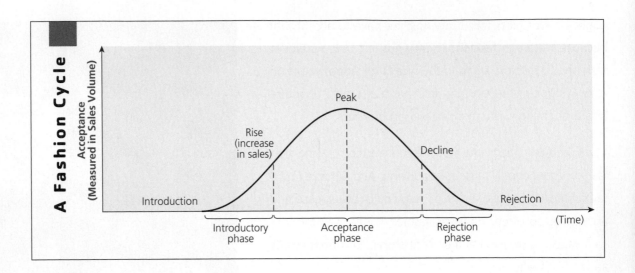

A Fashion Cycle

Acceptance (Measured in Sales Volume)

Introduction

Rise (increase in sales)

Peak

Decline

Rejection

(Time)

Introductory phase | Acceptance phase | Rejection phase

Taste An individual's preference for one style or another is referred to as *taste*. "Good taste" in fashion implies sensitivity to what is beautiful and appropriate. People who have good taste also understand quality and simplicity. Good taste is developed by extensive exposure to beautiful design. People also develop individual tastes, often referred to as "personal style."

Fashion Evolution

Generally, fashion change evolves gradually, giving consumers time to become accustomed to new looks.

Fashion Cycles

Fashion acceptance is usually described as a fashion cycle. It is difficult to categorize or theorize about fashion without oversimplifying. Even so, the fashion cycle is usually depicted as a bell-shaped curve encompassing five stages: introduction, rise in popularity, peak of popularity, decline in popularity, and rejection. The cycle can reflect the acceptance of a single style from one designer or of a "trend" (general style direction), such as cropped pants.

Introduction of a Style Most new styles are introduced at a high price level. Designers who are respected for their talent may be given financial backing and allowed to design with very few limitations on creativity, quality of raw materials, or amount of fine workmanship. They create new apparel and accessory styles by changing elements such as line, shape, color, fabric, and details and their relationship to one another. Production costs are high and only a few people can afford the resulting garments. Production in small quantities gives a designer more freedom, flexibility, and room for creativity.

New styles are shown to retail buyers and the press at collection showings and market weeks. At this first stage of the cycle, fashion implies only style and newness. Some wealthy people are able to buy these clothes because they want to wear them to important events. Some new styles are loaned to movie and TV stars to wear so that they will be seen by many people.

Increase in Popularity   When new styles are worn by celebrities on television or photographed in magazines, they attract the attention of the general public. Viewers and readers may wish to buy the new styles but perhaps cannot afford them.

Popular styles are copied or adapted by mainstream manufacturers to make them available to the general public. They use less expensive fabric and may modify the design to sell the style at lower prices. Some companies, such as ABS (Allen B. Schwartz), have built successful businesses imitating designer originals at lower prices. In self-defense, many couture and high-priced designers now have secondary, bridge, and/or diffusion lines, which sell at lower prices, so that they are able to sell adaptations of their original designs in greater quantities. Examples include Roberto Cavalli's "Just Cavalli" and Dolce & Gabbana's "D&G" collections.

Peak of Popularity   When a fashion is at the height of popularity, it may be in such demand that more manufacturers copy it or produce adaptations of it at many price levels. Some designers are flattered by copying, and others are resentful. There is a very fine line between adaptations and "knockoffs" (see Chapter 9)! However, volume production requires mass acceptance.

Decline in Popularity   Eventually, so many copies are mass-produced that fashion-conscious people tire of the style and begin to look for something new. Consumers still wear garments in the style, but they are no longer willing to buy them at regular prices. Retail stores put declining styles on sale racks, hoping to make room for new merchandise. Many shoppers today wait to buy when merchandise goes on sale, causing price deflation.

Rejection of a Style or Obsolescence   In the last phase of the fashion cycle, some consumers have already turned to new looks, thus beginning a new cycle. The rejection or discarding of a style just because it is out of fashion is called *consumer obsolescence*. As early as 1600, Shakespeare wrote that "fashion wears out more apparel than the man."[5]

Length of Cycles

Although all fashions follow the same cyclical pattern, there is no measurable timetable for a fashion cycle. Some fashions take a short time to peak in popularity, others take longer; some decline slowly, others swiftly. Some styles last a single selling season; others last several seasons. Certain fashions fade quickly; others never completely disappear.

Classics   Some styles never become completely obsolete, but instead remain more or less accepted for an extended period. A classic is characterized by simplicity of design, which keeps it from being easily dated. An example is the Chanel suit, which peaked in fashion in the late 1950s and enjoyed popularity again in the 1980s and 1990s. In the interim, the house of Chanel in Paris, as well as other manufacturers, have produced variations of these suits for a dedicated clientele at various price ranges. Other examples of classics include pea coats, blazers, cashmere sweaters, polo shirts, jeans, ballet flats, and loafers.

Fads   Short-lived fashions, or fads, such as pony prints or "charity" wristbands, can come and go in a single season. They lack the design strength to hold consumer attention for very long. Fads usually affect only a narrow consumer group, often begin in lower price ranges, are relatively simple and inexpensive to copy, and therefore flood the market in a very short time. Because of market saturation, the public tires of them quickly and they die out. Fads are more prevalent in the junior market.

Cycles within Cycles   Design elements (such as color, texture, or silhouette) may change even though the style itself remains popular. Jeans became a fashion item in the late 1960s and remain classics. Therefore, their fashion cycle is very long. However, various details, silhouettes, and other features came and went during that time.

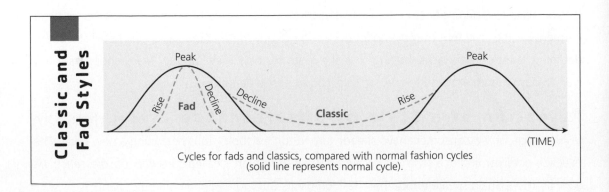

Cycles for fads and classics, compared with normal fashion cycles
(solid line represents normal cycle).

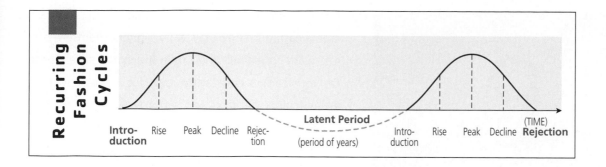

Recurring Cycles After a fashion dies, it may resurface. Designers often borrow ideas from the past. When a style reappears years later, it is reinterpreted for a new time; a silhouette or proportion may recur, but it is interpreted with a change in fabric and detail. Nothing is ever exactly the same—yet nothing is totally new. Designers are often inspired by nostalgic looks of the last century, but use different fabrics, colors, and details, which make the looks unique to today.

Consumer Identification with Fashion Cycles

How customers relate to the phases of fashion cycles has to do with the consumer group to which they belong.

Consumer Groups

Consumers can be identified with various stages of the fashion cycle. Fashion leaders buy and wear new styles at the beginning of their cycles; others tend to imitate: Manufacturers and retailers may also be identified as fashion leaders or followers, depending on which consumer groups they target.

Fashion Leaders The people who look for new fashion and wear it before it becomes generally acceptable are often referred to as fashion leaders. Fashion leaders are confident of their own taste or have a stylist to advise them. They dare to be different, and they attract the attention of others. Fashion leaders are a very small percentage of the public. They fall into two categories: fashion innovators and fashion role models.

FASHION LEADER
SARAH JESSICA
PARKER PRESENTS A
CFDA AWARD TO
NARCISO RODRIGUEZ.
*(COURTESY OF THE
COUNCIL OF FASHION
DESIGNERS OF
AMERICA)*

Fashion Innovators   Some fashion leaders actually create fashion. They may be designers themselves or just want to express their own individual style. These fashion leaders constantly look for interesting new styles, colors, fabrics, and ways to accessorize their clothes. They try to find unique fashion in small boutiques or vintage clothing stores, or they design their own clothes. They are discerning shoppers who like to wear beautiful or unusual apparel. They may give impetus to a certain style by discovering and wearing it. They may be referred to as *avant garde* (French for "ahead of the pack") or fashion forward. Italian designer Donatella Versace explained, "Many people give us inspiration, the way they put their clothes together, and some have a style that goes beyond the clothes."[6]

Fashion Motivators or Role Models   A few fashion leaders have the beauty, status, and/or wealth to become fashion role models. Designers lend new styles to celebrities, primarily film stars, to get publicity. They are seen at public events or on television and are photographed by the press. They become role models for everyone who identifies with them and, thereby, influence the way other people dress. For example, public interest in what actresses are wearing at the Academy Awards greatly influences the evening wear market. Because of their influence, fashion motivators are important to designers and to the fashion industry as a whole.

There are fashion leaders for every market segment. They can be any celebrity featured in the media, including royalty, politicians, TV and film stars, rock stars, and supermodels.

Fashion Victims   There are also those people with too much money to spend who become slaves to designer brands. Designer Jean-Paul Gaultier remarked, "Fashion victims are people who blindly and stupidly follow a brand without any discernment and without any analysis. As long as it's the latest rage, they buy it without thinking about adapting it to themselves."[7]

Fashion Followers   Fashion needs followers, or it would not exist. Most men and women seek acceptance through conformity and like to emulate world, national, or community fashion leaders to feel confident. Fashion followers imitate others only after they are sure of fashion trends. Consumers become fashion followers for one or more of the following reasons:

- They lack the time, money, and interest to devote to fashion leadership. Dressing fashionably takes time and energy.
- They are busy with their jobs and families and think that fashion is unimportant.
- They need a period of exposure to new styles before accepting them.
- They are insecure about their tastes and, therefore, turn to what others have already approved as acceptable and appropriate.
- They want to fit in with their friends or peer group or to be accepted by them.
- They tend to imitate people whom they admire.

There are various degrees of fashion followers. Many busy people want to be judged by their intelligence and not on how they look or what they wear. This is true for many people with a life full of work, children, or other interests.

Because of fashion followers, most manufacturers are copyists or adapters. From a marketing point of view, fashion followers are very important. They make mass production possible, because volume production of fashion can only be profitable when similar merchandise is sold to many consumers.

Individuality   A recent styling trend of mixing unexpected garments, prints, colors, and textures together has given more fashion decision making to individuals. Mixing unrelated pieces takes skill and practice to make the mix look fashionable. Women who grew up on suits and coordinated outfits find this eclectic look very difficult to achieve. Even designers have problems with it; Miuccia Prada said, "It is not easy to do those combinations."[8] However, it does give consumers the opportunity to develop individuality.

Fashion Leadership in Manufacturing and Retailing

Manufacturers and retailers respond to fashion leaders and followers in their product development and merchandising. They try to establish a particular merchandising identity with various consumer groups. Designer collections provide for the fashion leaders, whereas the majority of manufacturers provide merchandise for fashion followers.

Retailers, too, cater to fashion leaders or followers. Luxury brands featured at Bergdorf Goodman and Saks Fifth Avenue, for example, identify with and cater to fashion leaders, while Wal-Mart and Target are able to sell volume to the majority of followers. Stores like Macy's and the Gap fall in between. Retailer identification with fashion cycles is discussed fully in Chapter 15.

Adoption of Fashion

It is important to understand how new fashion ideas are disseminated, or spread, and how they are adapted to the tastes, lifestyles, and budgets of various consumers.

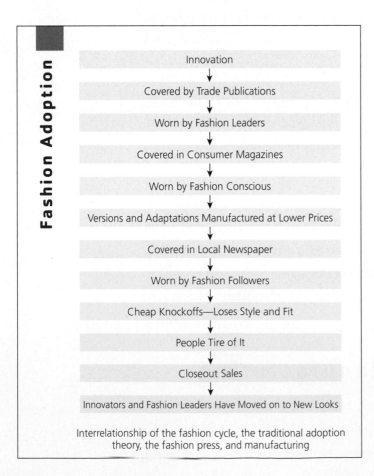

Fashion Adoption

Innovation
↓
Covered by Trade Publications
↓
Worn by Fashion Leaders
↓
Covered in Consumer Magazines
↓
Worn by Fashion Conscious
↓
Versions and Adaptations Manufactured at Lower Prices
↓
Covered in Local Newspaper
↓
Worn by Fashion Followers
↓
Cheap Knockoffs—Loses Style and Fit
↓
People Tire of It
↓
Closeout Sales
↓
Innovators and Fashion Leaders Have Moved on to New Looks

Interrelationship of the fashion cycle, the traditional adoption theory, the fashion press, and manufacturing

Basically, there are three variations of the fashion adoption process: traditional adoption, reverse adoption, and mass dissemination.

Traditional Fashion Adoption (Trickle-Down Theory)

The trickle-down theory is based on the traditional process of copying and adapting trendsetting fashion from Paris, Milan, London, and New York designers. Sometimes it is even difficult to know where an idea began. Because couture or "signature" designer fashion is expensive, it is affordable to only a few people. As new styles are worn by publicized fashion leaders or shown in fashion publications, more consumers are exposed to these new looks. To appeal to this broader group of consumers, manufacturers produce less expensive adaptations of these fashions. These are copied again and again at lower prices until they have been seen often enough to become acceptable to the most conservative buyer. The cheapest versions are seen at discount houses soon after. Consumers then tire of the look, and its popularity fades. Fashion implies newness and freshness. Yet, as a fashion is copied, modified, and sold at lower and lower prices, it loses its newness, quality, and other essential design elements.

Reverse Adoption (Trickle-Up or Bottom-Up Theory)

Since the 1960s, manufacturers and retailers have paid more attention to consumer preferences. Designers pay attention to what people are wearing. Dancewear and activewear, which began as functional needs of the consumer, also have influenced designer collections. Vintage fashion, purchased by young people in thrift shops, has influenced many recent collections. Designers now send out their own scouts or use shopping services to look for inspirational vintage styles.

Mass Dissemination (Trickle-Across Theory)

Modern communications bring fashion from around the world into our homes instantly. Consumers see the trends and want to look as fashionable as the celebrities. Manufacturers copy hot new styles almost immediately to meet the high demand; therefore, production speed is of the greatest importance. Mass dissemination is becoming the prevalent mode of fashion adoption. Oscar de la Renta commented that information is traveling a bit too fast—a denim coat from his collection had been copied and was selling at Bloomingdale's before his original version reached the stores.[9]

A DRESS FROM PRADA, THE MUCH-COPIED ITALIAN FASHION COMPANY. *(COURTESY OF PRADA)*

There is no longer one channel of fashion dissemination. Many separate markets have developed geared to various age ranges, lifestyles, tastes, and pocketbooks. What appeals to a junior customer would probably not appeal to a missy customer. Various designer and manufacturer labels appeal to various market segments at different price points. Increased diversity means that many different styles can be acceptable at the same time. There are many more options.

Motives for Consumer Buying

To help them make styling and merchandising decisions, designers, buyers, and other industry executives try to understand consumer motivation.

In the past, most people bought new clothes only when a need arose, for a very special occasion, or because their old clothes wore out. The average person simply could not afford to buy more than the basic necessities. In Western society today, discretionary income is larger, and people can buy new clothes frequently.

Therefore, buying motives have changed; people are able to buy clothes because they want or like them. Buying motives vary from consumer to consumer and from day to day. Motives are both rational and emotional:

To Fill an Emotional Need New clothes help people to feel better psychologically. Being secure in the feeling that they are wearing appropriate fashion gives them confidence and self-assurance. A growing body of brain research shows that shopping activates the chemical dopamine. However, dopamine can cause impulse buying (buying without careful consideration), bad decisions, and compulsive shopping problems.

To Be Attractive Consumers want clothes that are flattering, that make them look their best, or that show off their physical attributes.

To Be Fashionable People may buy new clothing to make them feel that they are trendy or at least in the mainstream of fashion. They may discard clothing that is still wearable only because it is out of fashion.

To Impress Others People may want to project a successful image or establish unique identities with fashion. They may want to exhibit their level of taste or income through clothing. Expensive brands have even served as status symbols.

To Be Accepted by Friends, Peer Groups, or Colleagues Average Americans have conservative tastes; they do not want to differ from their peers. They may want to identify with a certain lifestyle. Buying patterns suggest that consumers like some direction or guidance as a framework for their choices.

To Fill Basic Lifestyle Needs Based on their basic needs, individuals seek clothing for a particular event, climate or season, vacation, exercise or sport, job, or lifestyle.

Consumer Buying Patterns

Buying patterns change continually. To determine the acceptability of fashion, both designers and manufacturers find it helpful to consider these consumer shopping criteria.

- **Perceived value**—Consumers look for their idea of quality at reasonable prices; this is referred to as *perceived value*.
- **Item buying**—Consumers may buy only one item, such as a jacket, to update their wardrobes.
- **Multiple-use clothing**—Ideally, consumers look for comfortable, functional, multiple-use clothing.
- **Wear now**—People are buying closer to need, buying clothes they want to wear immediately.
- **Convenience**—With time and energy in increasingly short supply, consumers are looking for ways to make shopping easier. Consumers want to find what they need easily and quickly. In response to consumer needs, catalog and Internet shopping has increased.
- **Service**—Consumers are demanding personal service and in-stock assortments (clothing available in every size and color).

Fashion Selection

Customers are attracted to a particular garment or accessory by its styling features. There are also practical considerations, including quality and price, that the consumer usually evaluates before making a purchase.

Styling Features

Styling features, which are the same as the elements of design discussed in Chapter 9, are considered here from the purchaser's point of view, rather than the creator's.

Color People relate very personally to color, usually selecting or rejecting a fashion because the color does or does not appeal to them or is or is not flattering.

Texture The surface interest in the fabric of a garment or accessory is called texture. Texture usually gives a clue as to fiber content.

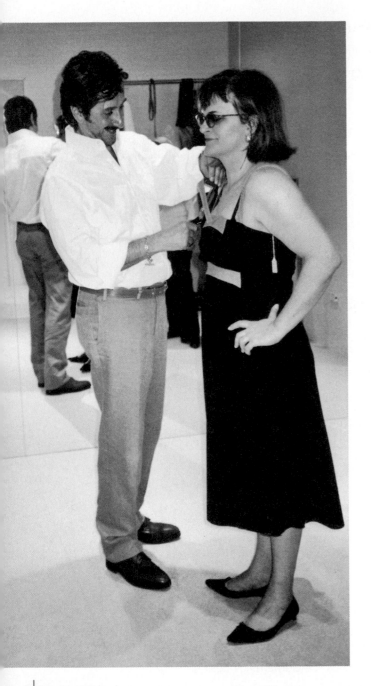

RALPH RUCCI
FITTING ONE OF
HIS DESIGNS FOR
A PRIVATE CLIENT.
*(COURTESY OF
RALPH RUCCI, PHOTO
BY GINI STEPHENS
FRINGS)*

Style   The elements that define a style include line, silhouette, and details. A consumer's selection is frequently influenced by his or her opinion of what is currently fashionable.

Practical Considerations

Price   Consumers want the best product at the best price. Price is probably the most important practical consideration for the average consumer. They must compare the total perceived worth of a style with the retail price and with their own budgets. As a result, discount retailers and inexpensive chains have taken market share away from middle market stores.

Fit   Sizing is not a guarantee of fit. The U.S. Department of Commerce has tried to set sizing standards, but it is difficult to set size ranges and grading rules to fit every figure. Each company tries its sample garments on models whose figures are typical of its target customers, which makes sizing vary from brand to brand. Fit Technologies has created a sizing system called Fit Logic, based on three body types. However, so far, Fit Logic and body scanning have not been widely adopted.

Comfort   Obviously, people need clothes to keep warm in cold weather or cool in warm weather. As the population ages and as travel increases, people also want clothes that are comfortable to move in, sit in, travel in, and so on. The increasing desire for comfortable clothes is one of the reasons for the popularity of spandex fiber (added to other fibers).

Appropriateness   It is important that consumers find suitable or acceptable fashions for specific occasions or to meet the needs of their lifestyles. Consumers consider their clothing needs for job and leisure-time activities, as well as what is appropriate for their figure type, personality, coloring, and age.

Brand or Designer Label   Brands are a manufacturer's means of product identification. Some consumers buy on the basis of a particular brand's reputation for styling or fit. Designer Giorgio Armani said, "A brand name is important as long as it is combined with a proper relationship of quality and price."[10]

Fiber or Fabric Performance and Care The durability of a garment or accessory and the ease or difficulty of caring for it are often factors in garment selection. Many consumers prefer easy-care fabrics because they do not have the time for or the interest in ironing or the money to pay for dry cleaning. Consumer concern for easy-care prompted the textile industry to develop no-iron finishes and made wash-and-fold cotton garments popular. To protect the consumer, government regulations now require fiber content and care instruction labels to be sewn into apparel.

Quality and Durability   Consumer demand for quality has risen in recent years. The designer or bridge customer considers clothing an investment and may not mind spending more for the lasting qualities of fine detailing and workmanship. Some consumers may look for a particular brand or name on the basis of a reputation for quality.

Fashion Categories

In response to consumer demand and changes in consumer lifestyles, manufacturers and retailers have developed various size and price ranges, as well as categories for styling and clothing type.

Variety in dress has resulted from manufacturers' responses to changes in our habits and roles and the increase in consumer purchasing power. Clothing for all occasions and lifestyles is available. Manufacturers specialize in clothing type (or have a separate label for each), age of target customer, price range, and often gender. Retailers have separate departments for each category, price range, and size range.

In our value-conscious marketplace, consumers seek multipurpose, multiuse clothing. They look for apparel that is wearable in a variety of settings: office, social activities, gym, home, or vacation. As a result, there is a breakdown of categories: gym wear has become streetwear; underwear is outerwear, and so on.

Women's Wear

Clothing Categories
There are many types of women's apparel, including dresses, social apparel, suits, outerwear, sportswear, activewear, and lingerie. There are also specialty categories, such as bridal gowns and maternity clothes, and a huge array of accessories.

Dresses are single garments or two pieces on the same hanger priced as one unit. Styles range from tailored to simple, business to casual. Dresses are easy to wear; no thought is required for coordination.

Social apparel includes special-occasion attire, such as long and short cocktail dresses, dressy pant ensembles, and evening or bridal gowns.

Suits are jackets and skirts (or pants) sold together as units. Suits range from casual to tailored. In spite of the trend to casual dressing at the office, professional women still want to wear suits.

Outerwear includes coats, capes, and jackets with a primarily protective function. Outerwear can be divided into four categories: traditional wool and wool blends, outdoor-ski anoraks in performance fabrics such as microfibers, leathers, and furs. All are available in both classic and fashion styles. Outerwear has become more casual.

Sportswear is any combination of tops and bottoms, such as jackets, skirts, pants, shorts, blouses, and shirts, that are priced separately so that the customer can combine them as desired. Sportswear lines are organized as separates or as coordinated sportswear (pieces intended to be mixed and matched). Sportswear is popular because of the variety of looks that can be made by combining separates. American designers have excelled in this category, which suits informal American lifestyles.

Activewear is one of the hottest categories of apparel today, fueled by the popularity of fitness. Activewear is worn by people who actively participate in fitness activities or sports, for spectator sports, or simply as streetwear. Activewear includes bike shorts, leggings, T-shirts, crop tops, jogging sets, unitards, sweatsuits, and jackets. More and more activewear companies are offering as many styles for women as for men. To make their clothing relevant, some manufacturers have the athletes that they sponsor give advice to designers and also feature these athletes in their ads.

■ ACTIVE SPORTSWEAR FROM PRADA SPORT. *(COURTESY OF PRADA, MILAN, ITALY)*

Swimwear includes one-piece suits, bikinis, and cover-ups. Manufacturers are beginning to cater to the baby boom market with bulge-concealers, push-up bras, extra torso length, and other inner construction. Manufacturers are also adding special sizes.

Lingerie, including innerwear, bodywear, sleepwear, and loungewear, is also enjoying increased sales. The popularity of lingerie is partly caused by the fashion of wearing corsets to show, as Karl Lagerfeld introduced under suit jackets, and the marketing style of Victoria's Secret. The more fitted look of today's fashion is also influencing the rise in sales of body slimmers.

Accessories, as discussed in Chapter 11, give consumers an easy way to update their wardrobes with scarves, hats, handbags, footwear, and hosiery. The popularity of particular accessories is cyclical, such as belts with waist interest. Functional accessories, such as backpacks and sun hats, have become fashionable as well.

Size Ranges   Each size range caters to a different figure type. Generally, today's sizing standards are based on more realistic measurements than in the past. However, each manufacturer has its own interpretation of standardized sizing. Designer clothes may deliberately be labeled one size smaller so that the customer can feel good about being a size 10 instead of a 12. Some manufacturers try to accommodate a variety of body types by using a variety of fit models. Manufacturers have been experimenting with body scanning for an individual fit and Fit Logic,

TABLE 3.1   TYPICAL RELATIONSHIP OF STYLE, SIZE, AND PRICE RANGES IN WOMEN'S WEAR

Style Range	Styling	Age	Size Range	Figure	Price Range
Designer	Unique, top-name designer fashion	25 and up	Misses 4–12	Misses: mature, slim	Designer
Bridge	Designer fashion	25 and up	Misses 4–12	Misses: mature, slim	Bridge
Misses	Adaptations of fashion looks	25 and up	Misses 4–14	Misses: mature, 5'7" block	Better to budget
Petites	Same as Misses	25 and up	Petite 0–14	Misses: under 5'4"	Better to budget
Women's or large sizes	Same as Misses plus some junior looks	18 and up	16–26W or 16–26WP	Misses: large size + some petite	Better to budget
Contemporary	Trendy	20–40	Misses 4–12	Misses: slim	Better to budget
Junior	Youthful, trendy, figure-conscious	13–25	Juniors 3–15	Not fully developed	Better to budget

a three-tier sizing system that would require stores to devote three times the selling space to carry brands tailored to three body types. Women's size ranges include junior, misses, petite, and large sizes.

Junior customers, sizes 1 to 13, have a less developed figure and a shorter back-waist length (a higher waistline) than misses figures. This figure is usually equated with a slim, young customer.

Misses sizes 6 to 16 (or 4 to 14) are for the mature female figure, usually based on a height of approximately 5 feet 7 inches. For misses separates, some blouses and sweaters are sized 30 to 36 (8 to 14); other may be sized small, medium, or large.

Petite sizes are created for the woman who is less than 5 feet 4 inches tall. Sizes range from 0 to 16. Most manufacturers limit the size range to 4 to 14.

Large or women's sizes range from 14W to 32W, but are usually limited to 16W to 26W. Sometimes these sizes are represented as 1X (16 to 18), 2X (20 to 22), and 3X (24 to 26). Large-sized petites are marked WP.

Fashion for petite and large-sized women was virtually ignored by the fashion industry until 1977. Statistics now show that 54 percent of the total female American population wears either petite or large sizes. Among women over 40 years old, 40 percent wear size 14 or larger. There is tremendous growth opportunity for manufacturers in special sizes because there are no extra costs for styling, only for new patterns. Now many manufacturers are catering to special sizes.

Manufacturers still have to deal with a majority of figures that do not fit sizing standards. One reason that sportswear is so popular is that it gives consumers the opportunity to mix sizes to accommodate their less-than-perfect figures. Women, too, do not have the benefit of free alterations at retail stores as men do.

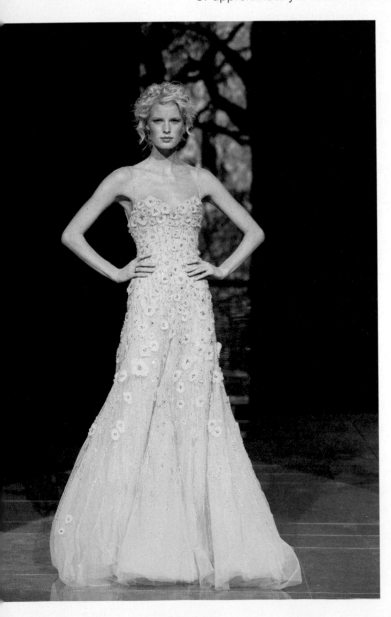

A COUTURE GOWN FROM ELIE SAAB, LAYERS OF GOLD TULLE SPRINKLED WITH FABRIC FLOWERS. *(COURTESY OF ELIE SAAB AND DENTE & CRISTINA)*

Styling and Price Ranges   Apparel is also classified by style range. Style ranges grew out of age groups, price, and size ranges.

Couture/Luxury This term is reserved for fashion that is made to order to fit an individual client's measurements. These clothes are the most luxurious and the most expensive, often between $5000 and $50,000 for a single garment and reserved for a *very* small international clientele. Examples of couturiers include Karl Lagerfeld for Chanel, Christian Lacroix, and Valentino.

Designer This category pertains to ready-to-wear from successful designers who own their own business or have a "signature collection" (with their name on the label). The high prices they charge, $1000 to $5000, allow them to use the best of fabrics and quality mass production. Examples of designer collections include Giorgio Armani, Donna Karan, and Ralph Lauren, as well as the ready-to-wear collections of the couturiers and all the designers listed in Chapter 8.

Bridge This styling and price range was created to give consumers a less expensive alternative to designer fashion. Bridge is simply a step down in price from designer, achieved by using less expensive fabric or different production methods. Some designers have secondary lines, such as CK from Calvin Klein, Donna Karan's DKNY, Marc by Marc Jacobs, or Emporio from Armani. Other collections, such as Ellen Tracy or Dana Buchman, cater specifically to the bridge market.

Contemporary This is a revived category aimed at the style-conscious woman who wants more fashion than missy styling provides, but does not want to pay designer prices; price ranges vary from bridge to budget. Resources include BCBG, Laundry, Max Studio, and Theory.

Misses This styling category provides more conservative adaptations of proven or accepted designer looks. Misses lines utilize less expensive fabrics and less extreme silhouettes. Misses styling is available in a variety of quality and price ranges: better, moderate, or budget. "Better" vendors include Jones New York, Liz Claiborne, and Lauren/Ralph Lauren. Moderate resource examples are Koret and Sag Harbor.

Junior This style range grew out of junior sizing—young styling for a young figure. Junior styling is heavily influenced by music and television celebrities and tends to be body conscious. A resurgence of this category is a result of the high birthrate after 1980. Typical labels include Necessary Objects and XOXO.

As manufacturers or designer names increase in popularity, they add lines in other categories so that their businesses can grow. Claiborne and Ellen Tracy now make dress lines in addition to

A SUMPTUOUS
VELVET COAT FROM
GIORGIO ARMANI,
MILAN, ITALY.
(COURTESY OF
GIORGIO ARMANI
SPA)

sportswear. Claiborne also added men's wear collections. Ralph Lauren, on the other hand, started by designing men's wear and later added women's apparel. They may also add different price ranges, such as secondary lines at higher or lower prices. Better manufacturer Liz Claiborne created the Dana Buchman bridge collection to reach another customer.

As women's designers enter the men's wear market, and vice versa, and with the popularity of men's sportswear, the production and marketing techniques in men's and women's wear are becoming similar.

Men's Wear

Men's clothing has also changed as a result of changes in men's interests and more casual lifestyles. Traditionally, men learned to look for quality, fit, and durability. Their wardrobes, formerly limited to suits, slacks, and sport shirts, have expanded along with their activities, and increased clothing choices have made them more fashion conscious. However, women still have an impact on the way men dress.

In the late 1990s, a shift to casual dressing at the office occurred. However, most men find it overwhelming combining the wide choice of sportswear separates. It is also difficult to judge what level of "casual" is appropriate for the office. Many businessmen still like to wear suits. However, casual dress is still prevalent for the electronic and marketing sectors, blue-collar jobs, and people working at home offices.

As a result of casual dressing, the men's wear industry has changed. Men's suit sales have decreased, whereas sportswear has enjoyed tremendous growth. In the past, suits represented half of men's wardrobe purchases; now purchases are divided equally among suits, furnishings and accessories, and sportswear. As tailored clothing becomes more casual, the category distinctions become blurred. There is an intermixing of business and leisure wardrobes, such as an Armani suit jacket over jeans.

Clothing Categories There are now as many categories available for men as there are for women. Many designers and manufacturers, including Ralph Lauren, Tommy Hilfiger, Hugo Boss, and Nautica, have lines in several men's wear categories. Stores have increased square footage in men's wear areas and use aggressive display and promotional techniques to lure their increasingly fashion-wise male customers. Categories include the following:

Tailored clothing includes suits, tuxedos, overcoats, topcoats, sport coats, and separate trousers for business and evening wear. Tailored clothing requires lengthy, time-consuming, costly production, and retailers need to inventory many sizes.

Furnishings include dress shirts, neckwear, underwear, hosiery, robes, pajamas, shoes, and boots.

Sportswear comprises sport jackets, knit or woven related separates, sweaters, and casual trousers that fill the demand for more leisure and casual wear.

Active sportswear includes all garments needed for sports or exercise, such as windbreakers, ski jackets, jogging suits, and tennis shorts.

Work clothes, such as overalls, work shirts, and pants required by laborers, have become popular for leisure wear.

Accessories include small leather goods such as wallets, shoes, boots, belts, jewelry such as cuff links, scarves, gloves, and eyewear.

Styling The styling creativity and diversity now apparent in men's wear are a result of men's desire to have appropriate clothing for their leisure acitivities. However, so far, there are not as many styling categories for men's wear as there are for women's wear.

Designer Styling Internationally recognized designers often set fashion directions in men's wear. Giorgio Armani led the way to casual, soft suits that can be worn at the office or for leisure activities. Italian collections, such as Armani, Brioni,

■ MEN'S SPORTSWEAR FROM GIORGIO ARMANI, MILAN, ITALY. *(COURTESY OF GIORGIO ARMANI SPA)*

Gucci, Kiton, and Zegna, are considered fashion forward. Calvin Klein and Richard Tyler are among the prominent American brands. Most designers have both suit and sportswear collections.

Traditional Styling Classic suit and sportswear makers like Hickey-Freeman, Hartmarx, and Brooks Brothers or designer collections like those of Tommy Hilfiger and Ralph Lauren are influenced by traditional tailoring. The primary interest is found in a wide variety of suiting and shirting fabrications.

Contemporary This styling is usually less expensive than designer apparel; it is trendier and aimed at a younger customer. Examples include Perry Ellis, KM by Krizia, Nautica, and Gap sportswear.

Price Ranges
Custom-tailored suits are made with the finest construction and fabrics. Suits from Savile Row in London, for example, cost more than $3000. Much of the inner, hidden construction is done by hand.

Designer ready-made suits at retail prices run upward from $1000, and sport coats cost upward from $500. Designer suits and sportswear are also made from fine fabrics, but they are not made-to-measure, and the quality varies.

Bridge suits and sportswear, as in women's wear, are a step down in price from designer. This can also mean a step down in fabric quality and workmanship.

Moderate suits have a broad range of retail prices, usually from $325 to $650; sport coats range from $200 to $450; and slacks cost from $40 to $90. Many large retailers, such as Macy's and Nordstrom, rely heavily on private-label merchandise for this price range to control price.

Popularly priced suits are those less than $325, the most affordable price range. Many discounters and mass merchants also offer private-label merchandise at this price range.

Size Ranges
Men's suits range in size from 36 to 44 (with additional large sizes to 50), originally based on chest measurements. Lengths are designated after the size number: R for regular, S for short, and L for long. European sizes are 46 to 54 (add 10 to each American size). Young men's sizes have a narrower fit in the jacket and hip than regular men's sizes. There has been an attempt to simplify men's sizing because traditional sizing requires a huge inventory of many combinations of chest and length measurements. An important innovation is the development of suit separates. Men also enjoy free alteration services at most men's stores and in men's clothing departments.

Dress shirts are sized by collar measurement (inches in America and centimeters in Europe) and sleeve length. Sport shirts and sweaters are sized in small, medium, large, and extra large. Trousers are sized by waist and inseam measurements. Dress slacks are left unhemmed to be finished by the store's tailor as a customer service.

Children's Wear

The children's wear business is very complicated because each size range is a separate market. Children's wear is also highly competitive because the consumer is extremely value conscious. Parents do not want to spend much money on clothes that their children will quickly outgrow.

Children's wear manufacturers often produce both dresses and sportswear to protect their businesses from shifts in fashion preferences. Some men's and women's wear companies, such as Esprit and Polo, also produce children's lines, but others have tried and found it a difficult business. Children's manufacturers, too, have had stiff competition from Baby Gap and Kid's Gap and all retail private-label programs. However, a steady domestic birthrate of around 4 million per year is keeping the children's wear market afloat.

Categories It is very difficult to categorize children's wear. Categories change with each size and price range. Also, boundaries between categories are becoming increasingly blurred. Some casual dresses fall into sportswear classifications; some dresses fall into tailored clothing classifications. Children's wear, too, has become more casual as today's children lead very active lives.

Girls' dresses are available in all style and price ranges. Holiday and spring are the biggest seasons for special-occasion dresses. Some girls' dresses, jumpers, jackets, and skirts are considered tailored clothing.

Boys' traditional clothing includes blazers, other dress jackets, suits, dress pants, and dress shorts.

Sportswear comprises T-shirts, jeans, pants, shorts, overalls, jumpsuits, leggings, girls' skirts, boys' shirts, sweatshirts, sweatpants, and sweatsuits in knits and wovens, particularly denim and fleece. Boys' wear has become very casual, and tops outsell bottoms.

Swimwear groups swimsuits and beach cover-ups.

Outerwear includes dress coats, all-weather coats, raincoats, ski jackets, windbreakers, and snow suits.

Sleepwear includes layette gowns and sacques, blanket sleepers, pajamas, nightgowns, nightshirts, and robes. A major issue in this category is the Consumer Product Safety requirement that sleepwear be made of polyester so that it can have a flame-retardant finish. However, many consumers want pure cotton and therefore are buying playclothes to use as sleepwear.

INTERNATIONAL FASHION FOR LITTLE GIRLS FROM OILILY, THE NETHERLANDS. *(COURTESY OF OILILY)*

Accessories include shoes, hats, gloves, scarves, hair accessories, sunglasses, jewelry, bags, backpacks, hosiery (tights and socks), and underwear; belts, caps, and ties for boys; and infant accessories, such as bibs and booties. Hats to protect children from the sun have become a fashion statement. Some manufacturers are including accessories with their apparel, priced as a unit.

Sizing   Children's wear sizing is separated by age groups.

Newborn sizes are layette (0 to 11 pounds), 3, 6, and 9 months.

Infant sizes are based on age in months, usually 12, 18, and 24 months. In Europe, sizes are based on the length of the baby or the height of the child.

Toddler apparel, for the child who has learned to walk, are sized 2T, 3T, and 4T.

At this point, sizes separate for boys and girls.

Girls' apparel is sized 4 to 6X and 7 to 16 (some companies manufacture sizes 2 to 10 or extra-small to extra-large); preteen sizes are 6 to 14; and the young teen wears young junior sizes 3 to 13.

Boys' sizes are 4 to 7 and 8 to 20.

Styling   The styling of children's wear changes considerably by size range. The only styling differentiation is traditional versus trendy.

Infants, Toddlers, and Young Children. In the case of young children, the consumer is a parent, grandparent, or other adult. Parents want their children's clothes to reflect their own taste. "There are still many parents who want people to look at their child and say 'that is the cutest outfit I've ever seen.'"[11] Many parents tend to dress their children more as little adults than as babies.

Ease of dressing, washability, durability, and versatility are important design considerations in clothing for young children. For infants and toddlers who have to be dressed, crotch snaps and generous necklines are important. For the toddler, ease of dressing, such as elastic waistlines, is also important because children want to dress themselves.

Novelty, color, and conversational prints are important in infant, toddler, and young children's wear. Apparel printed with licensed cartoon or television characters has also been a phenomenal success.

Older Children Older children have more definite opinions on what they want to wear, partly because of advertising, television exposure, and peer-group pressure. This development has had an effect on styling in that many childrens' wear manufacturers follow junior trends for girls and young men's trends for boys.

Because styling for older girls is often filtered down from the junior market, junior resources are finding success in the 7 to 14 size range and even in sizes 4 to 6X. In the same way, styling for older boys is influenced by young men's wear. Some men's wear companies, such as Tommy Hilfiger and Ralph Lauren's Polo, are making boys' wear. In this age range, too, printed apparel, with sports teams, celebrities, and brand names, such as Nike or Champion, has been extemely popular.

Price Ranges

In children's wear, price ranges are broader than in women's or men's wear. Also, some manufacturers produce lines in several price ranges and often manufacture for both boys and girls in multiple size ranges. The brand examples are a mixture of all size ranges.

Better resources provide fashion direction, quality fabrics, and workmanship. Vendors include Dorissa, Sylvia Whyte, Monkey Wear, Oilily, Polo, and Tommy Hilfiger.

Moderate includes a wide range of prices and labels at average prices, such as Baby Togs, Eagle's Eye, Esprit, Flap Doodles, Gotcha, Hartstrings, Little Me, Osh Kosh B'Gosh, Quiksilver, Rare Editions, and Youngsport.

Budget priced merchandise is offered by Byer, Eber, Carter's, Healthtex, and Rampage.

In children's wear, too, retailers often offer private-label merchandise in the moderate and budget-priced ranges.

SUMMARY

FASHION HAS THREE PROPERTIES: STYLE, ACCEPTANCE, AND TIMELINESS. CHANGE MAKES THE FASHION WORLD GO ROUND. NEW STYLES ARE INTRODUCED, RISE IN POPULARITY, THEN DECLINE INTO OBSOLESCENCE. SOME STYLES REMAIN FASHIONABLE LONGER THAN OTHERS. SOME COME BACK INTO FASHION AFTER A LATENT PERIOD. BECAUSE FASHION IS A PRODUCT OF CHANGE, A SENSE OF TIMING IS AN IMPORTANT ATTRIBUTE AT ALL LEVELS OF THE INDUSTRY.

CONSUMERS CAN BE IDENTIFIED WITH STAGES OF THE FASHION CYCLE. FASHION LEADERS, A VERY SMALL PERCENTAGE OF THE POPULATION, BUY AND WEAR NEW STYLES AT THE BEGINNING OF THE CYCLE; OTHER CONSUMERS IMITATE. THE MAJORITY OF CONSUMERS ARE FOLLOWERS, WHICH FACILITATES THE MASS MARKETING OF FASHION.

FASHIONS MAY SIFT DOWN FROM THE ORIGINAL IDEAS OF HIGH-FASHION DESIGNERS TO REAPPEAR AT LOWER PRICE LEVELS. OTHER STYLES ARE EITHER ADAPTED "UP FROM THE STREETS" OR ARE DISSEMINATED QUICKLY THROUGH MASS MARKETING. CONSUMERS BUY CLOTHES FOR MANY REASONS, INCLUDING THE DESIRE TO BE FASHIONABLE, ATTRACTIVE, IMPRESSIVE, ACCEPTED, OR EMOTIONALLY FULFILLED. CONSIDERATIONS IN FASHION SELECTION INCLUDE COLOR, TEXTURE, STYLE, PRICE, FIT, APPROPRIATENESS, BRAND, FABRIC PERFORMANCE, AND WORKMANSHIP. CONSUMER ACCEPTANCE IS A MAJOR INFLUENCE ON STYLING AND MERCHANDISING DECISIONS. THE FASHION INDUSTRY RESPONDS TO CONSUMER NEEDS WITH A VARIETY OF SIZE RANGES, PRICE RANGES, AND STYLE RANGES IN WOMEN'S, MEN'S, AND CHILDREN'S WEAR.

Terms and Concepts

Briefly define and discuss the following terms and concepts:

1. Fashion
2. Style
3. Acceptance
4. Sense of timing
5. Fashion cycles
6. Classics
7. Fads
8. Fashion leaders
9. Fashion followers
10. Fashion victims
11. Mass-market dissemination
12. Buyer motivation
13. Perceived value

Questions for Review

1. Name and define the three components of fashion.

2. How does fashion acceptance affect the timing of design?

3. Describe the phases of a typical fashion acceptance cycle.

4. Discuss the relationship of consumer acceptance to the fashion cycle.

5. What do consumers consider when buying clothes? How do you make buying decisions?

6. What are the similarities between style ranges and size ranges?

Projects for Additional Learning

1. Is there a well-known movie star or public figure (either male or female) in the news whom you believe to be a fashion leader? Write a short report documented with examples of how this person influences the way others dress. Clip (or photocopy) illustrations from publications.

2. From current fashion magazines, collect five examples of each of the following types of fashion: (a) high fashion; (b) mass fashion; (c) classic; and (d) fad.

3. In a local specialty or department store, compare two dresses of similar price from different manufacturers. Try them on. Which has the better fit? Compare fabric choices in terms of quality and suitability to the design. Compare styling: Which is more innovative? Taking all factors into consideration, which dress is the better buy? Discuss your findings in a written report. Describe or sketch the two garments.

4. In a local specialty or department store, compare the missy and junior departments. List the major manufacturers in each department, and explain the general styling differences.

Notes

1 As quoted in "King Karl," *Women's Wear Daily*, November 20, 1991, p. 7.

2 As quoted in "The Transformation of Vera Wang," *Women's Wear Daily*, November 16, 2005, p. 7.

3 As quoted in "Is the Designer Dead?" *Women's Wear Daily*, April 7, 1992, p. 10.

4 Quoted in "Fall Fashions: Buying the Line," *Time*, April 23, 1984, p. 77.

5 *Much Ado About Nothing*, Act III, 1598–1600.

6 As quoted in "Donatella Takes Charge," *Women's Wear Daily*, October 1, 1997, p. 4.

7 As quoted in "Les Fashion Victims," *Women's Wear Daily*, January 21, 1992, p. 4.

8 As quoted in "Hunting & Gathering," *Wall Street Journal*, December 17, 2005.

9 Review of Fashion Group International meeting, *FGI Bulletin*, May 2000, p. 1.

10 As quoted in "Europe Design Houses Face a New World," *Women's Wear Daily*, June 15, 1992, p. 6.

11 Natalie Mallinckrodt, president, Golden Rainbow, as quoted in "The Infant/Toddler Report," *Earnshaw's*, May, 1994, p. 51.

DESIGNER BETSEY JOHNSON IN HER
NEW YORK STUDIO, WORKING WITH
THE RESOURCES THAT INSPIRE HER.
(COURTESY OF BETSEY JOHNSON,
PHOTO BY GINI STEPHENS FRINGS)

4

FASHION RESEARCH AND RESOURCES

Career Focus

Before work on each new line or collection begins, every designer and merchandiser in the fashion industry is actively involved in fashion research. Market research consultants also study and report on demographics and consumer buying habits. Design services and fashion publications also need experts in fashion research and forecasting for every merchandise category.

CHAPTER OBJECTIVES

After reading this chapter, you should be able to:

1. Discuss the importance of research
2. Explain the need for market studies and fashion forecasting
3. Discuss and give examples of design resources

It is not easy to make or sell what people will want to buy in a future selling season. Awareness, research, and planning are needed for producers and retailers to make, buy, and sell what consumers will want. Fashion executives must be aware of what is going on in the world, including economics, politics, demographics, and social change, and how these events and conditions will affect their business. Without proper research, or with an unexpected turn of events, merchandise ends up on the sale racks, causing losses—and even business closures—for producers, manufacturers, and retailers alike.

This chapter discusses fashion forecasting, services, and resources that are used for product development at every level of the fashion industry. Research is done before any other design or merchandising activity at every level of the industry. It becomes second nature to every decision maker in the field of fashion. Because the very term *fashion* implies a state of flux, textile producers, fashion manufacturers, and retailers all need to absorb a constant flow of information to anticipate change and consumer preferences. Donatella Versace explained, "You cannot live in an ivory tower and make fashion or anything artistic. . . . You're to live in the real world."[1] Designer Karl Lagerfeld said, "I want to be informed, to know everything, see everything, read everything. . . . You mix all that, then forget about it and do it your way."[2] Ady Gluck-Frankel, owner and designer of Necessary Objects, explained, "It's the times that set the trends. We are all affected by the same issues: politics, ecology, economy, music, etc. We all just interpret them for our own markets."[3] Often, what seems to be intuition is actually clever assimilation and analysis of careful research.

Every executive, designer, and merchandiser in the fashion industry must be involved with research and analysis. They continuously study the lifestyles of consumers, shop the market, and read trend and design reports, fashion magazines, and newspapers to understand consumers and what they might want to buy. This research is absolutely necessary to make intelligent planning decisions regarding design, manufacturing, and sales.

Fashion Forecasting

Designers, merchandisers, and buyers must learn to predict trends, which are new directions in fashion.

It would be impossible to ask consumers what they will want to wear a year or two in advance—they would not even know themselves. Because designers, merchandisers, and retailers must work so far ahead of the selling season to produce or stock the fashions their customers will want, they must learn to anticipate customers' wants and needs—to be fashion forecasters of the future. Fashion forecasting involves the following activities:

- Studying market conditions—how the consumer's buying behavior is influenced by society, economics, technology, and the environment (see Chapter 2)

- Noting the lifestyles of the men, women, or children who are their customers (see Chapter 2)

- Researching sales statistics to establish sales trends

- Evaluating the popular designer collections to find fashions (colors, silhouettes, fabrications, lengths) that suggest new directions, or "trends"

- Surveying fashion publications, catalogs, and design services from around the world

- Observing "street fashions" (what people are wearing) and what celebrities are wearing

- Keeping up with current events, the arts, and the mood of the public

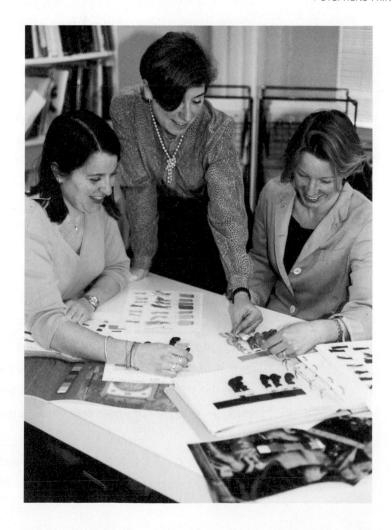

THE STAFF AT THE COLOR BOX, IN NEW YORK CITY, WORK ON COLOR FORECASTING. *(PHOTO BY GINI STEPHENS FRINGS)*

Market Research

As discussed in Chapter 2, manufacturers and retailers must constantly research their target market to learn buying habits and preferences.

Consumer Research Manufacturers and retailers may ask consumers directly about their buying preferences. Consumer reactions are compiled and tabulated to find preferences for certain garments or accessories, colors, sizes, or preferences for particular retailers. This information can be used to create new products to fit specific consumer tastes.

Methods of questioning consumers can be formal or informal. Buyers and sales associates may talk with customers in the store. Manufacturers or retailers may hire market research companies to make inquiries by telephone or mail and to hold consumer focus group meetings. Not every company can afford to hire market researchers, but they can speak with their customers.

- **Surveys**, by telephone or mail, are made by publications and market research companies for manufacturers and retailers. These surveys include questions about income, lifestyles, fashion preferences, and shopping habits.

- **Consumer focus groups** are meetings of target customers usually selected by a market research firm to meet with manufacturers or retailers. These groups discuss the pros and cons of merchandise or other aspects of shopping satisfaction.

- **In-store informal interviews** and "mall intercepts" can help researchers obtain information by simply asking customers what they would like to buy, what styles they like that are currently available, and what merchandise they want but cannot find. Because of their close contact with their customers, owners of small stores can often do this most effectively.

Shopping   To study what consumers want and need, designers and merchandisers also "shop" retail stores to see what merchandise is selling best. Designers and merchandisers compare the styling, price, fit, and quality of lines that compete with their own. Catalog designers and merchandisers also research competing catalogs and the Internet. Retailers observe competing stores to analyze which merchandise selections and presentation methods are the most successful.

Sales Records   Every manufacturer and retailer researches its own sales records. Rising sales statistics show what fashion trends are developing; declining sales show what styles have passed their peak (see Fashion Cycles, Chapter 3). Overall weak sales show that a style is not meeting consumer needs for fashion, quality, or fit. By carefully monitoring sales records, retailers can see trends: the rising popularity of higher or lower skirt and jacket lengths, softness versus tailored garments, new fabrics, certain colors, and so on.

Trend Analysis

Twice each year, top designers show their collections (see Chapter 12). From all over the world, retail buyers and fashion editors invade Paris, Milan, New York, and London. Editors and buyers try to analyze the collections for outstanding new ideas that might influence fashion direction. Traditionally, American manufacturers and retailers look at the European collections for an indication of the newest fashion ideas. International manufacturers and retailers are also interested in American designer collections, especially sportswear.

Fashion Trends   *Fashion trends* are the styling ideas that major collections have in common. They indicate the direction in which fashion is moving. Fashion forecasters look for the

A DISPLAY OF DESIGN FORECASTS AND REPORTS FROM D-CIPHER, PECLERS, INSIGHT, AND JENKINS. *(COURTESY OF ESP/ELLEN SIDERI PARTNERSHIP, INC.)*

styles they think are *prophetic*, similar ideas found in several successful collections that capture the mood of the times and signal a new fashion trend.

Several designers may use a similar fashion idea because they have been inspired by common sources. The trend may appear in a new or unique fabrication, silhouette, or other design element that appears in multiple collections. Very often, a new trend appears in small doses until it spreads to other collections. As the press notices similarities between collections and highlights them, the media exposure also helps to establish the trends.

Designers for mainstream manufacturers and retailers analyze the collections to understand trends. As designers are not invited to the shows, they must evaluate them by shopping in major fashion capitals or using design services, Internet sites, magazines, and newspapers.

For retail buyers, it is becoming a huge challenge to figure out which trends will become fashion basics and which are only fads. Buyers have to become very flexible in their buying patterns and cautious about inventory management. If the market becomes flooded with a new trend, consumers may react negatively to the overexposure. Ideally, retailers like to test a trend with a small amount of merchandise and buy more later, but this is not usually possible.

Empowered by the Internet and television, global trends are moving at an accelerating pace. The life span of a trend can be anywhere between five months and two years. For the junior market, the span may be only two or three months.

Trends for Target Markets Too often manufacturers and retailers get so focused on a single trend that they forget that there are many market segments. Diverse consumer age segments and lifestyles create many separate market niches, each with its own trends: trendy, junior, professional, family oriented, and so on. With today's segmented market, a trend may be confined to a single market niche. Designers and merchandisers must decide which trends best suit their own customers based on age range, income level, lifestyle, and fashion preferences.

Fashion Services and Resources

Fashion professionals rely on information sources such as design, color and video services, newsletters, books, magazines, newspapers, and Web sites to follow fashion trends.

Fashion Services

Fashion services are resources for fashion reporting, forecasting, and consulting available to the trade only on a subscription and/or fee basis. These services are very expensive, but many offer education rates. Most of these services can be found on Web sites, in New York City directories, or through sales reps in major cities. Some of the major fashion services are Doneger Creative Services, Carlin International, Dominique Peclers, ESP Trend Lab, Promostyl, Here & There, Fashion Box, and Trend Union. These services may provide market research, feasibility studies, collection reports, forecasting, slides, consulting, garments to borrow, and/or original designs.

Collection Reports Fashion services provide reports with the most immediate indepth source of information about the collections. The services work very quickly, getting their reports out on the Internet within hours and printed reports out within a week after the shows, whereas magazines take months. Fashion reports also analyze the collections in more depth than newspapers or magazines. They may include photographs and/or sketches, slides, fabric swatches, and descriptions. The collections can be so overwhelming in scope that even those who attend the shows may need the assistance of these reports to sort out ideas and identify major trends.

Trend Reports   Fashion services publish trend reports or "predictives" that include descriptions, sketches, fabric swatches, and color samples of garments they believe are prophetic or that are big sellers in Europe. They may project color or fabrication tendencies, forecast silhouette or other design elements, and indicate trends for particular target markets, often in separate books. Some include "street photos" of young people in major fashion cities, which are especially helpful to junior designers.

Most services offer information on both men's and women's wear. Some reports, such as *Bloc Note*, have separate books for children's wear, lingerie, or knits. The *Tobé Report* is aimed at retailers. Each service has its own special approach. Some of them, such as *Insights Footwear, Knit Point*, or *Mudpie Kids*, cater to special niche markets. There are so many of these reports that it is difficult to decide which ones to order. A German publication called *Styling News* (www. modeinfo. com) was created to make many of them known.

Consulting   Many services also offer personalized services, such as designing, brand development, market research, feasibility studies, customer profile analyses, and brand imaging, to help their clients to develop products. This can be on an individual consultation basis, or they may actually develop the entire line for a company. Peclers of Paris, for example, designs lingerie for Victoria's Secret.

Color Services

Some services specialize in color forecasting. Fashion and textile industry professionals meet at least twice a year to pool their knowledge of color cycles and preferences to project color trends for the future. Forecasts, including yarn colors or swatches, are sent out by the color services in time for designers and merchandisers to plan their color stories and purchase fabrics. Some fiber companies also supply color forecasts for their customers (see Chapter 6).

Color services include the International Color Authority (ICA) (British), Essential Colours and Colorace (German), OMS (Austrian), Orizzonti (Italian), L. A. Colours (Dutch), the Color Box, the Color Marketing Group, Concepts in Color, Colorplay, Doneger Creative Services, Huepoint, Color Portfolio, the Mix Global Color Resource, and more.

Color systems are another type of color resource. These companies, such as SCOTDIC (Standard Color of Textile Dictionaire Internationale de la Couleur) and Pantone, keep a permanent library of dyed colors in color families. They distribute color cards to their customers, who use the samples as standards for choosing colors for merchandise and dyeing fabrics.

Web Sites

Countless Web sites offer information on fashion. Almost every major manufacturer and retailer has a Web site. As the public's craving for fashion information grows, so do the number of Web sites. A few key resources (which change frequently) are included on the following list:

- www. fashioncenter. com The New York City Fashion Center site features an interactive database of over 12,000 apparel-related companies, a map of the garment district, and a trade show calendar.

- www. fgi. org The Fashion Group International's Web site lists events and business information for members. The site's "student center" gives information on fashion schools, internships, and jobs. Their newsletters and meetings are another good source of information on current developments in the fashion industry.

- www. doneger. com   Doneger Creative Services provides reporting and analysis on a fee basis for industry clients.

- www. firstview. com *First View* is a fashion publication available on a fee basis with photos of the latest fashion collections from Paris, Milan, London, and New York.

■ www. modeaparis. com Lists all members of the Fédération Francais de la Couture in Paris.

■ www. vogue. com *Vogue* magazine's Web site covers the designer collections, with celebrity and behind-the-scenes features.

■ www. wgsn. com Worth Global Style Network provides online fashion news, trade show calendars and reports, ready-to-wear and couture collections, and trend forecasts to businesses on a subscription basis.

■ www. wwd. com The online version of *Women's Wear Daily*, the daily fashion industry newspaper.

Video Services and Television

Video is another ideal medium for fashion reporting. *Videofashion News*, which offers collection coverage and behind-the-scenes designer interviews, appears regularly on Style Network, USA Cable Network's Trio Popular Arts Channel, and Cablevision's Metro TV. *Videofashion News* DVDs are also sold to stores, companies, and libraries.

A CD-ROM called *Fast Forward*, which covers major fashion events, is available by subscription.

Fashion Magazines and Newspapers

Fashion trend research also depends on a variety of trade and consumer publications. *Trade* magazines and newspapers are intended for people working in the fashion industry; *consumer* publications are created for the general public. Each fashion journalist edits fashion trends from a different perspective. Their collective editing can make or break the success of a designer and reinforce trends.

Fashion Editing The role of the fashion editor is to educate the public, to provide fashion information from all phases of the industry in all parts of the world, to make the industry or the consumer aware of all that is available, and to help the consumer

VOGUE EDITOR-IN-CHIEF ANNA WINTOUR WITH BELGIAN DESIGNER OLIVIER THEYSKENS. *(COURTESY OF THE COUNCIL OF FASHION DESIGNERS OF AMERICA, PHOTO BY DAN LECCA)*

to make wise and suitable styling and/or buying decisions. Fashion editors, together with journalists, stylists, and photographers, act as the eyes and ears of the consumer. They let the nation or the community know where to find the fashions that are currently on the market, and they report on how new fashions should be worn and accessorized.

The fashion editors of prominent newspapers and fashion magazines attend the collection openings, take notes on what they like best, and report on what directions they believe are important. They may request sketches or photographs of their favorite garments to use in their articles.

Articles for national fashion magazines are big productions. Editors book celebrities or celebrity models more than a year in advance. Editors sift through news releases and photographs that come into their offices for fashion story ideas. Photographers and studios or locations are chosen. Other preparations and costs include stylists, production assistants, props, hair and makeup artists, manicurists, transportation, and caterers. The fashion editor and stylist request clothes and accessories from designers for consideration. Photo prints are ordered, retouched (models aren't perfect), and color-corrected. For the cover, mock-up versions are made and then tested and rated by using an e-mail survey. Image is so important that it costs about $100,000 just to produce the cover!

Trade Publications Trade publications in the form of newspapers, journals, or magazines offer readers information on fashion trends and developments in the textile and fashion industries and retailing. Most specialize in a particular branch of the industry. Busy executives have time to read only a few of these, so they need to look for those publications that provide information relevant to their market. Fashion executives read these publications *daily*. The following are some examples:

Women's wear: *Women's Wear Daily*, the major American fashion industry newspaper, is published five days a week. Each day features different topics, and there are often special supplements on subjects such as accessories, sportswear, swimwear, or technology. *WWD* also publishes *W*, a monthly magazine. *Style* is Canada's trade magazine, *Gap* is published in France, and *Fashion Folio* and *Draper's Record* are published in England.

Men's wear: *DNR, the Daily News Record*, which is now actually a weekly, is the men's wear industry newspaper.

Children's wear: *Earnshaw's*

Sportswear: *Sportswear International, Sport & Street*

Accessories: *Shuz, FN (Footwear News)*, and *Accessories*

Textiles: *International Textiles, Textile World, Textiles Suisse Textile Arts Council Newsletter*, and *Textile View*

Apparel Industry: *Apparel Industry Magazine, Apparel Manufacturer, California Apparel News*, and *Apparel* (formerly *Bobbin*)

Advertising and marketing: *Advertising Age, Brandweek, American Demographics, Retail Ad World, SMM (Sales & Marketing Management)*, and *Communication Arts*

Retailing: *Stores* (National Retail Merchants Association), *Chain Store Age, Retail Intelligence, Retail Forward, Retail Merchandiser*, and *Shopping Center World*

Visual presentation: *Communication Arts, Display & Design Ideas, Inspiration, Lighting Dimensions, Retail Design & Visual Presentation*, and *VM & SD (Visual Merchandising & Store Design)*

International Consumer Fashion Magazines

These publications are aimed at the consumer and show fashion that is already available in the retail stores. Americans find foreign magazines helpful for forecasting because European designers often create these trends. Some of these magazines are published only two or four times a year to report on the collections. Many German and Japanese magazines include patterns.

Magazines are very important resources for designers, particularly when budget cuts eliminate design services. Designers buy only the magazines that provide suitable ideas for their specific product. For example, jeanswear designers buy contemporary and junior magazines that have ideas for that specific category. International magazines may be ordered through Overseas Publishers Representatives in New York City. The following is only a partial list of the hundreds of magazines on fashion:

Women's wear: *Collections, L'Officiel Collections*, and *Vogue* (France); *Line a Italiana, Donna, Moda, Harper's Bazaar Italia*, and *Vogue* (Italy); *Harper's* and *Queen*, and *British Vogue* (England); *Burda International, Madam, Fashion Guide*, and *Vogue* (Germany); *Élégance* and *Rendez-vous* (Switzerland); *Fashion Yearbook, Hi Fashion, Mode et Mode, Mrs.*, and *Madam* (Japan); *Style* and *Flare* (Canada)

Contemporary and junior (trendy): *Dazed and Confuzed* and *Options* (UK). *Elle, Dépêché Mode*, and *Jeune et Jolie* (France); *Moda In, Moda Viva*, and *Amica* (Italy); *Brigitte, Miss Vogue*, and *Carina* (Germany); *Non-no, 25 ans*, and *McSister* (Japan)

Children's wear: *Vogue Bambini, Donna Bambini*, and *Moda Bimbi* (Italy); *Sesame* and *Baby Fashion* (Japan) (Junior fashions are also a good source of ideas for children's wear.)

Men's wear: *L'Officiel Hommes* and *Vogue Hommes* (France); *L'Uomo Vogue, Linea Italiana Uomo, Mondo Uomo,* and *Uomo Harper's Bazaar* (Italy); *Männer Vogue* (Germany); *Men's Club, Mr.,* and *Dansen* (Japan)

Bridal: *Mariages* (France) and *Sposa* (Italy)

American Consumer Fashion Magazines Many established magazines are undergoing extensive facelifts, and there is a continuing influx of foreign publishers and editors into the United States. Some magazines have vanished, but there are always fresh attempts to reach new markets. American magazines as resources are best used to analyze appropriate fashion for specific target markets, to examine American designer collections, and to see what fashion is currently available in the stores. Each designer has his or her own favorites. Keep in mind that advertising takes up 50 to 75 percent of the magazine! Inspirational titles include *In-Style, Lucky, Teen Vogue, GQ,* and *Details.*

Catalogs

Designers also use catalogs as resources for ideas. Catalogs are essentially free magazines. A leather jacket shown in a sportswear catalog might be the inspiration for a corduroy nylon jacket for another fashion company, even another catalog business.

Design Sources

Historic and ethnic costume, the arts, and travel are sources of inspiration for designers.

Designing isn't all originality. Ideas do not simply materialize out of thin air. First, a designer does careful research, but what makes a designer's line special is his or her unique interpretation of design sources.

Historic and Ethnic Costume

Designers often turn to the past (recent or distant) or to folk costume for ideas and themes. Costume falls into two categories: *historic* costume, the fashion of a certain historical period, and *folk* or *ethnic* costume, traditional national or regional dress. Both are inspirational sources of design.

Historic Inspiration

Designers usually are sensitive to the combinations of colors, motifs, lines, shapes, and spaces in each historical period of costume. Some are inspired to use these in their collections. Nanette Lepore and James Coviello, for example, were both influenced by Edwardian England when designing their collections. Nostalgic looks are often used in today's fashion, reinterpreted for today. Carolina Herrera showed references to the late 1950s in her collection.

Design Company Archives

Most designer companies have their own fashion archives. The creation of a library of sketches, photos, letters, books, patterns, accessories, fabrics, and actual dresses and gowns has become an important way for these companies to relate to their roots. The creation of an archive is a daunting undertaking requiring space with temperature control, an archivist to label and categorize the materials, acid-free paper, and dust-resistant cabinets. The House of Balenciaga not only uses the archive for inspiration but also creates two small "editions" a year of old garments made in new fabrics.

Folk Influences

Designers find the same inspirational blend of colors, motifs, lines, shapes, and spaces in folk costume. Oscar de la Renta for example, was recently influenced by Indian and Russian dress. This has been expressed in the gypsy looks, beaded trims, embroidery, spicy colors, and tie-dye prints found in their collections. Chinese and Russian folk costume have also inspired many designers such as Michael Kors and Peter Som.

Vintage Clothing Shops and Services

Designers shop vintage clothing stores, flea markets, thrift shops, auctions, and online for old garments and fabrics to interpret for today's consumer. Stylists and services are available that search for vintage clothes for manufacturers. Hundreds of vintage fashion Web sites list fairs, flea markets, thrift shops, auctions, and online shops. Examples include www. rustyzipper.com, www.vintagevixen.com, and www.fashiondig.com. The Manhattan Vintage Clothing Show in New York is an example of a large market.

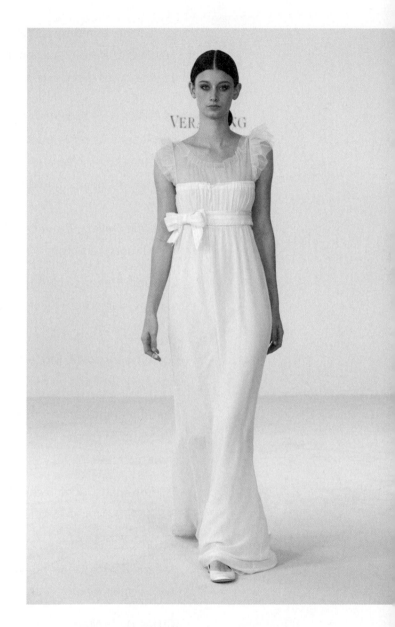

■ INSPIRED BY THE EMPIRE STYLE OF THE EARLY 1800S, VERA WANG CREATED THIS IVORY GEORGETTE GOWN WITH NET BODICE AND RUFFLES. *(COURTESY OF VERA WANG)*

Vintage fashion, especially couture, has become highly coveted. A Charles Worth gown was sold for $101,500 at a recent auction. Private collectors bid along with museums and antique dealers and design houses seeking items for their archives.

Museums Museum costume collections offer the unique opportunity of seeing actual preserved garments displayed on mannequins. A popular exhibit, such as the Cristobal Balenciaga exhibit at the Louvre in Paris, or "Anglo Mania" at the Metropolitan Museum in New York, can influence many designers. The following museums and galleries house important costume collections:

Costume Gallery, Brooklyn Museum 188 Eastern Parkway, Brooklyn, New York 11238
www.brooklynart.org

Costume Gallery, Los Angeles County Museum of Art 5905 Wilshire Boulevard, Los Angeles, California 90036
www.lacma.org

Costume Institute, McCord Museum 690 Sherbrooke Street West, Montreal, Canada
www.mccord-museum.qc.ca

Costume Institute and Antonio Ratti Textile Center, Metropolitan Museum of Art
1000 Fifth Avenue at 82nd Street, New York, New York 10028-0198
www.metmuseum.org

Fashion Institute of Technology (FIT) Costume Library and Gallery Seventh Avenue at 27th Street, New York, New York 20001-5992
www.fitnyc.suny.edu

Galleria d'Arte Moderna e Galleria del Costume Via della Ninna 5, 50122 Firenze, Italy
www.sas.firenze.it

Musée de la Mode et du Costume de la Ville de Paris Palais Galliéra, 10 avenue Pierre ler de Serbie, 75116 Paris, France
www.paris.fr/musees

Musée de la Mode et du Textile, Palais de Louvre 107 rue de Rivoli, 75001 Paris, France
www.ucad.fr

Museum of Costume Assembly Rooms, Bennett Street, Bath BA1 2QH, England
www.museumofcostume.co.uk

Rijksmuseum Stadhouderskade 42, 020 Amsterdam, the Netherlands
www.rijksmuseum.nl

Texas Fashion Collection School of Visual Arts, University of North Texas, Denton, Texas 76203-5100

www.art.unt.edu/tfc

Victoria and Albert Museum Cromwell Road, London SW7 2Rl, England

www.vam.ac.uk

Many regional museums have fashion collections, too, and almost every national museum of folklore includes ethnic costumes. Costume can also be studied in paintings in every museum.

Libraries and Bookstores Design ideas can also be gleaned from historic costume books and old magazines. Museum bookstores and libraries are excellent sources of costume references. Some colleges have historic costume books. Many libraries also have collections of old fashion magazines, including *Godey's Lady's Book* (from the 1830s to the 1890s), *Harper's Bazaar* (from 1867), and *Vogue* (from 1894). Many fashion designers build their own libraries of books on historic and ethnic costume, films, sports, artists, designers, and textiles.

The Arts

Film, video, television, art, architecture, music, and theater are also inspirational sources for fashion design. Designers are influenced by other designers and artists and, therefore, flock to large cities to soak up the creativity centered there. Excitement about a new idea acts as a catalyst for more creativity.

Art exhibitions often have an impact on design collections. Designers may also be inspired by a single artist or painting. Anna Molinari (for Blumarine), for example, was influenced by Gustav Klimt, and Badgley and Mischka by seventeenth century Flemish paintings. Designer Peter Som said he was inspired by Vermeer's painting *Girl with a Pearl Earring*.

Films often influence fashion. *Costume design* refers to the specialized field of creating apparel for film and theater. This kind of design involves period research and character enhancement. Actress Julianne Moore commented, "People in fashion go to the movies to get inspired and people in movies look to fashion to know how to dress, it's a very symbiotic relationship."[4] Ready-to-wear designers are often influenced by the clothes they see in films, both new and old. Peter Som was recently influenced by *My Fair Lady*, for example, and Matthew Williamson by Faye Dunaway in *The Thomas Crown Affair* of 1968.

Music and the exposure that video gives singers and musicians have made a significant impact on young people. Teens look to see what music celebrities are wearing; therefore, junior designers adapt these looks for their customers.

Television gives broad exposure to fashion as seen on sitcoms and reality shows. These clothes are either designed specifically for the show or are chosen from ready-to-wear collections. Because many programs are targeted to viewers under 30, the clothes worn by the stars disseminate youthful fashion trends. Some manufacturers and retailers pay to have their merchandise worn on popular sitcoms. Cable TV (as well as the Internet) also features runway collections. Bravo's *Project Runway* takes fashion a step further by providing exposure for aspiring designers.

The Academy Awards The gowns worn at the Academy Awards and the Golden Globes, and the outfits worn at the Grammys and other award shows, also have an impact on fashion. Top designers compete to dress the stars, particularly those nominated for the best actress award. Some designers, such as Armani, loan a few gowns for a celebrity to chose from, with the understanding that she will wear one of them. The film star may also hire a stylist to help her choose a flattering gown and to accessorize it. Since many people want to emulate the stars, these fashions are quickly copied.

ANDREW GN CREATED THIS ENCHANTING BLOUSE, INSPIRED BY THE LOVELY LACE-INSET FABRIC. *(COURTESY OF ANDREW GN, PARIS)*

Fabrics

Fabrics are the most important inspiration and resource for designers. There is no limit to their cost. One fabric may inspire an entire collection. A recent Matthew Williamson collection, for example, featured embroidered fabrics from India. Mainstream apparel and accessory designers are limited to the fabrics that are currently available in their price range.

Designers shop at international textile markets or fabric showrooms in New York and Los Angeles to see the current fabric lines. They also use fabric libraries such as the Design Library in New York or those at fiber and fabric companies.

Fabric designers do the same market and trend research as apparel and accessory designers. They also have the same sources of inspiration, especially fabric and costume collections, old or new interior decoration, or fabric market fairs. Certain textile swatch services specialize in vintage fabrics that can be copied.

Travel and Nature

Travel influences designers' collections. Designers like to visit visually and culturally stimulating places. Designers take working vacations because they are always using their awareness skills to absorb new stimuli. Nanette Lepore said she was inspired by a trip to the Amalfi Coast in Italy. Travel exposes designers to new ideas, but these ideas are not always obvious in their collections. The influences may be as subtle as a fresh color palette, a pattern for a fabric, or just a different way of looking at things.

Designers can be inspired by nature both at home and abroad. Natural forms and patterns can suggest a design for apparel or accessories. The colors of flowers or fall leaves might inspire a color story. Donatella Versace, for example, covered an entire dress with leaves cut from green-dyed python skin.

Form Follows Function

To borrow a phrase from architect Louis Sullivan, apparel designers, too, are inspired by necessity. The long-term demand for denim made jeans fashionable. When consumers became active, the fashion industry created activewear. As activewear became popular, it became fashion. The popularity of practical backpacks made them stylish. The desire for comfort and flexibility made spandex so successful. The use of spandex, in turn, led to body-conscious styling. Often, the need creates the fashion. Some designers also like to predict the future of fashion in their designs.

The Street Scene

Designers get ideas just watching people in the streets: people on their way to work, the trendy young people out and about, or the kids on their skateboards. They look in the shop windows. They take photos or make sketches of clothing that appeals to them. A designer at Levi Strauss made videos of "street fashion" to show to her colleagues to stimulate ideas. Photos of what the general public is wearing are often featured in *Women's Wear Daily* and fashion trend books.

Awareness

Designers surround themselves with photographs of ideas, fabric swatches, and anything else that will stimulate creativity. They leave their studios to shop, visit museums, study nature, attend the theater, or people-watch. They watch fashion on the Internet, videos, and television. Designers usually carry sketchbooks to jot down ideas whenever and wherever they find them. They hunger for information, letting ideas mingle and shape themselves into new forms.

Most fashion companies have their own resource centers. Large companies, such as Jones New York and Liz Claiborne, are able to provide extensive resources. Liz Claiborne, for example, has an 18,000-square-foot design resource center containing a vintage fabric library, periodicals, trend reports, consumer forecasts, art books, and a color lab.

Awareness is the key to creativity. Designers must learn most of all to keep their eyes open, to develop their skills of observation, and to absorb visual ideas, blend them, and translate them into clothes that their customers will like. It is impossible to predict where an idea will come from or which idea may inspire a whole group or line. Some people are more sensitive to good composition than others, but practice and observation make a person more aware, sensitive, and confident. Exposure to beautiful things helps a designer or buyer to distinguish genuine beauty and quality from fads and mediocrity.

SUMMARY

RESEARCH AND OBSERVATION ARE CRITICALLY IMPORTANT IN THE FASHION BUSINESS. BY OBSERVING AND RESEARCHING CONSUMER BUYING HABITS, WATCHING FOR DIRECTIONS IN DESIGNER COLLECTIONS, READING THE MOST APPROPRIATE FASHION PUBLICATIONS, OBSERVING FASHION TRENDS, AND BEING AWARE OF THE ARTS, MANUFACTURERS AND RETAILERS TRY TO PREDICT WHAT THE MAJORITY OF THEIR CUSTOMERS WILL WANT IN THE FORESEEABLE FUTURE. TO KEEP UP WITH THE CHANGING WORLD OF FASHION, FASHION AWARENESS SHOULD BECOME SECOND NATURE.

Terms and Concepts

Briefly define and discuss the following terms and concepts:

1. Fashion editing
2. Fashion forecasting
3. Fashion trends
4. Target market
5. Evaluating collections
6. Fashion services
7. Trade publications
8. Consumer publications
9. Awareness
10. Design sources

Questions for Review

1. What factors are involved in fashion forecasting?

2. How do designers use trend and information services?

3. Why is market research important for textile and apparel manufacturers and retailers?

4. Explain the difference between trade and consumer fashion publications.

5. What role does historic or folk costume play in today's fashion?

6. Give an example of how films have influenced fashion.

Projects for Additional Learning

1. Trend research: Make a survey of fashion resources available to you. Read the latest issues of fashion magazines and compare the contents with fashion looks six months ago and a year ago. From the information you find, try to analyze the fashion direction for the future. Organize your ideas into a few basic trend forecasts for color, fabrics, silhouette, and line.

2. Fashion magazine evaluation: Examine and compare the content of four different fashion magazines. How many pages are devoted to paid advertisements? How many pages are devoted to editorial fashion reporting? What do these magazines have in common? How would a fashion forecaster use this information?

3. Look through costume books for pictures of ethnic dress. Using these as inspiration, design a garment using the line, shapes, colors, and details from these garments in a new combination for today's lifestyle.

4. Develop a consumer survey. Type up questions you would like to ask. Be as specific as possible, such as "What length skirt do you prefer to wear?" Go to a local shopping mall and ask customers to answer your survey (explain that you are working on a student project). Tabulate your findings in a brief written report.

Notes

1. As quoted in "Donatella Takes Charge," *Women's Wear Daily*, October 1, 1997, p. 4.

2. As quoted in "King Karl," *Women's Wear Daily*, November 20, 1991, p. 7.

3. As quoted in "Juniors, a Trend Ahead," *Women's Wear Daily*, December 1, 1994, p. 6.

4. Julianne Moore quoted in "Starring Role," *Women's Wear Daily*, January 6, 2003, p. 16.

GIORGIO ARMANI'S EXQUISITE
DESIGN OF REPEATED RUFFLES
IN SHADES OF PURPLE.
(COURTESY OF GIORGIO ARMANI SPA,
MILAN, ITALY)

PART TWO

The Raw Materials of Fashion

To fully understand the production of fashion apparel or accessories, it is important to learn about the raw materials from which they are made. Collectively, the producers of these raw materials—fibers, fabrics, leathers, furs, and trimmings—are the suppliers to the apparel and accessories industries and the first level of the fashion industry.

- **CHAPTER 5** covers the *production of fibers and fabrics* for those students who do not have a background in textiles.

- **CHAPTER 6** describes the *marketing of these fibers and fabrics*, basic knowledge needed by anyone working in textiles or manufacturing.

- **CHAPTER 7** surveys *leathers and furs*, which are also raw materials for clothing, and *trimmings*, the necessary secondary supplies to finish apparel and accessories.

A FIELD OF FLAX.
(COURTESY OF THE INTERNATIONAL
LINEN PROMOTION COMMISSION)

5

TEXTILE FIBER AND FABRIC PRODUCTION

Career Focus

Careers in textile production require a technical education in textiles and/or engineering. As more and more textiles are imported, especially from Asia, there are fewer domestic career possibilities. Technical career opportunities exist in research and development, styling, plant technology, engineering, and management. While you may not plan to work in the textile industry specifically, it is important to understand the basic textile processes to prepare for a career in the fashion industry.

CHAPTER OBJECTIVES

After reading this chapter, you should be able to:

1. List the sources of fibers
2. Explain the processes involved in the production of fibers and fabrics
3. Describe the roles of mills and converters

Textiles is a broad term referring to any material that can be made into fabric by any method. Occasionally, the term *textile industry* is used to cover the entire apparel industry: the production and marketing of textile merchandise from raw materials to the product in the retail store.

More precisely, the textile industry encompasses the production and marketing of fibers, yarns, and fabrics, including trimmings and findings. This production and marketing chain includes the following steps: fiber production, yarn production, fabric production, dyeing, printing, and finishing. Defined in this way, the textile industry represents the first level of the fashion industry. Textile production will be discussed in this chapter, followed by textile marketing in Chapter 6 and trimmings in Chapter 7.

Fibers

Before the textile industry can supply fabrics to apparel manufacturers, it must first develop and produce both natural and man-made fibers.

Fibers are hairlike materials, either natural or manufactured, that form the basic element of fabrics and other textiles. They can be spun into yarn and then made into fabric by various methods, such as weaving and knitting. Fiber characteristics such as fineness, moisture regain, elasticity, luster, or crimp are inherent and, therefore, affect the properties of the yarns and fabrics made from them.

Total world fiber production is now 59.2 billion kilograms (130.5 billion pounds) per year, compared to 22 billion in 1970, 58 percent of which was for man-made fibers. Only one-half of worldwide fiber production is for apparel.

The vast differences between the *natural* and *man-made* fiber industries have resulted in markedly different operational and organizational forms, even though the final goal of both groups is the same: to produce fibers that fill consumer needs.

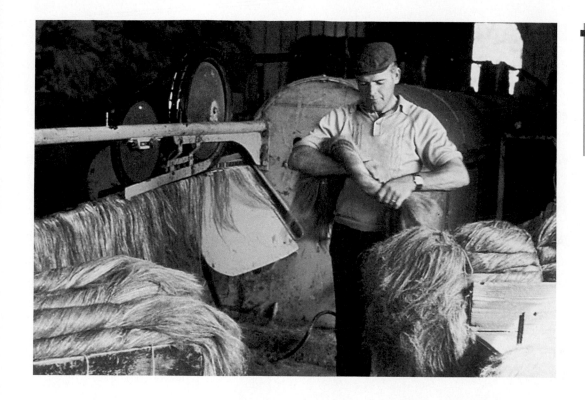

THE SCUTCHING PROCESS TO SEPARATE FLAX FIBERS FROM THE BARK AND STEM. *(COURTESY OF THE INTERNATIONAL LINEN PROMOTION COMMISSION)*

separated from the outer bark and the woody inner core of the stem. Further processing can include *hacking* or *combing* and drawing the flax into a continuous ribbon of parallel fibers ready for spinning into yarn to make the fabric called *linen*.

Linen is the oldest known textile, dating back as far as the Stone Age. At one time, linen was used extensively for bedding; this explains why we still call sheets, towels, and tablecloths collectively *linens*. Flax was an important crop in the United States until the invention of the cotton gin in 1792 made cotton cheaper to produce.

Today, flax makes up less than 1 percent of world fiber production or approximately 600 million kilograms annually. Eighty percent of the world's flax is grown in Russia; France is the largest producer of flax in the Western world. France and Belgium have the reputation for growing the best quality. Because the United States no longer grows flax, there have been no quotas on its importation. To revive their flax industry, some Russian entrepreneurs have developed flax-based fabrics that are as soft and flexible as cotton but more durable.

The cool, crisp qualities of linen make it especially suited for summer clothing. Renewed interest in texture and natural fibers has repopularized linen and linen blends, as well as linen look-alikes in the form of rayon and other fiber blends.

Bamboo

China used bamboo as a textile fiber 2000 years ago. Now, again, it is in some demand for clothing. The process to make bamboo fiber is similar to the one to make rayon. Stalks of bamboo are essentially crushed and pulped to enable it to be mixed with chemicals to convert it into textile quality fiber. Because it is lightweight and drapes well, it is in demand for lingerie. It also blends well with silk, cotton, spandex, and Tencel. However, it is difficult to obtain and expensive to produce.

Ramie

Ramie is a vegetable fiber similar to flax; it comes from the 5- to 6-foot stems of a nettlelike shrub. Ramie grows best in a semitropical climate and is imported primarily from India, China, and the Philippines. Ramie is even stronger than flax and has a smooth, lustrous appearance. The fibers dye easily, but are brittle and more difficult to spin and weave than other fibers. Therefore, it is most often combined with cotton to soften it.

Wool

SHEARING A SHEEP TO OBTAIN WOOL FIBER. *(COURTESY OF JUDITH WINTHROP)*

Wool fiber is a natural and renewable resource from the fleece of animals, most commonly sheep. The *fleece* is removed by the use of shears or clippers in the *shearing process*. Shearing takes place at various times throughout the year, depending on fiber-length requirements. Although wool is commonly understood to be fiber from the fleece of sheep, some other animal fibers are also classified as wool specialty fibers. They include angora, camel's hair, cashmere, mohair, llama, alpaca, and vicuna. With fashion's focus on texture, specialty fibers have become increasingly popular.

Wool fiber has an unusual ability to absorb and evaporate up to 30 percent of its weight in moisture. The crimp structure of wool fiber allows it to return to its natural position after stretching, which gives woven and knitted fabrics, make wool a fiber that can be worn in spring and summer. Wool fibers also absorb dye easily, allowing bright and clear colors to be produced.

Raw wool is scoured to clean the wool, then *carded* to separate and lay the fibers parallel, and *combed* to separate short fibers from long ones. The long fibers are spun into smooth, compact *worsted* yarns used for fabrics such as gabardine or crepe; short fibers make up the soft, dense *woolen* yarns used in textured tweeds and flannel.

Australia is by far the world's largest wool producer, followed by New Zealand and then China. Although more than 2.9 billion pounds (1.3 billion kilograms) of clean wool are processed each year, this represents only 2 percent of world textile fiber production.[1] The supply of wool changes yearly; sometimes there is a stockpile and other times a shortage.

Silk

Silk is the only natural fiber that comes in continuous *filament* form as opposed to short staple lengths. *Silk* is the protein filament secreted by a silkworm to make its cocoon. A silkworm uses the cocoon as a shell to protect itself during its transformation from caterpillar to moth. A typical cocoon will produce 600 to 2000 meters of continuous fiber, making silk the only natural filament fiber. Nevertheless, it takes over 500 silkworm cocoons to make a blouse.

Silk harvesters unwind the filament from the cocoon onto silk reels. The silk fiber is steeped and boiled in soap baths to remove the *sericin* or silk glue. The time and labor needed to cultivate silk make it a rare and, therefore, expensive fiber. World production of silk fiber is a mere 0.2 percent, or only 60 million kilograms annually. Asia produces nearly all of the world's raw silk filament fiber. Asia has decreased exports of raw silk and increased production and exports of finished silk fabrics. The most famous quality silk fabric mills are in Como, Italy, and Lyon, France, but the Koreans have learned their techniques.

There are four kinds of silk fibers. *Cultivated silk* comes from the domesticated silkworm. The filaments are almost even in size, their fineness indicated by a unit called *denier* (the weight in grams of 9000 meters of yarn). Cultivated silk is used for the finest silk fabrics, such as crepes, taffetas, and satins. *Wild* or *tussah silk* comes from the wild silkworm. Less secure environmental conditions cause the filaments to be coarser and more uneven. Therefore, fabric made from wild silk is not as smooth as that made from domesticated silk. *Douppioni silk* is the result of the filament sticking together at intervals while wrapped as a cocoon, causing slubs (lumps) and uneven yarn used to make shantung fabric. *Schappe* and *bourette* (*waste*) *silk* are composed of short fibers from damaged cocoons that are not strong or long enough to be used on their own. Yarn spun from waste silk also has irregular slubs from the joinings and is used in rough-textured silks.

Silk has always been used for the finest garments. The silk fiber is triangular and reflects light, giving silk its unique luster. Because it takes dyes with exceptional depth and clarity and has a luxurious feel, it adds elegance to any garment. Silk also has insulation properties, making the wearer feel cool in summer and warm in winter. Silk drapes exceptionally well, is very strong yet light-weight, and is comfortable as well as beautiful.

High-Tech Natural Fibers

High-tech fibers from alternative natural sources are being developed by modern science. Spider silk and casein are two examples. Other fibers, made from sasawashi leaf, lenpur, seaweed, and soybean, are in experimental stages of development.

Spider Silk   To capture the strength of spider filaments for use in fabrics, Nexia Biotechnologies in Montreal has introduced the spider protein gene into the genetic makeup of goats (it affects only the mammary gland). The protein is extracted from the goat's milk, processed, and spun.

Casein Fiber   Another interesting development is a silklike fiber made of casein, a protein found in cow's milk, manufactured by Toyobo of Japan. *National Geographic* Magazine pointed out the humor in a possible jersey-knit blouse made from the milk of a Jersey cow.

Man-Made Fibers

The phenomenal growth of the textile fiber industry was made possible by the development of man-made fibers.

Chemists began to experiment with synthetic fibers as early as 1850. In 1884, a Frenchman named Hilaire de Chardonnet patented a fabric he called "artificial silk," which is known today as *rayon* (or *viscose* in Europe). He discovered that silkworms use cellulose from mulberry leaves to make real silk, so he reproduced the process chemically. Rayon was first produced chemically in the United States in 1910, but not until 1939 was the first completely chemical fiber, *nylon*, introduced by DuPont.

Originally, the term *synthetics* was used to denote all chemically produced fibers. In the world market today, however, the term *synthetic* covers only the noncellulosic fibers. A true synthetic is made from the carbon atom of oil or coal, whereas viscose and acetate are regenerated cellulose. The textile industry refers to all chemically produced fibers together as *man-made* or *manufactured* fibers.

Man-Made Fiber Producers

Large chemical companies, such as BASF (Badische Anilin und Soda Fabrik), DuPont, and Celanese, pioneered the development of man-made fibers. The fiber divisions of these companies do extensive research and development of both fibers and fabrics; they work closely with their customers, the textile mills, and provide technical services to manufacturers and retailers.

Strong competitive pressures from imports forced the U.S. textile industry to reorganize, consolidate, and focus on those things that they do best. This specialization has led to international mergers and acquisitions. For example, Lensing of Austria bought the rayon division of BASF and is now the world's largest rayon producer. DuPont bought Zeneca's nylon facilities and, in turn, Zeneca purchased DuPont's acrylic division.

In contrast with natural fibers, man-made fibers are produced by a few chemical companies whose huge facilities enable them to take full advantage of mass production. These plants are located in areas where the combined cost of raw materials, labor, energy, and transportation is the lowest possible. Man-made fiber production depends mainly on the supply of petroleum products; therefore, it is subject to shortages and ever-increasing prices.

In 1960, man-made fiber production was only 22 percent of world fiber production as compared with more than 50 percent today (about one-third of this amount is used for apparel). The growth rate of man-made fibers is the result of many factors: fiber research and development by chemical companies, new technical developments in making new varieties of fibers, the scarcity and expense of some natural fibers, increased high-tech production, and increased demand.

China leads the world in man-made fiber production. China's production, combined with that of Taiwan, Japan, and Korea, makes Asia by far the largest producer, followed by the United States, and then the European Union (primarily Germany and Italy).

Of utmost importance is the use of man-made fibers in blends, either with each other or with natural fibers. Blends capitalize on the best qualities of each fiber. For example, spandex is often blended with a variety of fibers to add stretch. Polyester can be blended with cotton to give it easy-care properties. Continual experimenting with fiber combinations makes exciting new fabrics.

Man-Made Fiber Production

In very simple terms, all man-made fibers are extruded from a viscose solution of cellulose (purified wood pulp) or from chemical raw material. Originally, the chemical substances exist as solids and, therefore, must first be converted into a liquid state. The raw materials are converted into flakes, chips, crumbs, or pellets, which are then dissolved in a solvent, melted with heat, or chemically converted into a syrupy liquid and pumped through the tiny holes of a spinneret to form continuous filaments. The process of extrusion and hardening is called *spinning*, not to be confused with the textile yarn operation of the same name.

Unlike natural fibers, man-made fibers can be extruded in various cross sections (solid or hollow, for example) and thicknesses, called *denier*. These long fibers can be left as continuous filaments or cut into *staple* (short, uniform lengths) to be blended with other fibers.

Man-made fibers were first created to imitate the texture of natural fibers, duplicating their crimp, length, and thickness. Since then, scientists have learned how to vary the shape, composition, and size of fibers to achieve pleasing esthetic effects and higher levels of performance.

One of the most successful man-made fiber developments is that of *microfibers*, which contain individual filaments that are less than one denier thick, twice as fine as silk. Used primarily in polyester, these luxury fibers are giving polyester a renaissance. They can be used alone or combined with silk, worsted wool, or other fibers.

Regenerated Cellulosic Fibers

Derived chiefly from the pulp of wood, cellulosic fibers create a *hand* (the feel, body, and fall of a fabric) similar to natural fibers, as compared with chemical synthetic fibers. Cellulosic fibers include rayon, acetate, and triacetate.

Rayon (Viscose)
The first man-made fiber to be developed, *rayon* is composed of regenerated cellulose derived from wood pulp, cotton linters, or other vegetable matter. The cellulose is dissolved into a viscose solution and spun into fiber. Rayon has become very popular because it is a soft, lustrous, versatile fiber that can be treated and finished to produce a wide range of characteristics.

Soaring wood prices and the expense required to clean up the environment have made rayon very expensive to produce. The caustic materials needed for rayon's wet-spinning process cause pollution. The rayon fiber industry has had to incur heavy costs to conform to more stringent environmental standards.

Lyocell   *Lyocell* is the generic designation for a new type of solvent-spun cellulosic fiber produced by Tencel, Inc., a division of Acordis Fibers, and Lenzing of Austria. Lyocell is almost twice as strong as rayon, both wet and dry, is a good blending partner with many other fibers, and takes color well. Tencel A100 has been developed for use in knits.

Like rayon, lyocell is produced from wood pulp. However, lyocell is manufactured using a solvent spinning technique in which the dissolving agent is recycled, thus reducing waste that is harmful to the environment. Fiber producers are also experimenting with *lenpur*, made from a sustainably harvested pine wood pulp.

Acetate and Triacetate   Cellulose acetate fiber was first produced commercially in 1921 and advertised as a synthetic silk. *Acetate* (diacetate) and *triacetate* have been adopted as alternatives to rayon although they are not quite as strong. Triacetate can be heat-set to give it easy-care properties, but it requires such strong solvents that it is no longer produced in the United States. Diacetate can be dissolved in solvents that are easier to handle; therefore, it is more widely produced.

Acetate has a soft, silklike hand and excellent drape qualities and takes dye well. Acetate can be used alone or in combination with other man-made or natural fibers. It is used primarily in women's dressy apparel, bridal wear, and linings.

Synthetic Fibers

Made from chemical derivatives of petroleum, coal, and natural gas, *synthetic* fibers (also sometimes referred to as *noncellulosic* fibers) used in apparel include nylon, polyester, acrylic, spandex, and polypropylene. Synthetic fibers, particularly microfibers, have risen in popularity with the demand for lightweight, high-tech fabrics.

Nylon   One of the strongest and most durable man-made fibers, nylon is made of a long-chain synthetic polymer. Nylon filaments usually have an even, silky hand, but can also be textured to be soft and supple. Nylon is not only strong, but also flexible, washable, and colorfast. In apparel, it has traditionally been used in hosiery, lingerie, bathing suits, and active sportswear. However, the Italian designer Miuccia Prada has made nylon fabric fashionable for all apparel.

NEW USES FOR NYLON INCLUDE THIS QUILTED SUIT FROM PRADA. *(COURTESY OF PRADA, ITALY)*

MODERN MAN-MADE FIBERS, SUCH AS NYLON, SPANDEX, AND POLYPROPYLENE, HELP TO KEEP SKIWEAR FLEXIBLE, WARM, AND DRY. (COURTESY OF FILA, INC.)

Polyester Another kind of long-chain synthetic polymer, *polyester* is the most widely used man-made fiber in the world. Chemical companies can produce polyester fiber in the forms of filament, staple, or tow (short or broken fiber).

Polyester is highly wrinkle resistant and easy to care for. It was one of the first fibers to be developed in fabrics with permanent-press features. Polyester is used in many types of apparel, including textured knits and wovens, permanent-press blend fabrics, shirtings, suitings, and sleepwear. It is often blended with natural fibers to lend easy-care properties to them. The development of microfibers has made polyester even more adaptable and popular.

Acrylic *Acrylic* is yet another long-chain synthetic polymer. Because of the composition and cross section of the fiber, fabrics made of acrylic have a high bulk-to-weight ratio. This provides warmth in fabrics that are lightweight, soft, and resilient. End uses of acrylics include knitwear, fleece activewear, suits, coats, and fake furs.

Spandex A long-chain synthetic polymer comprised of segmented polyurethane, *spandex* can stretch 300 to 400 percent without breaking and return to its original length. Its elastic properties are unequaled by any other fiber, and it does not deteriorate as rubber does. Because of its tremendous stretch, spandex is generally added to other fibers, such as cotton, nylon, rayon, or wool, in small quantities of 2 to 20 percent to create stretch fabrics. This stretch characteristic makes it an excellent fiber for use in swimwear, hosiery, and active sportswear. Because of its comfort and fit properties, spandex is now widely used in many fabrics. It is used in stretch-wovens as well as knits and has even been used in stretch-satin for evening wear.

Polypropylene An olefin fiber made from polymers, *polypropylene* is very strong and resilient. It provides greater coverage per pound than any other fiber, yet it is so light that it actually floats. Although the major uses of polypropylene are in industrial and carpet applications, its good insulative properties make it useful in some high-tech activewear for which moisture transport is important.

High-Tech Fibers

Man-made fiber companies are striving to develop new fibers to meet consumer needs. Most of these, such as Kevlar, Nomex, and Zylon, which are strong or have high-temperature resistance, are examples of high-tech fibers used for the military, fire fighters, outdoor recreation, and apparel.

Modern technology is also creating a new generation of synthetic fibers based on renewable and biodegradable biological materials instead of oil. They are biodegradable and recyclable like natural fibers but with the performance of synthetics. Some of the new fibers are of interest to the fashion industry.

PLA PLA (polylactic acid), the generic classification for a corn-based polymer, is a recent fiber development from Cargill Dow Polymers. A cross between a natural and man-made fiber, it is made from the natural source of corn. The corn is processed into plant sugar and then fermented and transformed into a polymer, from which fiber is extruded. Ingeo, Cargill Dow's brand name for PLA, is used alone and in blends for both knit and woven apparel.

Generic and Brand Identification

When a completely new fiber is developed, the U.S. Federal Trade Commission assigns it a generic name, such as polyester. Many companies produce polyester, but they each call it by a different name in order to promote it independently. A *brand name* or *trademark* (identifiable symbol) is registered and is owned by the manufacturer. For example, Lycra is DuPont's brand name for spandex, and Dacron is its brand name for polyester. PLA is the FTC's newest generic designation. The Textile Fibers Products Identification Act requires that end products carry labels listing the generic names of the fibers used and the percentage of each.

It is possible to work within the basic generic composition of an existing generic fiber and modify it, both chemically and physically, to change the properties of the fiber to create variants. *Variants* are specialty fibers for special applications. Some variants are intended to imitate natural fibers. Some are blended with natural fibers to add easy-care properties to them. Others are engineered to add stretch, moisture wicking, or other comfort properties. Each fiber producer creates its own variants and gives them *brand names*. Thermax, for example, is DuPont's brand name for its insulating hollow-core polyester, whereas Coolmax is its moisture-wicking polyester. There are many variants of other man-made fibers; each producer gives them their own brand names.

Textile Yarn and Fabric Producers

Textile mills use fibers to produce yarns and fabrics. Converters may also finish fabrics. Both textile mills and converters are the suppliers to the apparel industry.

There are now only about 4000 apparel-related textile plants (fiber, yarn, fabric, and finishing) dispersed throughout the United States, and approximately 200,000 people are employed in domestic textile production. The industry originally located in the Southeast to be close to the source of cotton and to take advantage of less expensive labor. The Carolinas and Georgia together still account for more than half of all industry employment and production.

However, the growth of textile industries in China and elsewhere and competition from their low-priced imports have caused multiple mill closings in the United States. Others have filed for bankruptcy protection. In order to compete, many U.S. companies have opened facilities in Mexico and the Caribbean or formed alliances with companies in Asia and the Middle East. Others make only fabrics for home furnishings. Some have opened worldwide operations to handle their own sourcing abroad; U.S. textile companies have become importers themselves.

Textile Mills

Mills are the producers of yarns and fabrics. Some mills produce only yarns; others knit and weave fabric from their own yarns or from purchased yarns. Certain mills produce unfinished fabrics called *greige* (pronounced "gray") *goods*, which are sold to converters to be finished, or they may produce both greige goods and finished fabrics. Small mills usually specialize in one type of fabric, such as velveteen or corduroy. Large companies create separate divisions to do the same thing, grouping similar fabrics under one division.

The various stages in textile production may or may not be handled by firms under common ownership. Firms have tended to grow either forward or backward into the production or marketing chain to form large *vertical mills*, which perform all processes, from top to bottom (fiber to fabric). The newest trend is for companies to include apparel production in "garment-package" (or "full-package") deals. However, these operations are separated in specialized facilities. Milliken and Burlington are examples of U.S. vertical mills.

Mills have increased capital expenditures to purchase the latest technology to offset the low labor cost advantage of imports. Because of the huge investment needed for machinery and technology and the expense of changing it, the large mills tend to serve the mass market with volume fabrics. Most processes are computerized: the spinning and texturing of fibers and yarns; high-speed weaving and knitting; and automated material handling, dyeing, and finishing. The size of most U.S. mills is suited to high-volume production, but in recent years, as a result of competition from imports, they have begun to accommodate small runs and more design changes.

Textile companies invest heavily in research and new technology. They believe that technological advances will guide the future of fabric development in the twenty-first century. This is particularly true with the popularity of lightweight "performance" or "smart" fabrics, high-tech fabrics that are easy to care for and that move with the body.

Converters

Converters do only the finishing stages of production. They can be a division of a vertically integrated textile company or independent, such as Charter and Pressman-Gutman. There are fewer and fewer independent converters today, again due to competition from imports. Therefore, the industry has tried to cut costs by becoming vertical or forming alliances between levels of the industry. As a result, most large textile mills now do their own converting.

Converters *source* (find the best quality goods at the best price) greige goods from worldwide mills. The few independent, domestic converters that remain in business are sourcing most of their fabrics offshore, from Korea, China, Taiwan, or Mexico. They usually contract out all printing, dyeing, and finishing processes to specialized factories, rather than owning production facilities. This gives them the flexibility to change methods or products to keep up with changing fashion. The vertical mills are now trying to fill this role.

Yarn Production

Once a fiber is produced, yarn production is the next step in creating a fabric.

Textile manufacturers choose a yarn-making technique that can best achieve the texture or hand desired. Yarn can be made as coarse as rug yarn or finer than sewing thread. Finished yarn is then sold to fabric producers to be used for weaving and knitting.

Filament Yarn Processing

A *filament* is a continuous strand of fiber. Single monofilament, direct from the fiber producer, may be used as a yarn and knitted or woven into fabric. Multifilaments may also be brought together, with or without a twist, to create yarn. Filament yarns are smoother, have more sheen, and are more uniform than spun yarns.

Silk filament is twisted in a specialized silk spinning process. It is then ready for weaving or knitting.

Synthetic filament, on the other hand, is generally textured to provide bulk, loft, or elasticity. *Texturing* is a process used on filament yarn to change the shape or characteristics into some form of crimp, loop, curl, or coil. These characteristics are given to the fibers to make them suitable for specific end uses. After texturing, man-made filament yarn is ready for dyeing and weaving or knitting.

Spinning Staple Fibers

Spun yarns can be made from natural fibers and man-made fibers that have been cut into *staple* (short lengths that emulate raw natural fiber).

Natural fibers, such as cotton, flax, and wool, must go through a long and expensive series of processes to become yarn. Each fiber has its own special spinning system: the linen system, the cotton system, the woolen system, or the worsted system. To explain the systems in a very simple way, there are first several processes to clean, refine, parallel, and blend the raw fibers. Next, the fibers are drawn out into a fine strand and twisted to keep them together. This process gives them strength to withstand the spinning process.

Man-made fibers are cut into staple and spun on the same conventional spinning system used for cotton or on a new high-speed system to make yarn. The resulting yarns have characteristics similar to those of spun natural fiber. Both natural fibers and man-made fibers are blended to give yarn consistency, as not all the fibers have the same quality. Natural and man-made fibers may also be blended together. In fact, most man-made fibers that are cut into staple are used to mix with natural fibers.

Fabric Production

After spinning, the yarns are ready for weaving or knitting.

Fabric is material or cloth made from natural or man-made yarns by any of the following methods: weaving, knitting, bonding, crocheting, felting, knotting, or laminating. Most apparel fabrics are woven or knitted. Fashion preference for one or the other is usually cyclical.

Weaving

Woven fabrics are made by interlacing *warp yarn* and *filling yarn* (called *weft* in England and in handweaving) at right angles. Weaving begins with a process called *warping* during which yarns are wound onto a beam. The beams are combined via a "slashing" process to put 4000 to 12,000 yarn-ends onto a loom beam.

In the conventional method of weaving, filling (weft) yarns are fed into the loom by a shuttle carrying yarn wound on a bobbin. Originally, the shuttle was fed by hand. Modern technology has developed faster methods of weaving, such as the *rapier* loom that carries the filling yarns through the warp on steel bands. Faster speeds are obtained on air-jet and water-jet looms, which use a blast of air or water to propel the filling yarn across the warp. These looms operate at four to seven times the speed of shuttle looms and produce seven to eight times the amount of fabric at wider widths. However, loom speed and weave complexity are inversely related. The more elaborate the pattern, the slower the loom speed must be.

The warp yarns separate alternately (called *shedding*) to allow the filling yarns to interlace with them as they pass through the warp. The next step is *beating* the last row of yarns into the cloth.

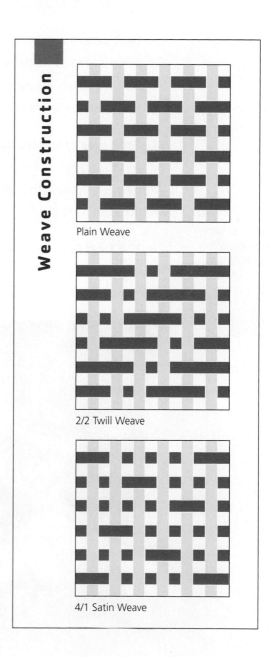

Weave Construction

Plain Weave

2/2 Twill Weave

4/1 Satin Weave

Kinds of Weaves   There are three basic weaves: plain, twill, and satin.

Plain weave is the simplest, most common weave. The warp and filling yarns alternately pass over and under each other, creating both horizontal and vertical surface interest. Fabrics woven by this method include a wide range of weights from broadcloth to duck.

Twill weave is created by passing the warp yarn over a number of filling yarns before going under one. The same pattern is repeated row after row, but each time the repetition begins on the next warp yarn, creating a diagonal weave that gives the cloth added strength and a diagonal surface interest. Denim is the most popular twill fabric.

Satin weave is achieved by one warp yarn crossing over the most possible filling yarns (or vice versa), creating floats on the face side of the fabric. The floats give the fabric luster and smoothness. But because they are caught into the fabric only at comparatively wide intervals, a satin weave does not have the same durability as the other weaves.

Pattern Created by Weaving   Pattern can be introduced by using yarns of different colors in the warp, the filling, or both, to create plaids, checks, or stripes. These *yarn-dye patterns* can be distinguished from prints because the patterns appear on both sides of the

COMPUTER SYSTEMS FEED PATTERN AND MONITOR WEAVING OF THIS JACQUARD LOOM. *(COURTESY OF BURLINGTON)*

fabric. Woven patterns may also be produced by reversing the direction of the weave in certain areas or in alternate rows, as in herringbones. Many variations of the three basic weaves are used to create unusual designs or patterns in fabrics, which are called *novelty weaves*.

Types of Looms   Weaves can be created on cam, dobby, or Jacquard looms. Cam looms are the fastest because they produce simple weaves. Dobby looms are used to do simple patterns. More complex patterns require more complicated yarn feeding and set-up and, therefore, slow down the speed of the loom.

Fancy woven patterns, such as brocade, damask, and tapestry, may be created on a *Jacquard* (jah-kard') loom. The pattern is programmed on a computer, which controls every yarn individually, creating the desired pattern. The Jacquard loom is the most flexible, but is therefore more expensive and slower than other looms.

Knitting

Knitted fabrics are made from one continuous yarn or a combination of yarns formed into successive rows of loops drawn through another series of loops to make cloth. The amount of stretch in the final product depends on the fiber and yarn construction, the density and type of knit, and the presence of spandex yarns. Various types of stitches in combination with several ways of knitting produce a wide variety of knit fabrics, from very bulky to fine gauge. Designs can be transferred to a computer tape, which operates electronic knitting machines automatically. A modern knitting machine can knit 1 million loops per minute.

Gauge or *cut* refers to the number of needles per inch in the knitting machine; a 10-cut machine has 10 needles per inch. However, the number of *stitches* per inch on the finished fabric may have more or fewer stitches than the number of needles per inch.

A 5-cut machine with 5 needles is the most commonly used for bulky knits. However, the resulting knit fabric can have as few as 3 stitches per inch or as many as 9 stitches depending on the amount and size of yarn fed into the machine. The more needles there are, the finer and closer the knit loops are. A fine jersey might be made on a 28-cut machine. The most common cut-and-sew jerseys and double knits are made on 18- to 24-cut machines.

Weft and warp knitting are the two basic methods of knitting fabric.

Weft Knitting   When the loops run horizontally across the width of the fabric, the process is called *weft knitting*. Weft knits can be made on either flatbed or circular machines, and

CIRCULAR (RIGHT
FOREGROUND) AND
FLAT (BACKGROUND)
KNITTING MACHINES.
(COURTESY OF THE
WOOLMARK
COMPANY)

circular knits may be either single or double knit. In single knits, all the stitches in a given *course*, or row, are made with a single yarn. In double knits, the stitches in a given row may be made by interlocking two different yarn feeds. Weft knits are made in a wide variety of single and double knits and generally have more stretch than warp knits.

Jersey is the basic construction of all weft knits. The front and the back of the fabric are different in appearance. The rows of stitches running vertically (parallel with the edges, like warp) are called *wales*, and the rows of stitches running across the fabric are called *courses*.

Jersey is the most common construction used in fine-gauge fabrics and stretches equally in length and width. Popular uses include pantyhose, underwear, and full-fashioned sweaters (see Chapter 10 for sweater and knitwear production). There are many variations on the jersey construction that are made by differing needle arrangements.

- **Purl-knit** is actually the reverse side of jersey and is used primarily for sweater knits.
- **Rib-knit** fabrics have a distinctive lengthwise rib on both sides of the fabric for added stretch in the width. A combination of jersey and purl stitches, rib is most often used in sweaters, socks, knit accessories, or trims, such as neckbands or cuffs.

- **Interlock** knit looks like jersey on both sides of the fabric. The stitches alternate a half-movement up or down to create a zigzag horizontally across the fabric.
- **Knit and welt** uses the front and back beds of the knitting machine to create a welt.
- **Float Jacquard** knits have a pattern on the face side. Yarns not being used on the pattern float on the back until they are needed again.
- **Full Jacquard** knits also have a pattern on the face side, but there is another simple pattern on the back instead of floats. This requires the use of both the front and back knitting beds and makes a double fabric, which is heavier.
- **Novelties**, including *tuck* stitches, *miss* stitches, and *pointelles*, can be created with other needle arrangements.

Warp Knitting   In *warp knitting*, multiple yarns are used, and the loops run vertically and zigzag across each other to form the fabric. Each stitch in a row is made by a different yarn that is fed from a sheet of yarns wound on a beam. Patterns and inlays can be introduced by various needle arrangements. The Missonis in Italy are famous for their beautiful warp knits. Warp knits include tricot and raschel.

Tricot knit fabrics are usually made with fine-denier filament yarns. They are soft, drape well, and are somewhat elastic. Popular uses include women's lingerie and uniforms for nurses.

Raschel is the most complex warp-knit structure, capable of making lacy, open stitches. Yarns may be heavily twisted filament yarns or spun yarns. Uses of this knit include thermal underwear, swimwear, shapewear, knitted lace, and crochet.

Nonwoven Fabrics

Nonwoven (or *engineered*) fabrics are made by bonding or interlocking fibers, filaments, or yarns into a web or sheet by mechanical (pressure, needle punch, or needle tufting), chemical, thermal (heat), hydro, or solvent means. Examples of such fabrics include nonwoven interfacings and nonwoven felt. Nonwoven fabric production usually includes four stages: (1) fiber preparation, (2) web formation, (3) web bonding, and (4) post-treatment. Nonwoven fabrics constitute one of the fastest growing segments of the textile industry.

Production Centers

China produces the most woven woolen apparel fabrics, followed by Italy. Hong Kong produces the most woolen knitwear, followed by Thailand, China, or Italy (varies from year to year). Better cottons come from Italy and Switzerland. The United States produces more denim than any other country. However, the largest cotton fabric producer is China, followed by Eastern Europe, and then India and the United States. Linen fabrics are produced in Italy, Belgium, Northern Ireland, France, China, and Poland. Italy produces the most printed silks, but only one-third of the total world silk fabrics. The other two-thirds are produced in Korea using Chinese silk.

It is difficult to calculate the production of fabrics from man-made fibers because so many are blends, and most industry and trade associations calculate production only in their own countries. The three major global centers of man-made and blend fabrics are Asia, Europe, and the United States.

Dyeing

Dyeing can be done at any stage of fiber, yarn, or fabric production.

Some of the most important methods of dyeing are the following:

- **Producer colored**—The producer or solution dyeing process, used for man-made fibers, adds the pigment or color when the fibers are still in solution before the filaments are formed.
- **Stock dyeing**—This method is used to dye loose fibers before yarn processing.
- **Yarn dyeing**—This is the quality method used to dye certain woven patterns such as stripes, plaids, and checks. It is done after the yarn is spun, but before weaving or knitting. It is most often used in shirts.
- **Piece dyeing**—Dyeing a piece of fabric after weaving or knitting is called piece dyeing. It is the least expensive and most widely used method of dyeing solid colors.
- **Cross dyeing**—This type of piece dyeing achieves a simple, less expensive two-color pattern. The cloth must be made of fibers having affinities with different dyes so that the cross dyeing can achieve varied color effects in one dyebath.

■ PIECE-DYEING CLOTH. *(COURTESY OF THE WOOLMARK COMPANY)*

- **Garment dyeing**—Greige goods are preshrunk and sewn into garments. The whole garments are dyed after they have been sewn. This method ensures quick delivery of needed colors as well as tops and bottoms that match.

Computers have been enlisted to help regulate dye mixing so that colors match from lot to lot.

If apparel manufacturers want a fabric in a color that is not regularly available, their order must meet a minimum yardage requirement. Solution-dyed fabrics require the largest orders and longest lead times.

Although domestic fabric producers are trying to be more flexible about minimums, mass production requires keeping machines and employees busy. Large domestic mills are most suited to servicing a large manufacturer, such as Levi Strauss or the Gap. Smaller manufacturers are often forced to seek fabrics outside the United States where minimums are lower.

Printing

Printing is used to apply design or pattern to fabrics. There are two basic printing techniques: wet printing and dry printing.

FLATBED SCREEN PRINTING. *(COURTESY OF THE WOOLMARK COMPANY)*

133

Wet Printing

In both engraved-roller printing and screen printing, dyestuffs are applied wet for optimum color penetration. In pigment printing, another method of wet printing, the pigment is attached to the fabric surface with a resin. Other wet prints use dyestuffs that have a chemical affinity to the cloth fiber and do not require resin. A new printing base is derived from milk protein. With wet printing, it is possible to achieve a soft, drapable hand.

Engraved-Roller Printing
In this technique, a separate roller engraving is used for each color in the pattern. The design is rolled onto the fabric as it passes through the printing machine.

Screen Printing
Flatbed screen printing uses a screen spread over a frame. The portions of the design to be printed are made of porous nylon fabric that allows the color to pass through the screen. The areas that are not to be printed are covered or coated. Color is poured into the frame shell and is forced through the nylon by means of a squeegee worked back and forth. Flatbed screen printing is versatile but expensive. The most expensive silk scarves require as many as 50 silk screens with separate colors to be printed in perfect registration.

Rotary screen printing is a mechanized version of flatbed screen printing. In this method, the roller itself is porous in the areas to be printed. Dye is forced into the roller cylinder and through its porous screen as it rolls over the cloth. This method is much faster than flatbed screen printing and is continuous, leaving no breaks between screens.

Dry Printing

Heat-Transfer or Paper Printing
In this process, rotary screens or rollers first print dyestuffs onto paper. The paper can be kept for use at any time. This process helps to keep converters' fabric inventories lean, inasmuch as greige goods are printed against orders and not for stockpiling.

To print on fabric, the paper and fabric are put through hot rollers; the dyestuffs sublimate into a gas, which moves from the paper base onto the fabric. The advantages of this method are that it gives a clean, fine line on knits with no mistakes or waste, and paper is a smaller investment than the elaborate equipment needed for the other methods. However, this method can cause the hand of the goods to become stiff, and the printed pattern transfers only to the fabric surface, with little penetration, creating potential *grin-through* (fabric showing through) problems.

The demand for prints, as well as developments in low-sublimation dyes, deeper-penetrating dyes, and better inks for a variety of fiber types, has given dry printing wider acceptance. Relatively little waste water and few harmful discharges are generated with this method.

Digital Printing

Used widely in offices and graphic arts, digital printing is an emerging process for the textile industry. A design on a CAD file can be downloaded directly onto cloth, thus eliminating the need to prepare screens. It is even possible to engineer a print design according to the shape of garment pieces. Digital printing is a flexible process that provides the opportunity for quick response changes in color or design as demand changes. This method is increasingly used for creating samples, short-run production, and customization.

Finishing

Finishes can radically alter fiber and fabric characteristics, performance, or hand.

Finishing is the term used to encompass all the processes used to enhance a fabric (usually after dyeing or printing). Finishes can be accomplished by chemical or physical change.

Physical Means of Finishing

- **Calendering**—A mechanical process of passing fabric between heavy rollers. By using different combinations of heat, pressure, and rollers, it is possible to produce a wide assortment of effects, such as glaze, watermark, or moiré. Calendering is usually done on synthetics, because it is not permanent on fabrics made of natural fibers.
- **Heat setting**—This is a final finish created by heating thermoplastic man-made fabrics (usually polyester) to just below their melting point. This treatment stabilizes the fabric so that there will be no further change in its size or shape and, therefore, improves the fabric's resilience.
- **Napping**—Fabric surfaces are raised and plucked with needles on rotating drums to create a woolly or flannel surface.
- **Shearing**—Fabrics are usually sheared to give the surface a uniform pile or to take off fuzz.

- **Sanding (or sueding)**—The process of mechanically rubbing the fabric with rollers coated with fine-grit sandpaper to create a soft surface.

- **Shrink control**—The preshrinking of cotton cloth so that it will not shrink during laundering; also known as Sanforizing or compacting.

Chemical Means of Finishing

- **Caustic reduction**—A process usually done on polyester to give it a silklike feel. The surface of the fibers is eaten away in a caustic bath, which reduces the weight of the fabric.

- **Decatizing**—The stabilizing of wool fabrics with the use of heat and moisture.

- **Durable press**—The application of certain resins to cotton or cellulosic fabrics so that they require little or no ironing (also called permanent press, although it is rarely permanent).

- **Mercerizing**—The treatment of cotton with a cold, strongly caustic chemical solution to achieve a lustrous silklike finish.

- **Water repellency**—Yarns or fabrics treated with chemicals and then woven to create cloth that permits air and vapor to pass through the fabric while keeping rain and snow out.

Other finishes can make fabrics flame retardant, ultraviolet light resistant, fade resistant, mildew resistant, bacteria resistant, or stain resistant. Advances in finishing and washing techniques have created unique fabric surfaces such as antique looks. *Nanotechnology*, a recent scientific development, allows enhancements to permanently attach to fibers at submicron level and, therefore, to last the life of the fabric.

When production is complete, fabrics are measured and rolled onto tubes. Each finished roll, called a *piece*, may have 40 to 100 yards on it, depending on the weight of the goods (heavier knits and wools have less yardage on a piece to make them easier to handle). Multiple pieces are shipped to manufacturers to fill production orders that can amount to thousands of yards. Smaller quantities, in the form of 3- to 10-yard sample cuts, may be ordered for designer styling, or *duplicate yardage* (perhaps 100 yards) can be ordered for multiple sales representatives' samples.

Eco-Friendly Fibers

The growing demand for more environmentally friendly products has generated a new awareness and ingenuity at each level of the textile industry.

The American Textile Manufacturers Institute has established an Encouraging Environmental Excellence (E3) program to urge producers to protect the environment. This includes environmental targets and audits to encourage recycling and environmentally efficient manufacturing and finishing processes. As a result, many textile firms now budget and plan for environmental improvements. For example, it is now illegal to produce rayon in the United States because the process severely pollutes our water supply.

Alternatives in Cotton Growing

It is estimated that the cotton industry is responsible for 10 percent of the world's pesticide use.[2] Now the public is beginning to ask questions about the social and environmental issues associated with cotton production. New standards are being set for the growing, processing, printing, and dyeing of cotton fabrics. New strains of cotton are being developed that are insect- and water-resistant and require little if any chemical insecticides or fertilizers. Organic farmers are striving for chemical-free cotton fibers. Some manufacturers are committed to using only organic cotton in their clothing; however, it costs about 30 percent more.

Recycled Polyester

Developments in recycled products include fabrics made from recycled soda bottles and polyester manufacturing waste that are cleaned, chopped, melted, and spun into fiber and used mostly in fleece for outerwear.

Alternatives in Fiber and Fabric Production and Finishing

Various companies are working to develop nontoxic pesticides; environmentally friendly alternatives to PVA and finishing detergents; citric-acid cleaners to replace phosphate and chlorine; natural oils to supplant petroleum lubricants; fiber-reactive dyes to decrease water use and chemical waste; resins to replace formaldehyde; and enzymes to replace acid washes.

"Green" Jeans

Formerly, the textile industry was dumping approximately 70 million pounds of scrap denim a year into American landfills. North Carolina State University, in conjunction with Burlington Industries, has developed a method to reclaim cotton waste and convert it into yarn for reweaving. The material, called Reused Denim, is made of 50 percent reclaimed denim yarn and 50 percent virgin cotton yarn. Companies are also making efforts to reclaim other scrap.

Costs of Environmental Improvements

Some American textile producers are against environmental improvements because of the expense. The costs to American and European textile companies to maintain health, safety, and clean air and water are astronomical. It is very difficult, therefore, for environmentally responsible producers to compete with the low prices from mills in Asia where producers do not pay to clean up their environment.

American textile manufacturers want to require imported textile products to be made under the same environmental, health, and safety standards to ensure fair competition as well as a clean environment throughout the world.

SUMMARY

TEXTILE PRODUCERS ARE THE SUPPLIERS OF FABRIC TO APPAREL AND ACCESSORY MANUFACTURERS. TEXTILE FIBERS ARE THE BASIS FOR FABRICS. THEY ARE CLASSIFIED AS NATURAL (COTTON, FLAX, WOOL, OR SILK) OR MAN-MADE (CELLULOSIC OR SYNTHETIC). YARNS ARE MADE FROM STAPLE FIBERS OR FILAMENTS AND ARE USUALLY WOVEN OR KNITTED INTO FABRICS. THE FABRICS ARE THEN DYED OR PRINTED AND FINISHED IN PREPARATION FOR SHIPMENT TO MANUFACTURERS.

THE MOST EXCITING DEVELOPMENT IN TEXTILES IS THE DEVELOPMENT OF BIODEGRADABLE FIBERS MADE FROM RENEWABLE RESOURCES. THE INDUSTRY IS ALSO MAKING ADVANCES IN THE DEVELOPMENT OF ENVIRONMENTALLY FRIENDLY PRODUCTION. HOWEVER, THE DOMESTIC TEXTILE INDUSTRY HAS SHRUNK DRASTICALLY DUE TO COMPETITION FROM LOWER-PRICED IMPORTS (SEE CHAPTER 6).

Terms and Concepts

Briefly define and discuss the following terms and concepts:

1. Textiles
2. Natural fibers
3. Flax
4. Casein fiber
5. Worsted yarns
6. Synthetic fibers
7. Man-made fibers
8. Cellulosic fibers
9. PLA
10. High-tech fibers
11. Generic fiber names
12. Man-made fiber spinning methods
13. Spun yarns
14. Filament-yarn texturing
15. Plain weave
16. Twill weave
17. Warp knitting
18. Types of dyeing
19. Printing techniques
20. Finishing methods
21. Mills
22. Converters
23. Garment packages
24. Nanotechnology

Questions for Review

1. Why is a study of textiles important to someone working in apparel production?

2. What determines the quality of cotton?

3. What are the two basic ways of making fabric?

4. How is knit yardage made?

5. Give examples of textile dyeing methods that can be used at three different levels of fabric production.

6. Why were specialization and consolidation important in the textile industry?

7. What is the difference between a mill and a converter?

8. Give three examples of high-tech fibers made from renewable sources.

Projects for Additional Learning

1. Examine the fiber-content labels in the clothes in your wardrobe. How many garments are made from natural fibers? How many from man-made fibers? How many from blends? How does the fiber content affect the care of the garment?

2. Visit a local fabric store and find examples of a plain weave, a twill weave, a satin weave, a novelty weave, a warp knit, a circular knit, and a nonwoven fabric. Ask for tiny swatches of each or purchase the smallest amount possible to illustrate your findings.

Notes

[1] David G. Link, textile economist, E-mail correspondence, February 2003.

[2] "Fair Trade Fashion Takes Off in Europe," *Women's Wear Daily*, May 3, 2006, p. 6.

BEAUTIFUL YARNS AND TEXTILES ARE THE BASIS OF
GOOD DESIGN. RALPH LAUREN USES WOOL YARNS
TO CREATE LUXURIOUS KNITWEAR.
(COURTESY OF RALPH LAUREN)

6

TEXTILE PRODUCT DEVELOPMENT AND MARKETING

Career Focus

In textile product development, there are career opportunities in research, design, and merchandising. In marketing, positions range from sales assistant to account manager, sales manager, marketing manager, and director of marketing. There are also the support areas of advertising and public relations to consider. Most of these opportunities are in New York City, Los Angeles, or other international textile centers. Because most fabrics are now imported, there are career opportunities for Americans willing to move to Asia to give them an American's perspective on marketing. It is also essential for anyone working in the fashion industry to understand the marketing forces that transform fibers into fabrics and then move these fabrics into the hands of the apparel designers and manufacturers.

CHAPTER OBJECTIVES

After reading this chapter, you should be able to:

1. Discuss the impact of imports on the textile market
2. Explain the importance of product development for both fibers and fabrics
3. Discuss the marketing strategies of the textile industry

Textile producers respond to consumer demand through their product development and marketing efforts. Textile consumers include the fabric manufacturers who use fibers, the apparel manufacturers who use fabrics, and the end users who buy apparel. *Product development* covers the trend and market research, merchandising, and styling involved in creating new products and updating existing ones. *Marketing* incorporates the entire process of planning, promoting, and selling goods, in this case, textiles.

This chapter discusses the impact that foreign competition and consumer demand have on the industry. It also describes how the industry is reacting with product development, new technologies, and new marketing strategies for fibers and fabrics. Product development, design, and marketing activities are centered in textile and fashion capitals such as Paris, Milan, Como, Lyon, London, New York, and Los Angeles.

The Global Textile Market

Globalization has made a huge impact on the textile industry.

Imports

As discussed in Chapter 2, globalization is the focus of the textile market today. Ever-increasing numbers of textile products are being imported into the United States because of the availability of cheaper labor abroad. American textile producers compete with labor rates of as little as $2.17 per hour in Mexico, 60 cents or less in India, and 69 to 75 cents in China.[1] As a result, imported fabrics are much cheaper than domestically produced fabrics.

Fierce competition from imports has caused the U.S. textile industry to lose more than 50 percent of its domestic market and has resulted in buyouts, takeovers, and consolidations to salvage the business that was left. Today there are only about 200,00 domestic textile employees, compared to 847,700 in 1980. Thousands of domestic plants have closed, more in the past 20 years than at any time since the Great Depression of the 1930s. Italy, too, has lost over 6000 textile companies since 2001.[2] Both the North American and European textile manufacturing bases are disappearing. These losses correspond to the enormous growth of the textile industries of China, Mexico, Canada, Pakistan, South Korea, India, Taiwan, Indonesia, Honduras, Thailand, and Turkey.[3] China is the leading supplier of imported textiles to the United States and Europe. They have developed a reputation for low-cost, quality production and have an almost inexhaustible pool of unemployed people moving to the cities in search of jobs.

To compete, U.S. and European textile companies have joined the stampede to import, because they find that fabrics produced and finished overseas are often 50 percent cheaper than those produced domestically. American textile companies may complete styling domestically, but most often buy goods from China, Korea, or India. American and European apparel manufacturers often buy textiles in a particular country because apparel production will also be done there.

Even with quotas phased out, tariffs (taxes) on certain goods of 12 percent on imports to Europe and 20 percent to the United States help to restrict imports somewhat. Special restrictions on imports from China are currently in place to help prevent China from completely taking over the global textile market. However, most manufacturers and retailers use alternative production in other countries as a safety measure.

Overseas Investment

Because labor and facilities are so much cheaper in Asia, many U.S. and European textile companies are forming joint ventures with Asian companies to produce fabrics there. Invista, International Textile Group (ITG), and Malden Mills, for example, have established production in China. Italian mills are also participating in joint ventures in China for both fiber and fabric production. In addition, some U.S. textile companies, such as Burlington, Cone Mills, and Guilford Mills, are among those that have built facilities in Mexico, the Caribbean countries, and other areas of Central and South America.

New Marketing Strategies

To compete with imports, U.S. textile producers have developed new marketing strategies.

The American textile industry was built on producing large volume, streamlining the product to be efficient, and offering quality at a reasonable price. In the past, companies were able to dictate products, prices, minimums, and production schedules. Now, with fierce competition from imports,

143

oversupply, and so many market niches, textile firms realize that they have to be market driven (responding to market or consumer needs), rather than manufacturing driven. In response to consumer demand for a variety of fibers and fabrics, textile producers have had to overhaul their marketing strategies completely.

The new strategies are difficult and expensive. Textile manufacturers are trying to provide innovative styling, improve quality, offer flexibility, and respond more quickly to the market. To be fashionable and flexible, however, it is necessary to produce smaller quantities, which costs more per yard.

Innovation

Innovation, which requires creativity, research, and new technology, has become an important part of the business. Textile companies strive to stay in the forefront of the market with new products. They invest heavily in research to develop new fibers, fabrics, and finishes.

High-Tech Fibers and Nanotechnology
As discussed in Chapter 5, textile manufacturers have developed new fibers such as spider silk, casein, and PLA that are applicable to fashion fabrics.

Nanotechnology, the science of precisely controlling the structure of matter at the molecular level, is used by the textile industry to develop high-strength, lightweight fibers that are 10 to 100 times smaller in diameter than synthetic fibers made by conventional methods. Nanotechnology allows the textile industry to create fibers with multifunctional properties. New thermal, heat-resistant, antibacterial, and antimicrobial fibers are being created for military or fire-fighting uniforms as well as athletic and recreational wear.

Performance Fabrics
In response to consumer demand for specific fabric properties, textile producers developed "performance" fabrics, especially for activewear for competing athletes, recreational sports, and exercise. Nanotechnology has created special finishes or treatments that can alter the hand or characteristics of fabrics or improve their performance. Intrinsic fabric properties might include muscle compression or moisture management, whatever is needed for each individual use. These fabrics must withstand vigorous activity and frequent washings.

Fabric Special Effects
Some designers and textile mills are experimenting with new fabric treatments. In Paris, Viktor and Rolf, for example, achieved a metallic look with a 47-hour process that includes applying electromagnetic paint and coating the fabric with silver. London's Giles Deacon and textile designer Fleet Bigwood applied glue to a fabric's surface, covered it with holographic foil, and placed it under a heat-transfer machine for another metallic

effect. Marc Jacobs, in conjunction with Swiss Mill Forster Willi, created a geometric lace by embroidering wool onto paper and then washing the paper away. Another example is Prada's use of a printed fabric that was unraveled and then rewoven for a blurred print effect.

Niche Marketing

Fabric producers separate their products according to market niches, such as juniors or misses in women's wear, in order to better serve their manufacturing and retail customers. They try to understand the needs of each customer: what type of garment they produce, how they are going to produce it, and how much they can pay for piece goods. They present only appropriate fabrics to each apparel-manufacturing customer.

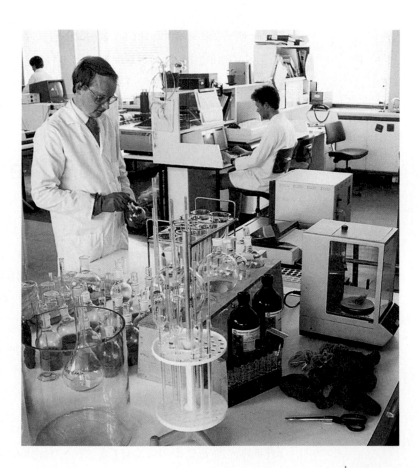

■ RESEARCHING NEW FIBER FINISHES IN A TEXTILE LABORATORY. *(COURTESY OF THE WOOLMARK COMPANY)*

Garment Packages

Many retailers have asked textile producers to supply them with *garment packages*. Retailers want to cut the cost of finished garments by eliminating middlemen and distribution charges. To meet this demand, many textile mills have extended their vertical operations to make finished garments. Although the mills do not want to alienate their apparel-manufacturing customers by competing with them, they also want to sell textiles. Burlington, for example, makes jeans at its manufacturing plant in Mexico; Galey & Lord produces khakis. Finished garment packages have become a popular way to compete against low-cost imports.

Shortening Lead Times

Textile companies are trying to speed distribution in order to meet ever-faster delivery requirements. Textile companies are sourcing fabrics close to apparel production facilities to eliminate time lost in transportation. Of course, this means that garments produced in Asia are made of Asian fabrics.

Some U.S. textile producers are able to sell to manufacturers using Mexican and Caribbean apparel-manufacturing facilities. They hope that this gives them an advantage over the competition of Asian imports that require a longer period of time for shipping.

Fiber Product Development and Marketing

To meet consumer demand, fiber producers do extensive research and product development. Textile marketers then promote and sell these fibers to yarn or fabric producers.

In the past, the marketing role of the natural fiber producer was relatively simple. The crops or animals were raised and harvested or sheared, and the fibers were sold at local markets to wholesalers who, in turn, sold the fibers at central markets. Sheep farmers and cotton growers did not have to be concerned with fabric and garment promotion.

Man-Made Fibers The development of man-made fibers and new marketing strategies changed the role of fiber producers. The giant chemical companies that produce man-made fibers invest a great deal of time and money in the research and development of new fibers and variants. This process may take several years (see Table 6.1). Several fiber companies may research the same problem simultaneously and might develop similar, competitive fibers. Then these chemical companies try to *create* a demand for the new fibers among yarn and fabric producers and apparel manufactures with sales promotion and advertising. They also educate consumers on the value and uses of these fibers.

Natural Fibers The need to compete with man-made fibers forced natural fiber producers to form associations to promote their fibers. Supported by growers, they include Cotton Incorporated, the Woolmark Company, the Silk Institute, and the International Linen Promotion.

Cotton Incorporated has a research and development center at its world headquarters in North Carolina and a marketing division in New York City, where it utilizes advertising and promotion to build demand for cotton. The Woolmark Company, based in Australia, has a research facility in Ilkley, England, and offices globally. Because wool represents less than 4 percent of global fiber

TABLE 6.1 TIMING OF PRODUCT DEVELOPMENT IN THE TEXTILE AND APPAREL INDUSTRIES
(The industry constantly strives to shorten lead times.)

Activity	Length of Time Before Retail Selling Season
Development of new fibers and variants	Several years
Fabric development (fiber firms working with mills to research and develop new fabrics)	1 to 2 years
Color predictions (fiber level)	18 to 20 months
Presentation of new fabric lines by fabric producers (Interstoff, Première Vision, Ideacomo, etc.)	1 year
Shopping fabric lines (by designers and merchandisers)	8 months to 1 year
Apparel design and line development	6 to 9 months
Apparel collection openings, market weeks, showing lines to retail buyers, taking orders	4 to 6 months
Apparel production	1 to 5 months
Shipping to retail stores	1 week to 1 month
Apparel for sale in retail store	0

production, the Woolmark Company's promotional activities are usually limited to research, development, and product innovation. However, they are now conducting a large marketing campaign in North America.

All the natural fiber associations work to improve fiber quality and processing, support fabric development, and promote their fibers to the trade and consumers. They have had to cut back dramatically, however, because their small market shares (other than cotton) do not support high marketing costs.

Blends   Natural and man-made fiber producers also work together to research and develop fiber blends. Textile engineers find the best properties of both man-made and natural fibers and combine them in satisfactory proportions to maximize their best characteristics. For example, cotton may be blended with polyester for easy care, with rayon for softness, or with spandex for stretch. In turn, these fibers will create new and interesting fabrics.

To foster sales, fiber producers create marketing campaigns to promote public recognition of their products. The man-made fiber industry has concentrated on consumer brand recognition and on explaining the uses of new fibers or variants. Natural fiber associations also want the public to be aware of the attributes of their fibers. Both use *trademarks* or *logos* for identification, such as the Woolmark Company's ball of yarn symbol.

To prepare for international textile trade shows such as Première Vision, fiber producers may have sample fabrics and garments made up to display. These samples show yarn and fabric producers how the fiber may be used effectively in a fabric.

Advertising and Publicity

The goal of *advertising* is to make consumers aware of natural fibers or man-made brands. For advertising, companies pay the media to run announcements about a product. Not only does the media itself cost a great deal, but ad production is very expensive. Ad production involves design; artwork; photography; copy for print media or scripting; and casting, rehearsals, and filming for television. As a result, advertising is very selective and usually is done only to stimulate interest in

■ COTTON INCORPORATED'S TRADE ADVERTISING CAMPAIGN FEATURING SILICONE CARICATURES, THE SPECIFIC BENEFITS OF COTTON, AND THE COTTON SEAL. *(COURTESY OF COTTON INCORPORATED)*

a new fiber or product. Fiber producers may use *cooperative advertising*, sharing the cost of advertising with fabric producers, manufacturers, and retailers that use their fibers. Tencel, Inc., for example, does cooperative advertising with Nordstrom and Bloomingdale's.

Fiber producers may advertise to fabric and apparel manufacturers in trade. However, they usually advertise their brands directly to the general public in magazines or on television. Cotton Incorporated's "Fabric of Our Lives" is an example of a national fiber advertising campaign. Television and magazine ads appeal to consumers' emotional association with the product by showing people wearing cotton in real-life situations. The ads run in conjunction with an interactive Web site. The aim of the campaign is to raise consumer awareness and demand for cotton. Other fiber associations and chemical companies also have ad campaigns.

Publicity is another way of sending a message to the consumer. In this case, a company cannot buy media time or space. The media editors choose information to write or talk about. Fiber companies and associations or public relations agencies send written information about fibers to media news departments in the hope that it will be used. They direct specific information to various media based on the interests of their readers, listeners, or viewers. The media choose what information they want to use and interpret the information to appeal to their readers. Because it cannot be purchased, publicity is especially important as it is more credible to consumers.

Customer Services

Fiber producers provide many services to their customers at both the manufacturing and retailing levels to promote sales.

Technical Advice Fiber producers offer advice to yarn and textile mills as well as to garment manufacturers. Fiber producers often commission fabric designers to work up new ideas for them. Samples of these ideas are woven or knitted in short runs, and swatches are sent to the mills. The fiber producers are also able to offer production advice to the mills.

Fashion Presentations Based on their research, some fiber producers make trend direction information available to mills, converters, and manufacturers, usually on a semiannual basis. A stylist representing the fiber producer may make presentations to manufacturers, showing garments, new and experimental fabrics, and color charts. Presentations are often targeted to specific needs, such as coat ideas for coat manufacturers or men's wear ideas for men's wear manufacturers. Market research and sourcing information may be included. Some companies also produce fashion styling reports or actual fabrics for their customers.

Color Forecasts Color directions based on color cycles, the economy, the arts, and international fashion trends are researched at the fiber level. These are combined with basics and seasonal colors to round out the color story. Some major companies decide on the colors that they think will be the most popular and dye yarn or fabric swatches to present to their customers. These are usually made available to fabric producers, converters, and apparel manufacturers to help them to plan their color stories.

Fabric Libraries An important service of the fiber producers is their fabric libraries, located in major fashion centers such as Paris, London, New York, and Los Angeles. Fabric libraries keep samples of fabrics from every mill or converter using their fibers. A designer can visit the library for an overall picture of what is available. If a designer is looking for a specific fabric, the library can help to locate a mill or converter that makes it. Some libraries now bar code the fabric samples. A scanner automatically reads and prints out the name and address of the mill and the contact person. At the same time, the designer's name is sent to the mill or converter so that they will know of potential customers.

Consumer Education Fiber producers continually provide information on their products to apparel manufacturers, schools, and the general public in the form of brochures, exhibits, lectures, audiovisual aids, and videos. This information covers every aspect of fibers and fabrics, including history, production, use, care, and benefits to the consumer.

A SELECTION OF WOOL COLOR CARDS AND YARN FORECASTS. *(COURTESY OF THE WOOLMARK COMPANY)*

Hangtags Some fiber producers provide apparel manufacturers with printed hangtags listing fiber properties and, perhaps, care instructions. Hangtags can be a useful form of publicity, as well as information for the consumer.

Fiber Distribution

Natural Fibers Fibers are sold to mills for yarn spinning and weaving or knitting. The farmers who produce natural fibers sell their goods at the markets, close to global sources, organized by their various trade associations. Farmers have no control over prices, which are set in the marketplace by supply and demand.

Man–Made Fibers The large chemical companies that produce man-made fibers have their own sales forces and set prices based on their costs. In some cases, when fiber producers and mills are vertically integrated into one large company, the producing company becomes its own market.

Fibers are often sold under certain obligations so that quality standards can be controlled. After spending a great deal on advertising to build a good reputation for a fiber's performance, the producer wants to preserve that good name. Restrictions on standards, therefore, are imposed when the fiber is sold under a brand name or a licensing agreement. There are no restrictions if the fiber is sold without the use of a brand name.

Fabric Product Development and Marketing

The next step in the textile marketing chain is the development and marketing of yarns and fabrics.

Fabric is becoming the driving force of change within the fashion industry. Karl Lagerfeld commented, "Fabrics bring the big changes now. Lycra, stretch and all that really make things possible that you could not do before, except in couture with 20 fittings."[4] Exciting innovations in fabrics, especially in blends and finishes, create interesting new textures and surfaces.

Textile Design

Specialization To focus on a specific target market, fabric producers usually specialize in one or a few types of fabrics. For example, their collection may center on only one fiber or fiber blend, a certain quality level, only knits, or only prints. Within that specialty, they offer a well-balanced line of fabrics and prices. Textile designers, too, tend to specialize in print, woven, or knitted design. They may work as full-time employees of mills, converters, or design studios, or they may sell their designs to textile companies.

Market and Technical Research Fabric merchandisers and designers try to anticipate consumers' needs by doing intensive market research. They also study international fashion and fabric trends and work to develop fashionable products having desirable fiber blends, finishes, and other properties. Merchandisers and designers must understand the physical attributes of fibers, the effects that can be achieved with the yarns that they are using, and the capabilities and limitations of the weaving looms or knitting machines to be used. They work hand in hand with textile engineers and have to understand textile processes to know if their ideas will work.

Focusing on End Use

It is very important for product managers, merchandisers, and designers to consider a fabric's end use:

- Fiber content and yarn sizes that are appropriate for the season and type of garment to be made
- Fabrics and prints that are appropriate for men's wear, women's wear, or children's wear
- Fabric prices that will fit into the price ranges of finished apparel

Concerned primarily with texture, textile designers generally use computer-aided design (CAD) systems to help them to experiment with visual representations of weave and pattern designs. A well-balanced collection of fabrics is created within the company's product line. Then a color story is chosen for the entire collection or for various groups within it.

Print Design

Print design ideas come from worldwide influences, including historic and folkloric motifs, wallpapers, old fabrics, architecture, nature, cartoons, and people's hobbies

LONDON DESIGNER JONATHAN SAUNDERS WORKS ON ONE OF HIS UNIQUE TEXTILE DESIGNS. *(PHOTO BY GINI STEPHENS FRINGS)*

and interests. Designers may shop worldwide for fabrics or garments as a source of new ideas. Many fabric companies maintain fabric archives to supply designers with ideas from the past for new prints. Print designers must consider the essential elements of color, texture, line, shape, and space. The *motifs* (repeated designs) for a print should have interesting shapes, a pleasing rhythmic pattern, and a harmonious relationship to one another.

Designers are concerned primarily with a two-dimensional surface, the flat fabric. Yet they must keep the three-dimensional end use of the fabric in mind if they are to create usable designs. Because print design is a continuous repetition of motifs, the designer must consider how cutting will affect the pattern.

Different types of prints may be designed for particular segments of the apparel industry. For example, florals and feminine motifs may be aimed at women's apparel; traditional geometrics at men's wear; and small, whimsical prints at children's wear. However, the use of prints is also cyclical; some kinds of prints are more popular than others at a given time.

Mills or converters may have their own design studios, or they may purchase original designs from independent print studios in Milan, Paris, London, Tokyo, or New York. Large print studios may also bring their design collections to New York and other textile centers for trade exposure. The original *croquis* (sketches) are then converted into a repeat design for fabric application. Variations, repeat work, restyling, and coloring may be done by the converter's own studio or by an independent studio. CAD systems are sometimes used to make the original design and most often are used for repeat work. CAD systems also transfer licensed artwork to be printed on T-shirts and sweatshirts, such as the Disney or Warner characters.

Coloring A print is usually offered in several *colorways* (color combinations). A new color combination is made by the textile firm's design department or by computer. If that is approved, a *strike-off* is run as a test on a short piece of fabric. Minimum yardage requirements for custom colors vary with the printing method.

The Fabric Collection The textile industry must develop fabrics early enough to allow apparel designers time to find and test suitable goods. Timing is very important. Every season, fabric producers prepare a new line or collection of fabrics to show to their customers, the apparel designers and manufacturers. Designers at Abraham AG, a trendsetting converter in Zurich, for example, create collections of more than 300 fabric designs twice a year.

It is very important for fabric merchandisers and designers to work directly with apparel manufacturers while developing the line. Cathy Valent, women's apparel merchandiser at Burlington Performancewear,

CATHY VALENT, DIRECTOR OF WOMEN'S WEAR PRODUCT DEVELOPMENT AND STYLING, PLANS HER FALL FABRIC AND COLOR LINE. *(COURTESY OF BURLINGTON WORLDWIDE)*

explained, "One can make the most beautiful collection; however, if one doesn't have distribution or the ability to place a product in the appropriate market, [the beauty] doesn't really matter."[5]

It is important for each fabric collection to be unique so that customers will not be tempted to buy something cheaper from another producer. Fabric producers have to be careful not to give swatches away because piracy is widespread. Fabric producers also offer their expertise to apparel manufacturers and sell sample cuts of fabrics for test garments.

Marketing

Fabric producers compete for the business of apparel manufacturers and for retail-level acceptance of products made of their goods. Marketing usually focuses on brand building. Textile companies educate the consumer about their product's characteristics to create consumer demand. The consumer learns to equate the brand name with those characteristics and to look for it. Fabric producers use advertising, publicity, and customer service to make their products known to their customers.

Advertising Large fabric producers advertise the brand names of their products. Like the fiber producers, and often in cooperation with them, they use television, newspapers, and magazines to reach national audiences. They also join apparel manufacturers and retail stores in cooperative advertising nationally or locally.

Publicity Fabric producers may also supply information on new fabric developments to the press in hope of editorial coverage.

Customer Services Like fiber producers, fabric companies provide services to their customers on both the manufacturing and retailing levels to promote sales. However, dwindling sales and profits have forced many companies to eliminate these services.

Fashion Presentations A few large fabric producers also employ merchandising and marketing experts who analyze trends and pass the information on to manufacturers and retailers. They invite customers to fashion presentations or take the presentations to customer offices around the world. They present photographs, fabrics, and/or garments from Europe, as well as the new fabrics from their own company and ideas on how to use them.

Other Services Many fabric producers also provide educational materials to consumer groups, schools and colleges, and the general public. Other services might include printed or visual materials, hangtags, brochures, in-store fashion shows, sales training sessions for retailers, and consumer education.

Fabric Markets

Twice a year, textile producers from all over the world display their lines at the following important international fabric shows in major fashion centers. Textile trade organizers try to make buying convenient and cooperate to plan cohesive fair schedules. Textile producers visit these shows to see the latest directions in fabrics. Manufacturers and their designers visit the shows to buy fabrics and gather ideas about how to use them.

> **Première Vision ("First Look")**—With approximately 650 exhibitors and 40,000 visitors, this market is held in March and October in Paris. Mod'Amont, a trimmings and supplies fair, and Texworld, presenting lower-priced fabrics and basics, are held in Paris at the same time as Première vision.

Tissu Premiere—A new fabric fair with approximately 285 exhibitors, this market is held each winter and summer in Lille, France.

Unica—The new unified Italian fabric fair now held in Milan in February and July, combining the former separate trade shows Moda In, Prato Expo, Ideabiella, and Ideacomo.

Eurotuch ("Euro-fabrics")—This fabric market, with approximately 100 exhibitors, is held each March and October in Düsseldorf, Germany.

Interstoff Asia—One of several international Interstoff fairs, this one is held in Hong Kong each April and October.

Intertextile Beijing—Organized by Messe Frankfurt, this Chinese textile fair has over 700 exhibitors from 18 countries each March and September.

International Fashion Fabric Exhibition (IFFE)—Showing fabrics from about 380 fabric producers, IFFE is held in New York in the spring and fall following the European shows.

Los Angeles International Textile Show (TALA)—Sponsored by the California Mart and the Textile Association of Los Angeles, TALA shows fabrics from approximately 140 producers each April and October.

THE DENIM-CORDUROY EXHIBITS AT PREMIÈRE VISION FABRIC FAIR IN PARIS. *(COURTESY OF PREMIÈRE VISION)*

Material World—Sponsored by the American Apparel and Footwear Association, this fair focuses on sourcing, technology supplies, and fabric information. It is held each March or April in Miami Beach, Florida.

Selling

Five times each year, fabric producers present their new lines to their customers. To get reactions to the line, fabrics are first shown to key customers. Then market weeks are held in the fabric producers' showrooms, usually in January, March or April, June, August, and October. However, the market is becoming increasingly seasonless, and new fabrics are continually being developed. Producers also have *open-line* fabrics that they can dye and ship quickly to customers (custom prints and weaves take longer to develop and produce).

Worldwide fabric producers have showrooms in major fashion centers such as New York, London, Paris, Milan, and Los Angeles. In New York City, these showrooms are on Sixth Avenue or in the Seventh Avenue Garment District area. Designers and merchandisers from apparel companies across the country come to these showrooms to see the new lines. Textile companies also work directly with private-label retailers, those who produce their own merchandise. Of course, no sales are needed for garment-package producers, as fabric and garments are produced within one company.

Sales Representatives Each fabric company also has sales representatives who visit manufacturers and their designers, showing them suitcases full of *headers*, head ends of fabrics. Most salespeople in the textile industry, especially for large companies, are salaried employees of the firms they represent. Independent sales agents or representatives may handle several textile lines and are paid by commission. They try to make contacts to gain new accounts, as well as show and sell fabrics to regular customers.

Jobbers Jobbers are independent agents who purchase leftover fabrics and *seconds* (damaged goods) at considerable discounts from textile producers and resell them at low prices. They may buy from several sources and put together their own line, or they may buy goods in hope of selling them later at a good markup during a period of peak demand. Selling leftover fabrics clears warehouse space and gives operating cash to the textile producer.

Brokers Textile brokers are also independent agents and act on behalf of apparel manufacturers. When there is a need for a particular kind of fabric at a certain price, brokers try to find it. They may first have to find the greige goods and then have a converter finish it to order. Brokers work on a commission, usually 1 percent, based on the volume of fabrics sold.

SUMMARY

PRODUCT DEVELOPMENT HAS BECOME VERY IMPORTANT, AND THE INDUSTRY IS STRIVING FOR INNOVATION AND FLEXIBILITY. THE INDUSTRY PROMOTES FIBERS AND FABRICS WITH BRAND-RECOGNITION ADVERTISING AND CUSTOMER SERVICES. INTERNATIONAL FABRIC MARKETS AND SALES REPRESENTATIVES PROVIDE THE LINK TO THE APPAREL MANUFACTURER, THE NEXT LEVEL OF THE FASHION INDUSTRY. THE ASIAN TEXTILE INDUSTRY, WITH ITS LOW PRODUCTION COSTS RESULTING FROM CHEAP LABOR, NOW DOMINATES THE GLOBAL TEXTILE MARKET.

Terms and Concepts

Briefly define and discuss the following terms and concepts:

1. Imports
2. Marketing strategies
3. Logos
4. Cooperative advertising
5. Consumer education
6. Hangtags
7. CAD systems
8. Motifs
9. Strike-off
10. Brand recognition
11. Customer services
12. Première vision
13. Headers
14. Jobbers
15. Brokers

Questions for Review

1. How have textile imports taken such a big market share in the United States?

2. What has been the textile industry's response to imports?

3. How does modern marketing differ from textile marketing in the past, when only natural fabrics were available?

4. How do natural fiber producers compete with the giant chemical companies?

5. What types of advertising do fiber producers use?

6. How are styling and color direction influenced by fiber producers?

7. What influences print design?

8. What are the major fabric markets in the world?

9. What function do jobbers and brokers perform?

Projects for Additional Learning

1. Select a print that you like from a book on historic costume or art. Trace (or modify to update, if necessary) and recolor the print in the current season's fashion colors.

2. Shop a local department store to compare fabrics used in designer or contemporary fashions.

   a. What fabrics look the freshest and most exciting?

b. What kinds of fabrics (knits, wovens, prints, solids) are used the most?

c. What are the predominant colors?

d. Examine hangtags and labels for fiber content. What kind of fiber is used more frequently in the garments, natural or man-made?

e. Can you identify the fiber brand names and generic names on the labels?

f. Can you identify fabric producers by the information on the labels?

g. Is enough information provided for the consumer about the fibers and fabrics?

h. Summarize your findings in a written report.

3. Shop a local department or specialty store and examine country-of-origin and fiber content labels in 20 garments.

a. Among the garments made of cotton, what country of fabric origin predominates? Where is each garment made?

b. Find the same information for garments made of wool, silk, ramie, and man-made fibers.

c. Make a chart showing fiber content, the country of fabric origin, and the country where the garment was made. Make separate sections for (1) foreign fabric and labor, (2) imported fabric but U.S. labor, and (3) U.S. fabric and labor.

d. Do you see a pattern forming? What conclusions can you draw from these data?

e. Are all garments adequately labeled?

f. How do prices compare between garments made overseas and those made in the United States? How do quality and detailing compare?

Notes

1 David G. Link, textile economist, e-mail correspondence, February 2003.

2 Scott Malone, "Turning to the East," *Women's Wear Daily*, March 22, 2005, p. 16.

3 "Top Fabric Exporters to U.S.," *WWD Book of Lists*, January 2005, p. 24.

4 As quoted in "King Karl," *Women's Wear Daily*, November 20, 1991, p. 8.

5 Cathy Valent, women's apparel merchandiser, Burlington Performancewear, correspondence, June 23, 2003.

LACE, FLOWER, AND RIBBON
TRIMMINGS GRACE THIS ELEGANT
CHIFFON GOWN BY ELIE SAAB.
*(COURTESY OF ELIE SAAB
AND DENTE & CRISTINA)*

7

TRIMS, LEATHER, AND FUR

Career Focus

Job possibilities for stylists, merchandisers, technicians, and marketers in the trims industries are very similar to those in the textile industry. Apparel manufacturers also need trim buyers. Most of the domestic leather and fur industry has been lost to imports, but there are still opportunities in marketing.

CHAPTER OBJECTIVES

After reading this chapter, you should be able to:

1. Explain how threads, interfacings, narrow fabrics, zippers, buttons, and belts are produced and used

2. Identify the sources of fur and leather and the steps in processing them

To complete our discussion of the raw materials of fashion, this chapter presents a survey of trims, leather, and fur.

Trims, covered in the first half of this chapter, are the secondary supplies necessary to complete a garment. The category of trimmings is very diversified, comprising both textile and nontextile areas. Thread, interfacing, and narrow-fabric manufacturing are extensions of the textile industry that have similar production and marketing procedures. Zipper manufacturing and button manufacturing, however, are entirely separate industries with their own resources and production methods.

Leather and fur sources and treatments are explored in the second part of the chapter. Leather and fur were used for clothing long before textiles were developed. Even today, leather and fur are important materials for the fashion industry. Leather is used for jackets and coats as well as for fashion accessories—shoes, handbags, gloves, and belts—whereas fur is primarily a garment material.

Trims

Designers and trimmings buyers need to know the best uses of a wide array of available trims.

Trims are the necessary supplies used to finish and adorn both garments and accessories. The huge array of decorative trimmings includes buttons, buckles, frog closures, belts, braids, ribbons, fringe, bows, laces, emblems, and sequins. Often, functional trimmings such as threads, elastics, tapes, fasteners, interfacings, and shoulder pads may be classified as *notions*. Trim buyers for manufacturers also buy necessary *sundries*, such as labels, hangtags, and hangers.

Use of trimmings varies with each segment of the industry. For example, men's wear manufacturers use more interfacings, construction tapes, and basic buttons, whereas activewear, swimwear, and underwear manufacturers use the most elastics. Women's and children's wear designers use a wider variety of decorative embroidery, ribbons, laces, and buttons.

Threads

Thread is manufactured by yarn producers from fibers. Formed by spinning and twisting textile fibers or filaments together into a continuous strand, thread holds a garment together, and its quality is vital to the durability of apparel construction.

Previously, cotton and other natural fiber threads met requirements of durability, appearance, and sewability because the majority of fabrics available were also made of natural fibers. However, the advent of man-made fibers brought about the development of many new fabrics, including knits. Because of their new characteristics, these fabrics demanded a stronger, more elastic thread. To meet these requirements, polyester, nylon, and lyocell threads were developed.

The following thread choices are available today:

- **Cotton**, used in cotton and garment-dyed apparel, is offered in soft, mercerized, and glacé finishes.
- **Core spun** is produced by spinning a staple polyester sheath cover around a core of filament polyester. This thread is strong, yet fine, and is used in better apparel.
- **Spun polyester** is strong, suitable for synthetic fabrics, able to withstand chemical and heat treatments, and inexpensive.
- **Continuous filament** can be made from nylon or polyester fibers.
- **Multifilament** is made from high-tenacity nylon or polyester filaments that are twisted and used for stitching tough materials. Polyester multifilament threads can be mechanically "textured" and heat-set to ensure bulk retention. Multifilaments can also be bonded with very little twist to create a monocord.
- **Monofilament** is produced from a single continuous synthetic filament but tends to be stiff and is not usually used for apparel.
- **Silk** is used in silk garments and some men's wear.
- **Embroidery thread**, made of rayon or polyester, is used for specific decorative sewing.

Threads are wound on cones in 1200- to 30,000-yard lengths for factory use. The Thread Institute has suggested metric conversions that approximate current yard lengths, which will eventually replace the numbering systems used now.

Manufacturers use various thread sizes, or thicknesses, according to end use, fabric, and quality needs. A metric system called tex has been suggested for measuring thread size. Based on the weight of 1000 meters of gray yarn, the tex number increases as the size increases; average thread sizes range from 10 to 500. Thread size for a blouse, for example, is lighter than that for jackets or pants.

Although a small part of the cost of manufacturing, thread quality is critical to the durability of a garment. In choosing a thread's weight, twist, or fiber content for apparel construction, consideration must be given to sewability, strength, shrinkage, abrasion resistance, colorfastness, and resistance to heat and chemicals. Thread selection is also based on strength requirements, stitch type and number of stitches per inch, the type of fabric being used, the kind of sewing machines being used, performance and quality expectations, and cost-effectiveness. Especially strong thread, for example, is needed for outdoor sportswear or children's wear.

Elastics

Elastic is used often in today's clothes, in swimwear, underwear, activewear, pull-on pants and skirts, and stretch cuffs. It affords an ease of dressing and comfort that many people appreciate.

Elastic is made from a man-made rubber called elastomer or from spandex. Elastic strands are covered (wrapped) with polyester, cotton, or acetate. They can be woven, braided, knitted, cut into flat strands, or made into thread.

Elastics are available in widths from 1/8 to 5 inches to fit manufacturers' needs. Types of elastic include the following:

- **Knitted elastics** are the most commonly used because they are the least expensive and retain their width when stretched. They are widely used for waistband tunneling.
- **Knitted spandex** is used in swimwear and dry-clean-only garments because it holds up in chorine and dry-cleaning solvents.
- **Narrow, braided elastic** is usually used for wrist and neck gathers, but the width gets narrowed when stretched.
- **Webbed elastic** wrapped in colored thread is used for decorative purposes such as stretch belts.
- **Woven elastic**, the highest-quality and most expensive product, is popular for exposed applications, such as logos woven into the elastic, as used for boxer short waistbands.
- **Elastic thread** (a strand of elastic wrapped in cotton, rayon, or polyester) is sewn into fabric to add stretch, as in shirring or smocking.

Interfacings

Interfacing is a layer of fabric placed directly under the garment fabric for structuring and support in tailored jackets and coats and to reinforce details such as collars, lapels, cuffs, pocket flaps, buttoning areas, and waistbands. Formerly, interfacings were made primarily of linen, burlap, or horsehair. Now, natural and man-made fibers and blends are used to make interfacings.

Types of Interfacings   **Nonwoven** interfacings are made of fibers held together by chemical, thermal, or spun bonding. They are the most widely used types of interfacing because they cost less to produce. Nonwovens are used in men's, women's, and children's wear; underwear; outerwear; and other garments.

Knit interfacings have been developed for use under soft fabrics in designs that require flexibility.

Woven interfacings are made by interweaving yarns, the same as most fabrics. These are used infrequently, mostly in tailored garments.

Interfacings are available in a wide variety of weights. Selection depends on the weight of the garment fabric, as well as the support and effect desired. Ideally, interfacing is never heavier than the actual garment fabric. Interfacings are also available in both sew-in and fusible forms. Fusibles, which are heat-bonded to fabrics, add body, make a smooth surface, and replace old-fashioned hand tailoring.

Narrow Fabrics

Narrow fabrics include narrow laces, ribbons, braids, other woven and knit decorative bands, piping, and cording. Woven, knit, and braid trims are produced by narrow-fabric manufacturers. Previously, most of the trims sold in the United States were imported from Europe. Now over 90 percent come from Asia, especially China, and U.S. manufacturers have virtually disappeared as a result of competition from cheap imports.

Narrow fabrics are either functional or decorative. The decorative trims industry is a fashion-oriented business, although there are really no seasonal lines. The fashion for trims is cyclical, like any other fashion. For example, when ethnic looks are popular, decorative trims are in great demand. Popularity is also based on seasons, regions, and customers.

■ A NARROW-FABRIC-WEAVING MACHINE. *(COURTESY OF JAKOB MÜLLER AG, SWITZERLAND)*

Types of Narrow Fabrics Narrow fabrics vary greatly and are specially made for different uses and methods of application.

- **Banding**—Narrow fabric having two straight or decorative edges that make it ideal for borders, edging, insertion, or accenting a design line

- **Beading**—Openwork trim, usually lace or embroidery, through which a ribbon may be threaded (this beading is not to be confused with beads used to create banding or edging for evening wear)

- **Binding**—Prefolded trim that encloses a raw edge, finishing and decorating it at the same time

- **Edging**—A trim having one decorative edge and one straight edge

- **Galloon**—Lace, embroidery, or braid having two shaped and finished edges; it can be used as a banding, border, or design-line accent or can be applied like insertion

- **Insertion**—A trim with two straight edges (also a method of applying trim by inserting and sewing it between two cut edges of fabric)

- **Medallions**—A chain of trims with individual motifs that can be used continuously as banding, edging, or galloons or clipped apart and used as appliqués

Laces The popularity of handmade laces led to the invention of lace-making machines. Although narrow-textile manufacturers primarily produce bands of lace, their methods can be applied as well to the production of lace fabric. Laces are used primarily for lingerie or bridal gowns, but like other decorative trims, they recurrently play an important role in fashion. Today, there are basically four types of machine-made lace.

Barmen lace has its roots in Germany and Cluny, France. The Barmen machine runs on a Jacquard system. *Jacquard* is a weaving system that uses a highly versatile pattern mechanism to produce intricate designs. Yarns are plaited together to resemble heavy, crocheted lace.

Leaver lace, named after Englishman John Leaver who developed the machine, is sheer bobbin lace. Also Jacquard programmed, the Leaver machine twists threads into a giant web that can have up to 180 bands, each connected by auxiliary threads. To separate the bands, auxiliary threads can be hand-pulled (as is usually done in Europe) or dissolved in an acetone solution.

Raschel knitted lace is less expensive than Leaver lace because of the high speeds at which it can be produced. This lace is also made in a giant web formed by linking chains of yarn. The bands are separated by pulling drawstrings.

Venice lace is made on Schiffli (see the following section) embroidery machines. The Schiffli machines are also controlled by a Jacquard system.

Embroidery Although embroidery is not confined to narrow fabrics, it seems appropriate to discuss its production after that of laces. As an allover or as a trim, embroidery has been used most often in lingerie and blouses.

Schiffli is continuous embroidery on fabrics or trims. Manufacturers can send out fabric panels to have them embroidered and then insert them into garments, as on a blouse front. The newest Schiffli machines are huge and highly automated, but require some labor to operate, including cutting and fastening threads. Schiffli machines are also used to make embroidered eyelet (cutwork embroidery) and lace.

Framework embroidery is used when a single motif is needed on a garment. Multihead machines operated by a computer embroider up to 20 pieces, such as a pocket, at one time. These pieces are cut apart and attached as decoration.

Ribbons Ribbons are another category of narrow fabrics. Many ribbons are woven at one time on looms with 2, 4, 6, 8, 16, 24, or 48 spaces. The width of the ribbon and the volume of production

A COMPUTER-AUTOMATED SHUTTLE EMBROIDERY MACHINE. (*COURTESY OF SAURER TEXTILE SYSTEMS, SWITZERLAND*)

determine the size of the machine to be used. Satin and velvet ribbons are made much like their fabric counterparts. Grosgrain is woven on a belting or dobby loom.

Solid color ribbons can be piece dyed after weaving to match manufacturers' color specifications. Patterns such as stripes or plaids may be woven with predyed yarns. For intricate patterns, Jacquard looms are used. Some motifs, such as company logos, are printed on woven, dyed ribbons.

Although most ribbons are produced in Asia, fine ribbons are imported from Europe: velvet from France, Germany, and Switzerland and plaids from England. Jobbers buy up huge quantities of ribbon and novelties from manufacturers to have them available for small manufacturers whenever needed.

Passementerie (Braids and Cords)
This category includes braided trims and woven and knitted decorative trims that are heavier than ribbons. Uniform and costume manufacturers use the most braids. Braided trims are made by interlacing three or more yarns to form a flat, narrow fabric. They include soutache, middy braid, braided cord edging, and rickrack.

Knitted braids, made by a few needles on a warp-knitting machine, include both flat and foldover braids.

Woven braids, made on textile looms, include flat and foldover braids and piping made with bias strips.

Patterned braids, like ribbons, are produced on Jacquard looms.

Fasteners

Zippers Whitcomb Judson, a Chicago inventor, first introduced a metal "slide fastener" in 1891. However, it was not until 1912 that Gideon Sundback developed a practical fastener made on narrow-woven fabric. These zippers were made by the Hookless Fastener Company in Pennsylvania, which later became Talon, Inc. In 1923, the B. F. Goodrich Company first used the term *zipper* to describe the fastener, and manufacturers began to use the device in fashionable garments. In 1960, the nylon zipper was introduced, which provided the industry with an alternative lightweight zipper that could be dyed to match any garment fabric. Today the Japanese company YKK dominates the zipper business.

Today, the three basic types of zippers, depending on the materials used, are polyester coil, metal, and plastic molded zippers.

AUTOMATIC BRAIDING MACHINES MAKING RICKRACK. *(COURTESY OF TRIMTEX, WILLIAM E. WRIGHT CO.)*

Polyester coil zippers, the most widely used, are manufactured from a continuous polyester monofilament that is either first formed into a coil and then sewn or woven onto a tape, or formed directly from the monofilament state into a zipper.

Molded zippers are made by injecting molded plastic teeth onto tapes.

Metal zippers are made by clamping interlocking metal scoops (teeth) onto narrow fabric tapes.

Zippers are sold in three basic forms: continuous chain (in long lengths), regular (closed end), or separating (open end). *Continuous chain*, sold on reels by the yard, can be cut by the apparel manufacturers and made into zippers. *Closed end* zippers are cut to specified lengths, and then metal staples are attached to the bottom and top. *Separating* zippers are also cut to length, then sliders, separating end components, and top stops are attached. Zipper thickness sizes range from a very fine size 02 to a large size 10. In lengths, 7 to 9 inches and 22 to 24 inches are the most common for use in skirts, pants, jackets, and dresses. Usually, zipper application is hidden under a placket-fold or at a seam. Sometimes fashion prescribes that zippers be displayed as garment decoration. In this case, the zipper color, size, and type become part of the design.

BUTTON STYLE AND SIZE CHART.

Buttons

Buttons are an important aspect of a garment for both functional purposes and fashion interest. When fashion emphasizes detailing, the market becomes stronger for buttons. Most button producers follow fashion trends in both color and styling.

Originally, shirting buttons were made from real pearl, so button production centers grew up in New York, near the Hudson River, and in Muscatine, Iowa, on the Mississippi River, both sources of freshwater pearls. Metal button production originated in Connecticut. Button manufacturing, like everything else, has been taken over by China and Thailand where labor is cheap. The Italians continue to make the most beautiful buttons, but they are quickly copied by the Asians.

Sew-through buttons have two or four holes that are sewn through for application. Decorative buttons can even have six or eight holes. Shank buttons are sewn through a hole in the shank back. Two-part metal buttons, as used on jeans, require special machinery for application.

Buttons are purchased by the gross (144), and all sizes are expressed in terms of *lignes* (one ligne equals 0.025 inch or 0.635 millimeter). For example, a 1-inch button is the same as a 40-ligne button. Self-covered buttons are made to order by contractors for apparel manufacturers.

Buttons can be made of natural materials, metal, or plastic.

Natural Traditionally, buttons were made from natural materials such as pearl, shell, wood, leather, porcelain, and bone. Manufacturers concerned with the environment are again promoting the renewable resources of natural materials. Tagua (also called Corozo) buttons, made from a nut that grows in Ecuador, have been popular, and their harvest helps to protect the rainforests. Mother-of-pearl, trocca, and mussel buttons are made from natural shells found in the waters around Japan, the Philippines, and Australia. However, most of these natural sources are expensive and, therefore, are copied in plastic. Also, due to U.S. Fish and Wildlife Department regulations, importers have to prove that the shells do not come from endangered shellfish. As a result of regulations, technological advances, and the wide use of synthetics, less than 10 percent of all buttons sold in the United States are constructed of natural materials.

Metal Metal buttons, which can be made from brass, stainless steel, or pewter, are either stamped or cast. Casting is expensive and constitutes only a small portion of the business. Stamped metal buttons (front and back are stamped separately and joined together), as well as metal rivets and snaps, are in great demand for jeans. Some environmentally concerned manufacturers are using buttons made from nonrusting alloys to avoid the hazardous sludge that is a by-product of electroplating.

Plastic Most buttons are now made of various types of plastics (melamine, urea, polyester, or nylon) because they can be made to imitate natural materials inexpensively, and they can be dyed to match fabric. These buttons can be cut out of plastic sheets, line cast, or molded. In the case of nylon, liquid nylon is poured into button molds to create unusual shapes, such as those used on children's wear.

Other metal and plastic fasteners include buckles, slide locks, snaps, and hooks and eyes. Tack-buttons (on jeans) and snaps are particularly popular.

Hook-and-Loop Fasteners
Hook-and-loop fasteners can be used to fasten apparel and shoes, to secure shoulder pads, and for many other applications. In the 1940s, the Swiss inventor George de Mestral came home from hiking with cockleburs on his trousers. His microscope showed that cockleburs were covered with hundreds of tiny hooks and that his trousers were made of hundreds of tiny loops. De Mestral decided to turn his discovery into a practical fastener. He

offered his new product under the trademark Velcro from the French words *velour* (velvet) and *crochet*. The first application in apparel was in skiwear.

In the apparel industry, most *hook-and-loop* (or *touch*) fasteners are made of woven or knitted nylon. The hook-and-loop tapes come in many stock colors or can be custom dyed. They are sold in 50- or 100-yard rolls in a variety of widths, 5/8 and 3/4 inch being the most common for apparel. A wide variety of shapes is now available, including linear tapes and cut pieces, straps, and custom forms. For example, to eliminate sharp edges for children's wear, the fasteners are often dye cut with rounded corners and applied by sewing.

Belts

There are two types of belt manufacturers. The *rack trade* (see Chapter 11) sells to retailers, and the *cut-up* producers sell less expensive belts to apparel manufacturers to be used on dresses, jackets, skirts, or pants.

Garment belts are usually made of inexpensive materials such as bonded leather, vinyl, or ribbon. The belt material is either glued or sewn onto a stiff interfacing or backing. Novelty belts can be made of any material needed to meet fashion requirements: webbing, plastic, braid, chain, rope, or even rubber. Self-belts (made of garment fabric) can also be made to order by a contractor.

Sundries

Labels Labels are the sources of identification for garments. Along the production line, various labels must be attached to the garment. These include manufacturer and/or designer identification, fiber content, care instructions, country of origin, size, and a union label if made in a U.S. union shop. Federal law requires listing fibers in order of percentage used, along with cleaning or washing instructions.

A label showing fiber content, care instructions, and country of origin must also be included in the garment. This information is usually on a separate small label under the brand label or on an inside seam.

Government regulations devote pages to fiber-content and country-of-origin labeling. Essentially, the predominant fiber in the garment is listed first along with its content percentage, followed by the other fibers in decreasing order of content. Care instructions are recommended and can be very specific. These instructions not only protect the consumer, but also protect the manufacturer against returns made by consumers who do not care for their garments as instructed.

A country-of-origin label is required by customs if the garment is made outside the United States. The label must say "Made in (name of country)" or "Made in USA of imported fabric." A "Made in USA" label is reserved for garments made entirely in the United States of U.S. fabric. Items made partially in a foreign country and partially in the United States must disclose these facts; for example, a tag might read "Assembled and sewn in the USA of components made in (name of country)."

Labels are made on narrow fabrics. The apparel or accessory manufacturer's name is often embroidered onto the label. Information labels are simply printed.

In addition, sportswear often has pressure-sensitive labels showing sizes on the outside of garments, particularly when they are folded. *Flashers*, printed cards that give product information, may be stapled to the outside of sportswear.

Hangtags *Hangtags*, printed paper tags, may be hung from the garment by plastic staple, barb, or string. Hangtags are designed to draw attention to the garment and are hung on the side of the garment so that the customer can see them easily. They usually show the brand name, perhaps the style number, color, size, and other product information. Sometimes hangtags are provided by fiber or fabric producers to promote fibers or finishes.

Marketing

Most manufacturers buy their trims from sales representatives who travel the country visiting their customers. Manufacturers may also visit one of the trimmings and supplies fairs to see new merchandise:

Mod'Amont—This trimmings and supplies fair is held at the same time as Première Vision in Paris.

Trimmings Expo—This market is held each November in New York for designers and manufacturers to see the newest in this important market.

Manufacturers may also buy their trimmings through distributors and/or jobbers. These people buy trims from trim manufacturers to have large inventories available when their customers, the apparel and accessory manufacturers, need them.

The trimmings industries use electronic data interchange (EDI) and automatic replenishment initiatives to speed up ordering, production, and distribution to apparel and accessory manufacturers. The Sundries Apparel Findings Linkage Council (SAFLINC) has established universal codes and linkage systems throughout the industry.

The Leather Industry

Designers, merchandisers, and manufacturers of leather apparel and accessories must know the sources, properties, and best uses of leather. Retailers, too, are interested in the quality of the leather products they sell.

Although much older than the production of fiber and fabrics, the processing of leather is not as sophisticated—and it takes much longer. Lately, however, production methods have improved, greatly increasing the supply and variety of leather. However, as in textiles, the domestic industry has shrunk considerably because of competition from imports.

Leathers are preserved animal hides and skins, by-products of the meat industry. Cattle hides provide the most leathers, but deer-, goat-, pig-, and sheepskins are also widely used. The world's largest exporter of cattle hides is the United States, most goatskins come from India and China, and most sheepskins come from Australia. Developing countries, particularly those with abundant raw material supplies, such as Argentina, Brazil, and India, impose export controls or taxes to encourage the growth of their own tanning and leather products industries.

Hides and skins are differentiated by weight. Skins come from smaller animals such as goats, deer, pigs, and calves and weigh less than 25 pounds. Hides come from large animals such as steers, cows, buffaloes, and horses and weigh more than 25 pounds each.

Leather Processing

Tanneries purchase and process skins and hides and sell the leather as their finished product. Companies usually specialize because processing methods depend on the nature of the skins treated and the end use of the leather. New equipment and technology have made the U.S. tanning industry more productive than any in the world. However, because of competition from cheap labor in developing countries and toxic waste, the tanning industry in the United States has shrunk to almost nothing.

The process by which hides and skins are made into leather can take up to six months and requires extensive equipment and skilled labor. The three basic steps in leather processing are pretanning, tanning, and finishing.

Pretanning Pretanning is basically a cleaning process. Skins and hides are cured to prevent them from rotting by applying salt, soaking them in brine, or just drying them. Then they are

LEATHER SHEEPSKIN JACKETS FROM GIORGIO ARMANI'S MEN'S COLLECTION. *(COURTESY OF GIORGIO ARMANI)*

soaked in water to rehydrate them and to remove dirt, salt, and some proteins. Hides and skins must also have hair and fat removed by additional treatments, which differ with each type of skin.

Tanning   Tanning involves the application of various agents that protect the hide or skin against decomposition. Treatment methods include soaking and powdering. The choice of agents depends largely on the end use of the leather. Tanning agents include vegetable products, oils, minerals, and chemicals.

- **Vegetable tanning** is generally done in large vats filled with tanning solutions made from water and tannin. Tannin is a bitter substance obtained from the roots, bark, wood, leaves, or fruits of various trees and shrubs and produces a firm, heavy leather.
- **Oil tanning**, using codfish oil that is rubbed into the skin, produces relatively soft and pliable leathers, such as chamois.
- **Mineral tanning** is performed with a tanning solution of chrome salts. Chrome tanning is much faster and is also more resistant to heat and scratching.
- **Chemical tanning**, a newer method, uses agents such as sulfonic acid.
- **Combination tanning** is the use of a combination of agents to obtain the desired effect. For example, many leathers are pretanned with chrome and then retanned with vegetable tannins.

Finishing   Finishing produces the desired thickness, moisture, and esthetic appeal. After excess water and wrinkles are removed from the tanned leather, it is shaved or split into a uniform thickness.

Color is applied to leather by brushing or by tray, drum, spray, solvent, vacuum, or tank dyeing. Special effects may be created by dabbing color on with a sponge, applying color through stencils, sprinkling, spraying, or tie-dyeing.

The dyed leather is treated with oils and fats, which provide lubrication, softness, strength, and waterproofing. The leather is then dried to fix the dyes and oils permanently. Dried leather is conditioned with damp sawdust to obtain uniform moisture content and then stretched for softness. Finally, the leather is coated with a seasoning or finish that improves its properties or character. For example, urethanes are used to add shine for patent leather. Leathers may be further treated with buffers, rollers, or presses to achieve glazed, matte, and embossed effects. Tanners in China and Korea add distressed finishes to less expensive pigskin and goatskin to make them look richer to compete with the more supple lambskin or calfskin.

Environmental Concerns The U.S. Environmental Protection Agency (EPA) has established standards to control the polluting wastes that tanners discharge, such as sulfides, chromium, and acid. Control of these wastes requires expensive primary and secondary treatment facilities. The industry is developing and adopting new tanning systems that will use nontoxic metal salts and other organic tanning materials to replace the chromium. The industry is also encouraged to adopt low-solvent or solvent-free finishes.

Leather Marketing

Like the fiber and fabric producers, leather producers market their products to apparel manufacturers, fashion editors, retailers, and consumers. Marketing is done by the individual companies or through trade associations such as the Tanners Council.

Leather markets are concentrated in Western countries. The United States imports more processed leather than it exports. It exports leather, but for nonapparel use, to more than 80 countries, primarily Japan and Hong Kong. It imports leather primarily from Argentina and Italy. The major importers of finished leathers are Europe and South America. Major exporters are Japan and China. International trade in leather is more than $1 billion per year. The footwear industry is the tanning industry's largest market.

Rising world population and incomes, along with new fashions for leather, have contributed to an ever-increasing demand for leather. To protect and expand their markets, leather producers must constantly strive to develop new leather finishes and colors.

The Fur Industry

The fur industry is another supplier of raw material for the fashion industry. Many apparel designers also design collections for fur manufacturers.

Fur is the hairy coat of a mammal. However, except in the case of lamb, fur is not a by-product of the meat industry. From prehistoric times, people have used animal fur for both its warmth and attractive appearance. Because fur has long been associated with wealth and prestige, the demand for luxury has played a major role in the development of the fur industry. Recently, however, an organization called People for the Ethical Treatment of Animals (PETA) has raised the American public's consciousness against the use of fur in fashionable clothing. Still, the use of shearling lamb is acceptable to many because lambskin is a by-product of the meat industry.

This section discusses the characteristics of various furs, the processes involved in preparing fur pelts for their use in the manufacture of fur garments, and the marketing of furs. The fur industry consists of three major groups: pelt producers or trappers, fur processors, and companies that produce fur garments for consumers (fur garment manufacturing is discussed in Chapter 11).

Fur Sources

INSPECTING FUR PELTS. *(COURTESY OF THE DEUTSCHES PELZ INSTITUT, GERMANY)*

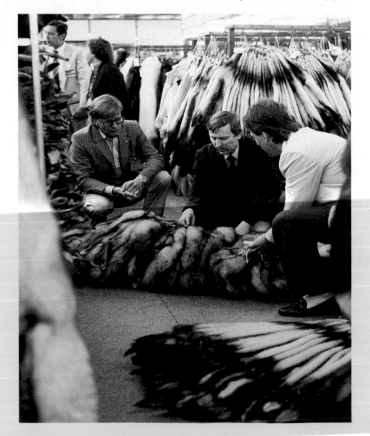

The international fur market is focused mainly on mink production. Scandinavia produces more than half of the world's mink supply, followed by the United States, Holland, and Russia. The major animals raised or trapped for the United States fur business are (in descending order of importance) mink, mostly bred; fox, trapped and bred; and sable, imported from Russia and Canada, where it is trapped. Other furs used in smaller quantities include muskrat, skunk, opossum, lamb, and rabbit. The industry obtains the pelts or skins of fur-bearing animals from the wild or, more often, from fur farms or ranches.

Wild Furs Wild furs for commercial use come from more than 80 countries on all six continents, but mainly from North America, which has the greatest variety (40 different types).

Endangered Species In the late 1960s, individuals, international organizations, and governments became concerned about the possible extinction of endangered species. As a result, some countries enacted legislation restricting or prohibiting the commercial use of particular animals, including certain monkeys, seals, and leopards.

Terms and Concepts

Briefly define and discuss the following terms and concepts:

1. Trimmings
2. Interfacing
3. Narrow fabrics
4. Jacquard system
5. Schiffli
6. Passementerie
7. Leather types
8. Tanneries
9. Fur dressing

Questions for Review

1. Briefly explain the difference between decorative and functional trimmings.
2. Discuss the various types of interfacings and their uses.
3. What categories are included in narrow fabrics?
4. Describe the four basic kinds of machine lace.
5. Describe the three basic types of zippers and their construction.
6. Why are man-made buttons used most often?
7. Briefly discuss the basic steps in leather processing.
8. Discuss the animal rights controversy and how it affects the fur industry.
9. Discuss the steps in the dressing of furs.

Projects for Additional Learning

1. Select one category of trim (lace, for example) and find a variety of samples at fabric stores. Ask if you may have or purchase just a small piece of each. Describe the pattern or construction of each type. Show examples (photos or actual garments) of their end use.

2. At the library, trace the origin and development of a specific trim. Explain the differences between how it was made by hand originally and how it is mass-produced today.

3. Visit a local department or specialty store and find five garments that use decorative and functional trimmings. List every trim on each garment. Discuss how the trims affect the total design of the garment. How do you think the manufacturers balanced the added cost of the trimmings with fabric and labor costs?

4. What impact do prevailing political attitudes and economic conditions have on the sale of furs?

5. Visit a furrier or fur dealer. Learn to identify various furs by their characteristics.

A CHARMING LACE AND RUFFLED GOWN
BY ELIE SAAB. (*COURTESY OF ELIE SAAB
AND DENTE & CHRISTINA ASSOCIATES*)

8

INTERNATIONAL FASHION

Career Focus

Every professional in the fashion business wants to be informed about what is happening in the fashion capitals of the world. Most designers, their business partners, other manufacturing executives, and promotional organizations are located in these major fashion centers where creative inspiration and suppliers are found and major business decisions are made.

CHAPTER OBJECTIVES

After reading this chapter, you should be able to:

1. Name the well-known international fashion creators
2. Explain the reasons for French fashion leadership
3. Discuss the growth in importance of the prêt-à-porter
4. List the reasons for the importance of New York as a fashion center
5. Discuss the role of international and domestic fashion centers

This chapter introduces the major fashion capitals of the world, the centers that are most influential in creating and marketing new fashion. You will read about the specialties of each and about the creators who have made them into fashion centers. Fashion centers develop as a result of concentrations of resources, supplies, skilled labor, and creative people. Designers are influenced by what other designers and artists are creating. Excitement about a new idea acts as a catalyst for more creativity. This is why many creative people gravitate to major cities.

Global Nature of Fashion

It becomes more and more difficult to discuss fashion by individual city or country.

Four cities have emerged as major fashion capitals: Paris, Milan, London, and New York City. American designers and brands score high when it comes to marketing savvy and making salable clothes that appeal to the whole U.S. population and have influenced the world with their approach to sportswear.

However, it is increasingly difficult to describe the characteristics of fashion by country or fashion capital. A clear division no longer exists between what is foreign and what is domestic; the fashion industry is becoming a worldwide exchange of ideas, talent, material, and products. Ideas come from all over the world; textiles are exported from one country to another; production is done almost everywhere, particularly in Asia; and nearly every country contributes in some way. Each company seeks to expand its markets through exports, and that makes them known internationally.

Designers move to other countries to work. Karl Lagerfeld, a German, works in Paris. Should we consider him a German designer or a French designer? John Galliano, an Englishman, designs the Dior couture collection in Paris. Marc Jacobs, an American, also designs the Louis Vuitton collection in Paris. The list is endless and it is, therefore, difficult to list designers by country. It is also confusing that some designers work in one country and show their collections in another.

The job of the international designer is not an easy one. Lagerfeld designs three major collections: his own signature line, Chanel couture, and the Italian Fendi collection. Some designers have time for little else than designing or promoting their designs. They supervise large design teams for several collections, visit factories, attend store openings, and make worldwide public appearances.

Promotion and Licensing

Designer names become famous because of extensive press coverage, their own advertising and promotional efforts, and success in the marketplace. With fame come requests for *licensing,* a process through which manufacturers are given permission to use a designer or brand name, and joint ventures (see Chapter 12). One major goal of fashion businesses is to market accessories and fragrances under the house (brand) name. As a result, fashion empires grow to the point that successful international designers have become stars.

Business Partners

A successful fashion business is not built on a good designer alone. Some designers try to serve as both designer and chief executive officer, but it is a difficult leap between mind-sets. Vera Wang finds that doing both is "the most profound challenge she has faced in her career. The freedom, extravagance and passion needed for the creative process often may be at odds with the discipline and control needed to run a business."[1] Most designers have astute business partners like Giancarlo Giametti at Valentino, or Peter Strom at Ralph Lauren. These people manage the finances, operations, and marketing sides of the business to enable the designer to concentrate on creativity.

AMERICAN MARC JACOBS DESIGNS FOR LOUIS VUITTON IN PARIS AS WELL AS HIS OWN SIGNATURE COLLECTION AND MARC BY MARC JACOBS IN NEW YORK. *(COURTESY OF LOUIS VUITTON, PARIS)*

Company Ownership

One trend in the fashion business is to try to build powerful, complex conglomerates or corporate groups. The fashion business is controlled by fewer large companies. The consolidation of retailers forces manufacturers to do the same to be able to supply all units of large chain stores. Manufacturing executives think that acquisitions are a means of survival. Large conglomerates develop in an effort to have the financial power to control image, source fabrics and production, and distribute worldwide. Megacorporations have greater negotiating power with suppliers, retailers, and advertising venues. Corporate executives also believe that it's important for them to diversify so that

185

when one brand is weak, others might be strong. They also argue that growth is necessary to sustain and increase the worth of their stock and to have the strength to compete with other large corporations. Many decisions are made to affect stock market ratings.

The French company LVMH Moët Hennessy Louis Vuitton, for example, owns Dior, Givenchy, Galliano, Kenzo, Celine, Louis Vuitton, Loewe, Donna Karan, Pucci, Thomas Pink, Joseph, and many more brands; Guerlain perfumes; Sephora cosmetic stores; and Le Bon Marché and Franck & Fils stores. The Gucci Group of Italy now owns Yves Saint Laurent, Balenciaga, Alexander McQueen, Stella McCartney, Bottega Veneta, and Sergio Rossi. Conglomerates like these aggressively vie for prestigious brands. Some manufacturers are happy to sell in order to have their brand survive. The parent company gives them capital to expand their businesses. As consumers, we are not aware that each company is part of a larger one. However, these large corporations must preserve the identity and autonomy of each brand. Some designers feel they lose control of their collections.

To compete on a global scale, a designer or manufacturer needs to open stores and expand business. This requires money, however, and a partner will assume financial risk only in return for ownership of the brand. The investor cares about getting a return on investment while the designer cares most about creating an identity and style. This can often lead to conflicts and splits. For example, if a designer leaves (or is forced to leave) his own namesake company, he will no longer have the right to use his own name in a new business, because the name is still owned by the corporation! Designers such as Jil Sander, Helmut Lang, Roland Mouret, and Hervé Leger have had to deal with this phenomenon.

Many private or family-run businesses, such as Ferragamo, believe that remaining independent allows them to be more flexible and focused on creating a quality product. Young designers have difficulty getting started because of the high costs involved.

France

Paris has long been the foremost city in the world for fashion, but has fierce competition from Milan and New York City.

Paris is the capital of France and is the Hollywood of the fashion world. Fashion is one of France's top three export industries with approximately 100,000 workers in the apparel sector (less than half of what it was in 1983) and roughly 400,000 employees in the combined textile, apparel, and related industries.

Chambre Syndicale de la Couture Parisienne, the managing body of the federation, dictates rules about workrooms and collections.

The couture has shrunk dramatically over the past 20 years. However, Giorgio Armani felt that couture was important enough to start his own "Privé" couture collection in 2005. American designer Ralph Rucci also shows his couture collection in Paris.

Ateliers To quality for the Couture-Creation list of the Chambre Syndicale de la Couture Parisienne, a house is required to have at least one *atelier* (workroom) in Paris with a minimum technical staff of 15 (20 for established houses), not including the director. A couturier may have anywhere from 15 to 200 employees in one or a combination of several ateliers. To get established, novice couturiers are allowed a two-year transition period during which they need have only 10 employees.

In large houses, where there is much work to be done, *modelistes* work under the head designer, executing the individual designs. The modelistes are the liaison with the ateliers, where they supervise construction of the *toile,* or sample garment.

Ateliers are separated into *flou*, where they make dresses, and *tailleur*, where they specialize in the tailoring of suits and coats. Each atelier is headed by a production manager or chief technician called the *premier d'atelier* (pre-me-ay' dah-tel-yay'). Working under the manager are the shop assistant(s), fitters, *midinettes* (seamstresses), and apprentices.

Parisian Couturiers

Karl Lagerfeld for Chanel (Gabrielle "Coco" Chanel, 1883–1971) brought international attention back to the couture when he took over as artistic director for the house in 1983. Born in 1938, Lagerfeld won the International Wool Secretariat design competition in 1954 at age 16 and was hired by Pierre Balmain as an assistant. In 1967, he began working for the Italian company Fendi. He was the designer for Chloé for 19 years before Bidermann Industries offered to back him in his own line. He also designs Chanel ready-to-wear, Gallery Lagerfeld, and Fendi, and does the photography for his advertising. His new lower-priced Karl Lagerfeld line is based in New York, actually owned by Tommy Hilfiger, and designed by Melanie Ward.

John Galliano for Dior (Christian Dior, 1905–1957), who was born in Gibraltar in 1960, moved to London in 1966 and later studied at St. Martin's School of Art. He presented his first signature collection in 1985, showing in London until 1990, when he began to show in Paris. In 1995, he was chosen to be the new designer for the House of Givenchy, but was soon

KARL LAGERFELD DESIGNS COUTURE FOR CHANEL IN PARIS. *(COURTESY OF KARL LAGERFELD)*

transferred to Dior, also owned by LVMH, where he presented his first collection in January 1997. He has won many fashion awards, including the British Designer of the Year award three times.

Jean-Paul Gaultier is known as the "enfant terrible" of the French fashion industry because of his outrageous designs. Born in 1952, Gaultier worked for Pierre Cardin and Jean Patou before showing his first signature collection in 1976. He has designed costumes for shows and films, and in 1997 began his Gaultier Paris couture collection. His other collections include Gaultier Classiques and JPG Jeans, as well as furs, eyewear, and fragrances. He is now also creative director for Hermès, the 165-year-old Parisian fashion house.

Christian Lacroix (La-kwa') is known for his extravagant costume looks, silhouettes, colors, and pattern mixes. Born in Arles in 1951, he studied art history, intending to become a museum curator. Chance brought him to Hermès in 1978 and then to Jean Patou in 1981. In 1987, Bernard Arnault, now chairman of LVMH, offered to back him in his own couture house. In addition to designing haute couture, prêt-à-porter, children's wear, jeans, and accessories, Lacroix has designed costumes for theater and opera.

Elie Saab is a Middle-Eastern designer with headquarters in Beirut, Lebanon. He opened his first atelier in 1982 at the young age of 18 and has since dressed royalty and international celebrities. In 2003, he was invited to become a member of the Chambre Syndicale de la Couture in Paris. He also has a prêt-à-porter collection, also shown in Paris.

Franck Sorbier was born in Fréjus, France, and studied at the Esmod Fashion School in Paris. He worked for Chantal Thomass and Thierry Mugler before presenting his first signature collection in 1987, backed by Cartier beginning in 1994. He began his couture collection in 1999. He also designs coats, shoes, and opera costumes.

Other couturiers include Adeline André, Riccardo Tisci for Givenchy, Dominique Sirop, and correspondent members Valentino and Armani from Italy. Felipe Oliviera Baptista, Walter van Bierendonck, Boudicca, Vanessa Bruno, Lefranc Ferrant, Maurizio Galante, Anne Valérie Hash, Adam Jones, Christophe Josse, Nicolas le Cauchois, Véronique LeRoy, Gustavo Lins, Martin Margiela, Yoichi Nagasawa, Richard René, Walter Rodrigues, Gerald Watelet, Viktor & Rolf, and Worth have been invited as "guest members." Yves Saint Laurent and Emmanuel Ungaro, two of the most outstanding couturiers, have retired, and their companies now produce only ready-to-wear.

Prêt-à-Porter

Prêt-à-Porter (pret-a-por-tay') is French for "ready-to-wear." Most French fashion is mass-produced, as it is in other countries. Mass production makes fashion less expensive. In this case, identical garments are manufactured in various sizes and colors. A customer needs only to try on a garment in a store to check fit and appearance, purchase it, and take it home immediately.

As couture garments became more expensive, mass-produced garments became more and more fashionable. By the 1960s, designer ready-to-wear became as influential as couture. The couturiers suffered from the competition and were no longer financially successful. Therefore, the couturiers began to produce their own prêt-à-porter collections.

Today, designer prêt-à-porter creations cost as much as couture used to. Whereas a couture creation might now cost from $5000 to $50,000, the upper-end prêt-à-porter range is roughly $1000 to $5000. However, despite its price, a prêt-à-porter garment brings no exclusivity with it. There is the same experimentation involved in creating original sample garments for ready-to-wear as there is for couture. However, ready-to-wear garments are made from much less expensive fabrics and

A STRIKING AND COLORFUL EMBROIDERED DRESS FROM PRÊT-À-PORTER DESIGNER ALBER ELBAZ FOR LANVIN. *(COURTESY OF LANVIN, PARIS)*

have no handwork. It is the mass production of these samples that makes ready-to-wear a profitable business.

Top Prêt–à–Porter Designers

Nicolas Ghesquiere for Balenciaga (Christobal Balenciaga, 1895–1972) Ghesquiere was born in Loudun, France, in 1971. He presented his first ready-to-wear collection for Balenciaga in 1997 and received the CFDA Outstanding International Design award in 2001. In 2001, Balenciaga was acquired by the Gucci Group.

Alber Elbaz for Lanvin Elbaz was born in Morocco in 1962, but grew up in Israel. He graduated from Shenkar College fashion school in Tel Aviv and then headed for New York City, where he worked for Geoffrey Beene for seven years. He was then ready-to-wear designer for Guy Laroche in 1996 and for Yves Saint Laurent in Paris in 1998. In 2001, Elbaz became the creative director at Lanvin (founded by Jeanne Lanvin in 1889), reinvigorating the label. He received the CFDA International Award in 2005.

Andrew Gn Born in Singapore in 1967, Gn moved to London to study fashion design and then studied in New York and Milan. He became Emanuel Ungaro's assistant in Paris and began his signature collection in 1994. In 1997, Gn was also artistic director for Balmain for a short time.

Olivier Theyskens for Nina Ricci Born in 1977 in Belgium, Theyskens always loved to sew. He attended Brussels' La Cambre Art Academy and began his signature collection in 1998. He presented his first collection for the house of Rochas in 2003 and received the International Award from the CFDA. Since 2006, he has been the design director for Nina Ricci.

Viktor (Horsting) & Rolf (Snoeren) Both born in 1969 in the Netherlands, they graduated from the Academy of the Arts in 1992 and a year later opened a fashion business together. For five years, beginning in 1996, they presented haute couture collections. Now they have both women's and men's prêt-à-porter collections and are known for their spectacular collection presentations.

Dries van Noten Born in Antwerp, Belgium, in 1958, van Noten attended the Antwerp Academy and launched his own men's collection in 1985. His flagship store, Het Modepaleis, opened in Antwerp in 1989. Van Noten began showing his men's collection on the Paris runway in 1991, following two years later with his women's collection.

Stefano Pilati for Yves Saint Laurent (who is retired) Pilati, born in 1966, was raised in Milan and worked for Giorgio Armani and Prada before coming to YSL as Tom Ford's assistant. The Gucci Group purchased YSL in 1999, and Pilati became design director in 2004.

Most of the couturiers also have prêt-à-porter collections, sometimes with separate designers. They also often have specialists as their accessory designers. The following are just a few of the hundreds of prêt-à-porter designers (some come from other countries to work in Paris): Haider Ackermann, Albert Kriemler for Akris, Antonio Berardi, Véronique Branquinho, Raffaele Borriello & Julien Desselle, Ivana Omazic for Céline, Paolo Merin Anderson for Chloé, Tao Kurihara for Tao Comme des Garçons, Ennio Capasa for Costume National, Ann Demeule-meester, Hedi Slimane for Dior men's wear, Yvan Mispelaere for Féraud, Ozwald Boateng for Givenchy men's collection, Martin Grant, Jerome l'Huillier, Antonio Marras for Kenzo, Sophia Kokosalaki, Hervé Leroux for Guy Laroche, Martin Margiella, Naoki Takizawa for Issey Miyake, Lucien Pellat-Finet, Patrick Robinson for Paco Rabanne, Gilles Rosier, Sonia Rykiel, Peter Dundas for Ungaro, AF Vandevorst (An Vandevorst and Filip Arickx), Giambattista Valli, Marc Jacobs for Louis Vuitton, and Yohji Yamamoto (Y's and Y-3 for Adidas).

To reach a wider audience, most designers also have a less expensive *diffusion line,* such as Yohji Yamamoto's Y's collection. Also, many less expensive prêt-à-porter lines are shown in exhibitions at the Porte de Versailles (see Chapter 12). Some of these brands have become world famous and influential.

Italy

Italian fashion has been a very popular export, but like other European countries, Italy is losing its manufacturing base to Asia.

Around 1940, only 30 fashion manufacturers operated in Italy, their production limited basically to men's wear. Since then, the Italians have built an international fashion reputation on

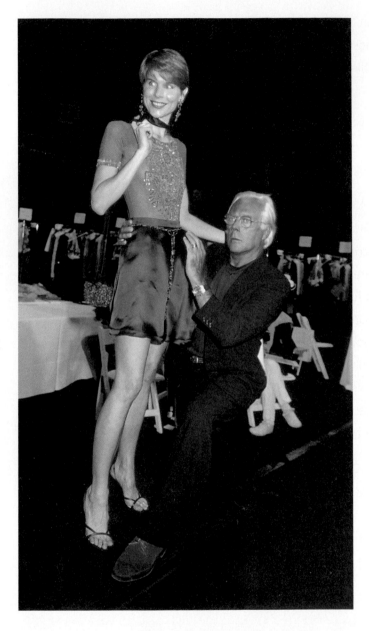

GIORGIO ARMANI
CHECKING THE FIT
OF ONE OF HIS
DESIGNS. *(COURTESY
OF GIORGIO ARMANI,
MILAN, ITALY)*

creativity, beautiful fabrics, knitwear, leather goods, tailoring, and quality production. The Italian fashion industry is primarily devoted to ready-to-wear and accessories.

Designers, manufacturers, and fabric companies work cooperatively, often as integral parts of a large vertical company. Some of these fashion companies are part of large textile firms, but, unfortunately, many of these companies have been forced to close due to competition from Asia. Italian trade organizations are trying to lure the young generation into manufacturing jobs. Companies such as Brioni and Kiton have set up in-house programs to teach apprentices sewing and tailoring. Bottega Veneta (Gucci Group) and a Vicenza trade school have jointly set up a three-year program to teach luxury handbag production.

Milano (Milan) has become the center for *moda pronta* (ready-to-wear) because it was close to the fabric sources of Como, Biella, and Torino. Italy also has a smaller fashion center in Florence, as well as fashion and accessory companies scattered around the country.

Designers

Giorgio Armani, born in 1934, learned apparel production at Nino Cerruti. He created his first men's wear collection under the Armani label in 1974 and added women's wear in 1975. His multimillion-dollar empire includes Emporio Armani (stores and a less expensive collection), A/X Armani Exchange (basics and jeans), Mani (Italy only), and licenses such as Armani Casa. His tailored style has set international trends. He has received many international awards,

Canali, Brioni, Forall (Pal Zileri), Corneliani, Urbis, Vestimenta, Paoloni, Luciano Barbera, Campagna, Kiton, and Zanella.

England, United Kingdom

London, the capital of England, is also the center of its fashion industry.

London enjoys a diversified international reputation for men's tailoring, classic woolen and cashmere apparel for women, and innovative young fashion.

■ GIEVES & HAWKES TAILORS AT NO. 1 SAVILE ROW, LONDON. *(COURTESY OF GIEVES & HAWKES)*

Savile Row

London has long been the respected world center for classic men's business attire and tailored country wear because of its famous Savile Row tailors and shirtmakers. Long-established tailors include Anderson & Sheppard, Dege & Skinner, French & Stanbury, Gieves & Hawkes, H. Huntsman & Sons, Kilgour, Norton & Sons, Henry Poole & Co., Strickland & Sons, Turnbull & Asser, and Bernard Weatherill. Savile Row employs more than 100 tailors. A *bespoke* (custom-tailored) suit requires two to three fittings, takes up to six weeks to complete, and may cost between £2000 and £5000 (approximately $3600 to $9000). These tailors are threatened by rent increases and have formed a Savile Row Bespoke lobbying group to protect British tailoring.

Sales for bespoke suits, however, have decreased by half during the past few years. To contend with sluggish sales and a stodgy image, some Savile Row tailors are trying to appeal to younger customers and to women. Therefore, they are adopting newer marketing and advertising tactics, renovating their shops, selling branded goods such as ties and watches, and licensing their names abroad.

BRITISH DESIGNER
ALEXANDER
MCQUEEN RECEIVES
A CFDA AWARD.
*(COURTESY OF THE
COUNCIL OF
FASHION DESIGNERS
OF AMERICA)*

In addition, Britain's well known men's ready-to-wear lines include Chester Barrie, Ozwald Boateng, Duffer of St. George, Timothy Everest, Richard James, and Paul Smith.

Women's Apparel

The young designers of the 1960s, such as Mary Quant, Jean Muir, and Zandra Rhodes, made London a fashion capital. The 1970s gave the junior fashion world the "Punk" look, and London designers are again setting fashion trends for the young. Many of them have small, undercapitalized operations, but their witty, wacky collections are good sources of ideas. A few of them have gone on to design collections in other countries.

Christopher Bailey, for Burberry Prorsum, was born in Yorkshire, England, in 1971 and went on to study fashion at the Royal College of Art in London. From 1994 to 1996, he was women's wear designer at Donna Karan and also for Gucci in Milan from 1996 to 2001. He joined Burberry in May 2001 as creative director, responsible for the design of all product lines as well as the company's overall image.

Stella McCartney graduated from Central St. Martin's Design College in 1995, and she immediately launched her own line. From 1997 to 2001, she was the creative director for Chloé in Paris. In 2001, she began her own signature collection, financially sponsored by the Gucci Group, which includes ready-to-wear and accessories. In 2004, she began a partnership with Adidas to design sport performance wear, and in 2005, she designed a one-time, sell-out collection for H&M.

Alexander McQueen was born in 1969 and served apprenticeships at Savile Row tailors and was Romeo Gigli's assistant in Milan. In 1994, after graduating from St. Martin's School of Art, he started his signature collection. He was given the British Designer of the Year award in 1996 and the CFDA International Designer of the Year award in 2003. McQueen designed couture for Givenchy from 1996 to 2001 but is now concentrating on his signature collection (financed by the Gucci Group), a secondary line known as McQ, a bespoke men's collection for H. Huntsman & Sons, Savile Row, and footwear for Puma.

Paul Smith, one of Britain's most successful designers, was born in 1947. He is known for his expert tailoring and 30 years as a men's wear designer. In 1995, he added a women's collection. He has expanded his business to include accessories and retail stores in Milan, Paris, and New York.

Other well-known British ready-to-wear designers include Antoni (Burakowski) & Alison (Roberts), Luella Bartley, Basso (Bruno) & Brooke (Christopher), Hussein Chalayan, Clements-Riberio (Suzanne Clements and Inacio Ribeiro, who also design for Cacharel, Paris), Emma Cook, Nicole Farhi, John Galliano (who also designs couture for Dior in Paris), Ghost, Margaret Howell, Eley Kishimoto, Julien MacDonald, Roland Mouret, Rifat Ozbek, Clare Waight Keller for Pringle, Antonia Robinson, Philip Colbert and Richard Ascott for Rodnik, Temperley (Alice) London, Vivienne Westwood, Matthew Williamson, Anna Valentine, Osman Yousefzada, and Ronit Zilkha. Some of these designers show their collections in Paris, Milan, or New York because they think they get better exposure there.

The British also have an international reputation for classic apparel, woolen country clothing, trench coats, and knitwear from such companies as Aquascutum, Austin Reed, Burberry, Daks-Simpson, Jaeger, McGeorge, and Pringle.

North of Oxford Street in London, in the area around Margaret Street, lies the West End "rag trade" district, which supports a conglomeration of fashion suppliers, studios, and showrooms. Actual production, however, has largely moved to Asia, Eastern Europe, and other countries with low-cost labor.

Canada

Canadian designers blend the European and American approaches to fashion and export many of their products to the United States.

According to Statistics Canada and Industry Canada, the Canadian apparel industry is the 10th largest manufacturing industry in Canada. Apparel manufacturing is located in every province and territory of Canada, but is most highly concentrated in Québec, Ontario, Manitoba, and British Columbia. Actual production is moving to Asia.

CANADIAN DESIGNER PHILIPPE DUBUC CHECKING THE FIT OF HIS DESIGN. *(COURTESY OF PHILIPPE DUBUC, PHOTO BY MARTIN RONDEAU)*

Although quite diversified, Canada's apparel industry is particularly known for exports of men's clothing, outerwear, furs, leather goods, women's sportswear, and children's wear. With a stagnant market, Canadian manufacturers export 30 percent of all apparel, primarily to the United States, followed by the United Kingdom and Japan. Since the implementation of the 1988 Canada–U.S. Free Trade Agreement (now part of NAFTA), exports to the United States have increased 550 percent and are still rising. In turn, the United States has become the main supplier of raw material for Canadian apparel.

Montréal, Québec

Québec is Canada's largest fashion-producing province, with approximately 57 percent of the apparel workforce, and 62 percent of total Canadian production. A large portion of the Québec fashion industry and fur industry is centered in Montréal. In fact, the apparel industry is the island of Montréal's largest employer. Showrooms and buyer's weeks are found in the Chabanel Street and the Place Bonaventure area.

Well-known Montréal area designers and brands include Jean Airoldi, Helene Barbeau, Dina Merulla for Boz, Arnold Brant, Lino Catalano, Simon Chang, Michel Desjardins, Philippe Dubuc, FFI Apparel, Dita Martin, Marisa Minicucci, Christian Chenail for Muse, Parasuco, Peerless, Hilary Radley, Rudsak and Mackage, Marie Saint Pierre, Samuelson, Debbie Shuchat, Nadya Toto, and Jack Victor.

Toronto, Ontario

Ontario is Canada's second-largest fashion center with more than 28 percent of the workforce. In Toronto itself, apparel manufacturing companies are located around the city, including the original King-Spadina fashion district. The city plays host to two Toronto Fashion Weeks per year, including designer runway shows and a market week, as well as two accessories trade shows.

Top Toronto-area ready-to-wear designers and collections include Lida Baday, Brian Bailey, Dominic Bellissimo, Joeffer Caoc for Misura, Sunny Choi, Wayne Clark, Judy Cornish and Joyce Gunhouse for Comrags, Jennifer Dares for Layer, David Dixon, Jim Searle and Chris Tyrell for Hoax Couture, Jennifer Halchuk and Richard Lyle of Mercy, Ian Hylton and Kim Newport-Mimran for Pink Tartan, Thien Le, Joyce Lo and Sabrina Albanese of Wolves, Linda Lundstrom, Ross Mayer, Pat McDonagh, Arthur Mendonca, Franco Mirabelli, Shelli Oh for Harebell, Crystal Siemens, and Olena Zylak. Internationally successful Toronto-founded manufacturers and retailers include Club Monaco (now owned by Ralph Lauren Inc.), Danier Leather, and Roots.

The United States

American manufacturers are largely headquartered in New York City, followed by California and other smaller regional manufacturing centers.

American designers and manufacturers naturally understand the domestic market best. American fashion blossomed during World War II, when communications to Paris were cut off. Since then, an American style has developed, especially for sportswear, which is now appreciated around the world. Recently, as a result of consolidations, company closures, and the shift of production to countries with low-cost labor, the number of apparel manufacturers has dramatically decreased.

Company Size and Ownership Traditionally, fashion businesses were small and family owned and operated. Their small size allowed flexibility in both design and production, which is needed to respond quickly to market needs. Today, however, the sizable advertising and marketing budgets of the large companies make it difficult for small companies to compete. As a result, small companies have been bought up by larger ones so that the number of apparel firms has decreased. The Jones Apparel Group, for example, now comprises Jones New York, Evan Picone, Rena Rowan for Seville, Sun Apparel, and Nine West and has the license to produce Lauren by Ralph Lauren and Ralph by Ralph Lauren. Another example is Liz Claiborne, Inc., which encompasses Liz Claiborne, Lizsport, Lizwear, Liz & Co., Elizabeth, Dana Buchman, Ellen Tracy, Sigrid Olsen, Russ, and the licenses for Kenneth Cole women's wear and DKNY Jeans.

Globalization American designers and brands have become very well known abroad. Their fashions are sold in stores in all the major cities of the world. Increasingly, American designers are working for European and Japanese companies. Examples include Tom Ford for Gucci in Italy and Marc Jacobs for Louis Vuitton of Paris. In addition, many foreign companies have invested in the United States, purchasing companies or production facilities. Takihyo, a Japanese firm, backed Donna Karan so that she could start her own business. The industry is full of similar examples.

Designers In companies that produce moderate- or low-priced clothing, the designer's name is usually unknown to the public. The company may use a fictitious name, such as "Ellen Tracy." Designers who have proved themselves may have their names added to the company's label, such as "Shelli Segal for Laundry."

Some designers are able to start their own businesses under their own names, called a *signature collection.* They may start small as Ralph Lauren did with neckties, or, if they have a good reputation working for a manufacturer, a financier might offer to back them in their own business. If their collections are successful and if they have skillful business and financial partners, quality production, and clever advertising, their names become well known.

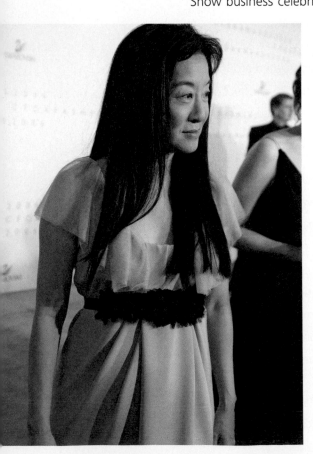

VERA WANG'S DESIGN HEADQUARTERS IS IN NEW YORK CITY. *(COURTESY OF THE COUNCIL OF FASHION DESIGNERS OF AMERICA, CFDA, PHOTO BY DAN LECCA)*

Show business celebrities are also getting into the fashion business. Gwen Stefani, for example, has created her own L.A.M.B. collection, and Jennifer Lopez has lent her name to the J-Lo Collection manufactured by Tommy Hilfiger. Celebrity brands are successful because of the lifestyle they represent. Companies try to lure entertainers to launch clothing and accessory lines and pay them high royalties for their names and images.

As in show business, however, designers are only as good as their last production. A designer is often a star today and forgotten tomorrow; the picture changes every season. It is increasingly difficult to name the most important American designers because they change from year to year. Reading fashion publications regularly is the only way to keep informed about current designer favorites and best-selling styles.

New York

New York became the U.S. garment center because creative talent, supplies, and skilled labor were concentrated there. However, fashion industry employment in Manhattan, New York City, has dropped to approximately 32,000 people working in design, manufacturing, marketing, and related activities.

The Seventh Avenue Garment District

Seventh Avenue gives its name to the entire garment district, which runs north to south from Fortieth to Thirty-fourth Street and east to west from Fifth to Ninth Avenue, on Manhattan Island in New York City. Art deco buildings, built in the 1920s, house design studios, showrooms, and offices. There is a sharp contrast between the plush showroom in front, for the outside world to see, and the cluttered design rooms in back. Many buildings in the garment district are known for certain apparel specialties. For example, 550 Seventh Avenue has traditionally housed high-fashion companies, one on each floor; 512 was known as the coat and suit building. Enterprises such as the Garment Industry Development Corporation and the Fashion Center Business Improvement District (FCBID) have been working to create incentives, in the form of tax breaks, to upgrade or expand manufacturing facilities. The FCBID has also installed bronze plaques honoring designers on the sidewalks of Seventh Avenue. However, advertising and media technology companies have moved into the area, driving up rents and forcing many apparel firms to move to side streets or other areas of the city with lower rents.

■ DONNA KARAN AT HER COLLECTION OPENING. HER COMPANY IS ONE OF THE FASHION FIRMS HEADQUARTERED AT 550 SEVENTH AVENUE. *(COURTESY OF THE DONNA KARAN COMPANY)*

Despite the advantages of proximity to the marketplace, over the past 30 years New York City has lost apparel production jobs to countries with cheaper labor. Only an estimated 1400 factories are left, located primarily in Chinatown, Queens, and Brooklyn. As New York City has lost its manufacturing base, many suppliers have also been forced out of business.

Noteworthy New York Designers

Tommy Hilfiger In 1969, Tommy began his business with a small store in Elmira, New York, his hometown, with a $150 investment. In 1980, he moved to New York City and designed for Seventh Avenue companies. In 1985, he was backed to manufacture his own men's wear collection. His company has enjoyed tremendous growth in men's tailored clothing, sportswear, and boys' wear since then.

Marc Jacobs Born in New York City in 1963, Jacobs attended the High School of Art and Design and Parsons School of Design. With his partner, Robert Duffy, he designed his first signature collection in 1986. After a stint at Perry Ellis beginning in 1989, he and Duffy launched Marc Jacobs International Company in 1993. He introduced his men's collection in 1996 and, since 1997, has also been artistic director for Louis Vuitton in Paris. He won the CFDA Womenswear Designer of the Year award in 1992 and 1997 and the Accessory Designer of the Year award in 1999 and 2005.

Donna Karan Born in 1948 in New York to parents in the "rag trade," Donna (Faske) Karan left Parsons to become Anne Klein's assistant. After

Anne Klein's death in 1974, Karan became head designer with Louis Dell'Olio. This was the first time that a U.S. fashion company was able to continue successfully without the original designer. In 1985, Tomio Taki offered to back Karan in her own business featuring luxury sportswear. Her bridge collection called DKNY (Donna Karan New York) has been extremely successful.

Francisco Costa for Calvin Klein The Calvin Klein brand began in 1968 with women's wear and expanded into sportswear, men's wear, jeans, and accessories. When Phillips-Van Heusen acquired the Calvin Klein brand in 2003, Brazilian Francisco Costa became design director. Born in 1967, Costa graduated from Hunter College and FIT in 1989 and worked for Oscar de la Renta and Tom Ford at Gucci before coming to Calvin Klein in 2002. Mr. Costa won the 2006 CFDA Womenswear Designer of the Year award.

Michael Kors Raised in Merrick, Long Island, New York, Kors enjoyed acting as a child, but later studied fashion at FIT. Kors worked at Lothar's boutique before opening his own business in 1982. He designs his own signature collection, the Kors by Michael Kors line, and he commuted to Paris to design for Céline from 1997 to 2004. He won the CFDA Womenswear Designer of the Year award in 1999.

Derek Lam Born in San Francisco in 1966, Lam graduated from Parsons School of Design in 1990 and worked as a designer for Michael Kors for eight years. In 2003 he launched his namesake collection and, in 2005, won the CFDA's Perry Ellis award for new designers. In 2006, Lam was hired as creative director for ready-to-wear shoes and handbags at Tod's, an Italian leather goods firm.

Ralph Lauren Born in New York City in 1940, Lauren began his career as a sales clerk at Brooks Brothers. In 1967, he started to design ties and by 1968 had established Polo men's wear with backing from Norman Hilton. The Polo name is perfect for his classic, Ivy League look in expensive fabrics. Lauren built the rest of his multimillion-dollar business on licenses for women's wear, a less expensive men's wear collection called Chaps, boys' wear, girls' wear, accessories, and home furnishings. In 1986, he opened a $14 million retail store on Madison Avenue and has Polo shops in stores around the world. He is the perfect example of a designer who was able to build an empire on a lifestyle.

Zac Posen Born in New York in 1980, Posen attended St. Ann's School for the Arts and then began the fashion program at Central Saint Martin's in London. Back in New York City, he spent two years as an intern at the Metropolitan Museum's Costume Institute and presented his first collection in 2002.

Jack McCollough and Lazaro Hernandez at Proenza Schouler Born in 1979, McCollough and Hernandez both studied fashion design at Parsons in New York City. They began their business in 2002 with business partner Shirley Cook and received the CFDA/Vogue Fashion Fund Award and the CFDA's Perry Ellis Award for Womenswear in 2003.

Oscar de la Renta Born in 1933 in the Dominican Republic, de la Renta studied painting, sketched for Balenciaga in Madrid, and afterward became assistant to Castillo at Lanvin. In 1962, he designed for Elizabeth Arden in New York and in 1965 became partner at Jane Derby, where he took over the business in 1966. His work, which enjoys a reputation for elegance, includes evening wear, suits and dresses, sportswear, men's wear, accessories, and the less expensive Miss O collection. He also designed couture for Balmain in Paris, the second American to do couture in Paris.

AMERICAN DESIGNER RALPH LAUREN AT A COLLECTION OPENING. *(COURTESY OF RALPH LAUREN, PHOTO BY CORINA LECCA)*

Narciso Rodriguez A Cuban American, Rodriguez graduated from Parsons School of Design in New York City in 1982. He began his career by designing accessories for Anne Klein and became Calvin Klein's assistant. Later he designed for Tse in New York and Cerruti in Paris. Rodriguez's signature collection is manufactured by the Italian company AEFFE and shown in Milan. He also designs a collection for Loewe (low-ay'-vay), a Spanish company (part of LVMH), which is shown in Paris.

Ralph Rucci After graduating from F.I.T. in 1980, Rucci presented his first signature couture collection. He is known for his beautiful fabrics and expert tailoring and technique. In 1994, he renamed his company Chado Ralph Rucci, to reflect the Japanese tea ceremony. His couture collection is shown in Paris twice a year as part of the Fédération Française de la Couture. He has received many fashion awards and is also a successful painter.

Vera Wang Born in 1950 in New York City, Wang was an art history major at Sarah Lawrence College and also studied at the Sorbonne in Paris. At age 23, she was named an editor at *American Vogue*. Later she spent a year as director of accessories for Ralph Lauren. She established her bridal business in 1990 and later added evening wear, ready-to-wear, furs, and footwear collections. She received the CFDA 2005 Womenswear Designer of the Year award.

Other successful designers in both men's and women's wear include Joseph Abboud, Kimora Lee Simmons for Baby Phat; Badgley Mischka (Mark Badgley and James Mischka), John Bartlett, Michael Vollbracht for Bill Blass, Thom Browne, Stephen Burrows, Julie Chaiken, Kenneth Cole, James Coviello; Eileen Fisher, Bruno Grizzo, Herve Pierre Braillard for Carolina Herrera, Nicole and Michael Colovos for the Helmut Lang label, Betsey Johnson, Ken Kaufman and Isaac Franco at Kaufman Franco, Christian Francis Roth for Anne Klein, Catherine Malandrino, Nicole Miller, Isaac Mizrahi, Josie Natori; David Chu for Nautica, Charles Nolan, Patrick Robinson for Perry Ellis, William Reid, Cynthia Rowley, Behnaz Sarafpour, Max Wilson for Sean John, Peter Som, Cynthia Steffe, Anna Sui, Elie Tahari, Vivienne Tam, Rebecca Taylor, Zang Toi, Richard Chai, Bryan Bradley for Tuleh, Carmen Marc Valvo, John Varvatos, Diane Von Furstenberg, and Yeohlee.

The Young Generation of Designers An unusual number of new collections have appeared in the last few years. Many of these young designers formerly worked as assistants for other designers listed previously. Collection names to watch: Yigal Azrouël, Octavio Carlin, Giles Deacon, Christopher Deane (C. Crawford & Angela Deane), Collette Dinnegan, Joseph Domingo, Doo.Ri (Doori Chung), Shari Gueron, Douglas Hannant, Peter Hidalgo, Henry Jacobson, L.A.M.B. (Gwen Stefani), Nanette Lepore, Marchesa, Joanna Mastroianni, Rozae Nichols, Thakoon Panichgul, Mary Ping, Tia Cibani for Ports 1961, Randi Rahm, Reem Acra, Tracy Reese, Brian Reyes, Jose Ramon Reyes, Kate and Laura Mulleavy for Rodarte, Jill Stuart, and Tocca (Samantha Sung).

Regional Fashion Centers

Although New York City remains the largest fashion marketing center, the trend toward decentralization is increasing. Some manufacturers have left New York City in search of more space. Other companies have started up in regional locations. The result is the growth of regional fashion centers.

California The California clothing industry is known for innovative styling, involvement with the entertainment industry, and the advantage of close proximity to sourcing in Mexico and the Pacific Rim. California also has a national reputation for developing private-label brands for major specialty retailers.

Much of the success of California designers is based on their ability to promote a certain lifestyle approach to fashion. California is especially known for sportswear, swimwear, and contemporary styling. Sales of the "California look" keep growing as Americans become more leisure conscious and as the population shifts toward the Sunbelt.

Los Angeles Greater Los Angeles is the largest U.S. apparel manufacturing center. Fashion and textiles are also the largest manufacturing sector in Los Angeles. The fashion district is part of the downtown Historic Core, built between 1920 and 1940. These Beaux Arts buildings are now being renovated into showrooms, lofts, and live–work spaces. Resulting higher rents, however, are pushing out many sewing contractors, fabric and trim suppliers, and small manufacturers. Los Angeles is also the second most important fashion marketing center in the United States (see Chapter 12).

Successful designers and brands in the Los Angeles area include Allen Schwartz for ABS, Max Azria for BCBG, Bradley Bayou, Magda Berliner, Michele Bohbot for Bisou Bisou, David Cardona (also designs for Cerruti, Milan), Randolph Duke, Desanka Fasiska, Geren Ford, Anthony Franco, Hajnalka Mandula for Gen Art, Jared Gold, Kevan Hall, Mintee Kalra, Anya Teresse for Kate and Kass, Jenni Kayne, Juicy Couture, Laundry by Shelli Segal, Cindy Lee, Monique Lhuillier, Hellen Yuan for Linda Loudermilk, Michelle Mason, Leon Max, David Meister, Mossimo (Giannulli), Juan Carlos Obando, Rick Owens (also designs for Revillon furriers, Paris), Rodarte (Laura & Kate Mulleary), Carlos Rosario, Tim Gardner for Saint John, Jeremy Scott, Michon Shur, Trina Turk, Louis Verdad, Sue Wong, Carol Young, and Petro Zillia.

San Francisco, California San Francisco is headquarters for the world's largest apparel brand, Levi Strauss. Recognized San Francisco designers include Julie Chaiken, Isda Funari, Christina Hurvis, Erin Mahoney, Jessica McClintock, Catherine Jane Mendoza, Colleen Quen, Lily Samii, Beverly Siri, Celia Tejada, and Jin Wang.

Other Regional Centers

Other important apparel manufacturing and design centers are scattered throughout the country.

Chicago, Illinois, has approximately 200 small design companies producing women's, men's and children's apparel and accessories. They have created a Chicago Fashion Advisory Council and Fashion Focus, a fall fashion festival.

Dallas, Texas, is home to designers and companies such as Michael Faircloth, Haggar, and Jerrel. There are textile, apparel, footwear, and accessory manufacturers and wholesale businesses in the state of Texas.

Miami, Florida, has a large number of children's wear, swimwear, sportswear, and activewear manufacturers. The city of Miami is producing is own official line of swimwear and apparel called Tropicool.

Seattle, Washington, manufacturers include Union Bay, Pacific Trail (now owned by London Fog), and Helly Hansen. Eddie Bauer produces sportswear and outerwear for its catalog.

Portland, Oregon, area manufacturers include Nike, Jantzen, Pendleton, Hanna Anderson, and Columbia Sportswear. Philadelphia, Pennsylvania, is the headquarters of Jones New York, J. G. Hook, and children's wear manufacturers. St. Louis and Boston are smaller centers for apparel and accessory manufacturing. Osh Kosh and Jockey are located in Wisconsin, Lee jeans and sportswear in Kansas, London Fog in Maryland, and Wrangler in North Carolina.

As regional manufacturing develops, each center becomes less and less specialized. The spreading of fashion centers throughout the United States and the world is helping to balance fashion influence and to diversify styling. Many large corporations own various subsidiaries located around the country. VF Corporation, for example, is based in Pennsylvania, but owns Wrangler of North Carolina, Jantzen of Oregon, Lee of Kansas, and Vanity Fair of Pennsylvania.

Other Global Fashion Centers

Fashion has become a global phenomenon.

Fashion centers around the world are growing and becoming more important. Germany's Escada (Brian Rennie), Rena Lange, and Hugo Boss are internationally known brands. Designers in Denmark, Australia, New Zealand, Japan, South Africa, India, Turkey, and Brazil are becoming internationally recognized as retail buyers scour the world seeking new resources.

HAN FENG (RIGHT) HAS MOVED HER BUSINESS FROM NEW YORK CITY TO CHINA. *(PHOTO BY GINI STEPHENS FRINGS)*

China, for example, which is known for inexpensive fabrics and labor, is developing its own fashion industry and designers. Chinese designers, such as Jeffrey Chow, Andrew Gn, Peter Som, Vivienne Tam, Zang Toi, and Vera Wang, have been working in New York or Paris. Now, with an emerging Chinese fashion industry, New York designer Han Feng has moved back to China. Chinese designers and brands with growing businesses, especially in Shanghai, include Hu Rong, Zhang Da, Wang Yiyang, Wang Wei, Lu Kun, Wan Yi Yang, and Shanghai Tang and Barney Cheng in Hong Kong. The China Fashion Awards were created to honor top Chinese designers.

SUMMARY

FASHION HAS BECOME A GLOBAL PHENOMENON. BECAUSE OF A CONCENTRATION OF RESOURCES, SUPPLIES, SKILLED LABOR, AND CREATIVITY, PARIS GREW TO BE THE FASHION CAPITAL OF THE WORLD. IT BUILT ITS REPUTATION WITH THE COUTURE, BUT PROFITS NOW COME FROM PRÊT-À-PORTER. MILAN AND LONDON ARE ALSO IMPORTANT INTERNATIONAL DESIGN CENTERS. CANADA HAS TWO STYLE CENTERS IN MONTRÉAL AND TORONTO. NEW YORK, ESPECIALLY THE AREA AROUND SEVENTH AVENUE, REMAINS THE FASHION CAPITAL OF THE UNITED STATES IN SPITE OF THE LOSS OF ITS MANUFACTURING BASE. LOS ANGELES AND SAN FRANCISCO MAKE CALIFORNIA THE LARGEST U.S. CENTER IN TERMS OF EMPLOYMENT. FASHION HAS BECOME BIG BUSINESS, AND THE TOP DESIGNERS ARE THE FASHION STARS.

Terms and Concepts

Briefly define and discuss the following terms and concepts:

1. Paris as a fashion capital
2. Couture
3. Prêt-à-porter
4. Atelier
5. Toile
6. Salon
7. Milan as a fashion capital
8. Savile Row
9. London as a fashion capital
10. Seventh Avenue

Questions for Review

1. Why does Paris continue as a fashion capital?
2. What are the requirements for membership in the Chamber Syndicale de la Couture?
3. Explain the two classifications of ateliers and discuss the organization of a typical atelier.
4. What are the differences between the couture and the prêt-à-porter?
5. What are the fashion centers in Canada? How are Canadian designers affected by the trade agreement with the United States?
6. What name is used to refer to New York's garment district? Explain why that name is used.
7. Discuss the growth of regional fashion centers in the United States.

Projects for Additional Learning

1. In a fashion magazine, find a photograph of a garment that you particularly like. Find the name of the designer in the description. Find other examples of that designer's work in older issues of fashion magazines until you have found 10 examples (in 10 separate issues) of his or her designs. Analyze the unique characteristics of the designer's style.

2. Peruse magazines that show Italian or French fashions. Find five of the designers mentioned in this chapter in ads or editorial photo credits.

Discuss the style characteristics of each design in a written report. If possible, illustrate with sketches or photocopies.

3. Shop a department store and examine an evening dress or suit in the $400 to $600 range. Then go to a discount store and look at an evening dress or suit in the $100 to $200 range. Make a written comparison of the quality of fabric, construction, and styling. Document your report with descriptions or sketches.

Notes

1 "The Transformation of Vera Wang," *Women's Wear Daily,* November 16, 2005, p. 6.

2 As quoted in "The Concorde Couturier," *Women's Wear Daily,* November 17, 1992, p. 24.

DESIGNER TOMMY HILFIGER PRESIDING AT A STYLING MEETING. *(COURTESY OF TOMMY HILFIGER)*

9

PRODUCT AND DESIGN DEVELOPMENT

Career Focus

The creative side of manufacturing offers highly competitive positions as designers, merchandisers, product managers, and patternmakers. In a large company, a designer, a merchandiser or product manager, and their assistants are assigned to each product group. A recent college graduate may obtain employment as an assistant in one of these areas.

CHAPTER OBJECTIVES

After reading this chapter, you should be able to:

1. Describe line development by item or by group
2. Explain the important elements and principles of design and their application to line development
3. Describe the process of creating a sample garment

A manufacturer's design or product development department plans and creates new styles within the company's image or identity. This chapter begins by explaining how a manufacturer's line is developed. To prepare for this, it is very important to first read Chapters 2, 3, and 4 to understand target customers, design influences, and resources. This chapter then goes on to discuss fashion design elements and principles, including color and fabrication and the creation of a sample line.

Product Development

Merchandisers or product managers, designers, and their assistants are all involved in the development of a line or collection of the fashion manufacturer's product.

Appealing to a Target Market

Each apparel manufacturer is defined by its customer and identified by its particular style. This involves finding a market niche around a particular lifestyle or need—ideally, a part of the market that is not served adequately or successfully by another manufacturer. Hedi Slimane, men's wear designer for Christian Dior, reflected on his creative approach; "I'm interested in [my customer] in the sense of where he lives, what sort of house [he lives in], what kind of car he drives, where he goes to eat. . . . In America, you call it life-style."[1] Manufacturers identify their customers as a group, develop a product that fits that identity, and stay with it.

Maintaining an Identity   A designer or manufacturer that develops and is recognized for a particular style, yet incorporates current trends into that style, attracts buyers year after year. Ralph Lauren is an excellent example of a designer with a distinctive style. Lauren himself said, "It's the most important thing for designers . . . to have an identity. . . ."[2]

Traditionally, manufacturers specialize in a particular styling category, price range, gender, and size range of apparel. As a company grows, it expands by adding diversified lines. Many manufacturers have broadened their product lines to include other style categories or size and price ranges, but they have separate divisions and/or label names for each. For example, Liz Claiborne started with women's sportswear and later branched out to include dresses, suits, accessories, and men's wear. Both Ralph Lauren and Giorgio Armani began with men's wear and later added women's wear collections. The addition of large-size and petite divisions offers

CHARLOTTE NEUVILLE, VICE PRESIDENT OF DESIGN AT NEW YORK NEW YORK, IN A MERCHANDISING MEETING WITH HER STAFF. (PHOTO BY GINI STEPHENS FRINGS)

manufacturers tremendous growth opportunity because very little new design is necessary, just additional patterns. As manufacturers diversify, however, they must maintain a consistent identity oriented toward their customers. Giorgio Armani reiterated, "Coherence is always the secret, I believe, behind a great company. There is an underlying philosophy to my designs that never changes."[3]

The Design or Product Development Team

Responsibilities for product development, design, and merchandising vary from manufacturer to manufacturer. Product development is the process of market and trend research, merchandising, design, and development of the final product. In small companies, the design team may be just a few people. In a large company, a designer, a merchandiser, perhaps a product manager, and their assistants are assigned to each division. H&M has 95 designers, and Zara has 300!

When the designer is the president of the company, he or she is obviously in charge. Manufacturers that are design driven, such as Liz Claiborne or Ellen Tracy, have designers in charge of product development. In companies that are merchandising or marketing driven, such as Levi Strauss, merchandisers and brand or product managers direct the development of the line. But in either case, in most companies, it is a team effort among managers, designers, and merchandisers.

Merchandising

Merchandising is planning to have the right merchandise at the right time in the right quantity and at the right price to meet the needs of the company's target customers. It is also the manner in which a group or line of garments is presented to the public—the way the line will look in the stores.

The merchandiser or product manager is basically a process manager, developing the blueprint of the line. Merchandising activities, which vary from company to company, usually include setting financial goals, budgets, and price points; making the merchandising plans; planning line size; planning fabric purchases; sourcing; scheduling production and deliveries; controlling product flow; presenting the finished line to the sales staff; and sometimes preplanning assortments for stores.

Cost Merchandising
Based on costs for last season's styles, merchandisers establish price points for garments to be designed. It is very important for merchandisers and designers to understand how fabric and production costs affect pricing. For example, higher fabric costs must be balanced by simpler construction.

Another important aspect of costing is whether the garment's perceived value is worth the price charged. Therefore, both the styling and the quality of a garment must appear to be worth the price and compare well with competing garments on the retail selling floor. Sometimes the price of a style may be adjusted slightly higher or lower to try to affect its sales potential. Occasionally, a manufacturer uses a *loss leader* (a garment with a low markup) to attract buyers.

Some companies figure an *average markup* so that their garments fit into a price line. For example, in sportswear manufacturing, shirts often cost out higher than pants and skirts because of expensive fabrications and labor. Therefore, the shirt price may be lowered so that it is more acceptable (a practice called *low-balling*), whereas the skirt and pant prices are raised (*high-balling*). In this way, the average markup is within an acceptable range.

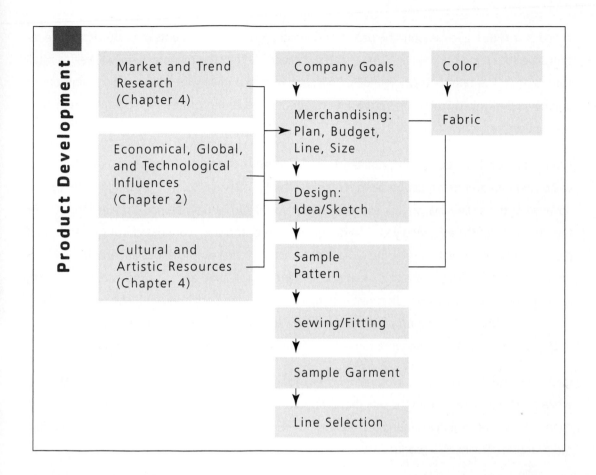

Even then, the stated price must often be inflated to compensate for expected discounts. Allowances in pricing must be made for the 8 percent discount retailers expect if their bills are paid on time and 25 percent markdowns.

Volume manufacturers may *reengineer* some of their first samples to meet their target price points if the garment in question is important to the line. This is accomplished by altering features such as the sweep of a hem or facings or pockets to reduce labor or fabric consumption. Pricing is discussed fully in Chapter 10.

Scheduling   Merchandising is responsible for integrating all the phases of product development, including design and production. The merchandiser, or product manager, sets up a schedule of deadlines for styling, finished samples, and production to meet the required shipping dates. These dates are, of course, coordinated with the production department. Merchandisers meet regularly with designers, the sales staff, and production managers to discuss company goals, budget requirements, line size, delivery dates, sizes, and so on. Merchandisers and designers have to plan production based on how they think the line will sell by group, color, and size in the stores.

Seasons Each season, the design and merchandising departments of each division are responsible for creating a new line, the seasonal collection, that the manufacturer will sell to retail store buyers. The terms are synonymous: *Collection* is used primarily in Europe and for high-priced apparel in the United States. *Line* is used more often in the United States for moderately and popularly priced fashion.

Work on a new line begins approximately 8 to 10 months before the selling season (a velvet dress to be sold in November must be designed in March). Sportswear design may begin a full year in advance of the selling season. For example, a sportswear firm usually beings work in February for the spring line of the following year. The design and merchandising team has about two and a half months to complete line development. At Jones New York, for example, designers and merchandisers research fabrics in February; work on the merchandise plan and group concepts in March; select fabrics and prints, work on sweater samples, and design bodies in April; and make final line selections in May. Yet the spring *line release* (when samples are shown to retail buyers) isn't until September 1.[4] That same line will be in the stores in late winter, to be worn in spring.

Designers and merchandisers work on two or more lines at once, designing a future collection while checking samples from the one that is about to be produced. They are finishing work on the spring line while beginning fabric research for summer. It is a continual process of creating new merchandise, "seamless" product development.

Most women's wear companies produce four or five seasonal lines a year: spring, summer, transitional, fall, and holiday or resort. Men's sportswear firms also have four line releases a year as compared to men's suit firms, which have just two. Children's wear firms have three or four, depending on the product focus. Most manufacturers have staggered delivery dates for each group within the line. Managing delivery dates in this way means that manufacturers are shipping to stores monthly, providing them with continual fresh merchandise. European companies that traditionally have shown two collections per year have also caught on to the need for fresh merchandise year round. Companies such as Zara or H&M design new merchandise continually and have no set seasons.

Some manufacturers are now trying to fit their lines into the financial calendar of the retail stores with a line per quarter: January to March for spring, for example. This makes it easier for the retailer to plan buying and deliveries. Manufacturers that have their own catalogs also do not follow traditional seasons. Instead, they plan their lines around planned catalog mailing dates.

The Merchandise Plan Each season, merchandisers have to develop a merchandise plan or business plan. They must decide how many apparel or accessory groups are needed to meet both the demands of retailers and consumers and the financial goals of the manufacturer. The previous year's actual sales are used as a basis for projected sales goals for each group. Spreadsheets are created to show what needs to be produced and sold per month to reach sales and profit goals.

The merchandiser has to determine the number of groups, fabrics, and styles required to meet these sales goals. This includes the number of styles in each group, styles in each fabric (wovens, knits, yarn dyes, prints, novelties), and colors per style (usually two to five). Price points are established so that fabric and labor cost limits can be determined. The plan also shows the *total units* that need to be manufactured and the *total net dollars* (value of these garments).

Design Development

The designer creates the styles for the collection, giving form to fashion ideas.

The current consumer demand for fashion and uniqueness has made creativity in design more important than ever. Couture and top ready-to-wear designers are able to enhance their creativity with expensive fabrications and beautiful workmanship because they are able to sell at higher prices. This freedom enables them to create trends. Mainstream designers must know how to interpret these trends to suit their own customers and select fabrics that fit into their company's price range. They are responsible for concepts, styling, and color selection. Designers must also supervise patternmaking, fit, and samplemaking, as well as see their lines through to a successful completion.

Line and Group Concepts   To begin work on a collection, many designers use concept boards to show their ideas to the management team. They make a collage of color and fabric swatches, sketches of ideas, and *swipes* (idea photos) from magazines that capture a mood or theme. These can also be developed on computer systems. When the concepts are approved, designers develop their ideas into specific themes for groups and individual garment designs.

Groups

Collections, or lines, are divided into groups of garments. Liz Claiborne and Jones New York, for example, do six to eight groups in each line release in each division. Each group has a specific *theme* based on a fabric, color, or a particular fashion direction. Ideas for the theme come from

■ AN ELEGANT SUIT
FROM GIORGIO
ARMANI'S MEN'S
COLLECTION.
*(COURTESY OF
GIORGIO ARMANI)*

research and environmental influences (see Chapter 4). The styling of each garment within each group creates variety, yet carries out the central theme. To present a visually pleasing group of dresses, gowns, sportswear, suits, or coats, a few common elements are needed. The recent trend to combine odd separates for an eclectic look is very difficult for manufacturers to merchandise.

Dresses Groups of dresses may begin with an *anchor*, a best-seller from the previous line with a change of color and/or fabric. Often, dress designers emphasize only a few silhouettes, called *bodies*, interpreting each of them in several prints, or they will feature one print in a variety of styles. Within the group, the garments must offer a variety of silhouettes, lengths, sleeve treatments, necklines, and/or other details. Women's suits and coats are also merchandised in this manner.

Suits and Outerwear

Men's suits are treated as individual units sharing only a basic silhouette. The manufacturer's objective is to include a variety of muted colors and suitings in the line, providing a wide choice for both the retail buyer and the consumer. The prime factors in styling men's suits are fabric and silhouette. Generally, few details change from season to season. The ideal suit is a timeless classic.

Women's suits, on the other hand, may be fashion oriented or classic. They are merchandised rather like dresses, with a variety of silhouettes, collar treatments, details, and fabrications.

Sportswear Sportswear pieces are designed to be worn together. A balanced mix of skirts, pants, jackets, shirts or blouses, and other tops is included in each group to give the consumer a choice of styles. There are usually two to three tops for every bottom (skirt or pant). There may be a basic jacket and a fashion-forward jacket, various skirt lengths, a basic pant and an updated version, and shirts and other kinds of tops with a variety of necklines. One garment ties all the group colors together, perhaps a striped or plaid shirt.

- **Coordinated sportswear** is designed to mix and match interchangeably and is sold as a package to the retailer.
- **Integrated sportswear or jeanswear** is also merchandised in groups. Parts are meant to be worn together, but do not constitute as obvious a relationship as coordinated sportswear.
- **Separates** do not show an obvious relationship and are sold individually.
- **Men's sportswear** is also merchandised in integrated groups or as separates. A group may include pants, jackets, vests, shirts, and sweaters. Fabrication mixes are very important inasmuch as basic styles do not change so much.

The number of pieces or styles in a group is determined by the statement the company wishes to make and the variety of pieces needed to complement one another as stated in the merchandising plan. The designer must think through what the customer can wear with what and how the group will look in the store. A top has to go with more than one jacket and/or bottom. Multipurpose clothing is very important in today's market.

In large sportswear companies, such as Levi Strauss and Eddie Bauer, designers may be specialists in one category of the group, such as bottoms, knit tops, or woven tops. In this case, the design director is responsible for the cohesiveness of the group.

Fashion versus Basics Every group must have a balance of fashion and basics. Even if the manufacturer is not a designer business, fashion pieces give the company credibility by showing retail buyers that the company is aware of fashion trends. However, basics are often what bring in the money to allow them to do the fashion. Even designer lines such as Ralph Lauren make most of their sales and profits on one or two hot basics, such as khaki pants or polo shirts. Tommy Hilfiger says that he begins with basics for the core of his men's wear collection and then adds newness and fashion to that.[5]

Some large manufacturers further divide groups into product segments for fashion and basic apparel. Basics, such as a turtleneck sweater or twill pants, are kept in stock for long periods of time and are available on a *replenishment* basis, on automatic delivery, when stock is low. New fashion styles are delivered to the stores every two to eight weeks to make the merchandise assortment fresh.

Items

Some manufacturers produce single *items*, garments that do not relate to each other. Items are popular styles that a consumer can use to update an existing wardrobe. Each garment must be strong enough to sell on its own, not depending on the strength of other garments in a group. Such garments are usually produced at moderate or budget price ranges at the request of retailers for private labels (see Chapters 12 and 13) and/or by a knockoff house.

Knockoffs A *knockoff* is a copy of someone else's design, usually a garment that is already a best-seller for another manufacturer. Knockoff companies simply buy a particular garment, make a pattern from it, order large quantities of the same or similar fabric, and have the garment manufactured. Production and fabric costs are lower because of the huge quantities made. The knockoff producer must have (1) an acute awareness of what garments are selling well at the retail level, (2) rapid production capabilities to capitalize on the success of the style while it lasts, and (3) lower prices. Now, in an age of instant global communications, copies often reach stores before the originals and at a fraction of the cost.

Many designers are understandably very annoyed with this practice. However, Oscar de la Renta called copying the "highest form of flattery. What would really upset me is if no one copied me." Allen Schwartz of ABS, the self-anointed King of Copycats, said, "The word 'original' does not exist in fashion. Everything starts from some sort of inspiration."[6]

Because this practice is very unfair to the original creator, some designers try to copyright their designs. Copyright is nearly impossible, however, because of the fast pace of the industry. The European Union has established an "unregistered design copyright" to help protect designs. However, by the time a design is granted a copyright, the garment is no longer in fashion. To protect their profits, some designers copy their own designs at lower prices, in a lower-priced line a season later.

Design Elements

Keeping the theme of the group in mind, a designer must incorporate a pleasing combination of all the elements of good design—color, fabric, line, and shape—into each garment. The ingredients of design, which are essential to every art form, are not a recipe for success and cannot substitute for experience. The designer does not think of these elements consciously; the use of them becomes inherent. Also, because fashion changes continually, there are no hard-and-fast rules. Sometimes trends defy good design!

Fabric Color is interpreted in fabric, the designer's artistic medium. Designers and merchandisers first select fabrics for each group in the line and specific fabrics for each style.

Fabric Selection *Fabrication* is the selection or creation of an appropriate style for a fabric, or the reverse, the selection of the right fabric for a design. Next to understanding the needs of the customer and interpreting trends for them, choosing a fabric suitable for a particular style is one of the most important aspects of designing. The designer chooses fabrics on the basis of fashion trends, quality, performance, price, and suitability.

Fabrics themselves often inspire garment design. For example, the softness and drapability of a jersey might inspire gathers in a dress. Christian Dior wrote, "Many a dress of mine is born of the fabric alone."[7] Other designers work the other way around, first getting an idea, perhaps developing it in a sketch, and then finding the appropriate fabric for it. However the designer works, he or she must ultimately decide which fabric will work best with a design, or vice versa. Designers must develop the ability to picture a design already made up in a fabric. This ability comes through observation and experience.

Many firms build a line or even an entire reputation on one fabric, such as denim or stone-washed silk. In sportswear, a *base fabric* is selected for jackets, pants, and skirts. In jeanswear, for example, the base fabric is always denim. An assortment of fabrics, solids and patterns, is chosen to go with the base fabric. The designer or merchandiser must be sure to include a variety of weights, textures, and patterns in a line, as well as a balance of fashion and classic fabrics.

Fabric Characteristics   Fabric suitability is determined by characteristics such as fiber content, weave, texture, performance, hand, pattern, and color.

Texture is the sensuous element of design. It is the surface interest of a fabric, created by the weave and by light reflection. Our eyes appreciate the play of light on smooth or rough surfaces, we feel the surface with our hands, and sometimes we can even hear the texture, such as the rustle of taffeta. Combinations of textures, such as suede with jersey (rough with smooth), create interest in a garment. Texture is a very important element in today's fashion.

Performance refers to a fabric's wearing and cleaning properties based on fiber content, weave, and finish. Fabric performance is an important consideration regarding the function and durability of a garment, especially in activewear and outerwear. A ski jacket must keep a customer warm in subzero conditions, for example.

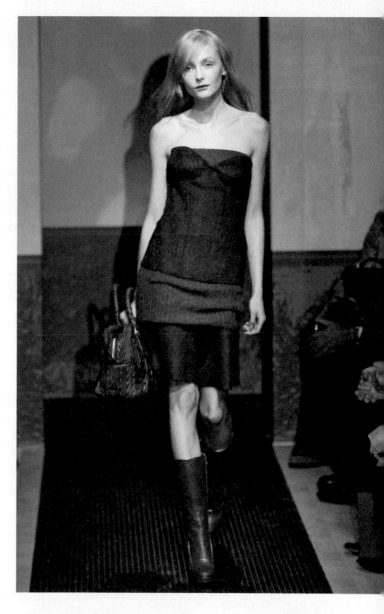

■ MIUCCIA PRADA USED KNIT AND WOVEN FABRICS TO CREATE A UNIQUE COMBINATION OF TEXTURES IN THIS LAYERED DRESS. *(COURTESY OF PRADA)*

Weight and **hand** dictate the silhouette of a garment. *Weight* is the heaviness or lightness, thinness or thickness of a fabric. *Hand* is the tactile quality: the feel, body, and fall of a fabric. A garment must be styled in a fabric that is compatible with the desired silhouette.

- *Firm fabrics*, such as worsted wool, gabardine, and linen, are needed to carry out a tailored look. These fabrics have both the crisp look and hand necessary to achieve the desired effect. Interfacing, a fabric sewn or ironed into the garment's inner construction, is used to give additional stiffness to finished edges, such as necklines, collars, cuffs, and buttoning areas.

- *Soft fabrics*, such as crepe, jersey, chiffon, and challis, are ideal for draped designs that delineate body shape. Additional fluidity can be achieved by cutting fabric on the bias grain so that the diagonal of the fabric falls vertically in the garment. However, bias is difficult to lay out on a *marker* (pattern layout) and thus expensive to produce. Softness may be increased by the additional use of gathers, shirring, smocking, and unpressed pleats.

Fabric weight must be suitable for the type of garment. For example, blouse weights are lighter than bottom (skirt or pant) weights. Manufacturers often buy fabrics in specific weights, such as a 5-ounce shirting or an 11-ounce denim. The weight is determined by the square yard for wovens and by the linear yard for knits.

Fiber Content　Fibers must also be appropriate for the season and styling suitability. Warm fabrics are needed for winter, and light, cool ones are needed for summer. Specific natural fibers have traditionally been considered appropriate for certain seasons. Wool is used for fall and winter because it is warm. Linen and cotton are used as warm-weather fabrics because they are light, cool, and washable. However, many fabrics are seasonless. A fabric such as jersey can be worn year round. Cotton, traditionally a summer fiber, can be woven into warm, bulky fabrics such as corduroy for fall and winter garments. Wools can be woven into lightweight fabrics for spring. Blends of natural and man-made fibers have become very important to create interesting new fabrics. Fabrics with spandex, to add stretch, are a major consideration for today's body-conscious styles.

Eco-Friendly Fabrics　Many manufacturers are concerned with the condition of our environment and want to do their part to try to improve the situation. They think that it is the fashion industry's responsibility to make environmentalism fashionable, because fashion is an important communicator of values to people. To do this, manufacturers may choose organic cotton, ingeo, bamboo, linen, wool, lyocell, or recycled materials that are treated with low-impact or bifunctional dyes, enzyme washes, and other safe finishes. A few designers, such as Linda Loudermilk and Carol Young, are using recycled fabrics in their designs. Some companies are also returning to natural materials for buttons and using nonelectroplated metal trimmings.

Patterns　The *scale*, or size, of a pattern must complement the design. To show a large print to its best advantage, it should not be cut up with seams and details, but rather allowed to be the most important element of the garment; so construction should be kept simple. On the other hand, if a design idea begins with dominating lines and details, then the fabric must be of secondary importance. Scale is particularly important in children's wear because the garment pieces are small.

The *repeat* of a print is the amount of fabric necessary for a floral or geometric pattern to duplicate itself totally. Large repeats are not usually suitable for trims or for children's wear. In addition, garments to be made in border prints must be carefully thought out so that fabric is not wasted in production cutting.

The designer must recognize patterns that require special matching because they increase the amount of fabric used and, therefore, the cost. Bold plaids and irregular stripes must match when sewn together. One-way prints and pile fabrics also use more yardage, because all the pattern pieces must be cut in the same direction. Many fabrics today are directional, and the manufacturer cuts them all one way to prevent variations in color.

Reviewing Fabrics   The designer's involvement in fabric selection for a manufacturer varies. Sometimes designers have the entire responsibility for fabric selection. In a large company, designers may share the responsibility with a fabric merchandiser, especially when an entire group is built around one particular fabric. The fabric merchandiser may also research the textile market for trends and sources and follow through with fabric purchases.

GIORGIO ARMANI USED AN UNUSUAL COMBINATION OF STRIPES AND DOTS TO CREATE THIS STRIKING SUIT. *(COURTESY OF GIORGIO ARMANI SPA)*

Before a new season, designers and/or merchandisers review the fabric market to research fabric trends. Designers may visit one of the international fabric trade fairs, such as Première Vision. This is the best way to keep abreast of the newest fiber or fabric developments that might be the source of ideas for both fabrics and garments.

Designers and merchandisers also frequently travel to a major fashion capital such as New York, where most textile mills and converters have headquarters and fabric libraries (see Chapter 6), for an overall picture of the season's textile offerings. Moreover, at these centers, the designers can discuss their ideas directly with textile designers and technicians. Designers often work directly

225

with mills or converters to develop a new pattern or fabric. Fabric mills or converter sales representatives also call on the designer at work. Each season, designers try to see as many fabric representatives as possible to learn about the variety of fabrics available.

Price Considerations   Fabric quality, and therefore cost, must be appropriate for the price of the line. An expensive designer collection is made of the finest fabrics; a moderately priced line requires less expensive materials. A general rule is that fabric and trimming costs must balance labor costs.

Sample Cuts   Color or swatch cards from textile companies help designers and merchandisers make fabrication decisions. To test the fabric, the designer orders a 3- to 5-yard cut of a fabric to make a sample garment. If the designer and merchandiser are very enthusiastic about a fabric, they may initially order enough for many samples, perhaps 100 yards or more. They also have to consider the availability of the fabric for orders and production. They may have to commit to a fabric order even before having a collection to show. Once fabrics have been selected, the designer can begin to create styles.

Color

Color is the first element to which consumers respond, often selecting or rejecting a garment because of its color appeal. Color is particularly important in today's fashion. Therefore, designers must consider their customers and provide colors that are both appealing and flattering. People connect certain colors with holidays and seasons. Although much less predictable than formerly, they expect to see some earth tones in fall clothing, jewel colors for the holidays, pastels in the early spring, and white for the summer. Many manufacturers include a few of these colors in their lines.

Color Dimensions   Color has three different dimensions: hue, value, and intensity.

Hue enables us to tell one color from another, such as red from blue or green.

Value refers to the use of darks and lights or the variation of light strength in a color. The value scale runs from white to black. White is pure light; black is the total absence of light. Adding white lightens a color, and adding black darkens it. The lighter values are called *tints* and the darker ones *shades*. Every garment has value contrasts, even if only those created by normal gathers and folds. Strong value contrasts (pure black against pure white is the strongest) achieve a dramatic effect.

Intensity or chroma is the relative saturation, brightness (strength) or paleness (weakness), of a color. Bright colors are considered high intensity, pale ones are low intensity. For instance, when paint is paled by adding water, the intensity of its color is lowered. For example, marine blue is high intensity, and soft pastel blue is low intensity.

Warm Colors   We classify red, yellow, and orange as warm colors because of their association with fire and the sun. Warm colors are stimulating, aggressive, and lively. Red is associated with matters of the heart: valentines, love, and romance; it is also exciting, fiery, and dangerous. A popular color for women's wear, it is one of the few colors used in high intensities for clothing in every season. Yellow is bright, sunny, cheerful, friendly, and optimistic. Orange has become popular in active sportswear.

Cool Colors The cool colors—blue, green, and purple—remind us of the sky and the sea. Blue is quiet, restful, and reserved. Denim blue and navy have become wardrobe classics. For this reason, most manufacturers include blue, especially in their spring or summer lines. Green is a soothing color, suggesting peace and calm. It is used primarily in a dark value in fall sportswear lines or mixed with neutrals to create earthy olive or loden. Purple, historically associated with royalty, has come to represent wealth, dignity, and drama.

Neutrals In apparel, neutrals such as beige, tan, taupe, brown, white, gray, and black are even more popular than the colors just mentioned. The reason is probably that they present a pleasing background for the wearer without competing for attention. Neutrals are part of every season's fashion picture, as either a strong fashion statement or a way to round out a color story.

White is associated with purity and cleanliness. Because it reflects light, it is cool in the summer. In Western culture, black has been connected with villains and death, but it has overcome these associations to become the most popular fashion basic.

MARK BADGLEY AND JAMES MISCHKA USED FABRIC OF AN UNUSUAL COLOR COMBINATION FOR THIS LOVELY GOWN. *(COURTESY OF BADGLEY MISCHKA, NEW YORK)*

Color Relationships There are no exact rules for the use of colors. Rather, colors are considered harmonious if they are used so that one color enhances the beauty of the other. Colors are now combined in many more unusual ways than ever before. Ethnic influences on fashion have changed our view of color combinations, making us more receptive to new ideas. In addition, colors run in fashion cycles just as styles do.

Color Naming An exciting color name can be important in promoting a fashion look. Fashion colors sometimes reappear with new names that make them seem fresh. "Plum" of one year might return as "aubergine" in another. Oil-paint color lists, as well as books featuring the names of flowers, trees, wood, fruit, vegetables, spices, wines, gems, and animals, can provide color-name ideas. To create moods, colorists and fashion journalists use exotic names such as "China Blue" or "Poison Green."

Color Selection   Within a line, each group is usually formulated around a *color story*, a color plan consisting of two or more colors. The color story might be all brights, or all muted, or a balance of darks and lights. The group may be anchored with neutrals, darks, white, or black. As trendsetters, couture and top ready-to-wear designers have the privilege of basing their color story on whatever inspires them.

Mainstream fashion designers usually rely on color forecasts provided by color and design services, trade associations, or fiber companies. By basing part of a color story on these trend forecasts, the designer is assured that the group will be in the mainstream of fashion. Usually, designers combine trend colors with their own choices to make their color stories unique.

Color choices must also reflect the season, climate, and garment category. Active sportswear, for example, employs many more vivid colors than business attire. Every line should include a range of colors that appeals to a variety of customers.

Line   After selecting the fabric, the designer must consider the other elements of good design. In this section, the term *line* refers to the direction of visual interest in a garment created by construction details such as seams, openings, pleats, gathers, tucks, topstitching, and trims. (It is confusing that the apparel industry also uses *line* to refer to a collection of garments.) Line direction should flow from one part of the garment to another and should not be meaninglessly cut up.

Straight lines suggest crispness, such as that of tailored garments; curved lines imply fluidity. However, a garment designed with only straight lines is too severe; a garment with all curves is too unstable. For optimal beauty, the two should work together. Straight lines are softened by the curves of the body, and full curves must be restrained to be compatible with the human form.

Lines have the power to create moods and feelings. Vertical lines remind us of upright, majestic figures and suggest

■ BY DRAPING SILK CHIFFON FROM THE BODICE INTO THE SKIRT OF THIS WHITE GOWN, VERA WANG CREATED VERTICAL LINE DIRECTION. (*COURTESY OF VERA WANG, NEW YORK*)

stability. Horizontal lines are like lines at rest; they suggest repose, quiet, and calm. Soft, curving lines express grace, and diagonal lines imply powerful movement and vitality.

Shape   Another function of line is to create shape. We use the term *silhouette* to describe the outline of the whole garment. Because the silhouette is what we see from a distance, it is responsible for one of our first impressions of a garment. Silhouettes tend to repeat themselves in cycles throughout history. At times a more body-conscious, natural (hourglass) silhouette is popular. At other times rectangular shapes that de-emphasize body contours may be prevalent.

A silhouette should be related to body structure, but some variation is needed to add interest. Sometimes one part of the silhouette, such as sleeves, hips, or shoulders, predominates. Bodies that do well in one season are usually updated in a new fabric or color for the next season.

Lines also divide the silhouette into smaller shapes and spaces by means of seams, openings, pleats, and tucks. The minute a waistline is added, a garment is divided into two new shapes: a bodice and a skirt. The sleeve becomes another shape. These parts create new spaces for smaller details, such as collars and pockets. The pattern of the fabric can create even smaller shapes.

Design Principles

Whether design elements are used successfully depends on their relationship to one another within the garment. Design principles serve as guidelines for combining elements. Designers may not consciously think of these principles as they work, but when something is wrong with a design, they are able to analyze the problem in terms of proportion, balance, repetition, and emphasis to create a harmonious design. These principles are flexible, always interpreted within the context of current fashion trends.

Proportion   *Proportion* is simply the pleasing interrelationship of the size of all parts of the garment. When conceiving a style, the designer must consider how the silhouette is to be divided with lines of construction or detail. These lines create new spaces, which must relate in a

VERA WANG CREATED AN INTERESTING SILHOUETTE WITH AN EMPIRE WAISTLINE AND BUBBLE SKIRT FOR THIS CHARMING TWEED DRESS. *(COURTESY OF VERA WANG, NEW YORK)*

pleasing way. Generally, unequal proportion is more interesting than equal proportion. Many mathematical formulas have been proposed as guidelines, but the best results come from practice in observing and analyzing good design. Standards of proportion change with fashion cycles along with the evolution in silhouette and line.

The height and width of all parts of a design must be compared. Individual sections of a garment, such as sleeves, pockets, and collar, must all relate in size to each other as well as to the total silhouette. A jacket length and shape must complement the length and shape of the skirt or pants.

The spacing of trimmings, pleats, and tucks must relate to the total design. Trimmings must not be too heavy or too light, too large or too small to harmonize with the space around them. Every line, detail, or trim changes the proportion because it breaks up the space even more. A designer continually experiments with subtle variations in proportion: line placement, hem length, and size and placement of trims. The designer gives the patternmaker specific measurements for these details.

B a l a n c e   *Balance* refers to "visual weight" in design. A garment must be balanced to be visually pleasing.

Symmetrical Balance   If a design composition is the same on both sides of the garment, then the design is considered symmetrical or formally balanced, following the natural bisymmetry of the body. Just as we have two eyes, two arms, and two legs, a symmetrical garment must have exactly the same details in just the same place on both sides. Formal balance is the easiest, most logical way to achieve stability and, therefore, is the most commonly used in design. Even slight deviations, when minor details are not exactly alike on both sides, are considered approximate symmetry. A sensitive use of fabric, rhythm, and space relationships is needed to keep a symmetrical design from being boring.

Asymmetrical Balance   To achieve a more exciting, dramatic effect, asymmetrical or informal balance can be used. Asymmetrical design composition is different from one side of the garment to the other and is achieved by a balance of visual

■ ALBER ELBAZ DESIGNED THIS INTERESTING CHOCOLATE GREEN SATIN ASYMMETRICAL DRESS FOR LANVIN. *(COURTESY OF LANVIN, PARIS)*

trimmings. Sketches must be clear so that the patternmaker can use the drawing as a guide. The working sketch usually includes notes on construction and measurements. Fax machines have been a big help in letting designers communicate their design ideas quickly to overseas offices and production facilities.

Computer–Aided Design (CAD)

Designers may also sketch on a computer with software such as Adobe's Illustrator. Using a vector program, designers "sketch" by connecting points with their mouse. They are able to show all construction detail specifications for length, widths, and so on. Computer graphics can also show the repeat of a fabric pattern, simulate fabric drape on the figure, and help designers to experiment with color and fabric changes quickly (see Chapter 6 for textile design).

An entire line of garments can be organized and edited on a product data management (PDM) computer system. Computer companies are also experimenting with the idea of converting sketches automatically into first patterns (see Chapter 10 for production patternmaking).

Style Board

To chart the development of the line as a whole, the designer arranges working sketches of all the garments in fabric and color groups on a large board, which is essentially a master plan. The board is posted on the wall of the design room. Styles are added and subtracted until the line is finalized. Again, in large companies, this is usually managed on a CAD or PDM system.

Developing a Sample Garment

The first sample garment or prototype is the test to see if a design is successful.

The First Pattern

The next step in the product development procedure is making the first pattern, which is used to cut and sew the *prototype*, or first sample garment. The pattern is made in a sample size, the one used for testing and selling purposes. Sample sizes are 5 or 7 for juniors, 6, 8 or 10 for misses, 34 for men's trousers, and 38 for men's suits. The patternmaker can use one of three methods to make patterns: draping, flat pattern, or computer generated.

CHECKING THE FIT
OF A JACKET.
*(PHOTO BY
ARNALDO CASTOLDI
MILAN, ITALY)*

Draping The patternmaker or assistant designer uses the *draping* method to cut and shape muslin or garment fabric on a dress form to create a pattern. Like fabric sculpture, draping is ideal for soft, flowing designs. This method is used mainly for couture dresses and evening wear. It enables the patternmaker and designer to see the proportions and lines of the design exactly as they will look three dimensionally on the wearer. The design is often altered as it develops on the form.

Everything must be carefully marked: center front, shoulder line, seams, armholes, buttonholes, and so on. When the designer is satisfied with the look and fit, the muslin is taken off the form and trued up. *Truing* is correcting the sketched lines with drafting curves, angles, and rulers. Finally, the pattern is redrawn on heavy paper.

Flat Pattern First, basic shapes, such as bodices, sleeves, pants, or skirts, are draped or drafted. *Drafting* is blocking a set of prescribed measurements on paper. These patterns, once tested for accuracy, become *blocks* or *slopers* that can be changed or adapted to each new style by moving darts and seams. The *flat-pattern* method uses angles, rulers, and curves to change existing board patterns.

Computer Patterns   Computer-generated patterns are discussed fully in the production pattern section of Chapter 10.

The pattern is laid out on the fabric, traced, and cut out by the assistant designer or the sample cutter to be sewn into the first sample or prototype.

Prototype

The prototype is made by a samplemaker, the best of a factory's sewers. Samplemakers must have factory sewing skills and know how to put an entire garment together. The design staff works closely with samplemakers to solve construction problems. Factory construction methods must be tested as the garment is sewn. Therefore, many manufacturers have their samples made abroad at the same factory where production will be done to test quality.

Fit   The next step is to test the sample for fit and total effect. The ability to create a good fit is the most important skill needed in the development of the garment. The garment must be fitted on a model to test comfort and ease of movement. Donna Karan likes to try on her samples herself.

The Designer Work Sheet

Records are kept on all styles as they develop. Each designer fills out a work sheet containing information that guides the production department in figuring costs and in ordering *piece goods* (the factory term for fabrics) and trimmings. Many companies now use product data management (PDM) or product lifecycle management (PLM) systems to collate this information. In this case, each department responsible (such as fabrics, trims, or design) enters its own data into the computer.

The work sheet or PDM form usually includes all or part of the following information:

1. The date the garment was designed

2. The selling season

3. The sizes in which the design will be made

4. The style number assigned to the design (each manufacturer has a code of numbers representing season, fabric, and pattern)

5. A short description of the garment

6. A working sketch of the design to make it easy to identify the garment

7. The colors or color combinations in which the design is offered

8. Fabric swatches of what is used in the garment

9. Material descriptions, including each fabric type and source, width, and price per yard

10. Marker width, usually one inch narrower than the fabric

11. Trimmings information: the kinds, sources, sizes, and prices of buttons, zippers, braids, lace, belts, elastic, and so on; special fabric treatments done by outside contractors, such as pleating, spaghetti straps, and ties, are also included.

12. Labor costs for grading, marking, cutting, sewing, finishing, garment dyeing, and washing; these may be listed either on the designer work sheet or on a separate cost sheet figured by the costing department (see Chapter 10).

The work sheet becomes an adoption form when the final line is selected.

Line Selection

Designers develop many designs for each line, which are then edited.

A designer must be objective in judging each design and develop an unbiased, critical eye—a difficult task when judging a personal creation.

Editing

Regular weekly or monthly progress meetings are held to analyze the development of the line. From all the samples, management, the designer, and the merchandiser choose the best for the line. Production and sales specialists are also consulted. Stylists are often hired to help edit the collection. Retail buyers are sometimes asked for their opinions because of their familiarity with customer preferences.

Some styles are weeded out, leaving only the most successful combinations of fabric, style, and price. Some designers think they need a closely edited line so that combination possibilities are not confusing to the customer. Some large companies like to give their customers more options. Jones New York, for instance, typically shows five groups of 32 pieces per season (or 800 pieces per year). On the other hand, Betsey Johnson shows an average of 100 pieces per season, 40 pieces per monthly delivery (or 500 per year). Recently, manufacturers have carefully edited their collections

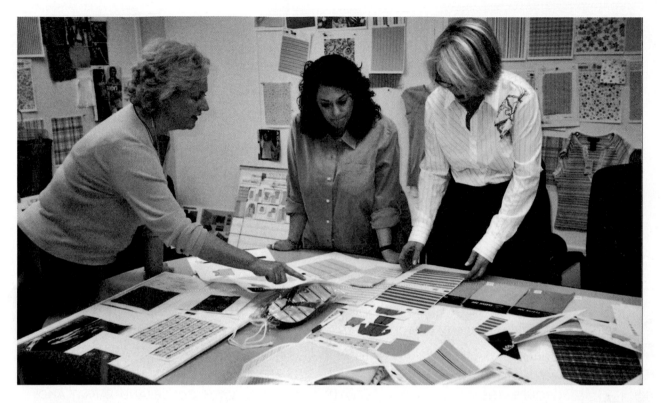

to reduce their size, to encourage larger sales per style, and to try to avoid cutting styles from the line that do not sell well enough to produce.

Reassessment of the Merchandise Plan

At this point, merchandise plans might be *reassorted*; if a group looks particularly strong, styles or colors could be added. The merchandise plan discussed at the beginning of this chapter might be revised so that it states the exact number of styles adopted, the actual price of fabrics chosen, and the yardage estimates for each style.

Line Presentation

Just before the scheduled line-release or collection-opening dates, the line is presented to the sales force. The designer or merchandiser must explain the line concepts, current fashion trends, and new developments in fabrications to the sales representatives and, sometimes, to retail buyers.

A consistent visual image created by a well-developed theme is a good selling tool on both the wholesale and the retail levels. Visual impact is what makes the line competitive once it is displayed in a retail store. The designer cannot be there to explain each style idea to the customer, so the product must speak for itself.

Product and design development is a challenge. Not only must designers be creative, but they must also understand production and know what sells. Claude Brouet, fashion director of Hermés, said, "There are plenty of designers with great talent, but one also needs to understand production, distribution, and on-time delivery. If you don't have those, even the most beautiful collection will be useless."[9]

Duplicates

After the line is complete, but before the line-release date, duplicates of the sample garments are made to keep in the showroom to show to buyers or to give to sales representatives to take on the road. These are made in the factory to test production. Basic styles are put into production according to sales projections before the line is sold.

SUMMARY

IN THIS CHAPTER WE DISCUSSED PRODUCT DEVELOPMENT, MERCHANDISING, AND DESIGN. THE COMPANY ESTABLISHES AN IMAGE AND A PRODUCT TO APPEAL TO A TARGET MARKET. THE MERCHANDISER PREPARES PLANS TO ACHIEVE SALES GOALS AND MEET CONSUMER NEEDS. THE DESIGN DEPARTMENT CREATES A SEASONAL LINE OF ITEMS OR GROUPS. THE DESIGNER IS ESPECIALLY CONCERNED WITH COLOR AND FABRIC AND OTHER DESIGN ELEMENTS TO DEVELOP ATTRACTIVE GARMENTS. AFTER A SKETCH AND FIRST PATTERN ARE COMPLETE, THE SAMPLE GARMENT OR PROTOTYPE IS MADE AS A TEST OF THE DESIGN AND FABRIC. FINALLY, THE LINE IS SELECTED AND PREPARED TO SHOW AT WHOLESALE MARKETS OR, IN THE CASE OF PRIVATE-LABEL RETAILERS, READY FOR SALE IN THE RETAIL MARKET.

Terms and Concepts

Briefly define and discuss the following terms and concepts:

1. Collection or line
2. Seasons
3. Merchandising
4. Merchandising plan
5. Designer
6. Items
7. Knockoffs
8. Planning groups
9. Theme
10. Elements of design
11. Color story
12. Fabrication
13. Texture
14. Performance
15. Sample cuts
16. Proportion
17. Asymmetrical balance
18. Repetition
19. Working sketch
20. First pattern
21. Draping
22. Flat pattern
23. Sample garment
24. Designer work sheet
25. Style board
26. CAD

Questions for Review

1. Describe how a designer uses CAD.
2. Discuss the merchandising function in relation to the design function.
3. Discuss the basic conceptual differences between merchandising sportswear and dresses.
4. Name the elements of design. Discuss briefly why it is important for these elements to be represented in a design.
5. What are the principles of design? How do they help a designer to analyze the effectiveness of a design?
6. Explain briefly the development of a sample garment.

Projects for Additional Learning

1. Write a short description of an imaginary or real person. Include the person's age, figure type, job, place of residence, interests, and lifestyle. This person will be the typical customer for your new sportswear line for the season eight months from now. Determine a price range and style range according to your customer's lifestyle. Design a group of 20 coordinating pieces or related separates. Develop a color story and suggest fabrications. (Merchandising students may cut pictures of sportswear items from magazines and display them on a board.)
2. Find examples of 10 successful designs in European and American fashion magazines. Describe the style of each in terms of line, silhouette, shapes and spaces, color, and texture (fabric, pattern, and trims), as well as balance, proportion, rhythm, and emphasis. Do all elements and principles work together harmoniously? What elements dominate? Find two garments that you feel are unsuccessful. Analyze them in the same way to discover what element or principle has not been properly used.
3. In a local specialty or department store, compare two dresses or two suits of similar price from different manufacturers. Try them on. Which has the better fit? Compare fabric choices in terms of quality and suitability to the design. Compare styling. Which is more innovative? Taking all factors into consideration, which dress or suit is the better buy? Discuss your findings in a written report. Describe or sketch the dresses or suits.

Notes

1. "Slimane Talks About Dior, YSL," *Women's Wear Daily*, July 5, 2000, p. 9.
2. As quoted in "Lauren at 25," *Women's Wear Daily*, January 15, 1992, p. 7.
3. Deborah Ball, "Armani Stands at Crossroads Amid Consolidations," *Wall Street Journal*, October 24, 2000, p. B17.
4. Robin Howe, former design director, Jones New York, interview, May 4, 2000.
5. Tommy Hilfiger, interview, September 23, 1994.
6. As quoted in "The Culture of Copycats," *Women's Wear Daily*, November 2, 1999, p. 8.
7. Christian Dior, *Talking about Fashion* (New York: Putnam's, 1954), p. 35.
8. "Lacroix Tells Us about Christian," *Marie Claire*, October 1998, p. 1.
9. As quoted by Katherine Weisman, "Hermès, Loosening the Reins," *Women's Wear Daily*, March 2, 1994, p. 15.

A FITTING IN THE LOUIS VUITTON
WORKROOMS IN PARIS. *(COURTESY
OF LOUIS VUITTON)*

10

APPAREL PRODUCTION AND GLOBAL SOURCING

Career Focus

Interesting technical job possibilities exist in apparel production and global sourcing. Technical training in both patterning and computers is needed for positions as patternmakers. Those interested in materials may consider positions as fabric and trimmings buyers. Numbers-oriented people might like to work in sourcing, cost analysis, and production planning. Most of these jobs, however, are now being done at factories overseas. To be effective, sourcing managers have to understand the production process and travel extensively to overseas factories.

CHAPTER OBJECTIVES

After reading this chapter, you should be able to:

1. Explain the costing of a garment
2. Describe, in order, the steps in garment production
3. Explain the various types of contracting
4. List all the uses of computers in manufacturing
5. Explain the differences between men's tailoring and men's sportswear production
6. Describe the two commercial methods of knitwear production
7. Discuss the importance of quality control

Production is one of the three integral phases of fashion manufacturing: design, production, and sales. Without design, there would be nothing to sell; without sales, there would be no reason to produce. Conversely, sales would not continue if orders were not produced properly and delivered on time. To keep its retail customers, each manufacturer tries to maintain a consistent price structure, quality of styling and construction, and timely deliveries. This chapter focuses on apparel production, from costing to quality control.

Production Planning

Based on orders or expected orders, a manufacturer has to decide how many garments of each style to produce.

Even before a collection is shown at market, production may begin based on sales forecasts. There are two philosophies of production planning: cut-to-order and cut-to-stock.

Cut-to-Order

The safest method of production is to *cut-to-order*, that is, to cut and produce only against orders. This means waiting until all orders are in and then working quickly to cut, sew, and deliver. This method is reserved for high-priced couture and designer garments and the newest fashion items in a line, when sales forecasting is difficult.

Cut-to-Stock

The method with the greater risk involves cutting based on estimates of projected sales, or *cut-to-stock*. Projections or forecasts (expected sales) are determined by the economy, sales histories of similar garments, the season, and the strength of the particular line.

The cut-to-stock method is necessary, at least for basics, to enable production to be spread out over time. The method enables the company to start work in slack months on those items with the highest projected sales. It is also necessary when orders for fabrics require long lead times, as is the case with yarn-dyed fabrics, sweaters, and imports from Asia.

Global Sourcing

Manufacturing has become a global phenomenon.

Most manufacturers (traditional manufacturers or retailers that produce private-label apparel) no longer produce apparel in their own factories. They are responsible for all phases of manufacturing, from design and merchandising to selling and shipping, but production is done by a contractor. A *contractor* is an independent producer who does sewing (and/or cutting and patternmaking) for manufacturers in their own factories.

By using contractors, manufacturers do not have to pay wages during slack seasons or be concerned with hiring, training, or wage demands of personnel. They also do not have to invest in plant facilities and machinery, which require large capital investment.

Contracting provides greater production flexibility, but it can involve problems. There is extra movement of goods, which results in more costs and some losses. There may also be communication problems or a possibility of late deliveries. However, manufacturers develop long-term relationships with contractors they can trust. Through global computer networks, information on design, specs, fabric, purchases, patterns, costing, and production is available to everyone who works on a particular style or group of styles. Computer technology makes it possible to coordinate production between countries.

Strategic Sourcing

Sourcing managers visit factories worldwide and meet with the factory owners. They evaluate the contractors' production capabilities and their information technology, equipment, cleanliness, and employee conditions to find the one who is most reliable and best suited for a particular job. Most contractors specialize either in a particular quality of sewing or in sewing on type of fabric, such as knits or wovens. A sample garment is provided, and the factory makes a trial garment. The selected contractor agrees to maintain a certain standard of workmanship and to finish work by a specific date. Some manufacturers may arrange to work exclusively with one or more contractors. They try to make long-lasting partnerships with reliable contractors for their mutual success.

Contractors can be located anywhere in the world where labor is abundant; wages are reasonable; and facilities, machinery, and transportation are available. In spite of technological advances, apparel manufacturing remains labor intensive. Therefore, manufacturers continually seek the cheapest sources of labor in Asia, Eastern Europe, Mexico, and the Caribbean. Apparel is manufactured in whatever country can produce the best garment for the lowest price. Manufacturers can visit sourcing expositions, such as the China Sourcing Fair in Hong Kong, to find the best deal. U.S. imports of apparel rise every year. Liz Claiborne, for example, sources, or contracts out, approximately 95 percent of its requirements offshore with some 300 independent contractors in 35 countries.[1] Currently, the largest producers of apparel for the United States are China, Mexico, India, Indonesia, Pakistan, Vietnam, Bangladesh, Honduras, Canada, India, and the Philippines.

Apparel production for the U.S. and European markets is vital to the growth of third world countries. Since World War II, Asian countries have used textile and apparel production to build their economies, which in turn raises their standard of living.

Some U.S. and Canadian manufacturers have purchased or opened their own production facilities in Asia, the Caribbean, or Mexico. Asian firms are counteracting by investing in the United States, Mexico, Central America, and the Caribbean Basin.

Asia Because Asian plants are very efficient and flexible and provide quality products, they are able to produce fashion apparel. Overseas production started in Hong Kong, which became the capital of Asian apparel manufacturing. Then workers in Hong Kong become so skilled and well paid that only the highest quality clothing is now made there. Manufacturers then sought cheaper labor sources in Taiwan, China, and South Korea. As these countries increased their skills and wages, other developing Asian economies, including India, Bangladesh, Vietnam, and Cambodia, and Southeast Asian nations such as Indonesia and Malaysia, were found as new sources. Compared with an average hourly wage of $12.97 in the United States, typical hourly wages (in U.S. dollars) are as little as 60 cents per hour in India or 62 cents per hour in China.[2]

China has become the primary producer of textiles and apparel shipped to the United States. China has hundreds of apparel companies, ranging from small shops to megafactories, from state-owned reminders of communism to privately owned symbols of capitalism. Luen Thai Holdings Ltd., for example, is a "superfactory" which employs 14,000 workers in 15 buildings in Dongguan. Bob Zane, former head of production for Liz Claiborne, feels that "China will continue to grow, eventually producing 50 to 80 percent of U.S.-destined apparel."[3] As discussed in Chapter 2, the overall trade deficit with China resulted in the passage of a new restrictive import agreement with China.

■ THE LUEN THAI FACTORY IN DONGGUAN, CHINA, WITH 14,000 WORKERS IN 15 BUILDINGS! *(COURTESY OF LIZ CLAIBORNE)*

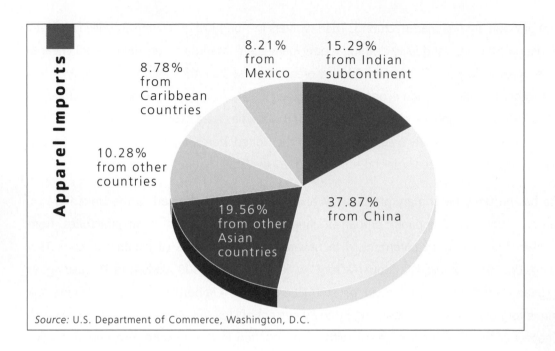

Source: U.S. Department of Commerce, Washington, D.C.

Mexico and the Caribbean Basin   Production in Mexico and the Caribbean Basin is encouraged by the U.S. textile industry so that domestic textiles can be sent there to be cut and sewn. Also, since NAFTA (see Chapter 2) was enacted, there are no tariffs on imports from Mexico. Several large U.S. and Mexican textile companies have created Textile City, an industrial park south of Mexico City, to serve as a base for U.S. apparel manufacturers. Mexico is already the world's sixth largest apparel-manufacturing country.

U.S. legislation has ended quotas (see Chapter 2) and duties for Caribbean and Central American countries that use U.S. yarn and fabric. The Central American Free Trade Agreement (CAFTA) covers the Dominican Republic, Costa Rica, Guatemala, Honduras, Nicaragua, and El Salvador. U.S. manufacturers like the quick turnaround time provided by the close proximity of these countries and so use factories in these countries to produce basic products that need to be quickly and steadily replenished.

Eastern Europe   Countries such as Poland, Hungary, Moldova, Slovakia, and Turkey in Eastern Europe, which used to supply the former Soviet Union, are providing cheaper skilled labor for European manufacturers. Some U.S. fashion companies, such as Liz Claiborne and Levi Strauss, are producing there as well. These countries have had to adjust from working in a command-oriented economy, where delivery schedules were not a problem, to working in a market-driven economy.

Importing Procedures

Importing, bringing merchandise in from other countries, involves numerous negotiators. Manufacturers need their own representative or an agent in the country where production is done, a customs broker to assist in processing the import application papers with the U.S. government to bring the goods into the United States, and a freight-forwarding agent to handle shipping. Manufacturers must rely on a good agent or company representative to keep control of quality, prevent late deliveries, and handle difficulties in communication caused by language differences. Or everything may be handled by a trusted contractor. Price negotiations are usually made in U.S. dollars because of the fluctuations in international currency exchange rates.

There are three basic methods of producing clothing overseas: a production package; cut, make, and trim; and offshore assembly.

Production Package   Now that many overseas contractors have sophisticated factories, they are capable of producing an entire *package*. The contractors are given sketches (via the Internet) or sample garments, specifications, and sizing standards. They are also given source information for fabric, buttons, and trims. Contractors order the fabric and trims. They also make the patterns and markers and do the cutting, assembly, quality control, labeling, and shipping. Contractors take full responsibility for production, quality control, and the delivery schedule.

Cut, Make, and Trim (CMT)   A manufacturer or its representative may buy fabric from one country—silk from Korea, for example—and have it sent to a factory in another country, such as China, to be cut, sewn, finished, and labeled.

Offshore Assembly   Fabric is purchased and cut in the United States and sent to Mexico or the Caribbean countries for sewing. This classification, item 9802 in the Harmonized Tariff Schedule (still referred to as the "807 program"), is being encouraged to promote the use of U.S. textiles. For this reason there is a guaranteed access level (large quotas) for this classification. Duty is charged only on the portion of labor done offshore.

Industry Concerns

Loss of Domestic Manufacturing   Consumer demand for reasonably priced clothing and investor demand for high profit margins have forced manufacturers to find cheap labor abroad. The Garment Workers' Union has been against overseas production because it takes jobs away from U.S. laborers. Since NAFTA was passed, thousands of apparel-manufacturing jobs

in the United States have been lost. The United States has shifted from a manufacturing base to service industries. Although it is unfortunate that the United States, Canada, and Europe are losing manufacturing, most young people in the United States are just not interested in this work.

Sweatshops Americans are deeply concerned about apparel contractor employees who work in deplorable conditions. It was found that many workers in Asia were physically or verbally abused, punished for petty mistakes, forced to work overtime, and interrogated by police if they complained.

Officials from industry, human rights groups, and organized labor have set up a task force to set standards for garment factories worldwide. The participants issued a Statement of Workplace Rights, setting guidelines for such issues as child labor, harassment, discrimination, health and safety, union organization, working hour limits, and wages. The task force wants to limit work to 10 hours a day and a 48-hour workweek, with a top limit of 60 hours including overtime. Wages would be tied to the cost of living for basic necessities, such as food and shelter, in each individual country. Companies complying with these rights would have to consent to have their factories monitored, but in turn would be able to advertise that they manufacture sweatshop-free products. Some U.S. apparel companies have initiated strict contracts and audit procedures regarding employee conditions at contracting facilities. The International Labor Organization has set up a factory-monitoring program in Cambodia as a model of how working environments can be improved in developing countries. They are trying to set a good example for human rights.

Costing

The production cost of a garment is mutually determined by the manufacturer and contractor.

Contractors determine the cost of producing a garment based on costs for materials and labor (the time it takes to make the garment). The contractor and/or manufacturer use the designer's work sheet, a prototype garment, and the production pattern to analyze materials and construction. Usually, final costs are mutually agreed on between manufacturer and contractor based on the production costs of similar garments made last season.

TABLE 10.1 MANUFACTURER'S COST ESTIMATES WHOLESALE PRICING FOR A HYPOTHETICAL DRESS

(Each company uses a unique pricing structure)

Direct Cost	Amount	Average Percentages
Fabric (cost depends on quantity purchased) 4½ yards @ $ 4.92	$ 22.14	18%
Trimmings	2.46	2
Labor and contractor fees (cost depends on number of garments sewn and in what country they are sewn)	23.37	19
Duties or sourcing agent fees	4.92	4
International transportation/freight	9.84	8
Total Direct Cost	**$ 62.73**	**51%**
Indirect Cost		
Design and merchandising staff salaries	4.92	4
General administrative overhead: management and office salaries, rent, insurance, utilities	14.76	12
Sales commissions	8.61	7
Retail discount	9.84	8
Retail markdown allowance	4.92	4
Advertising/marketing	4.92	4
Total Indirect Cost	**47.97**	**39**
Total Cost	**110.70**	**90**
Profit before taxes	**12.30**	**10**
Wholesale price of dress	**$ 123.00**	**100%**

Cost Considerations

Materials—The total amount of fabric needed for the garment is estimated and then multiplied by its cost per yard to find the total material cost per garment. Because higher volume allows more flexibility in making the marker and, thus, a more efficient use of fabric, material cost is somewhat reduced for high-volume styles.

Trimmings—The cost of trimmings needed for each garment is multiplied by the number of units to be produced. Dividing the total by the number of units gives the cost per garment.

Production patternmaking, grading, and marking—Many manufacturers and contractors allow for these costs in the general overhead or pay a fee to an outside pattern service.

Spreading and cutting—The contractor's fabric spreading and cutting costs are figured based on the number of garments to be cut, the number of pattern pieces for the style, and the layers of fabric required to accommodate the cutting order.

Assembly—Contractors calculate the average time it takes to sew the whole garment and multiply that by the factory's hourly rate. Pricing also depends on the time of the year and supply and demand. For example, a knit contractor may offer a low price to make classic sweaters in January to keep its factory busy.

Finishing—Costs are included to cover final preparations for shipping. In designer apparel, this may include some handwork. For most apparel, pressing and/or folding is sufficient. The cost for packing in preparation for shipping is also figured.

Freight—The cost of shipping completed garments from the contractor to the manufacturer's warehouse is calculated. A percentage of the air or sea freight cost must be added to the cost of each garment.

Duty and quota—In the case of imports, there are additional costs for duty and quota (now applicable only to non-WTO members and China).

Overhead—*Overhead* includes all the daily costs of running the business. *Fixed overhead* expenses, those that do not change from month to month, include rent, heat, lights, trash collection, insurance, salaries, taxes, and legal and auditing services. *Variable overhead* expenses include advertising, promotion, equipment repair, markdowns of leftover fabrics and garments, and losses due to fire and theft.

Wholesale Pricing

The manufacturer determines a wholesale price by adding the cost of labor (contractor), materials (unless part of the contractor's price), overhead, perhaps shipping, and a markup. The markup covers sales commission (usually 7 to 10 percent) and a profit, which is necessary for staying in business.

Most manufacturers add a markup of between 28 and 44 percent of the wholesale price. Budget companies usually take the lowest markup and hope to make a profit by volume sales. Today, with partnerships building between retailer and manufacturer, pricing often begins with the price wanted by the retailer. The manufacturer may work backward, trying to provide a garment that will sell at the requested price.

Purchasing of Piece Goods

Ordering the materials necessary to produce garments may be done by the manufacturer's piece goods buyer or the overseas contractor.

The piece goods buyer acts as a liaison between the mill or converter and the manufacturer and/or contractor. The buyer must know all the properties of fabrics and have information on prices, availability, and delivery. Often, piece goods are purchased as part of an overseas production package. In this case, the piece goods buyer supplies the contractor with fabric and trim source information.

PRODUCT DATA MANAGEMENT (PDM) KEEPS RECORDS OF FABRIC AND SUPPLY RESOURCES FOR PRODUCTION OF A VEST. *(COURTESY OF LECTRA SYSTEMS, FRANCE)*

Electronic data interchange (EDI) allows the exchange of piece goods ordering information by computer. As discussed in Chapter 2, this linkage has fostered partnerships between manufacturers and suppliers to ease purchasing procedures. Computer software uses sales figures to automatically adjust planned production and the amount of fabric and trim needed.

The following issues must be considered in the purchasing of piece goods.

Environmental Concerns   Consumer preference for environmentally safe products has led some manufacturers to look for fabrics made with organically grown or "fair trade" cotton, linen, wool, and lyocell; vegetable- and water-based inks in prints; fiber-reactive, low-impact dyes; and safe finishes. Some manufacturers, such as People Tree, now make special lines of fair trade and environmentally friendly clothing.

Volume Purchases   Generally, volume manufacturers purchase goods from large textile companies that can handle big orders. Ordering in quantity may give the manufacturer a cost advantage. The goal of a volume manufacturer is to obtain the lowest-priced goods at the widest width to use an efficient marker layout.

Small Orders   Conversely, small manufacturers usually deal with small textile firms, which can do shorter runs, or buy from fabric brokers. Shorter runs make it possible for manufacturers to buy smaller quantities. Lower minimum order requirements is one of the reasons (besides low-cost labor) that Asian textile manufacturers have become so successful.

Ordering

The manufacturer's or contractor's piece goods buyers must be aware of fabric prices at various mills and converters to negotiate the best price. The buyer must also calculate the amount of yardage needed to supply the cutting order. Orders for stock yardage are based on sales histories and on forecasts of future sales. Textile sales representatives encourage manufacturers to make a commitment early in the season to buy a specific amount of yardage. Ordering in advance ensures the availability and on-time delivery of a popular fabric, which may subsequently be in short supply. Volume orders may require a six- to eight-week *lead-time* for delivery. Now many Asian contractors handle fabric purchasing locally.

A manufacturer takes a great risk by stocking up for anticipated orders. To eliminate some risk, manufacturers often commit for greige goods, to be dyed later. Then, as sales information becomes more precise, colors can be *assorted*. In other words, the greige goods can be dyed to the colors needed, according to the sales percentage established for each.

Trimmings   The fabric or trim buyer buys trimmings and notions (functional trimmings). These are the materials used to finish garments or fashion accessories. Other sundries purchased by the trimmings buyer include labels, hangtags, hangers, and plastic bags.

Trim buyers must find the best trimmings available for each kind of application in each garment. Trimmings must have the same care properties as the fabrics used in the garment. For example, if the fabric can be safely washed, the trimmings must also be washable. Buyers must also ensure that the colors of all trimmings match the fabrics. They must also coordinate deliveries from each trim producer so that all trims for a particular garment are at the factory in time for the scheduled production of that garment. The contractor may also purchase the trimmings.

Fabric Quality and Dye Lots   In the past, fabrics were inspected for flaws, color differences, and variations at the apparel factory. If there were too many defects, the fabric was returned to the mill. Today, however, most manufacturers rely on the mills to inspect fabrics before shipping. For imported fabrics, a manufacturer can hire an outside inspection agency to check the goods before they leave the mill, or the contractor may inspect the goods.

Some apparel manufacturers build strong reputations on the reliability of their products. They perform washing, dry cleaning, steaming, and pressing tests to check tensile strength, durability, color cracking, color fastness, and shrinkage. They also test how the fabric holds up during sewing. Coordinate tops and bottoms must be cut from the same dye lot (or be garment dyed), and, at the very least, shipments to the same store must be within acceptable variations of color if from different dye lots (see Chapter 6 regarding garment dyeing).

Patternmaking

Accurate patternmaking is crucial for successful apparel production.

The Production Pattern

Strict attention must be paid to company size specifications, which are standardized measurements including ease (extra room for movement) for each size. When using fabrics that shrink, such as cotton, patterns have to allow for that shrinkage. Also, the seam lines of each pattern piece must exactly fit the piece to which it will be sewn, with notches marked perfectly for operators to follow. Grain lines, plaid lines, and other annotations are also marked on the patterns.

A PATTERNMAKER USES A STYLUS THAT AUTOMATICALLY RECORDS LINES IN THE ACCUMARK PATTERN DEVELOPMENT SYSTEM AND SHOWS THEM ON THE COMPUTER SCREEN. *(COURTESY OF GERBER TECHNOLOGY, INC.)*

In a small apparel factory, the production patternmaker might rely on the same methods used in the sample room to make patterns: draping, drafting, or flat patterning from standardized basic blocks; the same person may do both the sample and production patternmaking.

Computer Patternmaking   At most manufacturers or contractors, however, patterns are made on a computer. With *computer-aided design* (CAD) systems, the patternmaker manipulates small graphic patterns on the computer screen with a handheld control device. New patterns can be made or existing ones changed. *Geometry drivers* make an infinite number of changes to the shapes and sizes of the patterns, including creating new design lines or adding pleats, fullness, and seam allowances.

To make patterns manually on a computer, another system allows the patternmaker to work life-size on a sensitized table with traditional tools and a *stylus* that is attached to the table and the computer. The stylus picks up the lines drawn on the table and shows them on the screen. Changes can also be made directly on the screen.

In both cases, patterns are immediately available for other operations such as grading and marker making. Via global networking, this information is available to designers, merchandisers, and contractors.

Grading Sizes

Grading is the method used to increase or decrease the sample-size production pattern to make up a complete size range. For example, the sample size 10 pattern must be made larger to accommodate sizes 12, 14, and 16 and smaller for sizes 8 and 6. Each company sets predetermined grade *specifications*, or rules. For example, a misses manufacturer's grade rules might call for increments of one and a half inches in width and a quarter inch in length for each size.

Today, most manufacturers grade patterns on CAD systems. The patternmaker guides a *cursor* around the edges of the sample pattern on a digitized table. At each of the key points, he or she pushes a button to record a grade point. Each point is cross-referenced by a grade-rule table stored in the computer, which enlarges or reduces the pattern automatically according to predetermined increments and in a predetermined direction.

If the pattern was originally made on a computer, data already in the computer can be enlarged or reduced automatically. Preprogrammed grade rules for increase or decrease are automatically applied to the pieces at each grading location. Then the computer can print out the pattern in each new size. Manufacturers often use an outside service to make patterns, grade patterns, and make the marker. Overseas contractors usually make the patterns at their factories.

Making the Marker

From all the pattern pieces of varying sizes, a master marker is made. The marker is the cutting guide or pattern layout made on a sheet of lightweight paper the same width as the fabric. The purpose of the marker is threefold: to make a layout for the cutter to follow, to place pattern pieces close together to avoid fabric waste, and to accommodate the *cutting order* (ensuring that the correct quantities of each size are cut). The desired economical use of space is called a *tight marker*, which utilizes the highest percentage of fabric possible to avoid waste. Patterns are laid out so that each size and color are cut as needed (popular sizes are repeated on the marker). Grain direction, one-way prints, plaids, stripes, and naps are considered in making the marker.

Most manufacturers now make their markers on a CAD system or have it made by an outside service or contractor. Miniatures of the graded pattern pieces are displayed graphically on the computer screen. The operator can electronically position the pattern pieces into the most efficient arrangement. Once the marker is completed, a full-scale marker is printed by the plotter on a long sheet of paper. The patternmaker checks the arrangement on the screen or prints out a minimarker to check. Copies

■ A COMPUTER-
MADE MARKER.
*(COURTESY OF
GERBER
TECHNOLOGY,
INC.)*

of the marker are made to use in each cut. Miniatures of an entire marker can be faxed to locations around the world, or the entire marker can be printed out on a plotter wherever cutting is to be done.

Production Scheduling

The contractor schedules cutting and garment assembly in time to meet shipping dates.

Issue Plan

A production schedule, or *issue plan*, is created to ensure that delivery dates are met. This schedule is a reverse timetable, usually covering six months. The first date on the schedule is a shipping date that will meet the retail store's order requirements. The schedule progresses backward to include completion dates, cutting dates, and fabric delivery dates. Production scheduling is very difficult because it has to be organized to take maximum advantage of plant capacity as well as to meet shipping dates.

Plant Capacity

Plant capacity, the quantity of garments that can be made in a factory at a certain time, and construction difficulties must be considered in planning the production schedule. For example, some styles are more difficult to produce than others and, therefore, take more time. Operators are slower at their work when it is new to them; plant capacity builds as operators become accustomed to the sewing operation and are able to work faster.

Standard Allowed Hours Plant capacity is figured according to the time it takes to complete each operation or garment, as it is in costing. Plant engineers time each operation to find the "standard allowed minutes" it takes to complete a specific operation and the "standard allowed hours" to make a total garment. Standards are used to figure how many garments can be sewn in one hour or one day. For example, if 50 people can make 100 pants in one hour, then obviously they should be able to make 800 pants in an eight-hour day.

Inventory Control

The introduction of *computerized inventory control* has made planning more accurate. Computer systems are used to create issue plans and cutting orders. All fabrics and works-in-progress are given *universal product codes (UPCs)*, which identify style, color, size, price, and fabrication. *Product data management (PDM)* systems collate product data on a single program, forming an "electronic filing cabinet" of designer drawings, supply sources, pattern information, grading sheets, cost sheets, and cutting tickets. They also provide current information on the number of units that are cut, in work, or in stock. With these data, manufacturers can update fabric commitments and production plans to correspond with demand.

Spreading and Cutting Procedures

Using the markers made from graded patterns, in accordance with the issue plan, fabrics are cut to prepare for garment assembly.

Following the issue plan, the cutting order tells what to cut, what fabrics to use, and how to cut. A computerized cutting order uses programmed data to determine what markers should be made; how fabrics should be spread and cut, and the most cost-effective number of plies, colors, and size mixes.

Spreading the Fabric

A crane moves a roll of fabric into the *hopper* (fabric-feeding device) of a spreading machine. Conventionally, a spreader machine is guided along a table, laying fabric on the cutting table, the length determined by the marker. The fabric is cut at the end, the machine returns to the other end, and the next layer is laid face up on top of the first, in the same direction. Fabric is spread on the cutting table with one ply on top of another so that many layers can be cut at the same time. The number of layers is prescribed by the cutting order. Spreaders must be aware of how fabric finish, pile, stripes, floral designs, and other factors affect their work. More than 200 layers may be cut at one time, depending on the fabric thickness. Thinner fabrics may be more difficult to handle and are cut in lower stacks for more control.

In most factories today, spreading is done automatically with a computer-programmed spreading machine. In this case, a motorized spreader moves automatically up and down the table, unwinding up to 80 yards of fabric per minute.

Cutting Techniques

The marker is put on top of the layers of fabric. Using the traditional method, a skilled technician uses a straight-knife cutting machine, with a vertical blade, to cut through the layers of fabric following the pattern outlines on the marker.

Computer Cutting

Most cutting is now done by computer. A numerically controlled cutter reduces labor and improves the accuracy of the cut. A beam structure across the table holds the cutting head. The beam can move up and down the table, whereas the cutting head moves across. Movement is directed by marker data in the CAD system. The knife in the cutting head vibrates vertically to cut the fabric.

Laser-beam cutting is sometimes used for men's suits, which are cut a single layer at a time. The laser, a concentrated light beam, is also directed by a computer. *Water-jet cutting* is being used for some fabrics and leathers, especially in the shoe industry. A thin stream of water, also computer directed, is fired under high pressure through a tiny nozzle to cut the leather.

AUTOMATED COMPUTER CUTTER SHOWING THE CUTTING HEAD, BEAM STRUCTURE, AND MULTIPLE-LAYER CUT PIECES. *(COURTESY OF GERBER TECHNOLOGY, INC.)*

Environmental Concerns

Manufacturers of apparel are giving increased attention to environmental concerns. They are trying to identify ways to reduce and recycle their supplies. Their primary concern is the disposal of fabric scrap, which makes up a large percentage of production waste. One possibility for the disposal of this waste is to use an on-site incinerator to generate electricity. Some fabric scraps are shredded and spun into new yarn. Levi Strauss recycles its scrap denim to make blue letter paper. However, most environmental improvements and recycling are still too expensive for most manufacturers to implement.

Bundling

The process of sorting cut pieces and organizing them for assembly is referred to as bundling. Parts of garments and necessary findings must be grouped for the sewing machine operators.

Bar-coded identification tickets attached to each bundle constantly keep track of work-in-progress and each garment by size and color. Bundled work is distributed to machine operators in the factory.

Garment Assembly

**The next step in production is the actual assembly
or sewing of quantities of garments.**

Assembly Operations

The steps involved in garment assembly are called operations. A man's suit may have as many as 200 different sewing operations. No two contractors use all the same methods, but all follow the same basic order. A supervisor analyzes a garment's construction to determine the best and fastest way to sew the garments. An operation sheet is drawn up, listing all necessary operations in

GERBER'S PRODUCT
DATA MANAGEMENT
(PDM) SYSTEM
SHOWS
SPECIFICATIONS AND
NOTES FOR JACKET
CONSTRUCTION.
*(COURTESY OF
GERBER TECHNOLOGY,
INC.)*

sequence. This is usually part of a product data management computer system that collates all the information regarding the production of a garment style.

The introduction of specialized operations or new machinery requires additional training of operators, which results in higher production costs during the training period. As apparel manufacturing remains labor intensive, manufacturers and contractors find it necessary to rely on their operators as individual skill centers or as part of a small production team.

Individual Incentive Systems (Piecework)

Some sewing machine operators, finishers, and pressers are paid on a piecework rate. That is, they are paid a set amount for each operation they complete, rather than by the hour. Rates vary with the difficulty of the operation. As proof of work completed, the operator signs the identification ticket or removes one segment of it. Actually, most companies pay a guaranteed wage, with piecework acting as an incentive for operators to work faster and, therefore, earn more.

Assembly Systems

Sewing Operations must be performed in sequence. The three methods of construction are the progressive-bundle system, the tailor or whole-garment system, and the modular manufacturing system.

Progressive-bundle systems, which were used most often for sportswear, are fading out of use. They required each operator to repeat one assembly task, such as closing a shoulder seam or stitching on a pocket. Referred to as *section work*, machine operators are grouped to follow the order to production; they pass the joined pieces of garments from one section to the next as each operation is completed. The advantage of progressive-bundle systems is that the work area can be designed to complete a specific operation using the best machinery and trained operators for that job.

Whole-garment systems use a single operator to sew a whole garment together. This system is similar to the one used for sewing sample garments. In this case, finishing tasks may be performed by another operator who specializes in those operations. This system is used most often for dresses and couture.

Modular manufacturing is a team concept that involves the cross-training of operators and the development of small quality-circle production groups as initiated by the Japanese. Modular manufacturing involves a group of 4 to 17 people who set their own standards and work together to produce a finished garment. Each team member works on more than one operation, and group incentives may replace or supplement individual piecework. Modular manufacturing has many advantages, including shorter cycle times, enhanced quality, fewer incidents of cumulative trauma (resulting from movement from machine to machine) and injuries, and higher morale because the work is less boring.

Ergonomics is the development of workplace equipment designed to improve the safety, health, and efficiency of workers. Government regulations, the high cost of workers' compensations, and rising health care costs have activated economic strategies. As a result, new technology has produced quieter, easier-to-operate machines that reduce stress and injury and thereby build morale.

Computer Technology Used in Garment Assembly

Most factories have installed automated systems for the movement of goods and sewing to speed up production and cut lead time. Contractors attend international trade shows to purchase machinery and learn the newest technology.

Computer-aided manufacturing (CAM) applications include computerized cutting and programmable sewing machines.

Unit production systems (UPS) use conveyors to move garments automatically from one work station to the next where each operator is responsible for one stage of the assembly process.

Computer-integrated manufacturing (CIM) can connect these systems and share data for total automation. For example, a manufacturer can network data from a CAD patternmaking, grading, and marking system directly to a CAM cutting system.

Computer simulation allows for the viewing of a manufacturing floor plan on a computer screen before actual implementation. Through simulation studies, the type and number of machines and the number of operators needed may be determined before the assembly process begins.

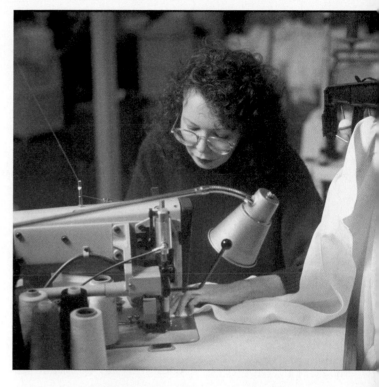

Flexible manufacturing is simply a variety of strategies used by one manufacturer. Not all garments lend themselves to traditional or automated technologies; a flexible system uses a combination of methods.

THIS UNIT PRODUCTION SYSTEM ALLOWS OPERATIONS TO BE PERFORMED WITHOUT REMOVING PARTS FROM THE HANGER, THEREBY REDUCING PRODUCTION TIME. *(COURTESY OF GERBER TECHNOLOGY, INC.)*

Power Sewing Machines

Three main types of power sewing machines are used in traditional factories: the lock-stitch, the chain-stitch, and the overlock machine.

The **lock-stitch machine** sews a straight seam on the same principle as a home sewing machine. This machine makes it possible for the top thread to go under the bottom thread around a bobbin, creating a lock. This is the most secure stitch possible, but it leaves an unfinished seam, undesirable in fabrics that ravel easily. Also, of course, operations must be stopped frequently to rewind the bobbin.

The **chain-stitch machine** works on a principle similar to crocheting: it makes a series of loops pulled through one another. The top needle goes in and out of the fabric, making loops underneath that catch into one another. The chain stitch is not as secure as the lock stitch, but because the chain-stitch machine does not have a bobbin, the operator does not need to stop in midoperation to rewind it.

263

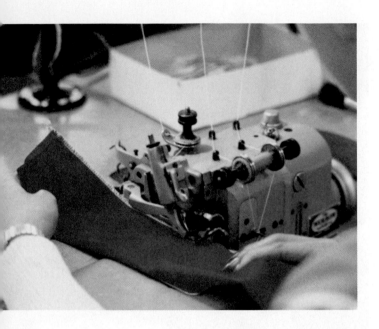

THE OVERLOCK MACHINE CREATES A FINISHED EDGE AS IT MAKES A SEAM. *(PHOTO BY GINI STEPHENS FRINGS)*

The **overlock or serging machine** is based on the same principle as the chain-stitch machine, and its stitch is also not as secure as the lock stitch. It was created to make an edge finish as well as to sew seams. In one operation it sews the fabric together, cuts off the fabric to make a smooth edge, and wraps thread around the edge. A simple overlock machine has one needle and two loopers (which look like thick, bent needles) and works with three spools or cones of thread. The needle and loopers work together in a reciprocating pattern, the loopers moving back and forth from the needle to the fabric edge. This stitch is ideal for knits because it gives with the stretch of the fabric.

The **safety-overlock machine** is a combination of the chain-stitch machine and the overlock machine. The safety factor is that if one row of stitching comes out, the other still holds the garment together. With a total of two needles, three loopers, and five cones of thread, it functions as two machines in one. It provides the straight chain stitch needed for factory assembling plus an edge finish.

The **blind-stitch hemming machine** is also based on the chain stitch. The hem is folded back and caught by the needle at even intervals.

Button machines sew buttons onto a garment. Button placement is marked on the fabric. A sew-through button is placed in a holder, which moves the button back and forth while the needle sews it onto the fabric underneath. A shank button is held in position sideways so that the needle can go through the shank on its back. Some machines have a hopper, a feeding device that automatically positions the button.

The **buttonhole machine** is essentially a zigzag lock-stitch machine with automatic devices to control the width and length of the buttonhole and to cut it open.

Programmable Sewing Machines

Generally, operators must first load fabric pieces into the sewing machine and press a button to start the sewing. Fully automated machines are microprocessor controlled and sensor activated, with an arm to grasp the cloth, align the fabric, and move it through the machine. Programmable machines have been very successful at surging or seaming basic pieces in garment assembly.

However, automated sewing is a difficult task because of the handling of different types of fabrics as they are sewn. Moving silk through a sewing machine is very different from moving wool, for example. The clothing industry remains labor intensive for two reasons. First, textiles are floppy and soft, which makes it difficult for robots to handle them and for computers to simulate their shapes. Second, since the industry is fashion sensitive, automated machinery must be able to change as fashion does, and it is very expensive to reprogram the machinery.

Finishing

Tailoring, the unseen quality handwork formerly done inside collars and lapels to form and hold their shape, has virtually disappeared because of the high cost of skilled labor. Most "tailoring" today is done simply by fusing or machine basting interfacings into the garment to give it shape.

Hand finishing is usually seen only in couture garments. In better garments, some hand finishing is necessary, such as sewing in linings or sewing on buttons, but this too is becoming rare. In moderate-and lower-priced garments, all finishing is done by machine.

Production of Men's Suits

The production of men's suits is one area in which tailoring is still used.

Traditionally, the men's clothing industry has been divided into firms that produce tailored suits, coats, and trousers and furnishing producers that make shirts, ties, underwear, and sleepwear. Tailored garment production used to dominate the industry, but with the trend toward casual dress for men, there has been a growing demand for sportswear. The production of men's sportswear is similar to that of women's.

Production of a man's suit, however, can require more than 200 steps. Inner construction to give a suit shape and body makes production lengthy, complicated, and costly. Formerly, the industry used a numbered system to rate the quality of men's suits, on a scale from 1 for machine-made suits to 6 for hand-tailored suits. This rating is no longer used because hand tailoring has virtually disappeared.

Modern technology has introduced automation into an industry that was traditionally hand-work oriented. Fusible interfacing has replaced hand-applied canvas in chest pieces, shoulders,

TAILORING WORKROOMS AT HUNTSMAN, SAVILE ROW, LONDON. *(COURTESY OF HUNTSMAN)*

lapels, collars, and buttoning areas to supply the required body and shape. Hand tailoring can be found in only the most expensive suits, such as Hickey-Freeman and Oxxford in America, or custom-made and other high-quality suits made in Europe and Hong Kong. At Oxxford, for example, tailors still put more than 2000 hand stitches into the lapels of each suit jacket to give them a lasting roll.

Production Steps The following basic steps are used in the mass production of men's suits:

1. Fuse or hand-stitch interfacings and jump-baste chest pieces and bridal tape on lapel crease for support.

2. Press, line, and stitch on pockets.

3. Join main pieces together.

4. Set in sleeves.

5. Set in linings by machine or, in the case of an unlined jacket, bind seam edges.

6. Sew buttons and buttonholes.

Production of Knitwear

The production of knitwear requires special skills and machinery.

The two commercial methods of knitwear production are cut-and-sew and full-fashioned.

Cut-and-sew is a method by which garments are made from knitted fabrics. This type of knitted garment requires the same patterning as that used for woven fabrics, except that patternmakers must take the amount of stretch into consideration when making the patterns. Stretchability is the key to knitted garments; therefore, an overlock stitch is used because it is flexible and gives with the fabric. Knitted braids and bands must be used as trims and finishes because all components must have the same stretchability.

Full-fashioned knits, mostly sweaters, are actually shaped on the knitting machine. The specifications for each piece are programmed into the knitting machine, which forms the shape as it is knit by adding or dropping stitches at the edge of each piece to widen or narrow it. Then the pieces are joined together. Most full-fashioned production is done in Asia because manufacturers saw the potential of cheaper labor there and invested in specialized machinery. Factories in Asia provide both affordable prices and variety of production.

Computers have also changed the production time and cost of knitting. Computer-aided design (CAD) systems permit designers to see a pattern or garment design on the computer screen or printed out on paper without having to knit a sample. Knitting machines tied into the computerized design screens will accept pattern and stitch changes in minutes rather than hours, allowing greater freedom for experimentation. Each type of sweater, whether it is intarsia, Jacquard, shaker, cable, or pointelle, has a different lead time, quantity and weight of yarn required, gauge (stitch size), finishing treatments, and special skill and machinery needed to produce it.

Pattern is introduced by Jacquard and intarsia knitting systems. Jacquard patterns are created by various needle arrangements on electronic knitting machines. *Float Jacquard* shows the pattern on

■ JOINING SWEATER PIECES ON A LINKING MACHINE AT A KNITTING CONTRACTOR IN HONG KONG. *(COURTESY OF KATRENA BOTHWELL MEYER)*

267

the face of the sweater while the yarns are carried on the back until needed again for the pattern. To create a *full Jacquard*, both the front and back beds of the knitting machine are used, creating a heavier, double knit. The main design appears on the front, with another simple pattern on the back to avoid floats. For *intarsia* patterns, the yarn is knotted and cut off in back when no longer needed for the pattern on the front.

Some sweaters are also hand-knitted or crocheted. Hand knits have the greatest variety of stitches and detailing. However, because of the time needed to make them, they are very expensive. Hand-knit garments for commercial marketing are usually made abroad, where labor is cheaper and more readily available.

The Final Steps of Garment Production

Pressing or folding, sometimes washing and garment dyeing, labeling, and quality control are the last steps in garment production.

Dyeing and Washing

To ensure a perfect color match between garments to be worn together, a few manufacturers dye the finished garments, which are in this case made with greige goods. This also allows manufacturers to assort colors later, according to actual orders. However, garment dyeing is expensive, and it is difficult to control dye baths to prevent shading.

In jeanswear, washing is sometimes used to finish garments. For a bleached look, environmentally friendly enzyme and stone washes have replaced acids. A popular trend in sportswear today, especially for denim, is simply to wash and fold the items.

Pressing

Pressing vastly improves the look of a garment. It can hide a multitude of imperfections, such as puckered seams and collars that do not lie flat. Garments are pressed during the course of construction as well as at completion. Steam irons are used for areas not easily accessible.

Various buck pressing machines, like those seen at a dry cleaner, are used on tailored garments to flatten jacket edges, crease trousers, and so on. Automated pressing is done by computer-controlled pressing equipment.

Quality Control

Quality control is the standardization of production using specifications as guides. The last garment sewn should be the same as the first garment. A samplemaker can make one garment neatly and accurately, but it is more difficult to control quality in the mass production of 500 or 1000 dozen garments. To ensure that production has been done correctly and to prevent returns, both work-in-progress and finished garments are inspected either totally or by random sampling. Quality controllers not only check for poor sewing, but also spot-check measurements against original specifications. Quality control teams may travel to spot-check quality at contractors' facilities. If there are mistakes in *first stock*, the production manager tries to correct them at the sewing or cutting source.

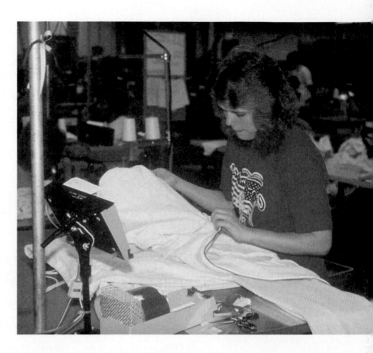

QUALITY CONTROL IS AN IMPORTANT PART OF APPAREL PRODUCTION. *(COURTESY OF THE NATIONAL COTTON COUNCIL)*

Production standards are very important and must equal the manufacturer's reputation and warrant the garment's price. It means nothing to have a beautifully designed garment if it is not produced well. Inferior garments may be rejected by the store and returned to the manufacturer, or they may look so unappealing on the hanger that customers will not buy them. Either event means a loss of reputation and future sales.

Computer bar coding or numbers on each garment's label identify the factory where the garment was made, enabling construction mistakes to be traced to their source. Besides construction mistakes, reasons for returns include poor fabric and fabric shading. The manufacturer tries to prevent these mistakes in future shipments.

Labeling

Labels are the sources of identification for garments. Along the production line, various labels must be attached to the garment. These include manufacturer and/or designer identification, fiber content, care instructions, country of origin, size, and a union label if made in a union shop. Federal law requires listing fibers in order of percentage used, along with cleaning or washing instructions.

Labels can help to establish the company's image. They tell the consumer the name of the brand and/or designer. Some people are attracted to a particular label or brand because of its reputation for quality or fit. The brand label is usually made of satin or twill ribbon and sewn inside the center-back neck, inside the waistband, or somewhere on the inside of the garment. It has even become fashionable to put labels on the outside of sportswear garments. Jeans often have a leatherlike printed patch sewn on the outside.

A label showing fiber content, care instructions, and country of origin must also be included in the garment. This information is usually on a separate small label under the brand label or on an inside seam.

There are pages of government regulations concerning fiber-content and country-of-origin labeling. Essentially, the predominant fiber in the garment is listed first along with its content percentage, followed by the other fibers in decreasing order of content. Care instructions are recommended and can be very specific. These instructions not only protect the consumer, but also protect the manufacturer against returns made by consumers who do not care for their garments as instructed.

A country-of-origin label is required by customs if the garment is made outside the United States. The label must say "Made in (name of country)" or "Made in USA of imported fabric." A "Made in USA" label is reserved for garments made entirely in the United States of domestic fabric. Items made partially in a foreign country and partially in the United States must disclose these facts; for example, a tag might read "Assembled and sewn in the USA of components made in (name of country)."

In addition, sportswear often has pressure-sensitive labels showing sizes on the outside of garments, particularly when they are folded. *Flashers*, printed cards that give product information, may be stapled to the outside of sportswear.

Hangtags, printed paper tags, may be hung from the garment by plastic staple, barb, or string. Hangtags are designed to draw attention to the garment and are hung on the side of the garment so that the customer can see them easily. They usually show the brand name and, perhaps, style number, color, size, and other product information. Sometimes hangtags are provided by fiber or fabric producers to promote their fibers or finishes.

Floor-Ready Standards

Striving for "seamless distribution" and hoping to trim distribution costs and put new merchandise on the sales floor more quickly, many retailers are requiring manufacturers to comply with "floor-ready" standards. Manufacturers are requested to preticket garments with bar-coded price tags provided by the retailer and to have the merchandise already on Voluntary Inter-industry Communications Standards (VICS) hangers. This eliminates the need for distribution centers to unpack shipments, tag and price goods, and put garments on hangers before repacking and shipping them to individual stores. VICS is also recommending improvements such as universal security tags, hanger recycling, and reinstituting direct shipments to stores. Radio-frequency technology (RF) allows garments to be embedded with tags that contain information on source of fabric, factory location, shipping, and importing.

Shipping

To further complicate matters, manufacturers have to choose from various combinations of transportation packages that must be negotiated. Manufacturers make these arrangements directly with contractors, through representatives, or through agents.

- **Free on board (FOB)** includes payment for the contractor to get the finished merchandise to the ship or plane in the country where it is made. The manufacturer has to arrange and pay separately for transportation and deal with *duties* (taxes on imported goods).
- **Landed, duty paid (LDP)** is a complete package, which pays the contractor to ship the merchandise, including paying duty, to the distribution center in the United States by a specified date. This costs more but is less bother.
- **Cost, insurance, freight (CIF)** pays for insurance and freight to the final destination.

Manufacturers must allow approximately 4 to 35 days for sea transportation, depending on origin, or 3 to 10 days for air delivery from Asia or Europe, plus trucking within the United States. Finished garments are returned to the manufacturer's distribution centers for shipping to retail stores.

Shipping to Retailers

At distribution warehouses, garments are checked for quality and then divided into groups according to style, size, and color and put into stock, a storage area where they may be hung on racks or stacked on shelves.

Retail orders for a certain quantity of units, on a form that includes entries for style number, color number, and price per unit, have been preanalyzed for a credit rating. Purchase order forms are becoming standardized, which makes ordering and shipping more efficient. The next step is to see what is available in stock to fill the order. Large orders and orders from important regular customers are filled first. Merchandise is pulled from stock to fill orders in the correct style, size, and color. Orders can be transmitted by EDI and then automatically translated into *advance shipping notices (ASNs)* and invoices. ASNs are sent to the store before the shipment arrives so that they know what it contains.

Garments are folded into shipping boxes and marked with the means of transportation specified by the retailer. Large manufacturers are using robotic automated warehouse equipment to speed packing. A packing slip (an invoice without prices) is enclosed in the box, while the actual invoice is mailed separately for payment. Manufacturers often use bar-coded "128" or "2D" cartons, which can be scanned at the retail distribution center to reveal the contents without opening the box. The boxes are labeled with addresses and then moved by trolley or conveyor belt to be loaded on the delivery truck and sent to the retailer.

On-time deliveries are extremely important to prevent cancellation of orders. On the basis of reliable production and delivery standards, a manufacturer builds and keeps a reputation for dependability that accompanies its reputation for innovative styling.

SUMMARY

IN THIS CHAPTER, WE DISCUSSED ALL THE ASPECTS OF GLOBAL SOURCING, GARMENT COSTING, PRICING, AND PRODUCTION SCHEDULING. WE HAVE SEEN HOW GARMENTS ARE MANUFACTURED, FROM PIECE GOODS PURCHASE AND INSPECTION, THROUGH PATTERNING, GRADING, MARKING, CUTTING, ASSEMBLY, AND FINISHING, TO QUALITY CONTROL. FACTORIES TRY TO USE THE NEWEST COMPUTER TECHNOLOGY, INCLUDING INVENTORY CONTROL AND ELECTRONIC DATA INTERCHANGE, AS WELL AS COMPUTER PATTERNMAKING, GRADING, MARKING, SPREADING, CUTTING, AND ASSEMBLY SYSTEMS TO REDUCE COSTS AND SPEED PRODUCTION. MEN'S SUITS AND KNITS PRESENT UNIQUE METHODS OF GARMENT PRODUCTION. QUALITY CONTROL AND ON-TIME DELIVERIES HELP THE MANUFACTURER TO MAINTAIN A GOOD REPUTATION FOR DEPENDABILITY.

Terms and Concepts

Briefly define and discuss the following terms and concepts:

1. Wholesale pricing
2. Cost sheet
3. Cost merchandising
4. Loss leader
5. Grading
6. Tight marker
7. Issue plan
8. Cut-to-order versus cut-to-stock
9. Piece goods
10. Contracting
11. Global sourcing
12. Laser-beam cutting
13. Offshore assembly
14. Piecework
15. Progressive-bundle assembly system

16. Computer-integrated manufacturing
17. Modular manufacturing
18. Unit production systems
19. Tailoring
20. Cut-and-sew knits
21. Full-fashioned knits
22. Quality control
23. Preticketing

Questions for Review

1. What factors are considered when costing and pricing a garment?
2. What are some of the things to consider when purchasing piece goods?
3. Discuss the differences between the cut-to-order and the cut-to-stock methods of production.
4. Briefly explain making and grading patterns on a computer.
5. Describe the differences among the major cutting methods.
6. Describe three ways in which computers aid apparel manufacturing.
7. Explain various systems of garment assembly.
8. Why do manufacturers use contractors?
9. Discuss what is involved in sourcing overseas production.
10. How has the construction of men's suits changed over the years?
11. Explain the two methods of producing knit garments.
12. Why is quality control so important?

Projects for Additional Learning

1. If there is an apparel contractor in your area, try to make an appointment for a factory tour. Observe production methods. Do operators do section work, or does one person sew one whole garment together? What computer technology is used in the factory? What production methods are unique to the product? Compare the wholesale price range of the garments being produced with the quality of production.

2. Investigate a major apparel manufacturer by interviewing managers, reading the company's annual report, reading trade newspaper articles about the company, or writing to the company for information. Write a profile of the company, including ownership, type of garments produced by each division, type of customer to which they appeal, type of production, price line, and where products are sold.

Notes

1 Bob Zane, former head of Manufacturing and Sourcing, Liz Clairborne, interview, April 30, 2003.

2 David G. Link, textile economist, E-mail correspondence, February 2003.

3 Zane, interview April 30, 2003.

OSCAR DE LA RENTA'S
MATCHING PRINT HANDBAG
AND DRESS.
*(COURTESY OF OSCAR DE LA RENTA,
PHOTO BY DAN LECCA)*

11

ACCESSORY AND FUR MANUFACTURING

Career Focus

Almost every category of accessories is a separate industry. Each area needs its own product developers, merchandisers, designers, patternmakers, production managers, marketers, and sales representatives. In the fur industry, production jobs are limited, but marketing careers are possible in major fur centers.

CHAPTER OBJECTIVES

After reading this chapter, you should be able to:

1. Discuss the unique design considerations of various accessories
2. Describe production methods for the major accessories
3. Explain accessory design and production centers
4. Discuss aspects of marketing for accessories
5. Explain fur garment production

This chapter discusses design, manufacturing, and marketing as they particularly apply to accessories and furs. Handbags, shoes, belts, gloves, and furs have in common the age-old use of animal skins as a raw material. Separate sections cover the styling and production of shoes, handbags, belts, gloves, hats, scarves, hosiery, jewelry, and furs, because each type of accessory has its individual methods for design and production. Although fur coats and jackets are wearing apparel, they are discussed separately because of the specialized methods used in their manufacture.

Fashion Accessories

Accessories are an important, integral part of the fashion business.

Over the last several years, the accessory industry has become one of the most exciting segments of manufacturing and retailing. Accessories are sometimes more important than ready-to-wear. Abe Chehebar, CEO of Accessory Network, explained, "Because accessories are so visible on the first floor of most retail stores, they communicate new fashion ideas, color, and designer or brand names to the consumer. Designers are communicating their image through their accessories."[1]

The shoe and hosiery businesses are dominated by large companies. Large international conglomerates own the luxury accessory brands. The largest is LVMH Moet Hennessy Louis Vuitton, followed by Compagnie Financière Richemont (Cartier), the Gucci Group (also owns Bottega Veneta), Chanel, and the Prada Group. In the United States, the handbag, glove, scarf, millinery, and jewelry industries have comprised many small firms all over the country. However, like the apparel business, there have been many consolidations, closings, and much competition from imports. This has led U.S. manufacturers to contract production overseas in order to offer competitive prices.

Product Diversification Well-known brands and designer names drive today's accessory business. Accessories such as shoes, handbags, belts, hats, and jewelry are designed to coordinate with apparel to create a total fashion look. Therefore, the fashion for particular accessories has been at the mercy of apparel designers and how they accessorize their designs on the runways.

Apparel Brands Add Accessories Apparel designers want accessories that are specifically created to go with their apparel collections. For this reason, many apparel companies have added accessory divisions through joint ventures or licensing arrangements (see Chapter 12) with accessory manufacturers. Even though the designer's name is on the product in the store, the product is produced and sometimes designed and/or marketed by an accessory manufacturer, marketer, or importer with expertise in that area. Accessory marketing benefits from the designer's apparel advertising and the resulting consumer name recognition. The house of Dior, for example, earns more than half its revenues from its accessories collections. .

Accessory Brands Add Apparel To balance product lines in the face of fashion cycles and to increase business by capitalizing on strong brand images, many accessory companies have diversified into other areas. One of the most notable developments in the fashion industry recently is the emergence of new apparel collections by accessory companies, such as Gucci, Hermès, Ferragamo, Louis Vuitton, Kenneth Cole (by Liz Claiborne), and Nine West (by Jones New York). Hermès, for example, launched its first ready-to-wear collection in 1997 and, in 2004, hired Jean-Paul Gaultier to design it. Ferragamo, the famous shoe manufacturer, also makes handbags, jewelry, and even ready-to-wear. Hermès has added ready-to-wear to its venerable line of scarves and leather goods. Kate Spade's handbag firm has added stationery, shoes, pajamas, luggage, scarves, and glove lines. Shoe designer Kenneth Cole has more than 30 licenses, including a sportswear line manufactured by Liz Claiborne. Accessories, however, usually generate the most profits for a company. Luxury brands such as Gucci, Louis Vuitton, Hermès, Prada, and Chanel make most of their money from a single accessory product group, leather goods.

■ AWARD-WINNING ACCESSORY DESIGNER KENNETH COLE NOW ALSO DESIGNS READY-TO-WEAR. *(COURTESY OF THE COUNCIL OF FASHION DESIGNERS OF AMERICA, PHOTO BY MARY HILLIARD)*

Product Development and Design The popularity of various accessories is cyclical and follows the same trends as apparel design. As fashion changes, so does the need for certain accessories. The fashion for belts is related to waist interest in apparel. Accessories such as jewelry and scarves become more important when clothing is classic and simply styled. Fashion in hats is related to hairstyles and weather. There are currently simultaneous trends for extravagant elegance and casual looks. Accessory manufacturers are catering to both.

Designers, merchandisers, and product managers of accessories must be aware of fashion trends to make accessories that successfully complement apparel. These individuals may attend the

Première Classe accessories show, held twice a year in Paris. They are influenced by the same factors as apparel designers (see Chapter 4) and develop their seasonal collections in much the same ways.

Accessory manufacturers have anywhere from one to five seasonal lines per year, depending on the type of accessory and its price range. Within each line, groups usually have a theme based on function, fabrications, quality, and/or price range.

Production   The differences in function and fabrication make production vastly different in each accessory area. Production methods are discussed separately under each category.

Each category of accessories is an industry unto itself. Shoes, handbags, and gloves share the same materials, but the skills and techniques needed to make them are very different. Scarves are basically textiles. Millinery uses textiles, straw, and leather. The jewelry industry, using metals and minerals, is totally different.

Except for hosiery, the accessory market is very involved with importing. High-end accessories from foreign manufacturers, such as Ferragamo and Gucci, are imported by retail stores. Other importers bring in merchandise to sell under retail store private-label brands. Also, because accessory production is labor intensive, many U.S. manufacturers have their merchandise produced in other countries where labor is cheaper: in Asia (especially China), the Philippines, Eastern Europe, and Central and South America. On the other hand, some U.S. accessory manufacturers have had success exporting.

Counterfeiting   One of the most difficult problems for luxury accessory firms is trademark infringement, or counterfeit merchandise sold illegally. These brands create desire with their advertising, and, therefore, everyone wants to have this merchandise. However, when it comes to counterfeits, luxury brands do not believe that imitation is the sincerest form of flattery.

Counterfeiting is difficult to control internationally because a design must be registered separately in every marketplace. The cost of registration and legal fees is very high, and these fees must be paid in every country. Luxury companies have invested millions of dollars in an enormous counterfeit crackdown, including investigations and lawsuits. These efforts make the products even more expensive. Some companies are trying to identify original products with holograms (encrypted codes), or with infrared and ultraviolet inks.

The U.S. Customs and Border Protection Service has confiscated millions of counterfeit accessories, particularly handbags and watches, 70 percent of which come from China. An agreement was reached between China and the United States to protect trademarks, but it is difficult to enforce.

Marketing   Marketing methods vary from company to company depending on the type of accessory and price range. Most manufacturers show their new collections in their New York showrooms during market weeks. They also may have showrooms in major market centers around the country, such as Los Angeles, Dallas, Atlanta, or Chicago, as well as sales representatives who call on retail store buyers across the country. Manufacturers may show their products at the AccessoriesTheShow or Accessories Circuit three times a year in New York City, showing spring and summer merchandise in January, fall merchandise in May, and holiday and resort merchandise in August (or at an additional show in Las Vegas in August). Accessory companies also advertise heavily; luxury brands spend 6 to 10 percent of total sales revenues on advertising.

Accessory manufacturers are using E-commerce and setting up Web sites. Initially, they used the Internet to make their brands known and to educate consumers. Some companies, such as Louis Vuitton, Dooney & Bourke, and Fossil, have online catalogs. Customers can see the products up close and three dimensionally. Sites are updated frequently to show seasonal and holiday merchandise.

In another effort to control merchandising and image and have direct access to consumers, many accessory companies have opened their own retail stores. In Europe, it is common for accessory companies such as Ferragamo, Gucci, and Aigner to own retail stores. Also, U.S. shoe companies have traditionally had retail stores in order to stock sufficient inventory and maintain trained sales staffs. However, retailing is a fairly new idea for most accessory manufacturers in the United States. Now accessory companies, such as Nike, Carlos Falchi, Robert Lee Morris, and Carolee, have opened their own specialty stores. These stores provide accessory manufacturers with increased brand awareness and the opportunity to present their entire collections unedited by buyers, as well as to make customer contact.

Accessory manufacturers also have merchandise representatives who work at multibrand retail stores to educate sales associates, arrange merchandise displays, and help customers. Accessory designers may make personal appearances in stores to promote sales and test consumer reactions to new styles. Many stores also have in-store boutiques featuring brand-name and designer accessories. Bloomingdale's, for example, has accessory boutiques for Salvatore Ferragamo, Louis Vuitton, Chanel, and Judith Leiber.

Large retail store accessory departments have traditionally been on the main floor. Now many retailers have opened additional accessory shops on their ready-to-wear floors next to apparel to help to sell accessories and to help the consumer find a complete outfit in one area. Retailers may also have accessories produced for them to sell exclusively.

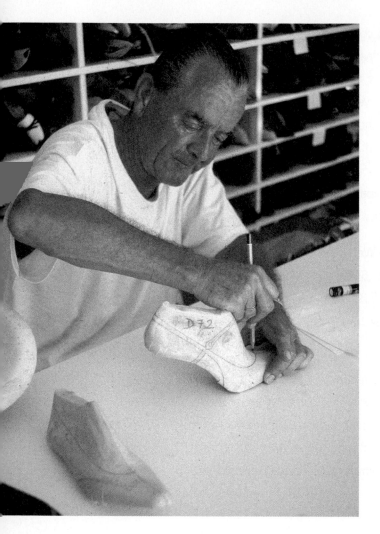

ITALIAN SHOE
DESIGNER ANDREA
PFISTER AT WORK IN
HIS STUDIO.
*(COURTESY OF
ANDREA PFISTER,
PHOTO BY MARY
TRASKO)*

Footwear

Footwear, including shoes, sandals, and boots, is the largest category of accessories. More than seven billion pairs of shoes are produced worldwide each year. Both functional and fashionable, shoes come in assorted materials, including calf, kid, suede, and reptile skins; imitation leathers; and fabrics such as canvas or nylon.

Today the shoe industry caters to both dress and casual trends. As a result of the enormous popularity of sport shoes, comfort has become an important element of shoe design. A number of popular shoe brands, from Beautyfeel to Ferragamo, have tried to combine style with the comfort of athletic shoes.

Design of Leather Fashion Shoes

Most dress shoe design direction comes from Europe. Shoe designers study fashion trends so that their shoes will coordinate with apparel. Creative international shoe designers such as Andrea Pfister, Manolo Blahnik, and Robert Clegerie set international trends for women's fashion shoes.

Many mainstream shoe company designers or *line builders* (product managers) attend the Lineapelle Leather Show in Bologna, Italy, and shoe fairs such as MICAM in Milan, Italy, to get ideas for a new shoe collection. Like an apparel merchandiser, the line builder begins with concepts for groups and works with designers who develop individual shoe styles. Designers are primarily concerned with materials, color, shape, and proportion. They must consider the view of the shoe from all angles.

Many shoe companies are using computer-aided design (CAD) systems that are capable of both two-dimensional design (design of uppers and size grading) and three-dimensional design (design of the last, a foot-shaped form, and projection of the drawing on the last).

Sometimes the line builder will buy *prototypes* (sample shoes) from a *modelista* (model maker) at a studio or factory. Or the line builder might forward a designer's sketches to a modelista, who makes the first model. If the line builder and modelista live in different countries, ideas and samples must be sent back and forth by the Internet or fax. The sample shoes are edited to form a balanced collection. Duplicates are then made for the sales staff, showroom, and trade shows.

Some shoe manufacturers develop collections for apparel designers through joint ventures or licensing arrangements. The shoe designer develops the shoes to complement the apparel designer's styles and colors. The apparel designers contribute design direction and have approval authority, but do not actually design the shoes.

Leather Sourcing

Leather sourcing is usually close to production: Italian leather for shoes produced in Italy, South American leather for Brazilian-made shoes, and Chinese leather for Asian-made shoes. However, leather is sometimes sourced in one country, sent to another for production, and marketed in a third country.

Imports

The increasing number of imports has had an enormous impact on the U.S. shoe industry. As there are no quotas on shoe imports, they have reached a new high of 98 percent of the 1.1 billion (nonrubber) pairs purchased in the United States.[2] China leads in shoe exports to the United States, followed by Brazil, Indonesia, Vietnam, and Italy.[3]

The highest-quality women's fashion shoes, such as Manolo Blahnik, Robert Clegerie, Patrick Cox, Ferragamo, Christian Louboutin, Bruno Magli, Andrea Pfister, Prada, Sergio Rossi, and Stuart Weitzman, are made by hand in Italy with the finest leathers. Some women's manufacturers, such as Magli and Ferragamo, also make men's shoes. Italian manufacturers such as Borri and Lorenzo Banfi specialize in high-quality men's shoes. Most high-end U.S. shoe manufacturers contract production in Italian factories.

Bridge lines, such as Ellen Tracy, Via Spiga, and DKNY, may be made in Italy or Spain. Better shoes, including Liz Claiborne, Nickels, Caressa, and Pappagallo, are typically made in Spain, Brazil, or China.

Moderate, budget, and sport shoes are usually made in China, Korea, or Mexico. Manufacturers are always seeking new, cheaper production sources. Some companies buy production time in overseas factories; others own facilities in Italy, Spain, or South America. China now makes 80 percent of all shoes sold in the United States.

Production of Traditional Leather Shoes

Traditional shoe production is complex, involving various measurements for length and width combinations. The full range of women's shoe sizes includes 103 width and length combinations between sizes 5 and 10. Shoes for the U.S. market are made according to U.S. sizing specifications. European shoes have only one width, whereas European shoes exported to the United States are usually made available in four widths.

Another factor contributing to the complexity of leather shoe production is the skilled labor needed to complete the number of operations performed. Two to three hundred operations can go into

TEST OF A
PAPER SHOE
PATTERN ON
A WOODEN
LAST. *(COURTESY
OF FERRAGAMO,
FLORENCE, ITALY)*

the production of a finely made fashion shoe. If a shoe is made in a factory, 80 different machines could be involved in its production. Shoe parts must be joined together for a smooth, perfect fit. Whether a shoe is handmade or mass-produced, there are usually nine basic steps:

1. **Making the last**—A foot-shaped form called a *last* is created. The original last is made of wood and requires as many as 35 different measurements. A shoe factory needs thousands of lasts, one for each size, width, heel height, and basic style. Duplicate polyethylene lasts are made from the master.

2. **Patternmaking**—A pattern is created based on measurements taken from the last and from the original *pullover model,* which is sewn and tacked onto a last. A trial shoe is made from this pattern. The line builder further assesses and refines style selections at this time, and the final line is closed or "frozen." Trials are duplicated as samples for sales representatives.

3. **Cutting**—Paper patterns are converted into steel dies that cut the leather. Modern factories use programmed continuous-cutting machines or water-jet cutters to cut the leather.

4. **Stitching and fitting**—The upper portion of the shoe is made, including buttonholes, topstitching, and all other upper design details. Then linings are added.

5. **Lasting**—The shoe upper is pulled over the last and attached to the innersole.

ATTACHING A LEATHER SHOE UPPER TO A LAST. *(COURTESY OF BALLY OF SWITZERLAND)*

6. **Bottoming**—The sole is attached to the upper by sewing, cementing, vulcanizing, nailing, stapling, or molding. Most shoe soles are cemented to the uppers.

7. **Heeling**—Heels, premolded in plastic and covered with leather or wood, are attached.

8. **Finishing**—The finished shoes are polished, and the last is removed.

9. **Treeing**—Shoes are dried and receive a final inspection. Tissue and sticks are put into the shoes to help them to retain their shape.

Large factories have a competitive edge because they have the capital necessary to invest in the most advanced machinery and computer technology. Widespread use of *computer-aided shoe-making systems* enables manufacturers to speed production, improve quality, and keep labor costs down. Programmable machines are now available for nearly every aspect of production, including sewing and lasting.

Domestic shoe production has declined so that there are only about 60 small shoe manufacturers left in the United States. The small amount of domestic shoe production left, primarily of men's shoes, is done in New England and the Midwest. These firms include better classic men's shoes such as Johnston & Murphy, Allen-Edmonds, Cole-Haan, and Alden, and moderate shoe lines such as Florsheim, Bass, Dexter, and Bostonian. In the future, it seems that weaker firms will continue to close, while stronger ones will consolidate plants and invest in new technology to narrow the gap between foreign and U.S. labor costs.

Marketing   Most shoe importers, such as Schwartz & Benjamin, are essentially marketers. They buy or license the designs and contract production. They operate this way because they believe they know what their customers in their own countries want and, therefore, can market the shoes more effectively than foreign manufacturers.

Shoe companies may have shoe lines in all price ranges and categories. For example, Nine West has acquired the Bandolino and Easy Spirit brands from the former U.S. Shoe Company.

Retail buyers shop important shoe fairs so they can see merchandise from all over the world at one time. MICAM, the prestigious international shoe fair, is held in Milan in March to show fall styles and in September to show spring styles. Other important international markets include the GDS footwear show in Düsseldorf, MIDEC in Paris, and FICC in Elda, Spain. The Fashion Footwear Association of New York (FFANY) holds six markets a year in New York. The largest shoe show is organized by the World Shoe Association (WSA) in Las Vegas each February and August. Retail buyers shop for early spring styles in June, for spring and summer styles in August, for early fall styles in December, and for fall and holiday styles in February.

Because of the large inventories needed to stock shoes in all styles, colors, sizes, and widths, many shoe manufacturers own their own stores. Nine West (owned by Jones Apparel) and Florsheim, for example, have their own shoe stores. Some also lease departments from department and specialty stores, but this practice is on the decline.

Shoe manufacturers use methods such as the Internet and seminars to educate consumers and sales personnel about quality and styling. Some shoe companies, such as Ferragamo and Nine West, also manufacture handbags.

Handbags

A handbag must be both decorative and functional; it must hold necessities conveniently as well as fit into the fashion picture. Handbag styles range from classic to trendy and constructed to soft shapes. Leather, including suede and reptile, still represents approximately half of handbag material; vinyl, fabric (tapestry, rug prints, needlepoint, silk, wool, nylon, and canvas), and straw make up the other half. Materials vary from year to year along with fashion trends. Some manufacturers, such as Louis Vuitton and Bottega Veneta, specialize in personalized fabrics. Fendi, Gucci, Marc Jacobs, Prada, and Tods are among the trendsetters in handbag design.

Product Development and Design

The elements of fabrication (leather or fabric), silhouette, and color, as well as current trends in ready-to-wear and footwear, are the most important components of handbag design. From an initial sketch, a sample is made from muslin or imitation leather. A final sample is made up in leather or fabric with appropriate supportive stays (made of treated paper). Felt, foam, and fabric interlinings may be layered around the stays to give the bag a nice hand and cushion. Hardware is also a key element in design, sometimes the main feature. Ornaments, closures, zippers, and/or handles must be chosen to complement the shape and fabrication. Linings differ with each type of bag and each fabrication.

Within a collection, groups may be based on fabrications, color, silhouettes, hardware, or other themes. Usually, a variety of silhouettes are included, perhaps in various fabrications (or types of leather). Several groups create a well-rounded collection. The product development team—the designer, patternmaker, samplemaker, production manager, and sales managers—critique the samples. The most successful designs are chosen for the collection.

Production

When the final line is chosen, cutting dies are made from the pattern and used to stamp out the pieces of leather, or the leather may be cut by water jet. Rising prices and reduced availability of leather in recent years have had a great impact on the styling and production of handbags. Fabric bags are cut by hand or by small rotary cutting machines.

Luxury Handbags The type and quality of workmanship varies greatly. At the top of the luxury market are Hermès handbags, which are entirely handcrafted. Production is deliberately limited and is allocated by the number of hours it takes to make a bag. For example, it takes 16 hours to make a "Kelly handbag," which costs over $5000. Each bag is dated and stamped with the craftsperson's initials. Distribution is limited to maintain exclusivity.

■ TOP LUXURY HANDBAGS ARE STILL MADE BY HAND. BEATRICE AMBLARD SEWS A HANDBAG AT APRIL IN PARIS. *(PHOTO BY GINI STEPHENS FRINGS)*

Luxury handbag manufacturers are now offering handbags in a variety of prices to attract a wider range of customers. Dior's saddle bag, for example, is available in 125 versions, from $600 for one made of canvas to $10,500 for alligator skin! Most luxury handbags are made in Italy, including those for Celine, Chanel, Bottega Veneta, Prada, Fendi, Tod's, and Ferragamo.

Interest in artisan skills and the traditional apprentice system is dying out in Europe and North America. Some Italian firms are trying to encourage young people to learn the technical skills needed to carry on the tradition of quality production of luxury leather goods. Companies such as Bottega Veneta (owned by Gucci), along with local trade schools, have set up three-year educational programs.

Designer and Better Handbags In the production of better handbags, both fabrics and leathers may be stitched by machine, but much of the assembly of linings, ornaments, handles, and closures is still done by hand. Although this handwork is expensive, some handbags are still made in the United States, primarily in New York, Maine, Connecticut, Massachusetts, and Florida. However, to keep costs down, most manufacturers source worldwide for the cheapest labor so that imports, especially from China, are increasing. Other handbag production sources include South America, Indonesia, Korea, Taiwan, and India.

Domestic designer handbag collections include Lambertson Truex, Carlos Falchi, and Kate Spade. Apparel designer handbag collections, such as Michael Kors, Oscar de la Renta, Marc Jacobs, and Donna Karan, are licensed to handbag manufacturers who pay them royalties for the use of their names; bridge brands include Coach, Etienne Aigner, and Dooney & Bourke.

Moderate and Inexpensive Handbags Moderate bags are sometimes made of leather, but usually of vinyl or fabric. Examples of moderate brands are Kenneth Cole, Nine West, Liz Claiborne, and Esprit. Moderately priced bags are primarily imported. Handbag imports have risen to approximately 80 percent of U.S. consumption, mostly from China.

Many retail stores create *private-label* handbags in all price categories in order to attain exclusivity and higher gross margins. The retailer works directly with a manufacturer or importer, labels the handbags with the store's private brand, and eliminates the cost of wholesale marketing.

Marketing Many handbag manufacturers show their collections at Mipel, the Italian trade fair, in Milan twice a year. U.S. collections are shown in New York and regional showrooms, as well as at trade shows such as Accessories Circuit and The Accessories Show. The two major handbag markets occur in February for the fall and in August for the spring.

MARKETING
DIRECTOR KAREN
WEISS SHOWING A
HANDBAG LINE IN
THE ACCESSORY
NETWORK
SHOWROOM.
*(PHOTO BY GINI
STEPHENS FRINGS)*

Makers of luxury handbags have attracted attention for their huge price tags that run into the thousands of dollars. Prices for European imports have risen so sharply in recent years, due partly to the weak dollar, that retailers are seeking domestic suppliers at lower price ranges. Now prices of less expensive designer bags are also rising as more companies enter the $400-to-$700 price range. However, although 7 percent of handbag sales were for luxury bags, most women spend far less.[4]

Belts

The fashion for belts in women's wear is *apparel driven* (corresponding to waist interest in apparel styling) and is, therefore, cyclical. In women's wear, a return to classic apparel means a rise in belt sales. Fashion belts are made of lightweight leathers and suedes, metallics, woven cord, metal chain, fabrics, and elasticized fabrics. Men's belts are strictly functional and must withstand everyday wear, so they are traditionally made of heavy (5- or 6-ounce) leather. Hardware, especially buckles, is extremely important, especially in classic belts.

287

Many apparel companies, such as Chanel, Donna Karan, Calvin Klein, and Liz Claiborne, have belts manufactured to accessorize with their clothes. Accessory companies such as Hermès, Ferragamo, and Gucci also make belts to coordinate with their handbags. These firms try to carry a design element throughout their accessory lines. A chain belt might repeat the design of a chain strap on a handbag, or a handbag clasp might be copied as a belt buckle.

Production   Leather and imitation leather materials are cut on *strap-cutting* machines or on computer-aided cutting machines. These machines cut the material into long, straight lengths of any desired width. Shaped belts are made either by die cutting or from Plexiglas patterns. With die cutting, the pattern is made into a die resembling a cookie cutter. A *clicker* machine presses the sharp edges of the die through the leather. Plexiglas patterns are used like paper patterns for single-layer cutting. The cutter must carefully cut around the patterns, using only flawless pieces of leather. Computer-automated cutting has helped to speed up production and ensure accuracy.

The cut leather is then sewn or laminated to a backing with a *walking-foot machine* or on computer-automated machines. Belt buckles, made from metal, wood, or plastic, come mostly from Italy (for high-priced lines) or Taiwan. Sterling silver buckles also come from the Southwest for western-inspired styles. Holes are made at one end of the belt by a foot-press or kick-press machine. The holes, the slit for the buckle, and the shape of the tip may also be cut by a die. In addition, a die can emboss a pattern onto the leather. Belts are finished with trims, such as stitching, cording, nail heads, or rhinestones, and may have an edge finish.

Belt manufacturers tend to be small firms. The industry is centered in the New York metropolitan area because of that city's proximity to suppliers, but production is also growing in California. A large investment in equipment is needed to finish leather well, but some of the operations can be contracted out. As in the manufacture of other accessories, belt production has moved extensively to Asia, especially China.

Markets   As with handbags, belt markets are held five times a year in New York and market center showrooms. Belt manufacturers also show at the Fashion Accessories Expo.

Gloves

Gloves are both functional and fashionable. They are needed to protect hands for work and sports or from the cold. The fashion aspect is cyclical; gloves are more in demand when fashion apparel is elegant.

Product Development and Design   Glove manufacturers have only one line per year, which is shown in November for the following fall and winter. This means that designers must work up to two years in advance of the selling season. The timing is very difficult because designers want their gloves to accessorize with apparel, particularly outerwear. Therefore, they have to be aware of apparel trends well in advance. Designers may travel to Europe to study apparel, as well as the Italian glove market, for ideas.

Like other accessories and apparel, glove collections are usually divided into groups. The basis for the groups might be function, such as dressy or sophisticated, tailored or classic, outdoor or country. Groups are also often based on materials: deerskin, pigskin, suede, shearling, cashmere knits, wool knits, fleece, or nylon. Linings are the second most important component and may be made of silk, cashmere, microfibers, olefin and polyester insulating fabrics, fleece, or wool.

A variety of colors is presented within each group. Black remains the most popular color for dress gloves, but brights are also included in glove collections. Natural colors predominate in casual leather gloves, and a variety of colors is found in fleece or ski gloves.

Production   Glove production in the United States was originally centered in Fulton County, New York. However, domestic industry employment is now only about 2000. Glove firms have remained small because of their specialized, handcrafted operations. Most gloves are still produced by a painstaking process that requires many hand operations.

Fine gloves are still table cut from patterns one at a time because this method is most precise. There are pieces for the front and back of the hand, the thumb, the *fourchettes* (pieces that shape the fingers between front and back), and sometimes *quirks* (small triangular pieces sewn between the fingers in expensive gloves). The leather is kept damp during cutting and sewing. Because of the curved seams, a glovemaker can only sew up to 12 pairs a day on a sewing machine, a French pique machine, or by hand. Gloves are hemmed and may be lined with knit, pile, or thermal fabrics. Dress gloves may be trimmed with real and fake fur, buttons, bows, braid, embroidery, lace, tassels, and zippers. Finished gloves are rolled or layered in damp cloths and then fitted on heated brass hands, called *laying-off boards,* which press them to take out wrinkles and straighten seams. Finished gloves are buffed to a glossy finish.

Less expensive gloves are made with less expensive materials and may have fewer pieces. They can be cut faster with patterns made into iron dies. In this case, a clicker machine presses the sharp edges of the die through the leather. Some gloves are knit, but even those are labor intensive because the fingers are closed by hand.

Some glove companies also produce scarves, hats, socks, or mittens. Aris Isotoner has added slippers, socks, and umbrellas to its product lines. Major U.S. manufacturers include Aris Isotoner, Fownes, Gates, and Grandoe. LaCrasia and Carolina Amato make high-fashion gloves. Glove companies continually work on production innovation, waterproofing techniques, and washability.

Imports   Almost all fine gloves are now imported. Italy has been a traditional leader in the glove industry; some Italian glove companies produce their own lines, as well as gloves for major designers. Portolano, for example, also produces for Moschino, Fendi, and Barry Kieselstein Cord. Many European and U.S. glove manufacturers have either purchased plants or use contractors in China, Hong Kong, or the Philippines. Grandoe, for example, has its own plants in the Philippines, China, and India. Some wholesalers (as compared to manufacturers), such as Shalimar, simply buy gloves directly from factories in Italy, Portugal, or Romania.

Marketing   Glove manufacturers show their dress lines in November and sport styles in January each year in their own New York showrooms and/or take part in one of the accessories exhibitions. Many glove lines are not marketed under the manufacturer's name, but carry the retailer's label. Grandoe, for example, makes gloves for the L.L. Bean, Nordstrom, and Saks Fifth Avenue labels. Gates makes gloves for Eddie Bauer. For branded gloves, manufacturers often provide hangtags with product care information and in-store training to educate salespeople and to promote sales. Like other accessory manufacturers, some glove companies are opening their own stores. LaCrasia, for example, has its own store called Glove Street.

Hats

In the past, the most important accessory was a hat. A woman bought a new hat to add a bright spot to her wardrobe; a businessman was never seen on the street without one. The trend toward more casual lifestyles changed that, and the *millinery* industry (traditional name for the hat industry) suffered a severe setback. Of course, functional hats to protect against the cold weather and the sun remained a necessity. Today, hats are enjoying something of a comeback, for fashion and for fun.

Product Development and Design   Hat manufacturers produce two seasonal collections per year. The spring collection is centered around a wide variety of straws and fabrics such as cotton and linen. Fall collections are dominated by felt and fabrications of velvet, velveteen, fake fur, and corduroy.

Hat collections are usually divided into groups organized around fabrications, color schemes, themes, or price ranges. Hat designers are aware of fashion trends, especially color projections, and use many of the same design sources as apparel designers.

HAT DESIGNER PATRICIA UNDERWOOD AT WORK IN HER SUNNY NEW YORK STUDIO. *(PHOTO BY GINI STEPHENS FRINGS)*

Designers and Manufacturers   Successful hat designers include Eric Javits, Stephen Jones, Kokin, Philip Treacy, and Patricia Underwood. Leading apparel designers such as Donna Karan, Ralph Lauren, and Calvin Klein also have hat lines to complement their clothing. These are usually made by hat manufacturers as joint ventures or via licences.

There are a few large hat manufacturers in the United States such as Betmar and Commodore, but most are small. More than 100 companies manufacture hats in the United States, primarily in New York City and the Los Angeles area, but also in Chicago, Texas, and Florida. World centers include Paris, Milan, Germany, England, and Australia.

Production   Designer millinery is made of the finest materials. Natural straw, imported from China, Indonesia, Japan, Ecuador, or the Philippines, or felt is first steamed and then hand blocked over wooden forms. *Blocking* makes the straw or felt into the shape of a hat. The edges can be hand trimmed and then wired or bound with ribbon. The best-quality ribbons, flowers, and other trims are applied by hand.

Hats in the inexpensive to moderate price range are machine blocked by a stamper (metal on metal) or a hydraulic press (a rubber inset mold presses on metal). New machinery from Italy

291

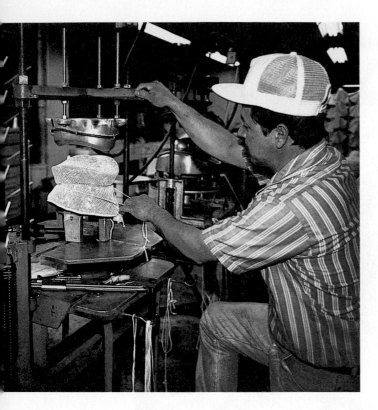

BLOCKING A HAT FORM BY MACHINE. *(PHOTO BY GINI STEPHENS FRINGS)*

automatically regulates the heat and timing for steaming and blocking. Decorative trims are applied by hand.

Soft hats and caps are made from fabrics. Patterns are made for the crown and brim of the hat and used to cut the fabrics. The pieces are sewn together, some over stiffening material, and then hand trimmed.

Marketing   Market week for early spring lines is in November, spring-summer market week is in January, fall market week is in May, and holiday-resort market week is in August. The manufacturers first show their collections in their New York showrooms, and then at regional markets. They may also show their collections at the Fashion Accessories Expo or Accessories Circuit in January, May, and August. Some designers show at the same time as the apparel shows. Manufacturers also have sales representatives at major market centers such as Los Angeles, Atlanta, Chicago, and Dallas. The Headwear Information Bureau gives annual "Milli" awards for outstanding hat design.

At retail stores, hat manufacturers use sales training and personal appearances in the stores to promote their designs. Many upscale stores create comfortable areas with chairs, mirrors, and special lighting for their customers to try on hats. Some stores are opening hat shops on apparel floors to help customers to accessorize their clothing purchases.

Scarves

The popularity of scarves, shawls, and stoles, like other accessories, is cyclical. Design is usually based on historic textiles, fine art, and ornate architecture, as well as apparel trends. A collection includes groupings based on motifs, fabrications, colorways, and scarf shapes. Scarf manufacturers may either buy a print design from a design studio or have their own in-house artist.

Scarves can be made of silk, wool, cashmere, cotton, or man-made fibers. Pashmina, a luxurious cashmere from the Capra Hircus mountain goat, is particularly popular for shawls and is often blended with silk. Fabrications include challis, sheers, metallics, and knits that can be printed, embroidered, or beaded.

SCARF DESIGNERS AND COLORISTS AT WORK AT ACCESSORY STREET, NEW YORK CITY. *(PHOTO BY GINI STEPHENS FRINGS)*

Production   The production of scarf fabrics, particularly silk, rayon, or polyester, is the same as for other woven textiles (see Chapter 6). The difference is in the printing and finishing. A small percentage of scarves, those made of the finest fabrics, are made in Italy and France. Most of the printing is done by silk screen, which lends itself to the square or rectangular shape of the print. Hermès, which makes the finest scarves, uses an average of 24 color screens and up to 50 screens for their highest quality! Less expensive scarves use only 4 to 10 color screens. The printed fabric is cut and then hand rolled, machine rolled, flat hemmed, or fringed.

Most scarf production is located in Asia, where expertise as well as inexpensive labor can be found. Many U.S. manufacturers buy their fabrics in Japan, Korea, or China and have the scarves printed there as well. Solid or textured scarves are cut and sewn from available fabrics from textile companies.

Designers such as Ralph Lauren and Donna Karan also have scarves made for them in licensing arrangements or joint ventures. Collection XIIX, for example, manufactures Anne Klein and Ellen Tracy scarves as well as its own brand. Accessory Street makes scarves for Oscar de la Renta and

Adrienne Vittadini to coordinate with their apparel collections. Echo produces scarves for Ralph Lauren, Laura Ashley, and Coach.

The three market seasons are spring-summer, shown to buyers in November and January; fall, shown in March; and holiday, shown in May and August. The high price of silk and the cost of labor have made the scarf business very competitive. Retailers have to order early to get on-time deliveries because of the long lead time involved in overseas production. Some retailers act as manufacturers by importing scarves and selling them under the store's private label. Scarf manufacturers have developed videos and brochures on how to wear scarves to help the customer and to promote sales.

Hosiery

Hosiery serves as both a fashion accessory and a practical covering to keep the feet and legs warm. Major changes in the recent history of the women's hosiery business include the development of nylon stockings in 1940, which were stronger and more uniform than silk, and the development

JOINING THE LEGS TOGETHER IN HOSIERY PRODUCTION. (COURTESY OF WOLFORD, AUSTRIA)

of pantyhose in 1965, which liberated women from gartered stockings, were more comfortable, and dominated the industry almost overnight. Today, hosiery is manufactured in a wide range of knits, colors, and categories, such as sheers, support, opaques, tights, and socks. The men's business, of course, is all socks.

Trends   Manufacturers of women's hosiery are now offering consumers more variety in large and petite sizes for better fit, and figure-enhancing products such as control-top pantyhose. Panty-hose are offered in a variety of styles, including leggings, opaque tights, fishnets, micromesh, lace, glitter, and multicolor patterns. In response to casual dressing, the sheer hosiery business has decreased, whereas tights and casual socks have grown to be a major part of the business. The fashion for pattern or color on the legs is cyclical and, as with other accessories, depends on what designers use on the runways and skirt lengths.

Product Development   The number of seasonal hosiery lines varies from two to four depending on the manufacturer and the price range. Some companies specialize in sheers and tights or socks; others make both. Collections are usually grouped by construction categories, such as pantyhose, control-top hose, support hose, stockings, thigh-highs, and socks. Constant research is done to develop better constructions and a variety of cotton, nylon, microfiber, and spandex com-binations. Within each group there is an assortment of colors and, in the case of socks, a variety of patterns.

Production   Hosiery is produced in knitting mills where machines run 24 hours a day. Panty-hose and socks are both knit on automated circular knitting machines with special techniques to shape the heel. Sock machines use thicker yarn and fewer needles. Knitting machines have become more productive, capable, and flexible with electronic patterning to enable individual control of every stitch. The steps involved in hosiery production are knitting, dyeing, drying, *boarding* (a heat-setting process), pairing (for stockings and socks), labeling, and packaging.

There are approximately 800 hosiery mills in the United States, located primarily in North Carolina, making hosiery the second-largest accessory industry. It is dominated by large companies, such as Berkshire, Ithaca, Kayser-Roth, Pennaco, and Sara Lee. Sara Lee, for example, owns both Hanes and L'eggs and has the Donna Karan, DKNY tights, and Liz Claiborne licenses. Kayser-Roth owns No-Nonsense, Burlington, and Hue Hosiery and has the Calvin Klein license. Sock manufacturers include Bonnie Doon, Burlington, Gold Toe (Great American Knitting Mills), Hot Sox, and Trimfit. Designers and designer brands such as Giorgio Armani, Kenneth Cole, Christian Dior, Givenchy, Donna Karan, Calvin Klein, and Ralph Lauren have hosiery and socks produced for them by licensing arrangements.

Hosiery manufacturers attend the biennial International Hosiery Exposition in Charlotte, North Carolina, every other April. There they look for information on the newest equipment and services, such as automated sewing machinery, linking and labeling systems, packaging, and display forms.

Marketing   Hosiery manufacturers also maintain sales headquarters and showrooms in New York City and sales representatives to work directly with their retail clients around the country. The two main markets are in March for the fall lines and in September for the spring lines. More fashion-oriented lines, such as Calvin Klein from Kayser-Roth, may be shown four times a year with apparel collections. Basic hosiery lines change little and are constantly replenished in the stores.

The hosiery business is extremely competitive. Hosiery manufacturers have huge national advertising budgets. They also invest in other promotional material, such as informative packaging, point-of-sale visuals, in-store events, and merchandisers. Merchandisers help to stock shelves, train salespeople, and generally do whatever is necessary to ensure that their products are well placed in the sales area.

Stock replenishment is especially important in the hosiery business. Manufacturers take responsibility to see that stores consistently maintain complete inventories of all sizes in each style category. Manufacturers use replenishment systems such as electronic data interchange (EDI) and bar coding to keep track of and continually replace inventory. Keeping a supply of undyed (greige) stock is a new inventory strategy offered by some mills; retailers can place special orders for specific colors, depending on consumer demand, that can be filled in a few days.

Jewelry

Because jewelry is made from metals and stones, it is a completely different industry from the other accessory businesses that use leather or fabrics. It would take an entire book to describe the many facets of the design, production, and marketing of jewelry. Both fine and costume jewelry have been particularly strong as fashion designers have been featuring jewelry in large doses on the runway. Following is an overview of fine, bridge, and costume jewelry.

Fine Jewelry   *Fine jewelry* is made of precious metals and gemstones; it is made by hand or with settings reproduced by casting. The quality of craftsmanship, the beauty of the design, and

JEWELRY DESIGNER ROBERT LEE MORRIS AT WORK IN HIS STUDIO. *(COURTESY OF ROBERT LEE MORRIS)*

the value of the metals and gemstones determine the cost. Because fine jewelry is usually a life-long investment, its design is often classic. However, there is increased demand for fashion and innovation in fine jewelry.

Metals Only precious metals such as 10-, 14-, or 18-karat gold, platinum, and sterling silver are used to make fine jewelry. Since precious metals in their pure state are generally too soft to retain shape or to hold stones securely, they are combined with other metals. Gold alloys are made with copper, silver, palladium, or nickel (white gold). Gold content is expressed in *karats;* 24 karats is pure gold; 14 karats is 58.3 percent gold. Platinum is mixed with silvery metals such as palladium. Silver must be 925 parts per thousand of silver to be considered sterling. Erwin Pearl has developed a pure silver, called 999 Super Fine, which is brighter and shinier than sterling. *Goldsmiths* use these precious metals to create jewelry and to make settings for precious gems.

Gemstones Precious gems are hard, natural stones selected for their beauty and cut or polished for use in jewelry. Gemstones include diamonds, rubies, emeralds, sapphires, aquamarines, topazes, tourmalines, garnets, jade, and opals. Semiprecious stones, such as lapis and turquoise, are also used. Price depends on clarity, color, cut, rarity, and size. The weight of gemstones is measured in *carats,* a standard unit of 200 milligrams. The term *carat* comes from the carob tree, the seeds of which were once used to balance the scales used for weighing gems. Gemstones are found mostly in Asia, especially Thailand.

Diamonds Diamonds have traditionally been the most valuable and coveted of gems, and prices are increasing. Diamonds are the strongest natural element known: a diamond can be cut only with another diamond. Sixty-five percent of the world's diamond production is controlled by DeBeers, a huge South African conglomerate. Botswana, Russia, Canada, South Africa, and Angola are the largest rough-diamond suppliers. The world's largest diamond market is located in Israel.

DeBeers is promoting the development of branded diamonds, engraving diamonds with invisible-to-the eye logos. Until recently, Tiffany and Zale were the only well-known diamond brands. Now diamond suppliers such as Lazare Kaplan International, Codiam Inc., and Schachter & Namdar and fashion houses Escada and LVMH have introduced branded diamonds, each promoting its own distinctive cut and style. Branding, however, may take business away from *diamantaires,* as gem dealers are called, whose business has traditionally been based on trust and a handshake.

Stonecutting Transparent stones such as diamonds and aquamarines are cut by a *lapidary* (stonecutter) into symmetrical facets to show off their beauty. At least 50 percent of a rough gem is wasted in cutting. Cabachon stones—the unclear stones such as jade, opal, and coral—are domed, carved, or left in their natural state. Cabachon rubies and sapphires are also treated this way, a process that results in star rubies and sapphires. Although computers have recently been programmed to direct the cutting of gemstones, it is by and large still a craftsperson's field. Major stonecutting centers are in Antwerp, Belgium; Tel Aviv, Israel; London; New York City; and Mumbai (Bombay), India.

Bridge Jewelry

Bridge jewelry is a category between fine jewelry and costume jewelry defined by lower price points than fine jewelry. However, it is still made of precious metals, such as vermeil (a process of electroplating a certain thickness of gold over silver) or sterling silver, 14-karat gold trim, and semiprecious or cubic zirconia (diamond look-alike) stones. Jewelry categories are blurring because semiprecious stones are also used in costume jewelry.

Costume Jewelry

Costume jewelry is mass-produced to provide consumers with a variety of styles to coordinate with each look in their wardrobes.

Classic costume jewelry simulates the look of fine jewelry, using base metals such as brass, palladium, aluminum, copper, tin, lead, or chromium *electroplated* (coated or bonded) with gold or silver. When shapes are cut or stamped out of the sheet, the edges must be covered with gold. Freshwater or faux (glass or plastic) pearls and enameling are also used to make classic costume jewelry.

Fashion jewelry is more trendy and utilizes metals that imitate gold and silver, as well as a wide variety of materials such as wood, plastics, leather, beads, shells, glass, clay, and/or feathers. Fashion jewelry is often colorful, and styles change seasonally in keeping with apparel design. This jewelry is not created to look like fine jewelry, but rather to make a fashion statement.

Product Development and Design

Like a successful fashion company, jewelry manufacturers try to identify their target customers and find a market niche. They develop a special look, perhaps concentrating on certain materials. The jewelry industries are flourishing with fashion's emphasis on glamour.

Jewelry design is often inspired by nature, with creative ideas interpreted into metals, beads, and stones. Designers are also aware of what apparel designers are showing on the runways and try to design jewelry to complement these clothes. Designers often go to the International Jewelry Show in Basel, Switzerland, each April to study jewelry trends. Trends in jewelry include layering necklaces in mismatched multiples, gold chains, fabric-like jewelry, obscure and rare stones, and now jewelry for men.

Major jewelry categories are rings, necklaces, earrings, and bracelets. A manufacturer might further subdivide categories into diamond, gold, precious, and semiprecious jewelry and then into price ranges. Each collection features a balanced variety of designs and materials based on the seasons and how the jewelry will be worn.

Jewelry Production

There are as many techniques of making jewelry as there are jewelry types. Artisans use various methods of carving, grinding, drilling, filing, hammering, and welding metal into desired shapes. There are also many ways to mass-produce jewelry by using sheet metal, metal cast in molds, and wire. In 2006, the Manufacturing Jewelers and Suppliers of America (MJSA) association presented its first trade show in Providence, Rhode Island, to make it easier for jewelers to find the supplies they need.

Flat shapes are usually stamped out of sheet metal and may be decorated with embossing or engraving.

Casting is a process used to produce three-dimensional shapes. Rubber molds are used to cast low-temperature metals, such as tin alloys. *Lost-wax casting* is used for high-temperature metals, such as gold, silver, and brass (for both fine and costume jewelry); wax is first formed in the rubber mold, and a new plaster mold is made over the wax forms. The wax is then burned out, and molten metal is forced into the plaster mold. Finally, the plaster mold is broken open to expose the shaped pieces of metal, which are then snipped off of a supporting tree structure and polished.

Electroform is a process that applies gold electrostatically around a base metal core. The metal is then chemically dissolved, creating a hollow shell of gold with a seamless surface.

Wire is used to make chains and various necklaces and bracelets. Band rings may be made by slicing tubes of metal. Fake jewels and pearls are made from glass.

Ornamentation may be applied with enamel. Enamel work is distinguished by the way it is applied; methods include cloisonné, champlevé, basse taille, and painting.

Resources

Fine Jewelry India, Turkey, Italy, New York, and Israel are international centers for the creation of fine gold jewelry. Retailers are sourcing jewelry from countries with lower manufacturing costs. There are approximately 2000 fine jewelry firms in the United States, mostly in New York, Rhode Island, and California. Major fine jewelry brands include Cartier, Charriol, Graff, Harry Winston, and Tiffany. Contemporary fine jewelry designers include Henry Dunay, John Hardy, and David Yurman. More fashion designers, such as Oscar de la Renta, Carolina Herrera, Vera Wang, and Diane Von Furstenberg, have launched jewelry collections.

Bridge and Costume Of the approximately 750 costume jewelry firms in the United States, the majority are concentrated in Providence, Rhode Island, and New York, although the number continues to shrink. However, companies such as Tiffany and Jay Strongwater still produce in Providence. Growing competition comes from imports from China, South Korea, Taiwan, Singapore, and Hong Kong.

Dominique Aurientis, Ted Meuhling, and Robert Lee Morris are among the well-known bridge jewelry designers. Designer costume jewelry manufacturers include Ben Amun, Carolee, Chanel, Christian Dior, Ciner, Carol Dauplaise, R. J. Graziano, Judith Jack, and Kenneth Jay Lane. Designers license their names to companies that have the expertise to manufacture jewelry. For example, Victoria Creations produces licensed Karl Lagerfeld and Bijoux Givenchy lines as well as Richelieu, its own pearl brand, and Worthington for J. C. Penney.

Marketing
Fine jewelry manufacturers usually have two collections a year. Fine jewelry collections may be shown at Bijoux in Milan, the Jewelers of America (JA) Show in New York each

February and July, and the JCK Show in Scottsdale, Arizona, in June. Asian markets, such as Hong Kong, Bangkok, and Mumbai, have grown as retailers seek less expensive resources. Formerly, fine jewelry was seen only at industry trade shows and high-profile awards ceremonies. Now, however, more jewelry and apparel designers are working together so that their designs complement each other and can be shown together in apparel runway shows. Robert Lee Morris, for example, has collaborated with Donna Karan for many years.

Costume jewelry is presented at the JA jewelry show in New York City and the United Jewelry Show in Providence, Rhode Island, each March, June, and September. Some costume jewelry firms bring out new collections five times a year in January, March, May, August, and November. Manufacturers have showrooms in New York City and major market centers, as well as sales representatives.

Fine jewelry was traditionally sold in luxurious salons, but many would-be customers felt intimidated. Therefore, fine jewelry companies are now building large, accessible stores that also show a wider array of merchandise to enhance the brand's image. H. Stern, for example, has a 5500-square-foot store in New York City, the largest of its 160 stores. Even chain stores such as Wal-Mart and J. C. Penney are selling fine jewelry.

Large jewelry vendors are emphasizing consumer and sales staff education to promote multiple sales. Trifari, for example, has full-time fashion accessory consultants on the selling floor of multi-brand stores who are paid in part by Trifari and in part by the store. Jewelry designers also make personal appearances at stores to promote their jewelry and get customer feedback. Some manufacturers also use booklets to show the consumer how to accessorize with jewelry and what styles look best on what facial structures and necklines.

Some jewelers, such as Erwin Pearl, have opened specialty retail stores devoted solely to costume jewelry. Other jewelry companies, such as Carolee, have in-store boutiques in various specialty and department stores as well as free-standing stores. Television shopping channels such as QVC, the Home Shopping Network, and ShopNBC rank among the biggest jewelry retailers.

Watches

Watches have become a fashion accessory. Because many consumers using cell phones no longer actually need a watch to tell time, watches have to provide additional functions or offer fashion styling.

Currently (although not new), "complicated" watches with multiple functions are in vogue. These watches include alternative functions, such as showing the phases of the moon; a dual dial showing the corresponding time halfway around the world; chronograph capacity, which also indicates brief time intervals; perpetual calendars; and/or an accumulator that indicates elapsed time. Skeleton watches, with a clear or partially transparent case allowing the movements within to be seen, are also popular. Watches may also be shock resistant and/or water resistant.

Luxury watches that are lifetime investments and status symbols are usually 18-karat gold, some with diamonds. The most expensive brands include Breguet, Blancpain, and Patek Philippe and can cost up to a million dollars. Other top-end luxury watches include Audemars Piguet, Gerald Genta, Ulysse Nardin, and Vacheron & Constantin. Less expensive luxury watches are Rolex, Ebel, Cartier, Baume & Mercier, Corum, Piaget, and Omega.

Fashion apparel and accessory companies, such as Prada, Louis Vuitton, Burberry, and Hermès, have created watch collections, manufactured by watch companies via licensing. Sector Group, for example, produces watches for the Valentino, Pireli, Moschino, and Roberto Cavalli brands. Some companies specialize in less expensive brands. Callanen International, for example, produces watches for the Nautica and Guess brands. Less expensive watch brands, such as Bulova, Citizen, Guess, and Fossil, are following luxury watch trends by adding chronographs, dual dials, moon phases, sweeps, and other complications. New brands are continually appearing as consumers buy watch wardrobes to accessorize every style of dressing.

Production   Historically, Switzerland has been the center of the watch-making industry. Their traditional watches were and still are considered a lifetime investment. Switzerland produces 95 percent of the world's luxury watches, but Japan and China have taken over the production of middle- and lower-priced versions.

In 1967, a Swiss firm produced the first quartz watch, which was copied by Japanese and U.S. fashion watch companies. By the late 1970s, the Swiss share of the world market had dropped from 43 percent to 15 percent due to competition from less expensive watches made in Japan and Southeast Asia. Unable to compete, many Swiss watchmakers were going bankrupt until the Société Suisse de Micro-electronique et d'Horlogerie (SMH) developed the colorful, pop-art Swatch in 1982. By limiting the number of components needed to make a good watch and by using synthetic materials, SMH was able to keep costs to a level low enough for mass production. The Swatch set a fashion direction for a whole new market of fashion watches at popular prices. To keep prices down, many watch companies are having Swiss parts assembled in Hong Kong or using Asian parts in Swiss watches.

Watches have intricately detailed mechanical works and are usually hand- or self-wound or quartz powered:

- **Mechanical**—A watch that needs to be wound by the wearer
- **Automatic**—A watch that doesn't require a battery; the energy source is the movement of the wearer's wrist via a rotor.
- **Quartz**—A battery-operated watch

Marketing Two important world markets are the Salon International de la Haute Horlogerie in Geneva and Baselworld, the Watch, Clock and Jewelry Show in Basel, both held in April. The United States is the largest importer of Swiss watches. Tourneau, the world's largest watch store at 16,000 square feet, is located in New York City.

Fur Garment Manufacturing

Furs were the earliest form of clothing and, like leather accessories, are made from animal skins.

The processing of fur pelts was discussed in Chapter 7. Once the pelts have been processed, the actual production of fur garments can begin.

Product Development

Fur garment product development begins during processing with the coloring and texturing of the pelts. Then, as in the styling of cloth coats, fur designers plan a collection of coats and jackets for one season a year, fall-winter. They may specialize in one type of fur or plan a variety of furs within their collections. Groups may be planned around themes. Designers also plan a variety of silhouettes, neckline treatments, and closures to please a variety of tastes, and some manufacturers also make accessories such as hats to go with their coats and jackets.

Creating a good fit and a light weight are important considerations for the designer of fur apparel. Collections are still dominated by classic, timeless styles because of the expense to the consumer. However, many designers add interest to a collection or build an entire reputation around trendy looks and innovation.

CANADIAN DESIGNER PAULA LISHMAN IS FAMOUS FOR HER KNITTED FUR JACKETS. *(COURTESY OF PAULA LISHMAN AND THE FUR COUNCIL OF CANADA, MONTREAL)*

Styling Trends In the past, a fur coat was a status symbol and a lifetime investment, resulting in classic styling. Now furs have become fashion products. Fashion trends influence the design of fur garments and the popularity of specific furs. Trends include shearling, sheared fur, dyed fur, recycled fur, knitted fur, and reversible leather-fur or cloth-fur coats. Saga has even developed washable mink, which has great merchandising appeal.

There is an increased use of fur as trim on cloth coats, suits, or jackets. Fur is also seen in accessories such as hats, scarves, and even handbags. Some apparel designers create fur jackets, coats, and accessories to go with their apparel collections, which are produced by fur manufacturers in a licensing arrangement. Some designers are making sportswear-oriented fur vests and jackets, using less expensive furs and less complicated production procedures to keep prices down. These trends cause a blurring of the boundaries between textile and fur garments to attract new, younger customers.

Industry Organization

Fur garment styling centers include Milan, Paris, Frankfurt, Hong Kong, Montreal, and New York. Famous fashion names in fur manufacturing include Alixandre, Nicolas Petrou for Dennis Basso, Ben Kahn, Birger Christiansen, Cassin, Corniche, Danzi, Fendi, Goldin-Feldman, David Goodman, Jean Crisan, Adrienne Landau, Maximilian, J. Mendel, Musi, Paula Lishman, Rick Owens for Revillon, Solecitti, Sorbara, Theo, Trilogy, and Zuki. Some well-known apparel designers, such as Oscar de la Renta for Alixandre, Ferré for Mondialpelli, or Michael Kors for Pologeorgis, create styles for fur manufacturers through licensing arrangements.

Manufacturing Centers A very small amount of fur manufacturing is still done in the United States and Europe by small companies. With increased competition from imports, especially from China, these companies have had to specialize in "high-end" (luxury) furs and innovation. The area of New York City between Sixth and Eighth Avenues and Twenty-sixth and Thirtieth interest in furs and luxury, including new markets in Russia, China, and Eastern Europe. Mink is by far the most popular fur with over 55 percent of world sales. New specialty fur retailers, such as J. Mendel, are opening stores to offer a variety of styles and skilled customer service.

SUMMARY

FASHION IN ACCESSORIES IS CYCLICAL AND RELATED TO APPAREL STYLING. MANY APPAREL DESIGNERS CREATE ACCESSORIES TO COMPLEMENT THEIR CLOTHING. IN THE SHOE BUSINESS, A MODELISTA MAKES THE FIRST MODELS OF SHOE DESIGNS, AND THEN THE LINE BUILDER ORGANIZES THEM INTO A BALANCED COLLECTION. THE PRODUCTION OF SHOES IS A COMPLEX PROCESS FROM LAST-MAKING TO FINISHING. MANUFACTURERS ARE USING COMPUTER-AIDED MACHINERY TO SPEED UP PRODUCTION AND SAVE LABOR. IN HANDBAG PRODUCTION, DUMMIES ARE FIRST MADE TO TEST A DESIGN. EXPENSIVE BAGS ARE MADE BY HAND OF QUALITY LEATHER, WHEREAS LESS EXPENSIVE BAGS ARE MADE OF IMITATIONS OR FABRICS. THE MANUFACTURE OF BELTS IS DONE AT MANY SMALL COMPANIES. GLOVE PRODUCTION INVOLVES MANY HAND OPERATIONS. DESIGNER HATS ARE HAND BLOCKED AND MADE OF THE FINEST MATERIALS, WHILE LESS EXPENSIVE FABRIC HATS MAY BE CUT AND SEWN. HIGH-END SCARVES ARE MADE IN ITALY, WITH MANY COLOR SCREENS ON THE FINEST FABRICS, WHILE LESS EXPENSIVE SCARVES ARE MADE IN ASIA. HOSIERY MANUFACTURING IS DOMINATED BY LARGE KNITTING MILLS. FINE JEWELRY IS MADE OF PRECIOUS METALS AND GEMSTONES AND TENDS TO BE CLASSIC IN DESIGN. BETTER COSTUME JEWELRY IS VERMEIL OR GOLD FILLED AND IS MADE OUT OF SHEET METAL, CAST METAL, OR WIRE.

MOST OF THE ACCESSORY MANUFACTURERS ARE SMALL FIRMS BECAUSE HIGHLY SKILLED CRAFTS ARE INVOLVED IN PRODUCTION; HOWEVER, THE SHOE AND HOSIERY INDUSTRIES ARE DOMINATED BY LARGE COMPANIES. VIRTUALLY ALL SHOES, HANDBAGS, GLOVES, AND SCARVES ARE NOW IMPORTED FROM COUNTRIES WHERE LABOR COSTS MUCH LESS.

THE FUR INDUSTRY PRODUCES COATS, JACKETS, AND HATS, AS WELL AS TRIMMINGS FOR TEXTILE AND LEATHER APPAREL. THE LARGEST CENTERS OF FUR PRODUCTION ARE CHINA, CANADA, KOREA, AND GREECE. THE TWO METHODS OF FUR PRODUCTION ARE SKIN-ON-SKIN AND LETTING-OUT. BECAUSE THE LATTER IS ESPECIALLY TEDIOUS AND TIME-CONSUMING, THE COATS AND OTHER FUR GARMENTS SO PRODUCED ARE VERY EXPENSIVE.

Terms and Concepts

Briefly define and discuss the following terms and concepts:

1. Accessories
2. Last
3. Line builder
4. Modelista
5. CAD
6. MICAM
7. Hermès
8. Clicker machines
9. Millinery
10. Blocking
11. Gemstones
12. Cabachon stones
13. Carat versus karat
14. Lapidary
15. Vermeil
16. Casting
17. Electroform
18. Letting-out method

Questions for Review

1. How do fashion cycles influence accessory production?
2. Discuss the pros and cons of an apparel firm expanding to include accessory collections.
3. Why are certain countries specializing in dress shoe production while others lead in casual shoe production?
4. Explain the major steps involved in traditional shoe production.
5. How are computers used in mass shoe production?
6. Name five important shoe designers or manufacturers.
7. What is the role of imports in the U.S. shoe market?
8. Briefly describe handbag production.
9. Explain how belt styles are driven by apparel.
10. Name three well-known hat designers.
11. What is the difference between fine millinery and inexpensive hats?
12. What is used to make the finest scarves?
13. What are the basic steps in hosiery production?
14. Why is most of the hosiery business still in the United States while many other accessories are produced overseas?
15. What materials are used to make fine jewelry?
16. What is bridge jewelry?
17. Briefly explain two types of jewelry production.
18. How has the Swiss watch industry responded to competition from lowpriced watches?
19. What is the effect of imports on accessory manufacturing?
20. Why has fur manufacturing remained basically free of mass-production techniques?
21. Discuss the differences between the two main fur manufacturing methods.
22. How do animal rights activists influence the fur industry?

Projects for Additional Learning

1. Arrange to visit the fur salon in a department or specialty store. Ask to see and feel a variety of furs. Note the fashion styling of today's furs. How do you feel about fur as wearing apparel?

2. Visit the hat department of a local specialty store. Note the differences between hats and fine millinery and the variations between func- tional and fashion styling. How do the millinery looks tie in with the apparel trends in the store?

3. Look for shoe advertisements in a fashion mag- azine. Collect pictures of five popular dressy styles and five popular casual or sport styles. How has function affected styling?

Notes

1 Abe Chehebar, CEO, Accessory Network, New York City, interview, May 4, 2000.

2 Nate Herman, international trade advisor, American Apparel and Footwear Association, e-mail, August 11, 2003.

3 "The Giants," *WWD Book of Lists,* March 7, 2005, p. 25.

4 "A Rally in Mid-Cap Purses," *The Wall Street Journal,* March 11, 2006, p. P6.

THE OPENING OF ELIE SAAB'S COUTURE COLLECTION IN PARIS FEATURES THIS GORGEOUS GOWN OF SILK TAFFETA. *(COURTESY OF ELIE SAAB AND DENTE & CRISTINA)*

Stefani's L.A.M.B., Jennifer Lopez's Sweetface and J Lo collections, Sean "Diddy" Combs' men's line, and Sean by Sean Combs women's collection. Also Hilary Duff, Beyoncé Knowles, Mary-Kate and Ashley Olsen, Jessica Simpson, and others have joined the stampede. They, too, may diversify and expand into fragrances and beauty businesses.

Building a Brand

Manufacturers strive to strengthen their brands by building their businesses. Successful manufacturers, such as Prada, Zara, H&M, Liz Claiborne, and Tommy Hilfiger, for example, are able to develop national or global brands. To do this, they can become multiproduct manufacturers, export their merchandise, and/or open their own retail stores.

Diversification Manufacturers add new categories and/or brands to build multiproduct businesses; a *brand portfolio* provides for many different demographic categories:

Secondary Lines Manufacturers may add secondary lines at lower prices, such as many designer-label manufacturers that have added bridge or "better" lines. Marc by Marc Jacobs, Prada's Miu Miu, and Donna Karan's DKNY are three examples.

Size Ranges Manufacturers often add large sizes and/or petites to an existing misses size range. Liz Claiborne, for example, successfully created its Elizabeth collection. This is lucrative because added sales can be achieved by simply grading patterns to the additional sizes.

New Product Divisions Manufacturers are diversifying their products in order to reach other consumer groups. A sportswear manufacturer may start a dress line, or vice versa; a women's wear company might start a men's division, or the opposite. Calvin Klein and Donna Karan, originally

RALPH LAUREN HAS BUILT HIS NAME INTO A GLOBAL BRAND *(COURTESY OF RALPH LAUREN)*

women's wear designers, branched out into men's wear; Ralph Lauren, first a men's wear designer, added women's wear. Liz Claiborne has built a clothing empire with "line extensions," such as Liz Sport and Lizwear, and spinoffs, such as Dana Buchman (bridge), to reach a wide variety of customers at many price levels.

Acquisitions   To gain new product divisions, manufacturers can also buy existing companies. Acquisitions help manufacturers to balance their offerings so they aren't too dependent on one brand. Through both new product divisions and acquisitions, manufacturers also boost their negotiating clout with giant retail chains such as Federated Department Stores. Liz Claiborne, again as an example, purchased Kate Spade, Ellen Tracy, and Juicy Couture to broaden its distribution. Through acquisitions, companies such as LVMH, Gucci, Liz Claiborne, and Kellwood have become megabrand corporations.

Accessory Collections   Manufacturers may include accessories in their product lines, usually via licensing arrangements or joint ventures. Donna Karan, Liz Claiborne, and many other designer names and brands have added accessories to complete their fashion statements. Some manufacturers find that their accessories are more successful than their apparel. Alternatively, accessory companies, such as Ferragamo, Hermès, or Tod's, have added clothing collections to their brands.

As manufacturers grow into multiproduct companies, they may oversee the manufacture of these new products themselves to maintain tight control over product and marketing or form joint ventures or licensing agreements.

Licensing

Licenses provide a means of diversification for the designer or brand without the risk of capital investment or the responsibility of production. Under *licensing agreements,* popular designers and brand-name manufacturers give other manufacturers permission to use their names. For this, the designer or brand name is paid a *royalty,* a percentage of wholesale sales. Ralph Lauren, for example, licenses his women's wear collection, fragrances, eyewear, hosiery, leatherwear, Chaps men's wear, luggage, and handbags. Some designers have made alliances with large retailers. Vera Wang does a collection for Kohl's, and Cynthia Rowley, Todd Oldham, and Isaac Mizrahi, for example, have designed collections for Target.

Licenses make it possible for designers to reach a broader audience, to produce a line of coats or accessories, for example, to complement and complete their fashion statement, things they could not make in their own company for lack of expertise or capital. The licensee has expertise in the production and marketing of a particular product, but in exchange gets the designer image to trade on. The licenses are supported by brand-name and designer advertising, and vice versa.

To protect the quality associated with their images, designers are being selective in allowing licenses, exerting more control, and participating more in the design and marketing process than they used to.

Joint Ventures

Joint ventures accomplish the same goals as licenses, but in a different business arrangement. They are a partnership between designer or brand manufacturers and specialty producers. For example, a coat manufacturer and a designer could arrange a joint venture to produce that designer's coats. It is a give-and-take relationship in terms of merchandising and marketing the line. The designer has more control over the product and the licensee has less risk, because payment is usually on the basis of profits.

Distribution

Manufacturers decide on a distribution policy to ensure proper merchandising of their apparel and accessories.

Distribution Policy

Bernard Arnault, chairman and CEO of LVMH-Moët Hennessy Louis Vuitton (owner of Louis Vuitton, Dior, and other companies), said, "If you control your distribution, you control your image."[1] A manufacturer's image, quality, and prices must be at the proper level to attract its target customers and, therefore, appropriate retail stores. For example, manufacturers of designer fashion sell to better department stores and fine specialty shops. Manufacturers of moderately priced apparel and accessories sell to a wider variety of department and specialty stores. Popular and budget-line manufacturers sell to discount and other price-oriented retailers.

The manufacturer must plan distribution so that (1) the appropriate stores buy the merchandise, (2) the merchandise is represented in desired geographical areas, (3) one store does not create

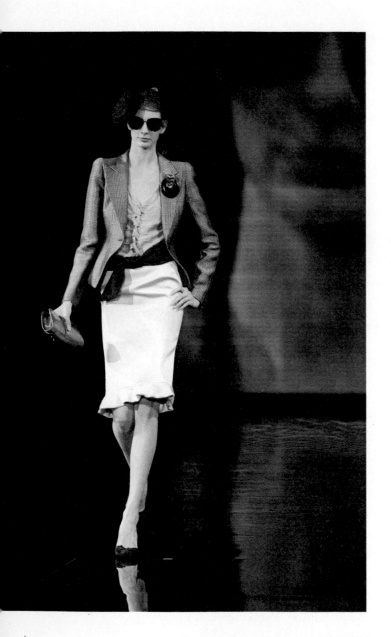

KNOWN GLOBALLY FOR HIS IMPECCABLE TAILORING, GIORGIO ARMANI USES A SELECTED DISTRIBUTION POLICY TO MAINTAIN EXCLUSIVITY. (COURTESY OF GIORGIO ARMANI SPA)

unfair competition for another, and (4) the estimated business volume is obtained. The manufacturer may have an *open distribution policy*, selling to anyone who can pay for the goods (which is most common), or a *selected distribution policy*, limiting the number of stores in an area. When Giorgio Armani opened Armani Boutiques in West Germany, he took the Emporio Armani line away from 150 retail clients to keep his clothes more exclusive. Manufacturers such as Hermès and Chanel limit the actual number of garments or accessories they produce to maintain exclusivity. Retailers often compete to be allowed to buy designer lines.

Some manufacturers *position*, or target, specific lines for specific stores. Liz Claiborne, for example, creates its Villager line for Kohl's and Mervyn's and Liz & Co. for J.C. Penney.

Exports

U.S. manufacturers are slowly learning to be exporters. Domestic markets are not growing; manufacturers are just competing for market share. Therefore, exporting (selling to overseas retailers or opening stores abroad) is one of the few ways for businesses to grow and find new markets. The Europeans are long accustomed to exporting. French fashion houses, for example, export four-fifths of their merchandise. Armani, for example, opened a store in Shanghai, and Chanel showed its couture collection in Hong Kong. U.S. manufacturers are now marketing to retailers in Europe and growing markets in Asia, Russia, and the Middle East (see Chapter 13 for examples).

However, while trade agreements are beginning to eliminate many barriers, manufacturers need research to understand the foreign consumer, make connections with foreign sales agents or retailing experts, understand customs regulations, and deal with problems of currency fluctuations and credit. Many manufacturers would like more support from the U.S. Department of Commerce. Some designers and manufacturers license their designs to local manufacturers in some countries.

advertising campaigns. The store has no rights to selection from the line, but must carry the entire range of merchandise. Escada of Germany, Hermès of France, Benetton of Italy, and Nicole Miller of the United States franchise at least some of their stores.

Leased Departments Manufacturers sometimes lease space in stores to sell their merchandise, although this practice is becoming rare. This arrangement requires no selling to a retail buyer. Leasing space is especially useful in retailing types of apparel and accessories that require salespeople with particular expertise. Fur, jewelry, and shoe manufacturers, for example, may lease departments because their sales associates must have special knowledge of their products.

Consignment Stores Small manufacturers may sell their merchandise on consignment. In this case, the retailer provides only floor space and personnel, but accepts no risks for the merchandise. The merchandise is lent to the store, and the store pays only when the merchandise is sold. The manufacturer must take back any unsold merchandise and try to sell it elsewhere, which, of course, is very difficult.

Jobbers In the fashion industry, merchandise is usually sold directly from manufacturers to retailers. The exception is the *jobber*, a middleman who buys goods from many manufacturers and resells them. These goods are usually overruns or markdowns bought at the end of a season at a large discount to clear the manufacturer's warehouse (especially if the manufacturer does not have an outlet store). They may sell in volume to small discount retailers or sell to the public in their own outlet stores. Stores such and Ross or Marshalls have grown from this concept.

Markets

International wholesale apparel and accessory markets are the means of distributing the manufacturer's finished products to retailers.

A *market* is the potential demand for a product, or the place, area, or time at which buyers and sellers meet to transact business. In this chapter, we refer specifically to the *wholesale* fashion market, in which the sellers represent fashion manufacturers and the buyers are fashion retailers.

This material is presented from the manufacturer's standpoint, whereas Chapter 14 discusses buying from the retailer's point of view, as part of their merchandising process.

Traditionally, fashion markets were located close to suppliers and manufacturers; therefore, most market centers were also production centers. However, with global sourcing, this is no longer the case. Newer market centers have been created in various locales for the convenience of buyers or where there is abundant convention and hotel space, such as Las Vegas.

This chapter addresses the international or global market and the domestic market (the United States). It covers the role of major international fashion market centers and regional fashion centers in buying and selling on the wholesale level. Although it is usually possible to buy year round, specific weeks are scheduled for collection openings or for the purpose of bringing buyers and sellers together.

Global Markets

Markets are the time and place where buying and selling occur.

After each manufacturer's collection or line is designed, it must be presented to retail buyers so that they can buy for their stores. This presentation can be accomplished by various means, including fashion shows, market weeks, showroom presentations, and contacts with sales representatives. The global marketplace is becoming increasingly smaller due to the Internet, mobile phones, fax, air travel, and container shipping.

The terms *collection opening* and *line release* are synonymous; both signal the first opportunity for retail buyers to see fashion merchandise for a new season. Most women's wear collections have four, five, or more lines per year. Some vertical brands, such as Zara and H&M, have no seasons; they constantly deliver new merchandise to their stores.

Only designer brands have runway shows. In spite of designing four or five collections (fall, holiday and/or cruise, spring, summer, and possibly pre-fall), these extravagant shows are held only twice a year to present spring and fall collections to buyers and the press. Scheduling both international and individual shows is difficult. Designers request particular time slots, and conflicts often arise. In any case, designer apparel is often sold to retail customers before the shows at "precollection" showings.

European Collection Openings

Couture   Paris continues as the world center for couture. American Ralph Rucci and some Italian designers, such as Armani and Valentino, show their couture collections in Paris. The spring collections are shown in January and the fall collections in July. These shows are by invitation only to private clients and the press. There are only about 300 couture clients in the world (mostly American, European, and Middle Eastern women)! Some couturiers try to attract attention with extreme fashion and theatrical productions. *Precollection* essential merchandise, which can represent a large percentage of sales, is often shown to buyers before the shows. Collections are largely shown at a new fashion center beneath the Place du Carrousel near the Louvre and other nearby venues.

The couture is highly regulated by the French Ministry of Industry and the Fédération Française de la Couture. Designers have to show a minimum of 50 pieces in a collection; new couturiers have to show only 25 pieces for a two-year transition period. It costs approximately $4 million a year for a large house to produce and show its two couture collections, including expensive fabrics, labor-intensive handwork, specially made accessories, highly paid models, a catwalk, and high-tech sound systems for the show. In addition, *houses* (couture companies) may show or send videotapes or a CD-ROM of the collections to private clients. However, these costs are amortized as part of the communications and business development budgets.

To compensate for the expense, the French government gives support to the couture to promote exports. DEFI, the commission for promotion of textiles and apparel, has developed a campaign called "La Mode de France." Government-owned French television gives the couture free exposure. This kind of publicity is more prestigious than costly advertising and helps to generate sales for ready-to-wear, perfume, and licensing businesses. In the past several years, the couture has generated more worldwide press coverage than ever before. Each show attracts more than 1000 French and foreign journalists.

ALBER ELBAZ'S BLUE SATIN "TWIST" DRESS AT LANVIN'S PRÊT-À-PORTER COLLECTION SHOWING. *(COURTESY OF LANVIN, PARIS)*

321

A ROMANTIC TIERED, RUFFLED DRESS BY ANDREW GN FOR HIS PRÊT-À-PORTER COLLECTION. *(COURTESY OF ANDREW GN, PARIS)*

Prêt-à-Porter Collections

European designer ready-to-wear shows are held twice a year: fall collections are shown in February/March and spring collections are shown in September/October in Paris, London, and Milan. A buyer needs more than two weeks to see the shows in all three cities. Some designers from other countries show their collections in Paris or Milan because they think they get better exposure. Buyers complain that the Paris shows are spread over too many days, that many shows do not start on time and are too long, and that many of the clothes are for editorial purposes only.

Retail-store buyers of better merchandise and approximately 2000 journalists from all over the world flock to see the individual showings of many designers. Most buyers see 10 shows a day, from early morning until late at night, taking notes to remember styles. After analyzing the collections from the point of view of their stores' needs, buyers place orders, usually at the designers' showrooms or through buying offices in each city. In lieu of a fashion show, a ready-to-wear collection may also be shown to buyers in the company showroom, and many manufacturers now present four or more collections per year in this manner, as in the United States. Deliveries are staggered so that new merchandise arrives periodically in the stores to capture customer interest.

Market Weeks and Fairs

Manufacturers also show and sell fashions at market weeks or trade fairs. Markets often coincide with collection openings or line releases. Markets in major centers are held first, followed by regional markets. Markets are held in specially built buildings (fairgrounds or "marts"), convention centers, or hotels. A market can last from three days to two weeks. European trade fairs are markets and not just expositions. In Germany, for example, businesses often sell 75 percent of their

merchandise at these markets. Markets are an excellent opportunity for the manufacturer to reach new stores, establish new accounts, and, in turn, help retailers looking for new resources. Market weeks are constantly competing for buyers' time and budgets.

Paris The French prêt-à-porter shows are not limited to the designer collections. Other shows and groups of exhibitors are spread out all over Paris, organized by various fashion associations. Prêt-à-Porter Paris (often referred to as "The Pret") is held at the Porte de Versailles. There are also other exhibit groups called Who's Next, Paris sur Mode, Atmosphere, Workshop, Le Dôme, and Tranoi. Some manufacturers show in hotels or restaurants. The city has launched a public relations campaign called "Paris Capitale de la Mode" to offer transportation, hotel reservations, maps, information booklets, and other services to visiting buyers.

Milan Milan Fashion Week is now held at the Fashion Milano Center plus three satellite marquees and the Vigorelli Velodrome. The Italian Chamber of Fashion also promotes Italian fashion internationally.

London Many London designers have been showing in New York, Paris, or Milan, so the British Fashion Council (BFC) has given London Fashion Week a makeover to bring them back home. Also, fashion calendar planners have allowed London more time between the Paris and Milan shows.

Around the World There are fashion shows and market weeks in every major city in the world, such as Berlin, Düsseldorf, Madrid, Istanbul, Mumbai, Hong Kong, Tokyo, Sydney, and Rio de Janeiro. Collection openings, fashion fairs, or market weeks are going on worldwide year round. Table 12.1 presents a calendar of the world's most important apparel and accessory fairs and market weeks.

■ BEIRUT DESIGNER ELIE SAAB SHOWS HIS READY-TO-WEAR COLLECTION IN PARIS. *(COURTESY OF ELIE SAAB)*

TABLE 12.1   **IMPORTANT INTERNATIONAL FASHION MARKETS AND COLLECTION SHOWINGS (SOME IMPORTANT FASHION–RELATED MARKETS HAPPENING YEAR ROUND THROUGHOUT THE WORLD)**

January

Pitti Uomo and Uomo Italia (men's)	Florence
Milano Collezioni Uomo (men's)	Milan
Designer Men's Wear Collections	Paris
The Accessories Show, Accessories Circuit, and Accessories Market Week	New York
Hong Kong Fashion Week	Hong Kong
NAMSB—National Association of Men's Sportswear Buyers Show	New York
Haute Couture collections (women's, spring)	Paris
Market Week (women's ready-to-wear)	New York
Los Angeles Market	Los Angeles
Pitti Bimbo (children's wear)	Florence
Salon de la Mode Enfantine (children's wear)	Paris
SIHM—Salon International de l'Habillement Masculin (men's)	Paris

February

Prêt-à-Porter Paris (women's ready-to-wear)	Paris
Première Classe (accessories)	Paris CPD
(Collections Premieren Düsseldorf) Woman · Man	Düsseldorf
FFANY—Fashion Footwear Association of New York and National Shoe Fair	New York
WSA—Shoe Show	Las Vegas
Mercedes Benz Fashion Week (7th on Sixth) and Market Week	New York
Prêt-à-Porter Designer Collection Shows	Paris
London Fashion Week	London
Milano Moda Donna and MilanoVendaModa (women's ready-to-wear)	Milan
MAGIC (men's and women's)	Las Vegas
The Super Show (sporting goods)	Las Vegas

March

MIDEC—Mode Internationale de la Chaussure (shoes)	Paris
MIPEL (leather accessories)	Milan

TABLE 12.1

MICAM (shoes)	Milan
NAMSB Show (men's wear)	New York

April

Los Angeles women's market	Los Angeles

May

The Accessories Show and Accessories Circuit	New York

June

Moda Prima (knitwear)	Milan
Milano Collezioni Uomo (men's designer collections)	Milan
Pitti Uomo and Uomo Italia (men's wear)	Florence
Pitti Bimbo and Moda Bimbo (children's wear)	Florence
NAMSB Show (men's wear)	New York
Market Week (women's ready-to-wear)	New York
Los Angeles Women's Market	Los Angeles
FFANY—Fashion Footwear Association of New York and National Shoe Fair	New York

July

Mode Enfantine (children's wear)	Paris
Designer Men's Wear Collections	Paris
SIHM—Salon International de l'Habillement Masculin (men's)	Paris
Haute Couture Collections (fall-winter)	Paris
Hong Kong Fashion Week	Hong Kong
Market Week (women's ready-to-wear)	New York

August

CPD Woman · Man	Düsseldorf
The Accessories Show and Accessories Circuit	New York
Los Angeles Ready-to-Wear market	Los Angeles
MAGIC	Las Vegas
FFANY—Fashion Footwear Association of New York and National Shoe Fair	New York
WSA Shoe Show	Las Vegas
Salon de la Mode Enfantine (children's wear)	Paris

(continued)

TABLE 12.1 (Continued)

September

MIDEC—Mode Intenationale de la Chaussure (shoes)	Paris
MICAM (shoes)	Milan
MIPEL (leather accessories)	Milan
Mercedes Benz Fashion Week (7th on Sixth and Market Week)	New York
Prêt-à-Porter Paris (women's ready-to-wear)	Paris
Premiere Classe (accessories)	Paris
Milano Moda Donna and MilanoVendaModa (women's ready-to-wear)	Milan
London Fashion Week (women's ready-to-wear)	London
Montreal Fashion Week	Montreal

October

NAMSB Show (men's wear)	New York
Market Week (women's ready-to-wear)	New York
The Accessories Show, Accessories Circuit, and Accessories Market Week	New York

November

Los Angeles market (women's ready-to-wear)	Los Angeles

December

Moda Prima (knitwear)	Milan
FFANY—Fashion Footwear Association of New York and National Shoe Fair	New York

Men's Wear The Salon International de l'Habillement Masculin (SIHM, men's and boys' wear) takes place in Paris each January and September. The Milano Collezioni Uomo (Milan men's designer collections) and the Pitti Immagine Uomo (men's wear) take place in Florence each January and June. Other markets of men's clothing are held in London in January or February and again in August or September. Many designer collections and markets now combine women's and men's wear.

Canada

Montreal Fashion Week (MFW), organized by Sensation Mode, is held each March and October. NSIA (activewear, footwear, and accessories) is also held in Montreal. The North American Fur and Fashion Exhibition (NAFFEM) in Montreal is the third-largest fur and leather show in the world.

CIMM, The Centre International de Mode de Montreal (The Montreal International Fashion Center), holds four market weeks a year.

Toronto Fashion Week, organized by the Fashion Design Council of Canada, features designer runway shows each March and October. The Ontario Fashion Exhibitors operates two large trade shows a year at the Toronto Congress Center, showing women's wear and footwear. The Jewelry World Expo is held in Toronto each August, and the Mode Accessories Show is held in both Toronto and Calgary.

FashionNorth Womenswear Show and the FashionNorth Menswear Show are both national shows held twice a year at Toronto's International Center.

Domestic Markets

Domestic market weeks and trade shows in New York City, California, and other regional centers are important wholesale markets for U.S. retail buyers.

New York

New York remains the major fashion market center of the United States. More than 23,000 apparel buyers visit the city each year for collection showings, market weeks, and trade shows.

Women's Wear

Fashion Week (7th on Sixth), sponsored by Mercedes Benz—Seasonal designer collections are usually presented to buyers and the press as fashion shows organized by "7th on Sixth" (Seventh Avenue on Sixth Avenue), held in two large tents in Bryant Park. Women's fall collections are shown in February, and spring collections are shown in September. Controversy over these dates is continuous. Some designers like the shows early, before Europe, to leave more time for production and deliveries; others prefer to show after Europe to have more time to order fabrics and prepare. Sixty to eighty shows in 10 days, sometimes with three shows running concurrently, present a huge organizational project as well as a hectic week for buyers. Some European designers are also showing in New York, which makes the schedule even more crowded.

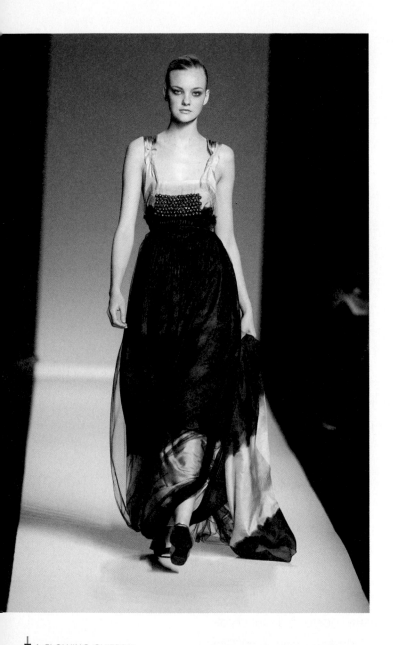

A FLOWING CHIFFON GOWN IN VERA WANG'S COLLECTION SHOW AT "7TH ON SIXTH," MERCEDES BENZ FASHION WEEK, IN NEW YORK CITY. *(COURTESY OF VERA WANG)*

New York Trade Shows—In addition, trade shows are organized by public relations or communications companies in hotels, convention centers, or other venues in New York City during market weeks. These companies rent showrooms or booths to manufacturers from across the country and around the world. They give the manufacturers an opportunity to show to visiting retail buyers. The larger groups include Fashion Coterie, Intermezzo, Sole Commerce, Femme, Designers & Agents, Moda Manhattan, AccessoriesTheShow, FAME, and Workshop NY. Smaller venues for young designers include MAO Space, Gen Art, South of Seventh, and Designer Debut. Other small hotel shows include American International Designers, Designers at the Essex House, Atelier, and Pacific Designer Collections.

Trade shows coincide with manufacturers' line releases (when the new lines are shown to buyers), which usually occur five times a year:

- Summer merchandise is shown in January.
- Early fall merchandise is presented in February.
- Fall II merchandise is shown in late March or early April.
- Holiday and/or resort merchandise is released in August.
- Spring merchandise is ready to see in November.

Children's Wear Formerly shown only twice a year, children's wear has now become so fashion oriented that it is shown three or four times a year, depending on the type of apparel. Dress manufacturers, for example, have major lines for holiday and spring, whereas sportswear manufacturers have three or four seasonal lines. Some trendier size 7 to 14 manufacturers have new lines almost monthly.

The International Kids Fashion Show is held in New York featuring fall fashions in March and spring fashions in August. The Florida Children's Guild Show is held in Miami in September. However, most children's wear companies show their lines only in their showrooms.

Men's Wear   The **Designers Collective Show** features upscale tailored suits and coats in late January for fall and in late August or early September for spring. 7th on Sixth also has shows of designer men's wear collections in February and July.

The **National Association of Men's Sportswear Buyers** (NAMSB) has increased shows to four times a year since the sportswear market has grown so much. Summer lines are shown in January, fall lines in March or early April, holiday and resort lines in June, and spring lines in October. These shows are followed by regional markets.

The **Clothing Manufacturers Association** (CMA), a men's wear trade organization, arranges tailored clothing market weeks in January for fall lines and August or September for spring.

Runway versus Showroom

Designer Narciso Rodriguez said, "It's easy to embellish something to make it a showpiece. It's much harder to make a very clean, exquisitely cut garment look new . . . and to get that across on a runway . . ."[2] Many designers, such as Galliano, McQueen, and Gaultier, present outrageous creations on the runway to attract attention. However, their showrooms (where buyers come to order) are also filled with salable merchandise! "Shock versus stock" is typical of the discrepancy between runways and showrooms.

A *showroom* is a place where manufacturers' sales representatives show samples to prospective retail buyers. Many manufacturers show their sample merchandise only in their own showrooms, usually next to design studios. Designers create many showstoppers just to get attention on the runway; however, the salable merchandise is seen in the showrooms. The showroom is the primary setting for selling merchandise to retail buyers, where the orders are placed.

In designer showrooms, fashions are often modeled or displayed on mannequins; in medium- to lower-priced apparel showrooms, clothes are displayed on hangers. The showroom is outfitted with display racks, sometimes mounted on the walls for greater visibility, with tables and chairs for the clients' comfort. Showrooms provide continual exposure for the line.

In Manhattan, New York City, apparel showrooms were traditionally located in the garment district, in the vicinity of Seventh Avenue and Broadway between Thirty-third and Forty-second Streets, close to the theater district. The district is also often referred to as "Seventh Avenue." They were usually grouped in buildings according to merchandise classification and price range. Grouping by apparel type was organized for the convenience of the buyer who does not have the time to travel all over

BETSEY JOHNSON'S WHIMSICAL SHOWROOM IN NEW YORK CITY. *(PHOTO BY GINI STEPHENS FRINGS)*

town yet must see everything offered in a particular category and price range. For example, the prestigious addresses of 530 and 550 Seventh Avenue were traditionally designer addresses. Showrooms for moderately priced women's wear are usually located on Broadway. Lingerie and intimate apparel are centered on Madison Avenue. Children's wear showrooms are grouped around Thirty-fourth Street and Sixth Avenue and at Thirty-third Street and Sixth Avenue. One large building at 1290 Avenue of the Americas has showrooms representing approximately 75 percent of domestically produced men's clothing. The Empire State Building houses showrooms of men's furnishings.

Now, however, these buildings have become less specialized as showrooms have relocated because of high rents, lease losses, or the need for more space. Advertising and Internet firms have moved into the area, which is changing the identity of the district and driving up rents. Many fashion companies have been forced to move to other areas, particularly the West Side of Manhattan.

Virtual Showrooms   The Internet is providing the opportunity for manufacturers to sell online. Stylesmart.com, for example, allows designers and manufacturers to display their merchandise to retailers via the Internet. Their Web site provides all the information a buyer would find in a real showroom, including close-up and three-dimensional views of the merchandise. The advantage of the Internet is its continual access to the global retail community.

National Trade Shows

MAGIC, the Men's Apparel Guild in California, has grown from a regional market to a national one. MAGIC produces the largest men's apparel trade show in the world, with more than 3500 exhibitors and 80,000 buyers attending. The interesting thing is that it is no longer held in California. It takes place in Las Vegas, Nevada, each February and August. MAGIC now encompasses four simultaneous markets: men's wear, children's wear, junior and contemporary (The Edge), and women's wear (in cooperation with *Women's wear Daily*).

Project, also held in Las Vegas, is a contemporary fashion trade show featuring approximately 600 vendors of men's, women's, and children's apparel and accessories, emphasizing new companies and new brands.

The Super Show, the world's largest sports product trade show, is held each February, alternating between Las Vegas, Nevada, and Orlando, Florida.

AN AERIAL VIEW OF SHOWROOMS AT MAGIC. *(COURTESY OF THE MEN'S APPAREL GUILD IN CALIFORNIA)*

Regional Market Centers

New York trade shows and market weeks are followed by regional markets. Most of these markets are held in cities that were first manufacturing centers. These markets cater primarily to independent specialty stores and regional retailers who do not have the time to go to New York. Many regional markets are known for particular specialties.

In many of these cities, large buildings of showrooms, called *marts*, have been built. Showrooms may be rented by manufacturers' sales representatives on a permanent basis, or space may be rented as needed for markets. Within the marts, showrooms are grouped according to category for the buyers' convenience. For example, men's furnishings showrooms may be grouped on one floor, women's lingerie on another, and so forth.

All the regional fashion marts host five major markets per year plus fashion shows and other specialty markets. Educational seminars on subjects such as trends, visual merchandising, management, and other activites may also be provided. Other facilities may include restaurants, auditoriums, hotels, hair salons, health clubs, printing services, and parking. To attract retailers and stimulate business, regional marts have developed aggressive new strategies. *Megamarts* (combined women's, men's, children's, and accessory markets) have been created for *crossover buying* so that buyers can make fewer or shorter trips to market and save travel costs. Other incentives include free or discounted hotel accommodations and airfares and more events throughout the year aimed at specific market niches. The major regional centers are as follows:

Los Angeles—Los Angeles has become the nation's second-largest fashion market center and is a showcase for California designers and junior and contemporary styling. California companies also develop private-label brands for major specialty retailers. The New Mart, the Cooper Design Space, the Gerry Building, and the California Market Center have formed "Intersection," a joint promotional effort for all four showroom buildings.

Dallas—Apparel and accessory showrooms have recently been relocated to Fashion Center Dallas in the Dallas World Trade Center and Fashion District Dallas in the historic Mercantile building. Dallas is particularly known for evening, bridal, and western fashion. The city also sponsors the annual Dallas Fashion Awards each October.

Chicago—The Chicago Merchandise Mart, serving the Midwest, opened in 1977 and has both permanent showrooms and temporary exhibit areas called Pavilion Suites. Many Canadian lines can be seen at the Chicago Merchandise Mart. Chicago presents an exhibition-style apparel show called StyleMax in March and October and Pulse, an "urbanwear" market in June.

Atlanta—AmericasMart, which serves the Southeast, opened in 1979. AmericasMart offers buyers the convenience of cross-marketing with an adjacent gift and merchandise mart. A recent remodel is designed to appeal to a younger audience. AmericasMart presents its Premier Show twice a year.

Miami—The Miami International Merchandise Mart opened in 1968. Due to its strategic location, it has also emerged as a wholesale center for the Americas, with many Latin American and Caribbean buyers attending its trade markets each year. The Swimwear Association of Florida holds the largest swimwear trade show in the world each February and July. Sobol Fashion Productions, producer of Miami Fashion Week, has launched "City Style," a multicultural lifestyle show.

Other regional marts are the Denver Merchandise Mart in Colorado; the Carolina Trade Mart, Charlotte, North Carolina; the Miami Merchandise Mart in Florida; the Northeast Trade Center, Woburn, Massachusetts; the Radisson Center, Minneapolis, Minnesota; and the Trade Center, Kansas City, Missouri.

Marketing Support Strategies

Manufacturers use specific marketing strategies, such as advertising and publicity, to make their merchandise known to prospective retail buyers and to the public.

Effective marketing can often mean the difference between success and failure for an apparel company. Although the term *marketing* can mean the entire process of making and selling merchandise, here marketing specifically refers to publicity, advertising, and other activities used to promulgate brand-name recognition and generate sales. Marketing strategies are adjusted globally to suit local habits, styles, and tastes. A global company may have one type of campaign in Europe, another in Asia, and yet another in the United States.

Collection Shows and Market Weeks

Designers and manufacturers have a press attaché, or hire a public relations (PR) firm and a trade association to handle the extensive arrangements for collection and market openings. For major collections, invitations are sent to journalists the world over, as well as to the manufacturer's best

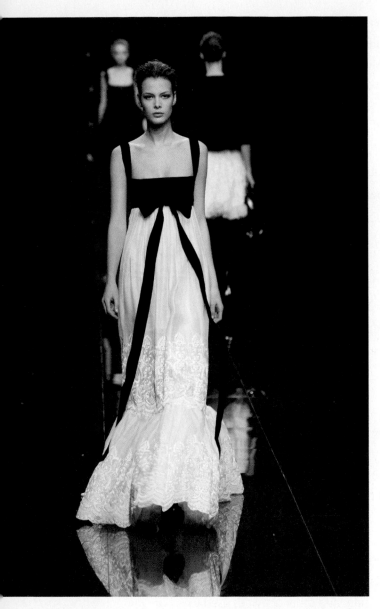

ELIE SAAB'S PRESS
KIT INCLUDES
PHOTOS FROM HIS
COLLECTIONS.
*(COURTESY OF ELIE
SAAB AND DENTE
& CRISTINA
ASSOCIATES, INC.)*

customers. A "run of show" (numbered list of models to be shown) is given out at the show. After the shows and market week, a "dossier" or press kit is prepared and sent to each journalist, usually by e-mail or a mailed CD. The kit includes photographs from the collection, a press release or analysis of the collection, and a biography of the designer.

With so many lines for buyers to remember, gimmicks such as distinctive invitations or souvenirs are used to draw attention to particular collections, and promotional items such as shopping bags or T-shirts with the manufacturer's name on them can serve as walking advertisements. Celebrities are hired to sit in front row seats to attract the press. Photographers often attend a show just to photograph a particular celebrity. This is invaluable publicity for the designer or brand.

Major designer fashion shows are very costly ventures. It costs at least $200,000 to present a seasonal designer collection show to buyers and the press. Typical expenses include approximately 20 models for a full day, lighting, set design, videotaping, accessories, rental of a facility, hairstylists, music, makeup artists, invitations, postage, and programs. As a result, some designers are making their shows less extravagant or showing only in their own showrooms.

Stylists   Stylists have become some of the most powerful people in the fashion industry. Stylists focus on the overall look and presentation of a collection. Their objective viewpoint helps designers edit their collections, and they often select what fashions will be shown on the runway along with the coordinating accessories. They may also coordinate the entire runway show and put together editorial photo shoots.

Publicity

Publicity is information given to the public regarding products, policies, personnel, activities, or services. Fashion manufacturers use in-house public relations or publicity staffs, consultants, or agencies to create publicity material and obtain *editorial coverage* of their collections in newspapers and magazines, on television, and on the Web. Fashion editors choose the material for their articles from information and photographs sent to them by the manufacturers. Although manufacturers do pay to create the publicity materials, they do not have to pay for the media coverage. Many small companies get valuable exposure on independent blogs that they might not get in mainstream media.

Advertisers are putting more pressure on publications for editorial coverage. Designer Michael Kors explained why editorial coverage is so important: "Advertising establishes your image, but editorial is it for prestige—and sales."[3]

Television and Films   Fashion programs on television are also an opportunity for designers to get publicity. E! Entertainment's Style Channel, CNN, and MTV's *House of Style* offer various approaches of giving free publicity to designers and brands. The Academy Awards has become the "world's largest fashion show."

Many companies aggressively campaign to get their products placed in feature films and especially on the most popular TV shows. In their quest to link their clothing and accessories with the biggest names in entertainment, they have to choose the appropriate film and celebrity to endorse their product and reach their target market.

Celebrities and Publicity   Having a celebrity photographed in a designer's creation is worth a fortune in publicity. Beginning with Giorgio Armani, designers have been donating or loaning gowns to celebrities to wear in public, particularly for awards ceremonies. Now the competition to dress the stars is fierce. Formerly, actresses were given gowns from several designers and did not decide what to wear until the last minute. The expense and disappointments involved have changed the system. Now designers make agreements with specific stars, that they will be provided with a choice of gowns only if they agree to wear one. Celebrities hired for a designer's advertisements may be expected to wear that designer's gowns at awards ceremonies.

Advertising

Advertising is the planning, writing, producing, and scheduling of paid announcements designed to attract potential customers' attention to the manufacturer's merchandise. Manufacturers have in-house staffs or hire outside agencies or consultants to develop and produce advertising campaigns. Large manufacturers of apparel, hosiery, and shoes advertise their brand names nationally or globally. Advertising budgets are usually 2 to 4 percent of projected business volume. Brands such as the Gap, Nike, Polo Ralph Lauren, and Levi Strauss & Company spend the largest amounts on advertising.

Media   Manufacturers use both trade and consumer media, thereby reaching both markets. Media buyers are faced with an overwhelming choice: publications, outdoor advertisements (billboards, painted walls, buses, bus shelters, taxis, and phone kiosks), radio, TV, the Internet, and event sponsorships.

Usually, an advertising campaign is supported in a variety of media. Peter Connolly, executive vice president of marketing at Tommy Hilfiger Corporation, commented, "You have to have a good mix. Not everyone just reads magazines, or just watches TV, or just looks at outdoor advertising. If you're trying to raise quick awareness for a new brand, then you might want to go with outdoor. To sustain an existing business . . . you want to go into the core fashion books. Where your brand is, is as important as the ad itself."[4] Many advertisers bombard consumers with impact units of 4- to 26-page ads in both trade and consumer magazines to achieve brand-name recognition. Advertisers also look for premium positions and a publication's event tie-ins.

A MAX MARA ADVERTISEMENT. *(COURTESY OF DENTE & CRISTINA ASSOCIATES, INC.)*

Television has become increasingly important as an advertising medium for the manufacturer. Also, many catalogs and Web sites are produced only for advertising purposes. Tommy Hilfiger's ad agency created a teen "soap" called *The Houseparty* on its Web site, just as an advertising vehicle. Advertising CDs are inserted in magazines that provide entertainment, such as designer interviews, as well as the opportunity to see merchandise close up from all angles.

Image Advertising   Designers and manufacturers may use *image advertising* to make the consumer aware of their names or brands. Image advertising tries to capture the spirit of the product and build brand identity. Product takes on a secondary role to build a distinctive brand image that transcends seasons. Image advertising tries to get the consumer to buy into a lifestyle, first on a psychological, emotional, or aspirational level and then on a product level. Because there are so many brands in the marketplace, marketers search for something that touches the consumer, that makes her choose to buy one brand over another. The most successful ad campaigns are those that manipulate feelings. This is done most often through visual imagery.

Ads with a multigenerational appeal are a recent trend. Companies such as Eileen Fisher, Ralph Lauren, Donna Karan, and the Gap use models of different ages to reach a wider audience.

Marketers have to differentiate themselves in some way to catch attention. Advertisements may use controversy, humor, celebrities, sex, or shock to get attention. "There is a brand for every life-style imaginable: Calvin is hip, Ralph is rich, Tommy is American apple pie, DKNY is city slicker, Diesel is outrageous, and Benetton is controversial."[5] Large fashion companies spend millions of dollars each year on image advertising.

Celebrities as Models   Celebrities, such as Angelina Jolie for St. John or Sarah Jessica Parker for Gap, command huge sums of money to help shape company images. They may be in a single campaign or have a contract for several years. Each celebrity is selected on the basis of his or her appeal to the target customer. Photographs of them wearing items from the collection are used in the company's advertising campaign, on posters, or in magazine ads, for example. Swim- and activewear companies are using athletes for models. Speedo, for example, sponsors medal-winning swimmers, divers, and triathletes. Their catalog features athletes wearing their clothes.

Item Advertising   When item advertising is desired, manufacturers choose one outstanding style from their collection to picture in an ad. With item advertisements, they are able to see direct sales response. Dana Buchman, for example, advertises one item twice a year.

However, fashion changes so quickly that it is often impossible to produce an ad of a specific style for national media. In addition, since each store carries different styles from any one line, it may be impossible to advertise one specific style for all stores.

Cooperative Advertising

Many manufacturers cooperate financially with textile producers and retailers on advertisements to make the public more aware of brand names. Manufacturers may offer to share costs with retailers who advertise their styles, or textile producers may help to fund manufacturers' ads if their fibers or fabrics are used. Textile and apparel manufacturers' co-op allocations may provide a retailer with up to 50 percent of its media costs. The cooperative ads carry the names and logos (brand or store symbols) of each contributing company.

Other Marketing Aids to Retailers

Manufacturers often provide retailers with aids that they can use in their advertising, publicity, and public relations. Each manufacturer constantly tries to develop more selling and promotional tools. A manufacturer may offer one or more of the following to stores that purchase its merchandise.

Personal Appearances Many designers make personal appearances at retail stores to draw crowds. These visits may be accompanied by a fashion show, talk, and/or luncheon.

Designer Trunk Shows This is a similar idea to the personal appearance, but in this case the designer brings the entire collection. Trunk shows are hard work, but very successful, because the line is not edited by a buyer. There is direct payback because customers can order garments in their own sizes immediately after a fashion show. Small manufacturers who cannot afford national advertising have found this method to be very profitable for them. Even some couturiers are trying this idea and arranging for fittings to be done in the stores.

In-Store Clinics Many manufacturers have discovered that their merchandise sells better if it is thoroughly explained to both salespeople and store customers. Therefore, the designer or a manufacturer's representative may visit stores to train and educate the sales associates and/or customers with demonstrations, slides, and a talk.

Videos Specific videos for training purposes demonstrate selling techniques and how pieces work together. Couturiers send videos to their best customers. Videos of fashion shows are often shown in stores. Accessory firms use videos to show customers in a retail store how to drape a scarf or wear a hat.

Image Books These booklets are mini catalogs that show a sampling of a collection. They may be distributed to retailers, the press, and customers. Dana Buchman, for example, offers "look books"

A MAX MARA LOOK BOOK FOR CUSTOMERS AND SALES ASSOCIATES TO LEARN HOW COLLECTION PIECES WORK TOGETHER. *(COURTESY OF DENTE & CRISTINA ASSOCIATES, INC.)*

for customers and/or sales associates to learn about the product and how pieces work together. Depending on the size and number of books sent out, which can be anywhere from 5000 to 250,000 per season, image books cost between $40,000 and $100,000 to produce.

Display Fixtures Manufacturers sometimes provide stores with fixtures to enhance visual merchandising. Ellen Tracy, for example, offers stores an *enhancement package* including mannequins and signing.

Radio Scripts and TV Commercials Stores can "tag" media spots provided by the manufacturer with their own names and run them in their local areas.

Glossy Photographs Photographs of merchandise may be provided to stores to be used for publicity or advertisements. Couturiers also send photographs, sketches, and swatches to their best customers.

Statement Enclosures Small mailing pieces, similar to pages in a catalog with photos of merchandise, can be provided for stores to send to customers in their monthly mailings.

Hangtags To help carry out a designer or brand image, a manufacturer's advertising department or agency may create consistent packaging, including hangtags for their garments or accessories.

Associations That Promote Fashion

Trade associations support manufacturers in promoting particular segments of the industry and organizing trade shows. The American Apparel Manufacturers Association (AAMA), the Council of Fashion Designers of America (CFDA), the Fashion Footwear Association of New York (FFANY), and the Fashion Association (TFA) are examples of specialized organizations.

The Fashion Group International, Inc., founded in 1931, fosters careers in the industry. Primarily promotional and educational in purpose, it now has over 6000 members with regional chapters in

OSCAR DE LA RENTA AND JEAN-PAUL GAULTIER RECEIVING AWARDS AT THE CFDA GALA. *(COURTESY OF THE COUNCIL OF FASHION DESIGNERS OF AMERICA, PHOTOS BY DAN LECCA)*

33 U.S. cities and nine foreign countries. The Fashion Group programs include slide shows of collections and industry executives as speakers, activities to raise funds to fight breast cancer, and "Rising Star Awards."

Fashion Awards Fashion awards presented by various organizations generate interest in fashion because of the publicity they create.

The Council of Fashion Designers of America presents annual awards in a minimum of four categories: men's, women's, accessories, and the Perry Ellis Award for new fashion talent. The winners are chosen by a committee of fashion editors and retailers. The CFDA has also organized "7th on Sale" to raise money to fight AIDS.

The Dallas Fashion Awards, which began in 1976 as a local awareness program, evolved into a recognition ceremony to honor U.S. designers. Three designers are nominated in many categories, and then national retailers vote for the winners by mail.

Selling to Retailers

Management and sales representatives carry out the activity of selling fashion merchandise to retail buyers.

In a manufacturer–retailer relationship, the manufacturer is often referred to as the vendor. The vendor sales team of management and sales representatives must communicate design and merchandising concepts to retailers. Sales teams also do more and more *assortment customizing* for each separate account so that the line or collection looks different at each store. Vendors recommend what part of the line should be purchased on the basis of the store's image, customers, and needs.

The two basic ways of selling fashion merchandise to retail stores are through corporate selling or sales representatives.

Corporate Selling

Most major vendors, including designer companies and large manufacturers, no longer have sales representatives. Fashion distribution to large store chains and groups has become so complex and so important to volume sales that the selling is now done *management to management*.

341

Marketing executives work at maintaining consistency of product and a good relationship with the store. Manufacturers and retailers are trying to build partnerships or alliances to help each other to do better business.

Sales Representatives

Some companies still employ sales representatives ("reps") to call on specialty stores that do not have the time or money to travel to New York. Sales reps are salaried or paid on a commission basis, ranging from 5 to 10 percent, on orders actually shipped to and accepted by the stores. Most commissioned representatives pay all their own expenses, including part of showroom or market costs, which can run as high as one-third of their income. Independent sales reps carry several small, noncompeting lines. Sales representatives belong to associations that sponsor market weeks.

After a line release, sales reps receive duplicate samples and take the line on the road to market weeks around the country and to towns and cities within their assigned geographical territories. The rep usually sets up a presentation in a mart showroom or centrally located hotel room where buyers from the area can come to see the line. To win new accounts or to introduce a new line, reps have to go to the buyers, because the buyers rarely have time to look for new resources themselves.

Selling Incentives

Retailers look for manufacturers whose styling, quality, and dependability they can trust and from whom they can expect the same level of styling season after season. Retailers expect the following:

- Consistent quality
- Continuity of styles (a guarantee that all styles ordered will be produced)
- On-time deliveries (buyers are shopping later and yet expecting prompt deliveries)
- Value
- Reorder performance (manufacturers that are able to fill reorders when needed)

However, styling, value, quality, and on-time deliveries are often not enough. As fewer and fewer retailers control retail distribution, they have the power to be more demanding with nonkey vendors, insisting on contributions for markdowns, advertising, and promotions. Small manufacturers have a difficult time competing with so many demands that eat into their profits. The manufacturer may offer or the retailer may demand one or more of the following so that the retailer can maintain a minimum profit margin:

- Incentive pricing (to allow for greater profit margins)
- Off-price or promotional goods (special buys at low prices, usually offered as a preselected package)
- Credit
- Markdown allowances (credit on goods that had to be marked down)
- Exchange or return privileges (allowing a retailer to return any unsold garments for credit or a refund)
- A discount of 8 percent if bills are paid on time (taken even if they pay late)
- Fines for violations of ticketing, packing, and shipping rules

A SALES REP PRESENTS HER LINE TO BUYERS AT THE DALLAS MARKET CENTER. *(COURTESY OF THE DALLAS MARKET CENTER)*

- Cooperative advertising allowances
- Promotional aids such as in-store clinics, designer trunk shows, and brochures
- Assistance in reordering (for those firms that reorder, reorder forms or direct reordering contact via electronic data processing terminals may be supplied)
- Merchandise representatives
- Customer service

Orders

Electronic data interchange can automatically put through a purchase-order transaction from retailer to vendor. Through computer networks, orders can be entered via telephone from anywhere in the world. *Inventory management systems (IMS)* can instantly report on what is in stock and what delivery dates a customer can expect based on the information that it has sorted and filed.

Customer Service Computer technology also helps the customer service department to follow up on a sale by automatically printing invoices, handling reorders, and even preticketing and premarking boxes for retailers. Fed the correct information, IMS systems keep track of shipments and adjust inventory records automatically. Some manufacturers use round-the-clock inventory management systems that provide up-to-the-minute reports of what is selling and what is not throughout the country. These systems enable companies to continuously monitor selling patterns and alter production accordingly. Customer service representatives follow up on orders, field questions from retailers, and solve problems to ensure customer satisfaction.

Merchandise Representatives Many manufacturers believe that stores have failed in their responsibility to train sales associates properly, so they have hired consultants to work *in* the retail store. Some work exclusively for a large store, whereas others are regional merchandisers servicing a cluster of stores in a particular area. Examples include Ellen Tracy's "retail merchandisers" and Laundry's "selling specialists." They check to see that merchandise is in stock and displayed properly. They educate both sales associates and customers on how the line should be merchandised, worn, and accessorized. They are in the position to give feedback to the manufacturer on competitive lines and customer reactions. It is very costly to maintain these consultants, but they drive multiple sales and full price sell-through.

Sales Analysis At the end of a season, merchandisers and sales managers use IMS records to compare actual sales figures with the original sales and profit plan to see if goals were met. These records also give merchandisers and designers specific information on what colors, styles, fabrications, and price ranges sold best, which helps them to plan future lines.

Manufacturer–Retailer Relationships

A breakdown has occurred in the traditional buy–sell relationship between retailers and manufacturers. Due to intense competition for market share, manufacturers and retailers are learning to work together to share risk and information on forecasting, product development, production scheduling, and distribution. They are developing partnerships or alliances, a sort of informal vertical integration, to exchange information and create seamless and cost-efficient marketing, production, and distribution. Usually, large manufacturers team up with large retailers, and small with small.

Automatic Replenishment Agreements between suppliers and retailers may allow manufacturers to automatically refill stock when inventory levels are low. Coded information on that style (including needed colors, fabrics, and sizes) immediately informs the fabric producer to send more fabric to the apparel manufacturer and the apparel manufacturer to issue new cuts. This arrangement needs the complete cooperation of each level of the industry, a willingness to supply on a reorder basis, and the flexibility to sell smaller quantities of fabric and issue smaller, more frequent cuts. This allows production to be done closer to the selling season to get reactions to sales data.

SUMMARY

THE RETAILER AND THE MANUFACTURER, WHO TRADITIONALLY REPRESENT TWO SEPARATE BUSINESSES, COMMUNICATE THROUGH WHOLESALE MARKETS. FASHION SHOWINGS AND MARKETS ARE HELD IN MARKET CENTERS ALL YEAR LONG AROUND THE WORLD.

BRANDS AND DESIGNERS EXPAND THEIR BUSINESSES BY ADDING PRODUCT LINES, EXPORTING, AND OPENING RETAIL STORES. MANUFACTURERS HAVE VARIOUS DISTRIBUTION POLICIES TO ENSURE THAT THEIR GOODS ARE MERCHANDISED PROPERLY. MANY OFFER INCENTIVES TO RETAILERS TO BUY THEIR MERCHANDISE. THEY ALSO USE PUBLICITY, ADVERTISING, AND OTHER PROMOTIONAL AIDS TO FOSTER SALES.

COMPUTER TECHNOLOGY HAS HELPED SUPPLIERS, MANUFACTURERS, AND RETAILERS TO FORM PARTNERSHIPS TO TRY TO SPEED TURNAROUND TIME FOR PRODUCTION AND DISTRIBUTION AND KEEP RECORDS OF INVENTORY AND SALES.

THE FINAL TEST FOR FASHION MERCHANDISE IS WHETHER THE CONSUMER BUYS IT AT THE RETAIL LEVEL. EACH SEASON BRINGS A NEW CHANCE FOR SUCCESS OR FAILURE. NO WONDER THE APPAREL INDUSTRY IS A COMPETITIVE AND OFTEN NERVE-RACKING BUSINESS.

Terms and Concepts

Briefly define and discuss the following terms and concepts:

1. Markets
2. Line release
3. 7th on Sixth
4. MAGIC
5. Showrooms
6. Diversification
7. Selected distribution policy
8. Corporate selling
9. Brand integrity
10. Licensing
11. Franchising
12. Factory outlet stores
13. Overruns
14. Trunk shows
15. Cooperative advertising
16. Image advertising
17. Brand-name saturation
18. Look books
19. Merchandise representatives
20. Enhancement packages
21. Assortment customizing

Questions for Review

1. What role do wholesale fashion markets play?
2. Name five important international apparel or accessory markets or fairs and their location.
3. Name five important international designer collections and the cities where they are shown.

4. What are two regulations regarding couture showings?

5. Why did regional, national, and international fashion markets develop?

6. How does the presentation of a high-priced collection differ from that of a moderate- or low-priced line?

7. Explain the difference between open and selected distribution policies.

8. How and why do manufacturers diversify?

9. Why are exports important for the U.S. apparel industry?

10. How do manufacturers act as retailers?

11. List five promotional aids that manufacturers offer to retailers.

12. Explain how computer technology aids marketing.

Projects for Additional Learning

1. Analyze the imported fashion merchandise and accessories at a large retail store. Make a list of the countries represented and the merchandise specialty of each.

2. Ask a local buyer if you can sit in when a sales representative shows a line. Is the line presented in groups? Did the sales rep premerchandise the line in terms of the store's needs? Do you believe that the line is successful? Why? Summarize your findings in a written report.

3. Sell the line you designed in Chapter 9 to your class, explaining its concepts and features.

Notes

1 As quoted in "Liberté, Fraternité—But to Hell with Égalité," *Forbes,* June 2, 1997, p. 88.

2 As quoted in "Narciso's Homecoming," *Women's Wear Daily,* December 6, 2000, p. 8.

3 As quoted by Teri Agins, "Editorial Plugs for Apparel Are in Style," *Wall Street Journal,* October 6, 1992, p. B-l.

4 Quoted in "The Media Maze," *Women's Wear Daily,* May 28, 1999, p. 6.

5 Lisa Lockwood, "Image, Is It Everything?" *Women's Wear Daily,* March 28, 1997, p. 16.

A GLAMOROUS DRESS IN CONTRASTING BLACK AND WHITE BY OSCAR DE LA RENTA. *(COURTESY OF OSCAR DE LA RENTA, PHOTO BY DAN LECCA)*

PART FOUR

Fashion Retailing

Part IV covers all aspects of fashion retailing from retail centers to marketing. It is important to have read Chapters 2, 3, 4, 8, and 12 to understand basic concepts before reading these chapters.

- ■ **CHAPTER 13** discusses retailing centers, types of retailing, and retail organization.
- ■ **CHAPTER 14** deals with retail merchandising and all the aspects of buying and selling fashion.
- ■ **CHAPTER 15** examines fashion marketing including advertising, publicity, special events, and visual merchandising.

BERGDORF GOODMAN ON FIFTH
AVENUE IN NEW YORK CITY.
(COURTESY OF BERGDORF GOODMAN)

RETAILING | 13

Career Focus

Retail store line management begins with a chief executive officer (CEO), director of stores, individual store managers, floor and area managers, department managers, and their assistants. Retailing careers are also possible in mail order, e-commerce, and television. Merchandising positions will be discussed in Chapter 14.

CHAPTER OBJECTIVES

After reading this chapter, you should be able to:

1. Explain today's retail situation and trends
2. Discuss the various types of retail stores
3. Explain the organizational differences between single-unit and multiple-unit stores
4. Identify the major international stores and famous shopping areas
5. Compare the organizational structure of a small store with that of a retail chain
6. Discuss the growing importance of nonstore retailing

Retailing is the link between the manufacturer and the consumer. Retailers may buy fashion merchandise from *vendors* (manufacturers), directly import merchandise from all over the world, and/or develop their own brands. They sell this merchandise to consumers in their stores, by catalog, and/or via the Internet or television. True success in the fashion business is finally achieved at the retail level by consumer acceptance measured in purchases.

Many factors go into the making of a successful retail store: skillful management, well-executed logistics, a convenient location, a pleasant atmosphere, efficient sourcing, exciting and appropriate stock, buyers with an understanding of customer needs, helpful salespeople, and customer service. Most important, a retailer needs a unique vision and to carry out this vision effectively. Too often, success also lies more in sheer scale than in superior merchandising vision or innovation.

This chapter examines the current retail situation, global retailing, types of fashion retail stores, nonstore retailing, and the organization of single- and multiple-unit stores and corporations. Chapter 14 covers the merchandising function, the buying and selling of fashion merchandise.

The Retailing Picture

Enormous changes have occurred in retailing methods, management, and ownership, which will have long-range implications for retailing.

Retailing's Roots in the Cities

Most of the world's top retail stores began in manufacturing and marketing centers, such as Paris, London, Tokyo, Rome, Milan, and New York. Certain city streets or areas have become famous for retailing: Fifth Avenue, Madison Avenue, and the Soho district in New York City; Oak Street in Chicago; Union Square in San Francisco; Rodeo Drive in Beverly Hills; the Faubourg St. Honoré, Avenue Montaigne, Boulevard Haussmann, Rue de Passy, les Halles, and the St. Germain district in Paris; Via Condotti in Rome; Via della Spiga and Via Monte Napoleone in Milan; the Ginza district in Tokyo; Causeway Bay in Hong Kong; and Regent Street, Bond Street, and the Knightsbridge area in London. Most *flagship stores,* the first or main store of a chain, have remained in the cities, and new ones have been added.

Revitalization of Downtown and Main Street Retailing In Europe, where cities have continued to be the centers of fashion retailing, many streets have been closed to automobile traffic, creating pleasant walkways between shops. In the United States, retailers and community groups are beginning to react to the consumer's need to be connected to community and the need for urban retail stores. Many cities and towns are conducting revitalization projects, including the refurbishing of older department and specialty stores and the construction of malls such as Water Tower Place in Chicago, Pacific Place in Seattle, and the Westfield San Francisco Centre. Madison Avenue in New York City has attracted upscale retailers from around the world. Cities and towns try to maintain their individuality with their own unique mixture of national and international stores, local shops, restaurants, and services.

Shopping Centers

The shopping centers that now line many of the world's highways developed as a result of the shift to suburban living that followed World War II, and their growth has been fostered by real estate developers in areas of housing developments. Location in relation to local demographics is the most important consideration in mall development. A *shopping center* is defined as a group of retail establishments that is planned, developed, owned, and managed as a single property, providing a concentrated place to shop. A *mall* is enclosed with a climate-controlled walkway between two facing strips of stores, whereas a *strip center* is an attached row of stores without enclosed walkways linking the stores. This discussion is limited to those centers with apparel and accessory stores.

The rest of the world has followed America's lead in creating shopping centers. The United States now has approximately 45,000 centers including 1175 regional malls, followed by Canada, Australia, England, France, Germany, Sweden, and Switzerland. The largest shopping center in the world is the 7-million-square-feet South China Mall in Dongguan, China. The other largest malls include the Golden Resources Mall in Beijing, China, the SM Mall of Asia in Manila, Philippines, and the West Edmonton Mall in Alberta, Canada. The West Edmonton Mall is the largest shopping mall in the Western Hemisphere, with 5.2 million square feet and more than 800 stores. The Mall of America, in Bloomington, Minnesota, is the largest mall in the United States with 4.2 million square feet and 520 stores. The Plaza & Court at King of Prussia, Pennsylvania, and South Coast Plaza, Costa Mesa, California, are third and fourth.

Regional Centers
The traditional regional center or mall is *anchored* by at least two stores, with many other small specialty stores in between. Formerly, anchors were department

stores, but today only a few names are left. Unconventional anchors are filling vacant department store spaces. Now anchors might be a moderate department store such as Macy's, a discount store such as Target, or a mass merchant such as Sears, with a variety of specialty stores catering to various market niches. The typical regional center is 400,000 to 800,000 square feet.

Unfortunately, many malls have become sterile, predictable, and indistinguishable, with similar shops. Most of the recently built malls just take market share away from other existing malls as shifting population densities change shopping patterns. Some regional malls in the United States are empty and others are run down. Some have been torn down or redeveloped. Many malls are competing by developing one of the following alternatives.

Fashion Specialty Centers

These centers are composed mainly of upscale apparel shops of high quality and price in a rich decor. They may be anchored by a specialty department store such as Neiman Marcus or Nordstrom, along with many smaller specialty stores in between. For example, the Collection at Chevy Chase, outside of Washington, D.C., is a luxury fashion center.

Power or Value Centers   Value retail centers, malls, or strip shopping centers, made up entirely of discount stores, are growing in number, size, and popularity. When older malls are faced with overwhelming competition from new ones, one option is to convert into value centers. Power centers are those dominated by large discount, off-price, or warehouse clubs, such as Target or Wal-Mart, with only a minimum of small specialty stores.

Outlet Centers   Manufacturer and retailer outlet or clearance stores are usually found in specially designated malls around the country. These malls are located away from traditional department and specialty stores to avoid competition with them. Examples of large malls that blend outlet, value, and off-price retailing are Franklin, Potomac, Gurnee, and Sawgrass Mills.

Recreational or Theme Centers   Competition has caused some malls to use entertainment to draw customers and to capitalize on the recreational aspects of shopping. These "retail-tainment" centers have become the new amusement parks. The West Edmonton Mall in Alberta, for example, incorporates an ice arena, a deep-sea theme park, a golf course, movie theaters, and 110 restaurants and snack bars and is Alberta's biggest tourist attraction. The Mall of America in Bloomington, Minnesota, includes movie theaters, an indoor theme park, a roller coaster, and a miniature golf course.

THE MALL OF AMERICA IN BLOOMINGTON, MINNESOTA, INCORPORATES 14 MOVIE THEATERS, AN INDOOR THEME PARK, A ROLLER COASTER, AND A MINIATURE GOLF COURSE. *(COURTESY OF MALL OF AMERICA)*

Town or "Mixed-Use" Centers   In the face of mall oversaturation, some are struggling to establish an edge by repositioning themselves as "town" centers. An outgrowth of both classic town planning and retail malls, these live/work/play/shop environments are cropping up across the country. In addition to shops, they provide cafes, restaurants, cinemas, libraries, meeting rooms, office space, and even townhouses to create centers that reflect community culture and architecture. Large empty spaces left by defunct department stores are sometimes converted to residential units. Developers have both recycled and created new mixed-use malls into open-air villages, simulating old-fashioned neighborhoods, with residences, parks, shops, theaters, and offices. Tattersall Park in Alabama, for example, recreates a small downtown from the 1940s complete with Main Street. Makeovers, such as the renovated Winter Park Village near Orlando, Florida, or Lakewood, Colorado, bring new life to old malls. Other new mixed-use centers include St. John's Town Center in Jacksonville, Florida, and San Tan Village in Arizona.

Urban Malls   To give city dwellers convenient shopping, some developers have created malls in downtown areas. This allows many shops to be built on a small area, often one square block, of high-cost real estate. Customers take escalators from one level of shops to the next. The San Francisco Centre, for example, is built on only 43,000 square feet of ground space, but its nine floors provide a total of 500,000 square feet of shops. Hollywood & Highland in Los Angeles comprises 8.7 acres of luxury shops, a hotel, cineplex, and the Kodak Theater, home of the Academy Awards. Atlanta Station, on the site of the former Atlantic Steel Mill, in north Atlanta, Georgia, is another example.

Transportation Centers   Some airports and train stations are being transformed into shopping centers. They make ideal malls because they have a steady flow of high-income passengers, resulting in much higher sales per square foot than traditional malls. Successful international airport malls have been developed at Heathrow, near London, Dubai, Schiphol in Amsterdam, and Frankfurt-Main, Germany, for example. Pittsburgh Airport and Union Station, Washington, D.C., made a success of the idea in the United States. Many retailers are finding transportation centers to be an innovative alternative location.

Ideally, shopping centers need to become more flexible, adding grocery stores, dry cleaners, and other services, and to become more imaginative and entertaining.

Retail Bankruptcies and Consolidations

Across the country, once solid companies have closed their doors, been purchased by other companies, or been forced to consolidate. Since 1980, long-established retailers such as Abraham & Straus, B. Altman, Bonwit Teller, Frederick & Nelson, Garfinkel's, Gimbel's, I. Magnin, Wards, and many others have either been acquired and absorbed by other retailers or closed due to heavy debt, fierce competition, sourcing and inventory control problems, real estate costs, and/or poor management. Many retailers are still consolidating, restructuring, or closing. Recently, an unprecedented number of sell-offs and consolidations have occurred. In 2006, Federated Department Stores purchased the May Company and closed Marshall Field, Strawbridge's, Hecht's, and Filene's, converting most of those stores to the Macy's brand. Now Macy's has over 800 stores in 45 states. Ames, Bradlees, Caldor, and Hills have closed. Sears has merged with Kmart. As a result, there is a great loss of independent and privately held apparel retailers. Surviving stores are trying to deal with a highly competitive marketplace, with more supply than demand.

Too Many Stores

In spite of bankruptcies and consolidations, too many stores still exist for the number of consumers in the United States. Although there are fewer retail names, there is an increasing number of stores. In the 1970s, an estimated 7 square feet of retail selling space existed for every person in the United States; now there are 18 square feet per person. Yet the big retailers are still getting bigger. Large chains such as Wal-Mart, the world's largest retailer, continue to open new stores. However, some retailers are closing stores to weed out unprofitable units, and others are cutting back on expansion. The reality of retailing is that it is a mature business with no room for growth because of a stagnant market. Retailing today is competition for existing market share.

Retailing Strategies for Success

With increased competition and a stagnant market, retailers try to reflect trends in consumer shopping habits and lifestyles to survive and be profitable.

Retailers are taking various approaches to compete. To be successful and improve *productivity* (sales per square foot), a retailer must create a competitive advantage and set itself apart by offering something special. Six areas of focus seem to be the most promising: uniqueness, new concepts, value, service, entertainment, and global expansion.

Unique Merchandising

With so much consolidation, uniqueness is often lost because most national retailers carry merchandise from the same large apparel manufacturers. As retailers narrow their vendor structures, many stores have become too mainstream and boring. Paul Delaoutre, director general of Galeries Lafayette, Paris, said, "We are not just a hanging place for brands." Differentiation is the key. Tom Herndon, CEO of RYA Design Consultancy, recommended "building the name brand of the store first, and brands in the store second."[1] Consumers prefer to shop in stores that offer a special experience. Retailers are trying to find new ways to provide unique styling with private-label merchandise (see Private Label, Chapter 14) and by finding exciting new vendors. With the renewed interest in fashion, uniqueness is especially important.

New Spin-Off Concepts

Specialty single-brand retailers are launching new store brands to reach wider demographics or to serve current customers with other types of apparel. Examples of these new specialty chains include Abercrombie & Fitch's "Ruehl," Gap's "Forth & Towne," American Eagle's "Martin + Osa," Polo Ralph Lauren's "Rugby," and J. Crew's "Crewcuts" (children's wear). Multibrand specialty store Neiman Marcus has also launched a new brand called "Cusp" to appeal to a younger customer. The antitheses of a typical Neiman Marcus, these smaller-format stores have an edgy decor and feature trendy contemporary clothes and accessories. Finding new ways to grow a business is very difficult; there are only so many voids in the market to fill.

HARROD'S OF LONDON IS A MAJOR TOURIST ATTRACTION. *(COURTESY OF HARROD'S)*

Value-Directed Retailing

Consumers look for value, convenience, and fair prices. Value-directed retailers include discounters, outlet stores, warehouse clubs, catalogs, or any retailer whose customers think they are getting their money's worth. Discount retailers have taken a considerable amount of business away from department stores. Successful retailers have the proper price–value and assortment relationship. They give customers what they want, where they want it, when they want it, at a fair price. Retailers are attempting to reduce expenses and become efficient to keep prices down.

Service-Oriented Retailing

Retailers are attempting to anticipate and focus on the needs of their customers and, in fact, to exceed their customers' expectations. They are trying to make shopping more convenient and friendly so that their customers will enjoy it and find what they are looking for. Many retailers are using capital investments to renovate existing units to create a warm, hospitable atmosphere. E-commerce and catalogs capitalize on convenience. Service-oriented retailers include Neiman Marcus, Nordstrom, and many mail-order and online retailers, such as L.L. Bean and Lands' End (see Customer Service, Chapter 14, for a full discussion).

■ HARVEY NICHOLS, A FASHION RETAILER IN LONDON, HAS OPENED STORES AROUND THE WORLD SUCH AS THIS ONE IN RIYADH, SAUDI ARABIA. *(COURTESY OF HARVEY NICHOLS)*

Entertainment

In an effort to keep stores alive, many retailers are trying to add excitement to the retail experience with entertainment. Stores are providing beauty makeovers, spas, cafes, musicians, DJs, personal appearances, special events, video walls, CD listening posts, computer games, and other sights and sounds to draw customers. Sometimes dubbed "lifestyle theme stores," they try to create an ambiance to attract customers. Entertainment may make it worthwhile for people to come into the stores; however, the merchandise has to be enticing enough to buy.

Global Expansion

Just as globalization has affected manufacturing, many retailers believe that one way to increase market share is through global expansion. Many European firms, such as Prada of Italy, Zara of Spain, and H&M (Hennes & Mauritz) of Sweden, have opened stores around the world, particularly in Japan, China, Russia, and the Middle East. Harvey

Nichols of London, for example, opened a store in Riyadh, Saudi Arabia, and plans to grow into an international chain of 10 or more stores. Retailers are looking at emerging economies for retail expansion, most notably India, Russia, Ukraine, and China.

Americans are following suit. The Gap has stores worldwide and plans 30 more in Singapore and Malaysia by 2010. Several American designers, such as Donna Karan, have stores in Europe. Saks Fifth Avenue has two stores in the Middle East. Japan has already attracted several U.S. retailers, such as Barneys, Brooks Brothers, Talbots, and Ralph Lauren. Brooks Brothers has 31 freestanding or in-store shops in Japan. Closer to home, J.C. Penney, Dillard's, Sears, Price Club, and Wal-Mart are expanding in Mexico.

In addition to opening stores in other countries, companies are investing in foreign retailing businesses. Renown of Japan, for example, acquired Aquascutum of London. Most retailers think that globalization is the only way to survive in the future. On the other hand, with global retailers opening stores in every major city, the same merchandise is available everywhere, and regional markets lose their identity.

Store-Based Retailers

Many types of retail operations have been created to try to serve customers' needs.

Over the past hundred years, various kinds of retail operations have evolved, including specialty stores, department stores, mass merchants, catalogs, television shopping channels, and electronic retailing, often referred to as E-commerce. The distinctions among these different forms have blurred. There are many overlaps among categories, and even retail experts do not agree on how to categorize stores. Retailing is continually evolving; new categories are emerging and old ones are combining.

Specialty Stores

Specialty stores cater to a particular target customer by providing a narrow focus of merchandise. Most specialty retailers stock merchandise within a certain price range, as well as in a specific category. In Europe, specialty stores have continually predominated in fashion retailing. Examples of international specialty stores are Harvey Nichols, Fenwick's, and Brown's in London; Le Bon Marché and Franck et Fils in Paris; and the traditional designer shops of Paris, Milan, Florence, and Rome, such as Hermès, Chanel, and Prada.

Specialty stores present a clear merchandising message to consumers. The customer can easily identify with a particular retailer by virtue of the merchandise, presentation, and advertising image. With smaller formats, specialty retailers are able to locate in downtown and neighborhood shopping districts. Specialty retailing has grown in the past two decades, overtaking department stores in market share.

There are four general types of specialty retailers: *single-line,* which carry just one category of merchandise; *single-brand,* which carry only private-label merchandise; *limited-line,* which stock related categories of merchandise; and *multiple-line* (sometimes categorized as department stores), which offer many categories.

Single-Line Stores

Single-line stores carry deep inventories of one specific classification. They have a very narrow focus catering to a specific consumer need, giving their customers a wide selection in one category of merchandise. They might sell only accessories, athletic shoes, ties, or socks. These stores can be small independents or may grow into regional or national chains (see Multiple-Unit Stores later in this chapter).

Single-Brand or Private-Label Retailers

Not to be confused with single-line stores, *single-brand* stores carry only merchandise sold under the store's name or *private label.* Private-label retailers maintain their own design departments or use the services of design studios, such as Mast Industries in Boston or Dominique Peclers in Paris, to design their lines. These retailers usually contract production of their product or may establish joint ventures with factories (see Chapter 14 for information on private-label merchandising). If the retailers do the manufacturing themselves, they are also considered to be *vertical* retailers because they perform functions on two levels of the fashion industry. Because they are vertical operations, they can be flexible and maximize a trend quickly. Gap, Brooks Brothers, and Ann Taylor are examples of single-brand or private-label merchants. They have established their stores' names as important apparel brands.

Limited-Line Stores

Limited-line retailers cater to narrow groups of consumers. They may carry just apparel and accessories for women, for example, just children's wear, or just men's wear. Within the limited category, they may carry different price ranges and brands.

Multiple-Line Stores   Multiple-line retailers carry a wider variety of categories, such as women's and men's apparel and accessories. In addition, they may have children's wear, cosmetics, and even gifts. Because they have many departments, some observers designate them "specialty department stores," and some even categorize them as department stores. Leading multiline, multibrand high-fashion specialty department stores across North America include Bergdorf Goodman; Saks Fifth Avenue; Neiman Marcus, based in Dallas; Nordstrom, based in Seattle; and Holt Renfrew in Canada. Smaller independent luxury multiple-line stores include Fred Segal in Los Angeles, Mitchells in Connecticut, Scoop in New York City, Wilkes Bashford in San Francisco, Stanley Korshak in Dallas, and Louis Boston.

Department Stores

In their heyday through the 1950s, department stores set the standard of good taste for the middle class. Beginning in the late 1800s, department stores dominated the American center-city retail scene and later served as the anchors and magnets that made regional malls successful. The term

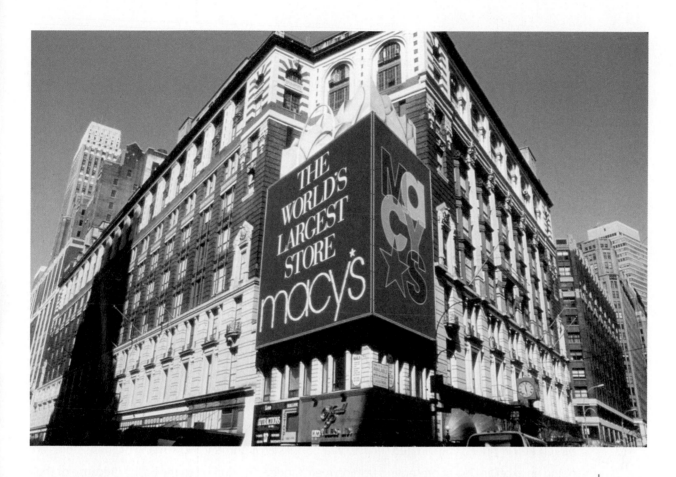

MACY'S, HERALD SQUARE, NEW YORK CITY, IS THE LARGEST DEPARTMENT STORE IN THE UNITED STATES. *(COURTESY OF MACY'S)*

department store comes from the practice of presenting many different kinds of merchandise, each in a separate department or specific selling space. Apparel and accessories for men, women, and children are sold along with household goods, such as furniture, lamps, linens, and tableware. (Department stores also used to carry appliances, toys, and other products that are now handled by individual specialty stores.) Department stores usually concentrate 70 to 80 percent of their merchandise in the moderate to upper-moderate price ranges. Women's wear usually accounts for more than half of the sales volume.

Internationally, Seibu in Japan claims to be the biggest department store in the world. GUM in Moscow is the largest in Eastern Europe, Harrod's of London is the biggest in Europe, and Macy's (part of Federated Department Stores) is the largest in the United States. Other leading international department stores include Liberty and Selfridges in London; Galeries Lafayette and Printemps in Paris; Rinascente in Italy; KaDeWe, Karstadt, and Kaufhof in Germany; and Matsuzokaya, Mitsukoshi, and Isetan in Japan.

Many established regional department stores, such as John Wanamaker, Marshall Field, Strawbridge's, Hecht's, Filene's, Jordan Marsh, Abraham & Straus, Bullocks, and the Broadway, went out of business or were taken over by national retailers during the past 30 years. The field is now dominated by just five retailing giants. Well-known national department stores include Federated Department Stores (owners of Macy's and Bloomingdale's), Dillard's, Kohl's, Sears-Kmart, and J.C. Penney. Sears, Penney's, and Kohl's are often categorized separately as "middle-market" department stores.

Initially, department stores attracted consumers by offering ambience, attentive service, and a wide variety of merchandise. Walter K. Levy, of Kurt Salmon Associates, explained, "It used to be that department stores created a concept and then developed an assortment around that idea."[2] Now all of them carry the same brands and have no individuality. Although they offer national and some designer brands, they have become overwhelming, difficult for customers to navigate, and dull. Their share of the apparel market has fallen to 40 percent from 70 percent two decades ago.

Mass Merchants

Mass merchandise retailers have built their businesses providing *commodity merchandise* (standard basics) at low prices, with limited service, in a no-frills environment. Now many of these stores are doing an excellent job of presenting fashion merchandise, in addition to the basics. Because of their ability to buy in volume, mass merchants are able to buy at lower prices and pass the savings on to their customers. Most retail consultants include discounters, off-price retailers, and factory outlets as mass merchants. Today, over 50 percent of all apparel is purchased at mass retailers (most of these stores are general merchandise retailers, but this discussion is limited to those that carry fashion apparel and accessories).

Discounters Discounters offer low prices by buying large quantities of lower-priced merchandise and keeping expenses down with low rent, a simple decor, and fewer salespeople. Consumers' quest for value and the popularity of casual dressing spurred the growth of discounters. Manufacturers are increasingly willing to supply them, and to enhance their fashion images they have hired designers, such as Isaac Mizrahi for Target, to design private-label merchandise for them.

The number of discount stores has more than doubled in the past 20 years and they have taken business away from the traditional department and specialty stores. Led by Wal-Mart and Target, discounters have become the largest retailers in the United States. Some discounters now have "supercenters," large megastores that include apparel, general merchandise, and groceries.

Off-Price Retailers Some retailers specialize in selling merchandise at low prices by offering special buys, closeouts, *overruns* (manufacturers' overproduced merchandise), last season's goods, off-colors, and manufacturers' returns. The need for low rents excludes them from high-rent malls and prime downtown areas. Examples of off-price retailers are Ross, Loehmann's, and Marshalls.

Outlet Stores Like manufacturers that sell overruns and out-of-season merchandise in their own outlet stores (see Chapter 12), retailers have found it profitable to run clearance stores for out-of-season or slow-moving merchandise. Macy's, Neiman Marcus, and Nordstrom are examples of stores that have their own outlets, such as Nordstrom Rack.

Warehouse Clubs These "big-box" retailers, which charge a small membership fee, offer consumers deep discounts on general merchandise in a warehouse setting. Although they do offer some clothing on racks, it is primarily casual or active sportswear. With stores ranging from 40,000 to 160,000 square feet, these retailers offer approximately 3000 to 5000 deeply stocked products. Examples are Sam's Club, owned by Wal-Mart, and Costco.

Promotional Stores

Any store that is price directed, be it a specialty store, department store, or mass merchant, is a promotional store. Some of these stores offer special buys from manufacturers and frequent sales in an effort to get customers into the store. Examples of promotional stores are Macy's, the May Company, Mervyn's, and Target. Whereas some stores have become more promotional, others are trying to get away from this strategy with consistent value pricing.

Consignment Stores

Although a very small part of the retailing picture, consignment stores and consignment selling are having a bit of a comeback. *Consignment* is the practice of retailers taking merchandise for their stores and paying vendors only if it sells. If the merchandise doesn't sell, it is returned to the vendor. Some retailers argue that consignment selling gives them the chance to try out new lines without risk. Although common in Japan, consignment selling in the United States is reserved mainly for fine jewelry departments in large stores and small designer or vintage clothing shops.

Retail Organization

Retail organizations offer many opportunities for a variety of experiences and responsibilities.

Retailing functions are generally divided into six areas of responsibility: merchandising, store operations, marketing, finance and control, real estate, and human resources. Merchandising, operations, and marketing are all responsible for sales. However, each store or corporation has its own unique structure.

Merchandising has the responsibility of planning, buying, and selling merchandise; the goal is to provide the store's target customer with the right merchandise at the right time, as discussed in Chapter 14.

Retail operations is responsible for planning, managing, and maintaining the retail building; protecting the store and merchandise; providing customer services; and coordinating the movement of goods and people within the building. In catalog and Internet retailing this would include maintaining the warehouse, orders, and shipping.

Marketing directs the focus and image of the retailer and is responsible for informing customers about goods and services through advertisements, displays, publicity, special events, and public relations (see Chapter 15).

Finance controls expenditures and keeps records of money spent and received: accounts payable (goods received but not yet paid for), payroll, taxes, credit (customers' charge accounts), and inventory.

Real estate or store planning oversees store location, property investment, building and construction, and fixtures.

Human resources staffs the store with people who are qualified and trained to handle the work that needs to be done and ensures compliance with state and federal labor laws.

Small Stores

The typical small store is often managed by one person, usually the owner, who assumes many roles in the store's operation, such as manager, buyer, salesperson, stockperson, and bookkeeper. In some cases, several people jointly run a store, each assuming responsibility for the jobs he or she is most capable of doing. As sales grow, the owner hires employees who perform a wide range of activities. Successful stores may grow in size, open additional locations to become a "chain," or be purchased by a larger company.

Small stores can offer their customers highly personalized service that larger stores cannot, such as wardrobe planning. They can also get to know the needs of their customers through personal contact. Although small stores are often unable to buy from large manufacturers due to high minimums, they can buy from small manufacturers, offering their customers unique merchandise in a unique setting, or buy through a *buying office* (see Chapter 14) together with other small stores.

Small independent specialty stores have a difficult time competing. Some observers say that the needs of today's customers are not satisfied by the small specialty store that does not have the assortment that a Neiman Marcus or a Saks Fifth Avenue has. On the other hand, the small specialty store may be the only avenue left for the unique fashion made by small manufacturers. For this reason, there is a resurgence of small fashion boutiques, such as Berlin's, Janet Brown, Linda Dresner, Fred Segal, Jeffrey, Julian Gold, Lilly Dodson, Louis, and Scoop.

Large Stores

As sales increase, an owner may hire more employees and increase space. As additional managers are hired, specialization occurs; the retailing functions are divided among people who are specialists in the performance of their respective jobs. Individual managers are responsible for separate functions, such as merchandising, operations, human resources, or finances. A store may hire an outside financial service and an agency to do the advertising and publicity. The larger the store—by sales, square footage, or number of stores—the more complex the organizational structure.

Stores within a Store

In-Store Designer Boutiques
Popular designers or brands often require that a retail store furnish a permanent location and *real estate* (a certain amount of square footage) within the store devoted solely to their merchandise. The retailer provides space and purchases the product. The designer or brand vendor prescribes how the merchandise is to be visually merchandised and accessorized. They negotiate with the store regarding the creation of boutique environments and may supply the fixtures.

In-store boutiques allow designers and brands to present their entire collection and strengthen their image. They can also present their own accessories together with the clothes. In so doing, they present the consumer with "the world of" Giorgio Armani, Calvin Klein, or Ralph Lauren. Wal-Mart has even opened a "vendor store" where manufacturers are permitted to take charge of selecting and displaying their own merchandise.

To present a cohesive store image and promote in-house brands, some department stores are phasing out in-store shops. They are returning to grouping apparel by category to make shopping easier for their customers.

Leased Departments
To provide additional services for their customers, many stores lease certain departments to an outside organization better able to handle a particular

THE D&G (DOLCE AND GABBANA) IN-STORE SHOP AT HENRI BENDEL. (COURTESY OF HENRI BENDEL, PHOTO BY GINI STEPHENS FRINGS)

specialty. Leased departments in retail stores are merchandised, owned, and operated by an outside firm, rather than by the store itself. Departments such as furs, shoes, and fine jewelry are sometimes leased because special training for sales associates is necessary. Today, however, leasing is used less frequently because it is more cost-effective for a store to run its own departments.

Multiple-Unit Stores

A successful *single-unit* store may open additional locations to grow into a *multiple-unit* operation. These range from small retail organizations with just a few locations to national retail *chains* with hundreds of stores and thousands of employees. The success of the multiple-unit retailer is based on its ability to buy in large quantities and distribute the merchandise and operating costs throughout the organization.

National and global single-brand stores, such as the Gap and Ann Taylor, and department stores, such as Sears and J.C. Penney, are chain organizations. Even many luxury designer stores have become chains; Polo Ralph Lauren has over 350 units and Giorgio Armani has over 300. Some chains have become megaretailers. Wal-Mart, the world's largest retailer, has over 1570 stores, 1250 supercenters, 520 Sam's Clubs, and 1200 international units. The Gap operates over 3000 stores worldwide, including Gap Kids, Old Navy, Banana Republic, and Forth and Towne. Zara of Spain has over 5000 stores worldwide; Swedish H&M operates over 1000 stores in 14 countries. Retailing is increasingly dominated by large chains.

Chain Organization Naturally, the management of a chain is much more complex than that of a small retailer, especially because individual stores, referred to as *doors,* are often geographically far apart. Most chains have similar organizational structures. The chief executive officer (CEO), the chairman or president, is the head of the management team. Vice presidents are responsible for separate functions, such as merchandising, marketing, store operations, regional stores, planning, visual merchandising, finance, human resources, and customer service. In the operations division, a general manager or store manager is responsible for

TALBOTS IS ORGANIZED AS A NATIONAL CHAIN. *(PHOTO BY GINI STEPHENS FRINGS)*

each store. Group sales managers, sales managers, and sales associates work in specific areas of each store.

Senior executives work at company headquarters or at regional centers. Merchandise managers and buyers may also have offices in New York City, to be close to national markets (organization of the merchandising division is discussed in Chapter 14). Centrally purchased merchandise is distributed to all stores from a central or regional distribution center. Individual store managers are in charge at each store throughout the chain.

Types of Ownership

Another way to classify retailers is by their type of ownership.

Sole Proprietorships

Most independent fashion stores are sole proprietorships; they are owned by a single person. Although many of these businesses exist, they do only a small fraction of the total retail business. Most of these stores are owner-managed. The owners have direct contact with their customers, are not bound by corporate rules, and, therefore, can be flexible and respond quickly to customer needs. However, these owner-managers have to have a broad range of capabilities to operate their businesses effectively. They usually hire outside financial services and advertising agencies. Small, independently owned retailers are enjoying a resurgence, due to consumers' disenchantment with the merchandise sameness in national chains and department stores.

Partnerships

A partnership is a business owned by two or more persons under a contractual agreement. In this case, each partner assumes responsibility for separate functions. One owner may manage merchandising and the other might be in charge of finance and running the store, for instance. As the store hires more employees, the jobs become more specialized. As a partnership or sole proprietorship grows, it is usually converted into a corporation.

Corporations

Virtually all fashion retail chains are corporations or divisions of larger corporations or holding companies. Stockholders finance the corporation and elect a board of directors. They, in turn, select a chairman and other corporate officers to run the company. The main functions of the management team are to set policies and make sure that strategies are carried out properly. Officers manage specific areas of responsibility, depending on their expertise.

As we discussed at the beginning of the chapter, considerable consolidation and restructuring of corporate retail chains has occurred. Each acquired retailer becomes a separate division within the corporation. Usually, each division is a semi-independent unit with its own central merchandising and management. However, corporate management handles overall organization, strategic planning, and finance. All the divisions share communication, information, and distribution systems; private-label development; catalog production; and E-commerce development, which helps to reduce costs. Retailing executives think that consolidation is necessary because large companies have more buying power. Fewer corporate chains now dominate fashion retailing, but they keep growing by adding new stores.

Nonstore Retailing

Nonstore retailing has developed for the convenience of the consumer.

Many consumers dislike the inconvenience of traffic, parking, crowds, and going from store to store in search of a coordinated wardrobe. Also, many busy people do not have the time to go shopping. They want to buy clothing and accessories quickly and efficiently. To answer their needs, mail-order, cable television, and Internet shopping offer consumers the convenience of shopping from home. Large retail corporations have separate divisions to handle catalogs and E-commerce.

Although home shopping is still just a small segment of retailing, it is growing rapidly. Many major store-based retailers are also selling via catalogs and the Internet. The wave of the future is multichannel retailing—traditional stores, catalogs, and the Web working together because consumers expect merchandise to be available anywhere at any time. However, although non-store retailing is convenient, customers cannot touch the merchandise, see the details up close, or try it on.

Mail-Order Merchants

Mail-order retailing offers merchandise to consumers in a catalog or direct-mail format. Mail-order catalogs provide consumers with the opportunity to compare merchandise and prices while sitting at home. Direct mail offers merchandise in brochures, often sent with retail store billing statements (see Advertising, Chapter 15).

Many mail-order businesses, including Talbots and J.C. Penney, also have retail stores. Some opened stores after their catalog businesses became successful; others were already established retailers. In fact, all retailers are finding that mail order complements their store merchandising and

THE FIRST PROOF, SHOWING CORRECTIONS, OF A PAGE FROM AN EDDIE BAUER CATALOG. *(COURTESY OF EDDIE BAUER)*

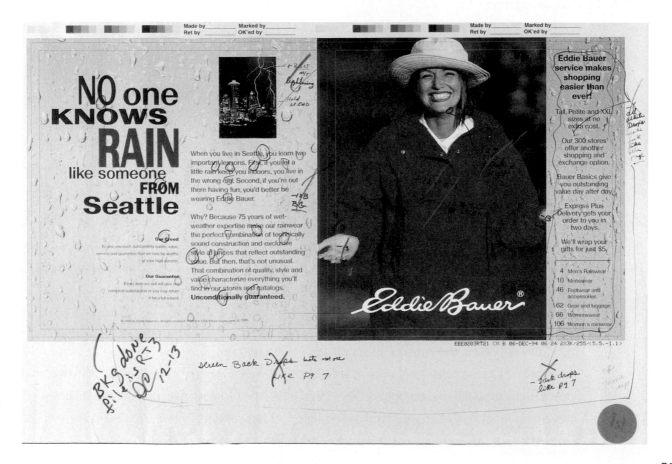

brings them increased business. Apparel catalog retailers include J. Crew, Lands' End, L.L. Bean, and Talbots. Catalog size runs the gamut from J.C. Penney's semi-annual 1000-page book to Talbots' 48-page catalog. Some of these companies also have microcatalogs that focus on specific niche markets.

Catalogs are a difficult business, however, and success often depends on how carefully a company organizes production and distribution. The length of time needed to design, develop, and distribute catalogs makes it difficult to respond quickly to new trends in fashion. High production and paper costs and postal rates make catalogs expensive to produce and send. J. Crew, for example, mails out approximately 80 million catalogs annually to a mailing list of millions. When customers call a toll-free number to place orders, operators can access information about past purchases, making it easier for customers to order.

To increase business, some mail-order merchants have extended distribution to foreign countries. However, foreign languages, higher postal rates, and the absence of 800 numbers are some of the barriers they face. To meet the competition of online shopping, many catalog retailers are selling via the Internet.

E-tailing

E-tailing is the retailing industry's term for online retailing via the Internet, or *e-commerce*. The customer and the retailer communicate through an interactive electronic computer system. The retailer transmits information and graphics to the customer's computer via the Internet, and the customer can order merchandise directly through the interactive system. Price-Waterhouse-Coopers analysts equated the Internet with "a gigantic electronic vending machine for everything on sale on Earth."

The Internet opens up global markets. It reaches many people without the cost of running a store. Online apparel sales are now fourth after media (books and music), travel services, and computer software. Almost every retailer now has a Web site, including small boutiques such as Scoopnyc.com.

Consumers like the convenience of shopping anytime, day or night, and shopping at stores that are not in their area. They want to have easy access to a site, find what they want quickly, and have the merchandise delivered promptly. Sites need to be easy to navigate, updated frequently, and have clear graphics that convey a retailer's image. Retailers continually evaluate design elements of their Web sites to find the best presentation to engage consumer interest. Successful e-tailing is also dependent on how well a company can monitor inventory, fill orders, and handle customer service. E-commerce is easiest for catalog companies that already have warehouse and distribution systems in place.

Research indicates that consumers are gravitating to retail Web sites that are tied to stores they already know and where it is easier to make returns. Stores with Web sites are referred to in the press as "brick and click" retailers. The companies with the largest apparel sales online are eBay, QVC, and Victoria's Secret, followed by JC Penney, Coldwater Creek, Home Shopping Network, Lands' End, Old Navy, Eddie Bauer, and L.L. Bean.[3]

Online shopping services, such as Style.com, ShopVogue.com, and Glam.com, offer shopping at various retailers. Ideally, electronic catalogs will eventually enable shoppers to custom search among many e-tailers for a product by size, brand, and price range and zoom in for a closer look at the item. The future of retailing is multichanneled, giving customers the option of phone, Internet, or in-store shopping.

Television Shopping

TV home shopping includes shopping networks and infomercials that allow consumers across the country to see merchandise in their own living rooms, order it by phone, and have it delivered. The major cable networks are QVC and Home Shopping Network (HSN); however, only 20 percent of their business is fashion. Some designers do special collections for cable television, such as Randolph Duke for HSN and Carole Hochman for QVC.

Industry analysts do not see much growth potential for television shopping; most people do not want to wait for specific times when certain merchandise is shown. As a precaution, both major shopping networks see the Internet as a natural extension of their businesses; HSN has acquired the Internet Shopping Network, and QVC launched its own QVC shopping service on the Web.

SUMMARY

THIS CHAPTER EXAMINED THE RETAILING SITUATION OF CLOSURES AND CONSOLIDATIONS DUE TO FIERCE COMPETITION AND STRATEGIES FOR IMPROVING BUSINESS IN THE FUTURE. RETAILERS ARE TRYING TO COPE BY MEETING CONSUMER NEEDS WITH VALUE, SERVICE, ENTERTAINMENT, UNIQUE MERCHANDISING, AND GLOBAL EXPANSION. THERE IS A RENEWED INTEREST IN INNER-CITY RETAILING, AND MALLS ARE DIVERSIFYING AND RENOVATING TO STAY IN BUSINESS.

RETAIL OPERATIONS INCLUDE SPECIALTY STORES, DEPARTMENT STORES, MASS MERCHANTS, AND MAIL-ORDER AND ELECTRONIC RETAILERS. THERE ARE BOTH SINGLE- AND MULTIPLE-UNIT STORES, SOME GROWING INTO LARGE CHAINS. STORE FUNCTIONS INCLUDE MARKETING, MERCHANDISING, STORE OPERATIONS, FINANCE, REAL ESTATE, AND PERSONNEL. IN SMALL STORES, THESE JOBS ARE HANDLED BY ONLY A FEW PEOPLE; IN LARGE STORES, EACH FUNCTION IS DIRECTED BY A DIFFERENT EXECUTIVE.

TO MAINTAIN A COMPETITIVE POSITION, A RETAILER MUST BE FOCUSED ON THE NEEDS OF ITS TARGET CUSTOMER. TO APPEAL TO THIS CUSTOMER, THE STORE MUST HAVE A UNIQUE YET APPROPRIATE IMAGE CARRIED OUT IN ITS MERCHANDISE, MARKETING, AND SERVICES.

Terms and Concepts

Briefly define and discuss the following terms and concepts:

1. Retailing
2. Lifestyle centers
3. Fifth Avenue
4. Chain stores
5. Department stores
6. Specialty stores
7. Deep-niche retailing
8. Flagship stores
9. Private-label retailers
10. Off-price retailers
11. Promotional stores
12. E-tailing
13. In-store boutiques

Questions for Review

1. What is the purpose of retailing?
2. What is causing restructuring and consolidation in retailing?
3. What strategies are retailers using to compete? Which do you think are the most effective and why?
4. How does globalization affect retailing?
5. Explain five different types of shopping malls that have emerged in the United States.
6. How does a department store differ from a specialty store?

7. Explain the differences in organization between a small store and a large store.

8. Why has off-price, discount, and warehouse retailing increased?

9. Briefly explain the growth of mail-order retailing.

10. What impact might Internet retailing have in the future?

11. Describe the basic functions of a retail organization.

12. How can small stores compete with large ones?

Projects for Additional Learning

1. Find out whether one of the department or specialty stores in your community is owned by a retail corporation. Find out what other stores are part of the same corporation.

2. Research the history and growth of a large store in your area. Contact the store's public relations department for information, and check your college or local library for further information.

3. What is your favorite retail Web site? Why? Analyze the merchandise offered, graphics, and ease of ordering.

Notes

[1] As quoted by Melissa Drier, "Department Store Parley Focuses on Adaptation," *Women's Wear Daily,* May 22, 2006, p. 5.

[2] Walter K. Levy, managing director of retail trends, Kurt Salmon Associates, as quoted in "In the Black or in the Red," *FGI Bulletin,* Fashion Group International, Issue 4, 2003.

[3] "Retail Therapy Online," *Women's Wear Daily,* April 6, 2006, p. 12.

THE EMILIO PUCCI STORE
IN FLORENCE, ITALY.
*(COURTESY OF
EMILIO PUCCI SRL)*

RETAIL FASHION MERCHANDISING | 14

Career Focus

Fashion merchandising is most often directed by retail management, merchandise managers, and sometimes a fashion director. However, the actual buying and sell-through of merchandise are the responsibility of buyers, planners, and their assistants.

CHAPTER OBJECTIVES

After reading this chapter, you should be able to:

1. Discuss the buying and selling aspects of merchandising
2. Explain buying procedures
3. Describe all aspects of inventory control and evaluation
4. Discuss the importance of customer service and sales associates

Merchandise is the term used to define articles for sale; it derives from the word *merchant,* the actual seller or retailer. *Fashion merchandising* includes all the planning and activities necessary to supply the fashion wants and needs of retail customers. In the past, fashion merchandising was usually associated only with women's apparel and accessories. Today, stores use aggressive merchandising techniques for men's and children's clothing, too. Fashion influence has also spread to all other areas of retailing, from cosmetics and home furnishings to cookware and iPods.

This chapter covers the planning and carrying out of buying and selling activities including the responsibilities of buyers. It follows the flow of merchandise from arrival in the store to purchase by the consumer.

Merchandising Organization

Every area of merchandising responsibility needs planning and organization to make it function properly and to ensure successful buying and selling.

In small stores, a few people carry out all buying and selling functions with freelance or agency help from outside. In large retail chains, merchandising responsibilities are usually divided between two chains of command. The *buying line* has responsibility for merchandise content and assortment; the *store line* is the liaison between the merchandise organization and customers. The buying line works behind the scenes; the store line interfaces with customers on a daily basis. The goal of both is to sell merchandise at a profit.

Responsibilities of the Store Line

The main responsibility of the store line is operational:

- To coordinate receiving and the movement of goods and people within the store
- To train sales associates
- To provide customer services
- To control expenses
- To maintain the building
- To maintain security

Above all, store-line executives must work together with merchandise managers, buyers, and sales associates to produce positive sales results. Everything and everyone involved in the operation of the store must be organized to achieve this goal.

The director of stores, who heads the store line, supervises individual store managers in multiple-unit organizations. Store managers are responsible for sales, employees, merchandising, and the general success of the store. They, in turn, usually delegate responsibilities to group sales managers, floor managers, or area managers, who supervise department managers. Department managers and their assistants run the department, communicate and distribute information about merchandise to and from management and buyers, put out stock, mark sale merchandise, and supervise sales associates. Although buying careers interest most retailing students, there are more opportunities as managers. It is also very important for buyers to have the experience of working with customers in the store line. Many retail training programs require trainees to have store-line experience to gain a better understanding of customer satisfaction (see Appendix).

Responsibilities of the Buying Line

The merchandise managers and buyers of the buying line must do all the planning and other activities necessary to bring the right merchandise into the store at the right time to meet sales and profit plans and satisfy customers' needs.

General Merchandise Managers The retail chief executive officer (CEO) delegates merchandising responsibilities to several general merchandise managers (GMMs) or corporate merchandise managers (CMMs). They set merchandising policies for the entire store and are responsible for sales volume. The general or corporate merchandise managers are in charge of several divisions. The divisions may be related, such as a general merchandise manager for women's wear and accessories, or the divisions may be totally unrelated.

Divisional Merchandise Managers Merchandising responsibility is further segmented into single divisions, such as women's sportswear or men's furnishings, directed by divisional merchandise managers (DMMs). For example, in the women's area, a divisional might be in charge of misses dresses, misses sportswear, junior dresses, or junior sportswear. A national retailer with decentralized buying has regional merchandise managers (RMMs) instead.

Buyers Each division is composed of departments. These departments may be based on lifestyle, styling categories, price ranges, or vendors. If based on lifestyle, women's dresses might be divided into social occasion, career, and so on. If categorized by price ranges, the departments might be divided into designer, bridge, better, contemporary, moderate, and budget. Accessories are subdivided into handbags, hosiery, hats, jewelry, and so on.

MARIAN GOODMAN, DIVISIONAL MERCHANDISE MANAGER FOR READY-TO-WEAR AT BLOOMINGDALE'S WITH HER STAFF. *(PHOTO BY GINI STEPHENS FRINGS)*

Each department is further segmented into *classifications,* a related group of merchandise. Depending on store size, a buyer is responsible for the success of one or more classifications, one department, or several departments. For example, one buyer may buy just a few bridge or designer collections. Each retailer has it's own unique breakdown of classifications and buyer responsibilities.

Fashion Merchandising Direction

Fashion direction is established to maintain cohesive fashion merchandising in line with a distinctive store image (see Chapter 15). In single-unit stores, the owner usually acts as fashion director and buyer. Upscale large stores or chains usually employ a fashion director. The fashion director is the bridge between corporate marketing policy and actual merchandise buying decisions. He or she works with merchandise managers, buyers, and advertising executives to suggest what merchandise to choose and how to present it.

Along with management and designer collection buyers, the fashion director may attend European and U.S. collection shows to study fashion trends. These trends are analyzed (see Chapter 4) in relation to the store's image, and this information is passed on to buyers as a guide to merchandise planning and advertising. The fashion director may also work with buyers to select appropriate merchandise, develop the store's private label, and coordinate their buys with merchandise in other departments. A fashion director also prepares seasonal fashion presentations for the store line, including sales associates.

Buying Preparations

Careful planning is done to help merchants to buy apparel and accessories efficiently and successfully.

The Merchandise Plan

Management determines a fashion merchandising policy, a long-range standard for fashion buying, selling, and related activities. Merchandise managers make up a merchandise plan within the framework of the policy, goals, and fashion direction set by management. Actual sales figures and evaluations (see end of chapter) from the corresponding season of the previous year, recorded in computer-based forecasting and planning systems, are used as a basis for the new plan.

The merchandise plan is a financial plan allocating specific amounts of money to each department or division for the purchase of an appropriate assortment of fashion merchandise that will meet consumer demand and sales and profit goals. Usually, management determines financial plans for the company as a whole, divides the totals, and assigns sales goals to general merchandise managers. These plans are then further subdivided and given to divisional managers and buyers, who work on developing their part of the plan.

Planning Sales Goals The retailer's goal is to exceed its own merchandise plan and beat last year's sales figures. To make a realistic estimate of prospective sales, merchandise managers and buyers must consider the following points:

- Economic conditions—anticipating a recession, buyers tend to buy conservatively, whereas in a good year they may buy more in hope of an increase in business
- Market and trend analyses (see Chapter 4)

LIBERTY OF LONDON'S MERCHANDISE PLANS HAVE REFLECTED RECENT INTERIOR ALTERATIONS. *(COURTESY OF LIBERTY OF LONDON, PHOTO BY GINI STEPHENS FRINGS)*

- Shifts in population

- Local retail competition

- Variations in consumer demand

- Seasonal consumer demand—swimsuits for resort and summer, and back-to-school, for example

- Weather—mild winters result in poor coat sales, for example

- Holidays—how holidays will affect buying patterns, including the number of shopping days, especially weekends, between Thanksgiving and Christmas, whether Easter is early or late, or the length of time between Easter and Mother's Day, Father's Day, Labor Day sales, and so on

- Physical expansion or alterations needed in the store

- An individual department's ability to house and display the merchandise effectively

- Which marketing activities are needed to support the merchandise

- Basic stock, merchandise in consistent demand throughout the year or during the same season each year

- The effects of casual dress in the workplace—casual clothes are less expensive than dress clothes, which means average sales are lower

- The retail price of the average purchase—are customers buying multiple items of high-priced garments and accessories per purchase or only single items at low cost?

Merchandise plans are based on a fiscal calendar, are determined four months to a year before the selling season, and cover a six-month or one-year period: the spring season (February through July) and/or the fall season (August through January). The plans are developed on computer spreadsheets, which show beginning-of-season stock and merchandise to be purchased and sold per month in order to reach sales and profit goals.

Merchandise Plan Components

- Receipt plans—cost of goods (at retail value) that need to be received to sell in the store

- Sales plans—how much merchandise must be sold to reach sales and profit goals

- Markup plans—setting retail prices to cover costs for both merchandise and operations

- Markdown plans—reducing prices to move goods

- Promotional plans—special purchases from vendors at lower costs

- Beginning-of-season stock levels—goods coming into the store

- End-of-month stock levels—goods that are in the store

- Weeks of supply—how long it will take to sell out merchandise

- Inventory shortages

- Gross margin (profits)—a retailer cannot be successful without profits

- Stock turn—figured by sales divided by average stock

- Discount taken—retailers take a 6 percent discount off their vendor invoices
- Units—the plan may also exactly specify the *units,* or number of garments and accessories, to be purchased to meet these sales goals

Planning Stock The next step in planning is to determine the amount of stock, in terms of dollar investment, necessary to meet consumer demand and thereby to support planned sales. Stock must be brought to a maximum just before the expected time of peak selling, and enough units must be available to fill the floors. Stock plans are part of the retailer's computer-organized financial systems.

The Buying Plan

Working within the merchandise plan, buyers draft their market strategies. The *buying plan* is a description of the types, quantities, prices, and sizes of merchandise that a buyer expects to purchase from vendors within a specific period of time. The totals state exactly how much may be spent on merchandise in each category in line with sales goals and the financial merchandise plan.

The more detailed the buying plan is, the less confusing buying decisions will be, allowing the buyer to concentrate on the fashion aspects of the merchandise during the seasonal market. The plan must be flexible enough, however, to allow for revision if conditions change or buyers do not find what they want in the market.

Assortment Planning A merchandise *assortment* is a collection of various styles, quantities, and prices of related merchandise, usually grouped under one classification within a department. The buyer plans to buy a balanced assortment of merchandise to meet consumer demand and appeal to a particular group of target customers.

Open-to-Buy Considering stock on hand at the beginning of any given month (BOM) and the end of each month (EOM), the buyer has to calculate the amount of purchases that can be made if stock and sales are to be kept in balance.

The difference between actual stock and planned stock equals *open-to-buy (OTB)*, the value of planned purchases.

$$\text{Actual stock} - \text{Planned stock} = \text{Open-to-buy}$$

The open-to-buy budget is adjusted according to business. When business is good, stock is low and needs to be replenished. When business is slow due to an economic downturn, buying has to be reduced to prevent markdowns. In addition, open-to-buy often has to be based on the amount of space or "real estate" that a buyer has available for specific categories and merchandise or for particular vendors. However, open-to-buy has to remain flexible enough to leave money for reacting to trends.

The Buying Process

The buyer purchases merchandise in accordance with the merchandising plan and sales and profit goals.

Preparation

Experience   A buyer's knowledge of merchandise stems from both education and experience. The ability to evaluate merchandise and judge whether it is suitable for a customer develops over years of examining all types of merchandise for quality, styling, and price. It is also very important for buyers to have store-line experience; they need to be on the sales floor to learn about customers' wants and needs. Leslie Wexner, founder of the Limited, said that his "experience of being in stores, watching customers' reactions to merchandise and its presentation, and overhearing their comments" helped him to develop a retail sense.[1]

Research   Market and trend research becomes second nature to the buyer. As discussed in Chapters 2 and 4, buyers must constantly research the following influences:

- Demographics and psychographics
- The effect of economic conditions on demand for certain types and prices of merchandise
- Global influences on styling and sourcing
- Market and fashion trends
- Influence of the media and celebrities on fashion
- Competitors' merchandise offerings

CHAPTER FOURTEEN | RETAIL FASHION MERCHANDISING

The Bottom Line versus the Creative Aspects of Buying

The buying process is part analytical and part creative. The mechanics involve a knowledge of sales histories and the development of a merchandising plan. Their increased responsibilities to the bottom line leave many buyers no choice but to be just administrators. In industry jargon, they must find a balance between being "number driven" and "merchandise driven." The creative side of buying is the ability to spot trends and buy merchandise with sizzle that will appeal to customers. Department store buyers tend to play it safe, but they need to take more risk, especially now that the market is more fashion oriented.

The Buyer as Editor   Buyers can influence consumer buying to a large degree by their selection of merchandise, which narrows the choice for the consumer. By determining what parts of a collection will be sold in the store and in what quantity, the buyer affects the public perception of a manufacturer's collection.

Buyer–Planner System   Some retailers separate buying functions into a *buyer–planner system,* a team effort to maximize business. Under this system, buyers are able to focus on shopping the market and merchandise selection, as well as financial control, while planners concentrate on distribution within the chain.

Planners shape the size of the buy and plan distribution to individual stores. Planners analyze regional differences, designating appropriate merchandise for particular stores based on sales histories of color preferences, lifestyle needs, climate variations, ethnic tastes, and so on. They also reallocate merchandise to stores where it is selling best and make sure basic merchandise is kept in stock. Most stores now have computer-based forecasting and planning systems that include allocation.

Micromerchandising versus Macromerchandising

Target Customers   Buyers try to select the right styles, color assortment, and fabrics at acceptable prices for their target customers. Buyers need to keep in touch with their customers' lifestyles to buy merchandise to fit their needs. One San Francisco–based buyer of long formals and evening dresses spent a late spring evening sitting in the lobby of a downtown hotel to see what young people's preferences were in prom dresses (see Target Marketing in Chapter 2).

THE GAP
PRACTICES MACRO-
MERCHANDISING;
EVERY STORE IN
THE CHAIN
CONVEYS A
UNIFIED IMAGE.
(COURTESY OF GAP)

Micromerchandising Because of the large number of market segments, based on age, ethnicity, and lifestyles, there is increasing need for customizing merchandise. *Micromerchandising,* identifying and serving one market niche, is in response to the recognition of a diverse society with diverse tastes and needs. This means that national retailers must differentiate their merchandise from region to region and store to store. Retailers such as J.C. Penney have decentralized buying systems that allow local buyers to vary assortments according to the needs of individual stores. At retailers with central-ized systems, planners use computer-based allocation systems to distribute merchandise appropriately.

Macromerchandising Some national retailers, such as the Gap, are *macromerchandisers* that prefer to convey a unified image throughout the chain. They make some concessions to climate, but they want consumers to find the same Gap merchandise in every store.

The Buyer's Role in Marketing

Decisions on how to market and sell merchandise are usually made well in advance of the selling season (although shifts in trend directions or other ad opportunities may arise midseason). Buyers make plans for advertising, including direct-mail and electronic retailing, visual merchandising, and special events (see Chapter 15).

Advertising Buyers request ads on the basis of their merchandise plans and negotiate with ven-dors for co-op money (see Chapter 15). They help determine the kind of ad and type of media.

They must provide merchandise and complete information about it to the advertising copywriter and check the ad copy for accuracy. They must then make sure that the merchandise has been delivered and is on the selling floor when the ad runs.

Visual Merchandising Buyers may also request window and in-store displays for particular merchandise. They must also make sure that a good selection of that merchandise is on the selling floor for possible customer purchase.

Special Events Buyers may initiate special events and fashion shows. For example, the buyer of a designer collection might arrange with the fashion office for a designer to make a personal appearance to introduce a new collection.

To evaluate marketing strategies, buyers compare sales statistics before and after the ad, presentation, or event. They try to determine whether these strategies were successful in promoting sales.

The Buying–Selling Cycle

The buying and selling cycle is related to the fashion cycle of consumer acceptance (as discussed in Chapter 3). Therefore, a buyer's responsibilities involve a complete cycle: planning what to buy; searching the markets and selecting the right merchandise; working with advertising, display, and special events to promote merchandise; training sales personnel; and marking down leftover merchandise.

The buying–selling cycle is constantly overlapping: new goods come into the store and reach their sales peak while other goods decline in sales. By comparing current sales of a particular style with the previous week's or month's figures, a buyer can determine whether sales are rising or declining. Thus, the buyer's job of identifying and interpreting consumer demand and evaluating current sales is a continuing process.

Broad Assortment Buying Ideally, buyers would like to buy a *broad* (many styles) but *shallow* (only a few of each) assortment of merchandise at the beginning of a season to test consumer reaction, and then, as certain styles emerge as best-sellers, increase stock in depth. However, reorders are usually difficult, as best-selling merchandise may no longer be available from the manufacturers.

Narrow and Deep Buying If a category of merchandise is very popular, or if the buyer feels strongly about a style, he or she may buy *narrow* (just a few styles) and *deep* (many garments in each size and color).

THE L.K. BENNETT SHOP AT FENWICK OF LONDON, WHICH PRACTICES SHORT-CYCLE BUYING IN ORDER TO HAVE TRENDY MERCHANDISE. *(COURTESY OF FENWICK LTD., PHOTO BY GINI STEPHENS FRINGS)*

Short-Cycle Buying Buyers use *short-cycle buying* (buying closer to the selling season) in order to judge market conditions and trends and to respond quickly to the market, particularly for junior and contemporary fashions. Also referred to as *just-in-time merchandising*, short-cycle buying helps to reduce inventory. This is completely dependent on the manufacturer's production cycle and the availability of merchandise.

Planning Promotions Buyers have to plan ahead for *promotions*, special buys at low prices. When a particular item is popular, such as cashmere sweaters, a buyer might arrange for a volume purchase at a special price. Many retailers would like to cut down on the practice of constant sales and promotions, but it is difficult because consumers expect them.

Planning Markdowns Although buyers hope to select merchandise with full *sell-through* (selling at full price), they also have to plan ahead for inevitable markdowns. Many stores mark down prices after the merchandise has been on the selling floor for approximately 8 to 12 weeks. Retailers speed inventory turnover by marking down and clearing out stale merchandise. Merchandise may be left over because it has passed its peak of popularity or because of *broken sizes and colors* (incomplete assortments resulting from customer purchases).

Retailers usually charge manufacturers for *markdown allowances* to help offset their losses. Some manufacturers may even suggest to the retailer when it is permissible to mark down merchandise to make room for new deliveries. Many consumers have a "markdown mentality"; they shop only for sale merchandise. "To combat this mentality," Julie Dugoff, better sportswear merchandise manager for Federated Merchandising Group, explained, "retailers cut back on inventory, carefully editing their buys, to encourage full sell-through."[2]

Shopping the Market

After the buying plan has been established, fashion buyers shop the market to view the merchandise available for the coming season. For the retailer, the manufacturer is the *supplier, vendor,* or

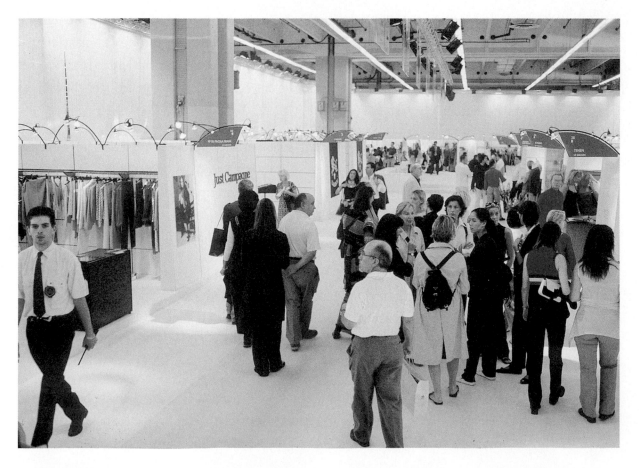

■ BUYERS FROM ALL OVER THE WORLD AT THE PRÊT-À-PORTER MARKET IN PARIS. *(COURTESY OF PRÊT-À-PORTER PARIS, PHOTO BY JEAN-MARC HANNA)*

resource of fashion goods. Buying trips are timed to cover markets that are important for the buyer's particular category of merchandise.

Buyers visit different market centers for different needs. Many people imagine a buyer's job to be a glamorous one involving many trips to Europe. However, only designer department buyers and fashion directors of large stores attend the European collections. Even then, with packed appointment schedules leaving little time to eat or relax, business travel does not remain glamorous for long. Many French and Italian designers now have New York showrooms so that buyers do not necessarily have to go to Europe.

In the search for uniqueness, buyers from small specialty stores are now scouring the world to find new talent as far away as China, Australia, New Zealand, Turkey, Brazil, India, and South Africa. "We could spend all year going from one fashion fair to another all round the world looking for new designers, but it wouldn't be cost-effective," says Selfridges' head of fashion Anna Garner.[3] Buyers try to find something wonderful before the competition does. They often try to hire a local scout in each country to look for new designers.

Designer and bridge buyers go to New York to see the U.S. ready-to-wear collections. Contemporary, better, junior, and special size buyers go to specific market weeks for their specialty in New York, Los Angeles, and elsewhere. Men's and children's wear buyers, too, may go to New York for their markets. Moderate- and budget-priced apparel buyers may go to manufacturers' showrooms at regional markets.

Regional stores may also do all their buying at regional markets. Buyers from Dillard's, for example, buy approximately half of their merchandise at the Dallas markets. Merchandise may also be bought from manufacturers' sales representatives who call on small stores for the convenience of owners who may not be able to get away to markets. Some retailers, such as J.C. Penney, show selected merchandise to their buyers in Texas via teleconferencing.

Line Buying versus Trend Buying
Buyers shop both key resources and new ones. *Key resources* or *core vendors* are those who have maintained a reputation for dependability and whose merchandise sells through because of appropriate styling, quality, price, and/or a nationally advertised brand name. The practice of buying from these major resources is called *line buying.*

Matrix System Some retailers are requiring that 80 to 90 percent of all merchandise be purchased from core vendors! The most restrictive is the *matrix system,* strict centralized merchandising used at Dillard's. Some large retailers want to deal with equally large vendors that can supply all their stores.

Buyers are limited to a list of core vendors and are not permitted to buy from other manufacturers. Of course, this system cuts out small apparel manufacturers who cannot supply all the stores in a large chain or corporate group and contributes to monotony and a lack of choice for consumers.

Trend Buying   Seeking merchandise for its innovative styling is referred to as *trend buying.* Trend buying is especially important for leading fashion stores. Because buyers do not always have time to seek out new resources, some retailers provide *vendor days* when manufacturers can come to the store to show their merchandise. Finding an exciting, unique resource can mean an important merchandising statement for a fashion store. Since there is an increased focus on fashion, newness, and uniqueness, most retailers do some trend buying, especially small independent fashion stores.

Market Procedures   Buyers visit the showrooms of manufacturers who produce the specific types and price lines of merchandise that they need. As the entire line is shown to them by management, a merchandiser, or a sales representative, buyers take notes on *line sheets,* forms provided by the vendor that list style numbers, descriptions (and sometimes a sketch), size and color ranges, fabrication, and wholesale price.

COLORFUL MERCHANDISE AT HENRI BENDEL, A STORE THAT SPECIALIZES IN TREND BUYING. *(COURTESY OF HENRI BENDEL, PHOTO BY GINI STEPHENS FRINGS)*

Buyers look for styling, quality of fabric and production, good fit, sound company management and financial backing that support the product, and on-time deliveries. Julie Dugoff at Federated said, "A buyer has to believe in the resource and see its long-term potential."[4] Buyers must evaluate whether styling and quality compare favorably with other merchandise they have seen in the same price range. Retail store square footage is limited; when a buyer tries a new resource, it takes space away from others. Buyers also consider the possible sales potential of each style for their stores and how the clothes will look on the selling floor. At the end of the market trip, buyers review their notes, eliminate the less desirable styles, and decide which styles to purchase.

Corporate Buying In the case of a major store making a large purchase, buying is often done management to management by a group of executives including the buyer. Wal-Mart, for example, tries to do all of its buying in this manner. In this case, the buyer is part of a buying team.

Retailer–Vendor Alliances
Manufacturers and retailers try to work together toward mutual success. Vendor executives, designers, merchandisers, and/or sales representatives suggest appropriate merchandise for each retailer's particular customers. Manufacturers may preassort merchandise for their customers. Buyers and sales representatives continue to work together throughout the selling season regarding advertising, reorders, markdowns, and sell-through. Buyers also provide vendors with weekly selling reports.

Purchase Orders
Placing an order for merchandise is considered a contract between the store and the vendor. Therefore, writing an order commits the store to taking the merchandise if it meets quality expectations and delivery requirements. Standard purchase orders specify the date of the order, the name and address of the resource, the terms of sale, shipping instructions, ship and cancel dates, the store's shipping address, the name of the department, the quantity ordered, descriptions and prices of styles ordered, and obligations between buyer and seller. Purchase orders are most efficiently done by Internet vendor-linked computer systems, which can instantly supply information on what goods are available or are in work and what shipping dates are expected. The purchase order information becomes part of the retailer's total merchandise information systems (MIS), which keeps track of merchandise as it is ordered, received, and finally sold.

Deliveries are timed so that sufficient quantities of merchandise are in the store to meet various peaks in the consumer demand cycle. The vendor is committed to meeting these delivery dates or the order may be cancelled or a discount required for extension. An early delivery means that merchandise will be on the selling floor longer and have a better chance at *sell-through* (selling at full price).

Automatic Replenishment
In an effort to maintain stock of basic merchandise, retailers use automatic replenishment, made possible by electronic data interchange systems

that link them to vendors. To implement automatic replenishment, retailers must be willing to adopt a *continuous open-to-buy position* for basic merchandise to let suppliers replenish depleted stock without any retail management approval or review. Large retailers develop systems to allow suppliers to keep each store stocked at all times. These systems send sales and inventory information directly to vendors so they can plan production. The use of automatic replenishment is especially important for underwear, hosiery, and shoes, to make sure that all sizes, colors, and so forth, are in stock.

National Brands versus Private Label

Retailers provide their customers with house brands to differentiate themselves from the competition.

Multibrand retailers across the country try to provide their customers with a wide selection of popular national brands. *National brands,* manufacturers' brands that are available nationwide, help the customer to identify with a consistent standard of styling, fit, and quality from season to season. However, as retailers stock more and more of the same national brands, exclusivity tends to decrease and stores look too much alike.

Exclusivity has long been an important aspect of a fashion retailer's uniqueness. Buyers seek distinctive fashion looks from out-of-the-way sources in foreign markets or from little-known, aspiring young designers to give their customers something that no other store has. Some retailers work with manufacturers to produce *exclusive brands* for them. Many retailers also turn to private label.

Private Label

In an effort to save costs and provide quality, value, and uniqueness, most multi-unit retailers sell private-label merchandise. *Private-label* merchandise carries the store's label, such as "Saks Fifth Avenue," or a fictitious name, such as Macy's/Federated's "I.N.C.," Nordstrom's "Classiques Entier," or Wal-Mart's "George." The general public is usually not aware of the difference between a retailer's private label and a national brand; to the consumer, they are all brands.

Cost Savings Private-label merchandise can be produced less expensively than premium national brands because no wholesale marketing expenses are necessary. Lower costs allow the retailer

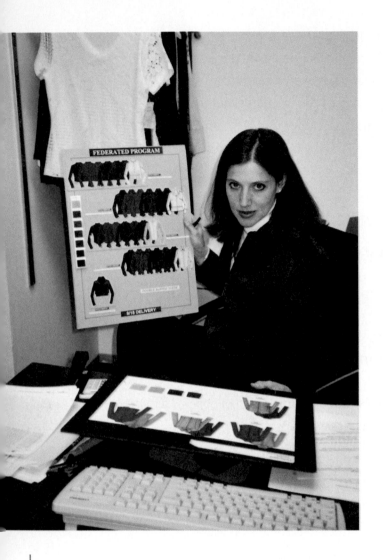

MERCHANDISE MANAGER JULIE DUGOFF SHOWING HER PRIVATE-LABEL SWEATER COLLECTION PLANS FOR FEDERATED MERCHANDISING GROUP. *(PHOTO BY GINI STEPHENS FRINGS)*

higher markups, thereby improving gross margin. The store can also pass some of the savings on to customers.

Exclusivity Private-label merchandise also provides retailers with merchandise that is exclusive to them. Previously limited to basics such as polo shirts, retailers are now providing quality fashion merchandise under private label. These fashion collections or pieces help retailers to differentiate themselves from their competition. Mass retailers are even hiring designers to produce exclusive merchandise such as Vera Wang's "Very Vera" collection for Kohl's and Isaac Mizrahi for Target.

Retailers as Manufacturers
Retailers have private-label merchandise made directly for them to their specifications by guaranteeing a quantity order. Manufacturing may be arranged in several different ways.

- Retailers may simply have a "hot" item copied by a contractor.
- They may have a line created for them by a design service, such as Peclers, and then have it produced.
- They may set up their own design and merchandising department, which works with contractors. Zara's 300-member design staff create 20,000 designs a year.
- They may work with a manufacturer that specializes in private label, such as Cygne Designs, or one that produces both branded merchandise and private label, such as Tahari.

Retailers started private label for basic merchandise, such as hosiery, underwear, and basic furnishings. Now many retailers manufacture fashion apparel, too. Private-label manufacturing allows them to produce closer to the selling season and, therefore, to react quickly to new trends. Major retailers today have hundreds of lines of private-label clothing, which account for at least 20 percent of all men's and women's apparel sold. Private label accounts for half of J.C. Penney's merchandise. Retailers are trying to find the right balance between national brands and private label.

Many retailers have developed private labels that can compete with national brands, such as JCPenney's Original Arizona Jeans Company or Macy's I.N.C. As discussed in Chapter 13, many specialty chains, such as Gap, Brooks Brothers, H&M, and Ann Taylor, sell only private-label merchandise.

Buying Offices

To facilitate buying, many stores are affiliated with resident buying offices located in international and domestic market centers or have their own corporate buying offices.

Although the term *buying office* is still used in the industry, its role has greatly expanded to fill a wide variety of functions. The two primary types of buying offices are independent and store owned.

Independent Resident Buying Offices
Independently owned and operated, these buying offices charge fees to noncompeting stores for market services. The current largest is the Doneger Group, which represents more than 400 stores.

Store-Owned Resident Buying Offices
There are basically two types of store-owned buying offices: associated and corporate.

1. **Associated buying offices** are jointly owned and operated by a group of stores. Member stores usually have similar sales volume, store policies, and target customers

CREATIVE DIRECTOR DAVID WOLFE AND HIS TEAM PROVIDE SERVICES FOR THE DONEGER GROUP. *(COURTESY OF DONEGER CREATIVE SERVICES)*

but are in noncompeting locations. Operating expenses are allocated to each member store on the basis of the store's sales volume and the amount of services rendered. Associated Merchandising Corporation (AMC) is a well-known example.

2. **Corporate buying offices** are owned and operated by the parent organization of a group or chain of stores. At Federated Department Stores, 70 percent of the buying for member stores is done centrally by the parent company, while the other 30 percent is done by individual member stores.

International Buying Offices

Many large retail stores have their own buying offices abroad or use foreign *commissionaires,* agents representing stores in foreign market centers. These offices are equipped to handle import–export transactions in the language of the country, check quality control, figure currency exchange rates, provide a consolidated center for shipping, and wade through customs red tape.

Buying Office Services

Buying offices act as market representatives for member stores. Their merchandisers see the lines of vendors, prepare market analyses, and send out bulletins to their member stores reporting on new fashion directions, best-sellers, trends, and special price offerings. However, unlike buyers, they do not make final decisions as to purchases and do not place orders unless specifically asked to do so by the buyer of the retail store. Buying offices also organize group purchases for small stores so that the total order is large enough to meet the minimum order requirements of large or important manufacturers.

Buying offices also offer many other services to their clients, such as color and trend forecasting, product development for private label, sourcing, facilitating imports, assortment planning, advertising and promotional support, online services, and advice and information on all aspects of retailing. They provide members with information by means of reports, newsletters, workshops, and consultations.

Retail Pricing

Retail selling prices are based on predetermined store pricing policies and wholesale costs.

Markup

Markup is the difference between the wholesale cost and the retail price of merchandise. It can be figured as a percentage of retail value or calculated on the basis of cost.

TABLE 14.1 PRICING OF A TYPICAL DRESS

Pricing of a Typical Dress
Retailer's Costs

Wholesale cost ($123 less 8 percent discount for prompt payment)	$113.20	
Allowance for markdowns (averaged over all dresses in stock)	$10.00	
Allowances for shortages and pilferage	6.00	
Salaries and benefits (averaged per garment)		
Sales staff	14.00	
Merchandising and buying staff (including expenses)	16.00	
Clerical and stockroom (receiving, marketing deliveries, and other expenses)	10.00	
Advertising, display, and sales-promotional staff	16.00	
Administrative staff (executives, credit and accounting officers, including expenses)	22.00	
Employee fringe benefits	4.00	
Overhead (rent, insurance, utilities, cleaning, and security)	20.00	
TOTAL	$231.20	
Profits before taxes	16.80	
SELLING PRICE	$248.00	Retail price
	—$113.20	Cost
54% Markup	$134.80	Markup

*These are approximate figures. Percentages vary depending on the kind of store. Markup percentages vary according to volume and store.

Most retailers calculate markup as a percentage of retail price. This method is used because expenses and profits are commonly expressed as a percentage of net sales based on retail prices. The markup must cover markdowns, shortages, and operating expenses and still create a profit. Operating expenses include salaries, travel expenses, sales promotion, and overhead, including rent, utilities, and store maintenance.

$$\frac{\text{Retail price} - \text{Cost}}{\text{Retail price}} = \text{Markup}$$

Price Points Several price points are offered in each department or merchandise category. The term *price range* refers to the span between the lowest and highest price points. Merchandise of comparable quality usually falls into the same price range. Within a price range there must be enough difference between price points that variations in quality at each level are obvious to customers.

Receiving

Merchandise purchased by buyers is received into a regional distribution center and then into the store, where it is entered into stock and put on the selling floor.

When buyers place orders at the market or with sales representatives, they indicate delivery dates that are usually staggered so that new merchandise is constantly on the selling floor.

Merchandise is accepted into a *central* or *regional receiving and distribution* warehouse where it is counted and checked for quality. Merchandise is ticketed according to information stated on the buyer's purchase order. The ticket includes bar-code numbers for vendor, season, classification, department, and retail selling price. When this information is recorded into the retailer's merchandise information system, the data are used for automatic ticket printing, record keeping, and accounts payable. Efficient receiving is achieved when manufacturers send *advance shipment notices (ASN)* and *preticket* merchandise with information they obtain through electronic data interchange (EDI).

CENTRAL RECEIVING AT MARKS & SPENCER IN ENGLAND. *(COURTESY OF MARKS & SPENCER)*

Retailers try to reconcile *fall out*, differences between actual shipments and purchase orders, and decide whether to accept or reject partially filled orders, substitutions, or late shipments. If the order is unacceptable to the buyer for any of these reasons, it may be returned to the manufacturer, or an unfilled order may be cancelled.

Retailers use *chargebacks* to withhold payments to vendors to cover manufacturers' mistakes such as late shipping, incomplete orders, missing paperwork, or incorrect assortments, and even customers' returns and advertising fees. Over the past decade, chargebacks have become a contentious issue between retailers and manufacturers. Retailers claim that chargebacks are a way to maintain gross margins. On the other hand, a group of manufacturers has formed a Vendor Coalition for Equitable Retailer Practices to address these issues and suggest guidelines to improve fairness.

Planners decide on the proper distribution of merchandise to multi-unit stores, which is based on the needs of that unit's customers. Then merchandise is sent to individual stores and on to departments. The department manager also checks and verifies both the count and the information on the price tag. If approved, the merchandise moves into a stockroom or onto the selling floor.

Record Keeping

Retailers need to keep control of inventory, what merchandise is in stock and what has been sold, so that they are able to evaluate what to buy in the future.

Unit Control

To track and maintain records of *units,* or items, retailers use a *unit control system,* part of their overall computer-based merchandise information system (MIS). Unit control is a system for recording the number of units of merchandise purchased, on order, received, in stock, or sold. Records are kept of additions to or subtractions from stock, from the time an order is placed with a manufacturer until the merchandise is sold. Information for unit control comes from receipts, sales records, and *merchandise transfers* (movement of merchandise from one store to another or elsewhere).

The major advantage of unit control systems is that the records enable a buyer to keep track of consumer demand. If certain styles are selling quickly, the buyer may reorder them; if styles are selling too slowly, the buyer may make markdown plans. Unit control systems also give a realistic growth picture in inflationary periods, when dollar volume increases may be misleading.

Inventory Control

Inventory control keeps records of the *dollar value* of merchandise on hand. Most stores use the retail method of inventory control, which involves figuring inventory at retail prices, rather than on the basis of the wholesale cost.

Computer *inventory management systems* (IMS, part of the retailer's financial systems) record receipts, sales, additions to and subtractions from stock, stock transfers from one store to another, and returns by customers in dollars. When merchandise is sold, the point-of-sale terminal automatically feeds this information into sales records and deletes it in inventory records. Retailers integrate their unit and financial systems when possible.

Physical Inventory

A *physical inventory* is the actual item-by-item count of all merchandise on hand, taken one to three times annually to confirm computer records and to comply with accounting regulations. In case of discrepancies between the computer records and physical inventories, the physical count prevails and the inventory records must be adjusted accordingly.

Stock Shortages and Overages   Discrepancies between computer and physical inventory are described as stock shortages or overages.

Shortages mean a lower physical inventory than computer inventory and are the result of theft, damage, or clerical error. Shortages are common, and allowances must be made in initial pricing to cover these losses. Retailers are investing in new loss-prevention technology and video analysis software to combat theft.

Overages indicate a higher physical inventory than computer inventory and may be caused by clerical error, misticketing, or shipment to an incorrect location.

Customer Service

To many consumers, and in many stores, service has become just as important as fashion.

American retailers were pioneers in offering customer service. Years ago, Montgomery Ward and John Wanamaker, retailers that were established in the 1800s, instituted guaranteed-refund policies. The success of Nordstrom and Wal-Mart, where customer service is a priority, has paved the way for

THE SHOE DEPARTMENT AT NORDSTROM, A PACESETTING RETAILER FOR CUSTOMER SERVICE. (COURTESY OF NORDSTROM)

a renewed interest in improved service in every store. The service in these stores has become the yardstick by which other stores now measure their own levels of customer service.

Many retailers are attempting to become *customer driven* (to anticipate and focus on the needs of their customers), in fact, to exceed customers' expectations. They train sales associates to be knowledgeable and helpful and may offer an increasing number of services:

- To be "in stock"—having merchandise the customer needs available in all sizes, styles, and colors
- Special incentive programs for core customers (such as Neiman Marcus's "InCircle"), which identify and reward high-spending customers, using proprietary credit cards
- Customer appreciation days or courtesy days, usually offering customer discounts
- Newsletters or look books sent to customers
- In-store events such as wardrobe-planning clinics
- Interactive videos that supply information on product location
- Comfortable dressing rooms with call buttons or phones to ask for assistance
- Alterations
- Gift registries and gift wrapping services

- In-store services such as photo finishing, restaurants and snack bars, packaging and mailing, and banking
- Free use of telephones for customers waiting to be fitted
- Appropriate music
- Free personal shopping services
- Knowledgeable and helpful sales personnel who will check stock at other stores
- No-question return privileges
- National credit card acceptance
- 800 telephone numbers
- Extended store hours
- Convenient restrooms and comfortable places to sit
- Free local delivery and valet or free parking
- Ordering kiosks in the store for catalog and online ordering

Luxury retailers, such as Neiman Marcus, Barney's, and Saks Fifth Avenue, have been very successful in the past decade. Due to the high prices for designer and luxury products, their customers expect first-class service, and these stores compete to attend to clients' needs. They shower them with perks such as gifts, special events, lunches, and even visits to customers' homes to organize their closets.

Retail Sales

Selling techniques have become very important in trying to establish repeat business and customer loyalty.

In many stores, customers have to hunt for assistance. At mass merchants and discount stores, sales help is often limited to cash register clerks. Training sales associates to be more knowledgeable and attentive helps to maximize sales and profitability.

Sales Training

Fashion selling requires special training that gives sales personnel merchandise information, confidence, and motivation. In small stores, training is informal, usually based on experience on the selling floor. In larger stores and chains, training is usually more structured. H&M, for example, pairs new recruits with seasoned mentors. Chanel retail stores give intense training aimed at teaching the selling staff how to establish ongoing relationships with customers to build loyalty and repeat business. Large chains have formal training programs.

At the beginning of a season, new merchandise is presented, often on video, to show sales associates how garments should be worn and accessorized. The fashion director or buyers explain the selling features of merchandise so that the selling staff in turn can point out quality, fashion, and performance features to their customers. Buyers try to infuse enthusiasm into the sales force, hoping that it will be transmitted to the customer.

Selling

Sales are the key to success in retailing. Of course, much depends on the buyer's selection of fashion assortments and whether the merchandise is in stock to meet consumer demand. However, success also depends on the ability of sales personnel.

Personal Selling   *Personal selling,* the method involving the most customer contact, is used most often in specialty stores for luxury merchandise. With this method, sales associates

■ PERSONAL SELLING AT HERMÈS.
(PHOTO BY GINI STEPHENS FRINGS)

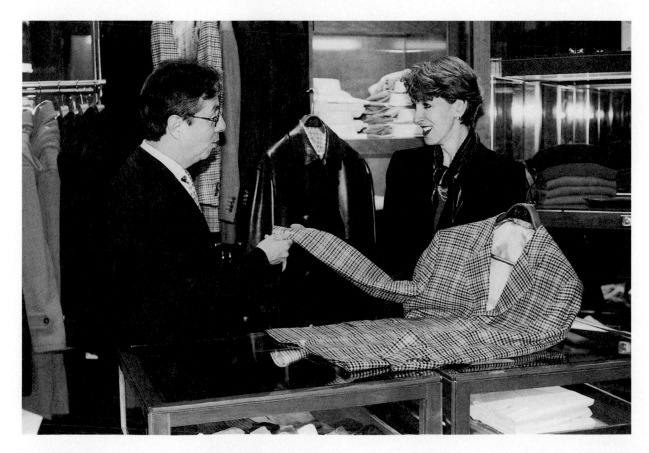

actively help customers to choose merchandise suited to their tastes and needs. These associates are given extensive training, everything from product information sessions to instruction on how to write thank-you notes. Sales associates are encouraged to greet customers at the door and to treat them as guests, tell them about the store's merchandising concepts, and ask questions about their lifestyles, needs, and preferences. To build a multiple sale, associates are ready with alternative selections, wardrobe extenders, and accessory suggestions.

Sales associates keep files on customers, noting style and color preferences, sizes, and other pertinent information. New computer-based systems create and maintain electronic profiles of customers, including sizes, style preferences, physical measurements, career and social clothing needs, and sometimes even digital photographs. When new merchandise comes in that seems appropriate for their customers, these sales associates call or write a note to these customers. Many transactions at the luxury level are conducted by recommendations on the phone, without customers setting foot into the store.

Sales Incentives

Some retailers offer their sales staffs incentives to increase productivity. These incentives, which may take the form of higher salaries or commissions, help to attract better sales personnel. Nordstrom, for example, offers its sales associates a commission, good benefits, and stock options as incentives.

Merchandise Representatives

Vendors are getting much more involved in retail sales. Some manufacturers are supplying *merchandise representatives* or *sales specialists* to train salespeople and help customers. For example, Ellen Tracy's representatives conduct seminars on merchandising, presentation, and selling. Vendors often supply other aids to selling, such as videotapes, slide shows, look books, and brochures (see Chapter 12).

Cooperative Salesperson Programs

Vendors become directly involved in retail selling by contributing to the salaries of *selling specialists* through various types of programs. Some vendors share the cost of salaries, offer bonuses if sales plans are met, and/or provide clothing allowances; others pay the entire salaries of exclusive salespeople recruited either by the vendor or the retailer.

Point-of-Sale (POS) Transactions

When recording a sales transaction, sales associates not only collect payment but record information such as style number, vendor, size, and color for use in analyzing department success and planning for future buying. As public concerns over identity theft have mounted, retailers have had to meet strict computer-security standards set by a consortium of credit card associations. Security precautions that retailers need include firewalls, antivirus software, no-default passwords, encrypted cardholder-data transmissions, and restricted access to cardholder data.[5]

Merchandising Evaluation

Evaluation of the success or failure of a season helps buyers to plan for better merchandising for the future.

Retailers use intranet (internal) communications systems and access their merchandise information systems (MIS) to make merchandising evaluations during and at the end of each selling season. These systems organize information about suppliers, merchandise, and customer preferences based on point-of-sale data. Retailers might use MIS to find out what colors, sizes, or vendors are selling best. They may be able to analyze sales information by store or by item on a daily, weekly, or monthly basis. They can combine statistics in various ways to analyze their business. Each retailer's system is different and yields different information. Managing data and information technology will be the key to retail success in the future.

How Merchants Use Data
By evaluating exactly what merchandise has been sold, retail executives are better able to plan for the future, thus beginning a new cycle of buying and selling. With this information, they are also able to measure the merchandising impact on the store's profitability and the achievement of financial goals. These evaluations can be ongoing or periodic processes.

Vendor Analyses A buyer may compile a *vendor analysis* showing the initial markup, markdowns, and profit percentages gained on products from an individual resource. A vendor must maintain a high percentage of regular-price *sell-throughs*. Although a vendor may have one or two bad seasons, the store will most likely drop a resource whose merchandise consistently offers no profit.

Comparisons Sales data can also be very revealing in relation to other important information. When compared with the previous year's data for the same period, the numbers show whether the store's volume grew over the year. When compared with the merchandise plan, the results show how well the store met its objectives established at the beginning of the period and, therefore, how well planning was done. The ultimate goal is to have exceeded objectives. When compared with inventory on hand and on order, as well as with customer returns, the figures can indicate whether merchandising, planning, and promotional activities were successful.

Sales-Related Ratios Sales data are also used to determine important ratios such as average gross sales, sales per square foot, and stock or inventory turnover. These sales-related ratios are used not only to evaluate a department or store, but also to compare different stores within a retail chain. Due to fierce competition in a nongrowing market, retailers experience pressure for higher gross margins, growth of average sale, more sales per square foot, and growth of market share.

NEIMAN MARCUS ENJOYS A HIGH SALES-PER-SQUARE-FOOT RATIO DUE TO ITS POPULARITY. *(COURTESY OF THE NEIMAN MARCUS GROUP, INC.)*

Average gross sales—Total dollar sales for a given period divided by the number of transactions for the same period provide *average gross sales.* This ratio indicates the dollar volume per transaction. An increase in the ratio can indicate higher prices, which result from better merchandise, inflation, or multiple sales per customer.

Sales per square foot—Total sales for a period divided by the number of square feet of selling space of a floor or store provide *sales per square foot,* an internationally used indicator of productivity. Sales per square foot are monitored seasonally or sometimes monthly. In their desire for internal growth, many stores are focusing on raising dollars per square foot in existing units, often through renovation. As a result, new departments may be created, or existing ones may be increased or decreased.

Stock or inventory turn—Stock turn is basically the number of times stock (inventory) is sold out and replaced in a given period. A high turnover is usually very desirable because it speeds the buying and selling cycle and frees funds for renewed use, thus increasing the profitability of the retail operation. *Stock turn* is calculated by dividing total sales by average stock or inventory. For example, if seasonal sales total $1 million and average stock is $500,000, then the stock turn is 2.

Gross margin—Because the only source of income for most retail stores is the sale of merchandise, the projected sales must cover more than expenditures to produce gross margin objectives. The *gross margin* is the fundamental income from which expenses (including cost of goods, shortages, salaries, sales promotion, and store operations) are deducted to obtain the necessary profit to stay in business.

Net sales − All expenses = Gross margin

Planning Ahead All these indicators are used by buyers and management not only to measure the success of the retail merchandising operation, but also to refine and improve the long-range planning of future merchandising activities. Sales data can help show a buyer what styles, colors, sizes, and price ranges should be purchased in the future. Evaluation and the establishment of new and more accurate goals result in a more profitable retail operation.

The major drawback of merchandising evaluations is that they cannot determine what styles, colors, or sizes customers wanted but could *not find* at the store. So far, this information can be learned only informally through conversations with customers. Retailers hope to gain this information in the future via direct consumer responses fed into databases.

SUMMARY

AS MERCHANDISERS, RETAILERS MUST BUY THE RIGHT GOODS AND HAVE THEM IN THE STORE WHEN THEIR CUSTOMERS WANT THEM. MERCHANDISING IS GUIDED BY THE FASHION DIRECTOR AND MERCHANDISING MANAGERS; RESPONSIBILITIES ARE DIVIDED BETWEEN THE BUYING LINE AND THE STORE LINE. STORE POLICIES AND LONG-RANGE PLANNING HELP RETAILERS TO DO THEIR JOBS EFFECTIVELY. THE MERCHANDISE PLAN ALLOCATES SPECIFIC AMOUNTS OF MONEY FOR THE PURCHASE OF FASHION ASSORTMENTS. ASSORTMENT PLANNING IS EXPRESSED AS A BUYING PLAN THAT INCLUDES DESCRIPTIONS OF THE TYPES, QUANTITIES, PRICES, AND SIZES OF MERCHANDISE NEEDED. RETAILERS PROVIDE THEIR CUSTOMERS WITH BOTH NATIONAL-BRAND AND PRIVATE-LABEL MERCHANDISE.

BUYERS' RESPONSIBILITIES COVER BOTH THE BUYING AND SELLING ASPECTS OF RETAILING. BUYERS PLAN WHAT TO BUY, SEARCH THE MARKETS FOR GOODS THAT WILL MEET THEIR CUSTOMERS' NEEDS, PROMOTE SALES, AND SUPERVISE MERCHANDISING AND SELLING, ONLY TO BEGIN THE CYCLE AGAIN FOR A NEW SEASON.

MERCHANDISE INFORMATION SYSTEMS AID IN THE PLANNING, MONITORING, AND EVALUATION OF RETAIL SALES. INTERNET DATA EXCHANGE ALLOWS FOR AUTOMATIC REPLENISHMENT OF BASIC MERCHANDISE, AND COMPUTER RECORDS OF BUSINESS TRANSACTIONS KEEP RECORDS OF SALES AND INVENTORY. MERCHANDISE INFORMATION SYSTEMS ALSO HELP RETAILERS TO EVALUATE SALES IN ORDER TO MAKE FUTURE MERCHANDISING PLANS.

CUSTOMER SERVICE HAS BECOME VERY IMPORTANT, AS HAVE SALES TRAINING AND INCENTIVES. CUSTOMER ACCEPTANCE IN TERMS OF SALES IS THE BASIS FOR SUCCESS AND PROFITABILITY IN RETAILING. RETAILERS FACE A CONSTANT CHALLENGE TO SERVE THE PUBLIC MORE EFFICIENTLY AND EFFECTIVELY TO ENSURE CONTINUED GROWTH AND DEVELOPMENT.

Terms and Concepts

Briefly define and discuss the following terms and concepts:

1. Fashion director
2. Buying line
3. Classifications
4. Merchandise plan
5. Assortment planning
6. Stock turn
7. Open-to-buy
8. Vendor
9. Key resources
10. Corporate buying
11. Line buying
12. Matrix system
13. Resident buying office
14. Private label
15. Central receiving
16. Markup
17. Unit control
18. Personal selling
19. Sales incentives
20. Customer service
21. Markdowns
22. Sell-through
23. Sales per square foot
24. Merchandise information systems
25. Vendor analysis
26. Merchandise representatives
27. Gross margin

Questions for Review

1. How are merchandising responsibilities organized?
2. Explain the differences between the store line and the buying line.
3. How can the merchandise plan be either management or buyer directed?
4. Describe the buying–selling cycle.
5. What are a buyer's responsibilities?
6. Why must a buyer research fashion trends?
7. What is the difference between line buying and trend buying?
8. Describe the difference between broad assortment and short-cycle buying.
9. What is the difference between a national brand and a private label?
10. What services does a buying office provide?
11. Describe inventory control systems.
12. Name five customer services. Are they effective?
13. Discuss the techniques and advantages of personal selling.
14. Explain the difference between promotions and markdowns.
15. Why is merchandising evaluation important?

Projects for Additional Learning

1. Interview a local store's fashion buyer. Ask how and where he or she buys fashion merchandise: At a market? From a sales representative? Through a buying office? From a catalog? What type of merchandise is purchased in what way? What is the buyer's favorite method and why? How often does the buyer go to a market center? Which one does he or she attend? Summarize the answers in a written report.

2. Visit the contemporary sportswear department in a retail store and examine the merchandise. Is it all from one manufacturer, or has the buyer mixed garments from several vendors to carry out a fabric or color theme? Who are the major vendors in the department? What are the price ranges? Which manufacturers have the most innovative looks? Ask salespeople which groups are selling the best and why they think so. Does the department have a good selection of sizes, colors, and styles? Write a critique of the department.

3. Shop a large department store. Study the three different ways to merchandise the suit look. Compare suits in (a) the misses coat and suit department (the suit is priced as a single unit), (b) the sportswear department (components are priced separately), (c) the dress department (components are priced as a unit, usually a dress with a jacket). What suit styles do you find in each department? Compare the selection (assortment), price ranges, quality, and fit in one department with those in the others. Which department has the best value and selection?

4. In a local store, evaluate a sale rack. Is the merchandise marked down, or is it a special purchase (garments purchased at a lower price and offered as a promotional event)? Why was the marked-down merchandise marked down? In your opinion, was it because of broken assortments, styling, poor timing, poor construction, poor fit, unattractive colors, or too high a price? Summarize your findings in a short report.

Notes

[1] As quoted by Pete Born, "Wexner Shares Trade Secrets at FIT," *Women's Wear Daily,* February 23, 1989.

[2] Julie Dugoff, merchandise manager, better sportswear, Federated Merchandising Group, New York, interview, April 28, 2003.

[3] As quoted by Avril Groom, "The Next Small Thing," *How to Spend It, Financial Times,* September, 2005, p. 29.

[4] Julie Dugoff; see note 2.

[5] "Retailers Rush to Secure Data Against Theft," *Wall Street Journal,* April 15, 2005, p. B1.

A CHANEL WINDOW AT NEIMAN MARCUS.
(COURTESY OF THE NEIMAN MARCUS GROUP, INC.)

RETAIL FASHION MARKETING | 15

Career Focus

Marketing provides a wide variety of interesting and creative career opportunities. Retail marketing executives have the responsibility for, or work together with, those in charge of advertising, public relations, market research, and new business development. The advertising director works with in-house and agency creative directors, E-commerce managers, ad managers and copy chiefs, layout artists, writers, media buyers, merchandise coordinators, and photographers. Corporate directors of fashion, special events, and/or public relations have regional managers or store coordinators to carry out responsibilities in individual stores. The visual merchandising director of a chain of stores oversees regional or individual store visual merchandising managers and a staff of designers.

CHAPTER OBJECTIVES

After reading this chapter, you should be able to:

1. Explain the purpose of marketing
2. Explain how a store's fashion image is conveyed to consumers
3. Explain the purpose, goals, and procedures of advertising, publicity, special events, and visual merchandising
4. Describe various types of media and their relation to target customers

Marketing

Marketing is the responsibility of everyone in retailing from management to sales associates.

In its broadest sense, marketing encompasses all of the activities needed to sell merchandise to consumers. *Marketing* involves communicating a retail fashion image and/or the availability of a product. It is also an attempt to attract the type of customer for whom the merchandise is intended. The primary challenges of marketing are to differentiate the store from competitors, attract new customers, get customers into the store, generate sales, and increase market share by inspiring new and current customers to buy more.

Retailers strive to differentiate themselves from their competitors; they try to show why a consumer should prefer their store, catalog, or Web site over another. Ideally, retailers should have several channels of distribution; store retailing should be balanced with online and catalog merchandising so that the customer has alternative ways to find merchandise. In retail stores, fashion marketing more specifically refers to the efforts to further those sales by means of advertising, publicity, special events, and visual merchandising.

This chapter deals with all aspects of retail fashion marketing, including market research, fashion leadership and image, visual merchandising, advertising, public relations, and special events. All these efforts tie into and complement each other. The methods used by retailers to market fashion vary considerably. Merchants must choose the approach best suited to their customers, the merchandise they carry, and the size of their business and budget.

Market Research

Whether setting up a new store or reevaluating an existing one, retailers study the types of people who live in the community, their lifestyles, and, ultimately, their shopping wants and needs. Massimo Ferragamo explained, "You can't take the customer for granted and just hope they come floating into the store. We want to know who they are, their likes and their dislikes."[1] As discussed in Chapters 2 and 4, retailers use telephone and online surveys, focus groups, feedback from sales associates, and point-of-sale (POS) data to study their customers.

Retailers analyze sales data on a store-by-store basis to uncover differences in customer buying habits. They issue their own credit cards to get even more precise information about their customers. All this information is entered into databases for use in store planning, merchandising, and marketing. Retailers develop *customer profile systems* that record the type, sizes, and frequency of merchandise purchased for each customer. They also use these databases to establish loyalty programs to reward good customers.

Retail Target Customers

Retail management decides which group of consumers it wants to reach and how it wants to reach them. The term *target market* describes the group of consumers the store wishes to attract. As discussed in Chapter 2, customers comprising a specific target group are within a general age range, have similar lifestyles, and, therefore, have similar needs and tastes. No retail store can be all things to all people; it must select one or a few groups of people to serve.

While specialty stores may aim at one market segment, a department store tries to appeal to several categories of target customers. Separate departments, areas, or floors are created for each category. Once retail executives determine their target market(s), they tailor the store's image, merchandise focus, and marketing efforts toward these consumers.

Fashion Leadership

Each store plays a role in fashion leadership according to the customer it wants to reach. Fashion leadership can be separated into three loosely defined categories:

- **Fashion-forward stores,** such as Bergdorf Goodman, Saks Fifth Avenue, Neiman Marcus, and Henri Bendel, seek leadership by carrying high-priced fashionable merchandise from around the world. These stores cater to the top 1 percent of the population, while Bloomingdale's and Nordstrom target the top 20 percent of the population. There are fewer of these stores because the percentage of customers who can afford their high prices is relatively small.

- **Mainstream retailers** identify with consumers who want fashion adaptations available to them at moderate and upper-moderate prices. Most of the department stores, such as Macy's and Dillard's, fall into this category, as do some specialty stores, such as Banana Republic and Gap.

- **Mass merchants** such as Wal-Mart and Target appeal to people who simply cannot or will not spend more money on their clothing. However, even at this price level, mass merchants find that they need a balance of fashionable and basic merchandise.

The Retailer's Image

Consumers are overwhelmed with so many choices, and it is often difficult for them to understand a store's message. It is important for a retailer to define its *image* clearly, the personality or character that it presents to the public. This image or uniqueness reflects its degree of fashion leadership and its market niche and, therefore, appeals to its target customers. Ralph Lauren said, "Retailers have to have a point of view. It's the most important thing for retailers to have an identity, a sense of who they are."[2]

In keeping with that image, retailers strive for a store atmosphere that is both a complementary background for merchandise and an inviting, fun, and entertaining environment for the customer. The store's merchandising, advertising, interior decoration, and customer services develop, maintain, and reflect that image and try to generate excitement about the merchandise to create a desire to buy.

Planning and Direction

The sales marketing director, fashion director, advertising and creative directors, visual merchandising director, merchandise managers, and buyers work together to plan and coordinate marketing strategies.

In small stores, a single person may direct all marketing activities with the help of outside consultants or agencies. In a large store, a marketing director may coordinate the joint efforts of advertising, special events, visual merchandising, public relations, and the fashion office. (Sometimes the fashion office is part of merchandising, and visual merchandising is part of store planning.) In large chains there may be a vice president to head each area.

■ A BERGDORF GOODMAN WINDOW FEATURING CELINE FASHIONS FROM PARIS, WITH THE VISUAL MERCHANDISER'S USUAL SENSE OF HUMOR. *(COURTESY OF BERGDORF GOODMAN, PHOTO BY ZEHAVI & CORDES)*

Buyers recommend plans for marketing activities in conjunction with their projected merchandise plans. The marketing director, fashion director, advertising and/or creative directors, visual merchandising director, merchandise managers, and buyers must agree on marketing strategies and how to reach their target market. At planning meetings, they discuss how to communicate fashion trends and important designer or brand promotions within the context of the store's image.

Stores schedule marketing activities for seasons and holidays throughout the retail calendar year as an integral part of the year's merchandising plan. Advertising and promotional events, such as holiday sales and customer appreciation weeks, are often scheduled up to a year ahead of time. In spite of all the scheduling, however, new promotions and other events can supersede all the best laid plans. For example, plans for scheduled activities could be cancelled in order to launch a new product and to react to new trends or the world situation. Marketing has to be flexible.

Visual Merchandising

The corporate visual merchandising director, store planning director, architects, regional creative directors, and individual store visual managers and designers create a store's visual image.

Visual merchandising, or visual presentation, is one means to communicate a store's fashion, value, and quality message to prospective customers. The purpose of visual merchandising is to entice the customer into the store, enhance the stores' image, effectively present the merchandise the store has to offer, and show the customer how to wear that merchandise and accessorize it. With increased competition, retailers are trying to create more exciting and aggressive presentations. They use a variety of methods, such as humor, shock, elegance, and minimalism, to get attention or enhance store image. As visual presentation is an opportunity to create uniqueness, each retailer has its own approach.

The Visual Merchandising Team   Visual merchandising is a team effort involving management, including the fashion director and the marketing director; store planners; merchandise managers and buyers; the visual merchandising director, designers, and staff; the sign shop; and individual department managers and sales associates. The actual presentation set-up is done by staff designers.

Store Planning

The building design plays an important part in establishing a store's image. Although building and renovations are managed by a separate *store planning division,* it is helpful to discuss them as a background to visual merchandising. A store's effectiveness and uniqueness lie in the retailer's ability to plan, create, and control the store's image in relation to the physical building. Store planning management must consider store image, location, architecture, and interior layout.

Store Location   The location of a store is very important in relation to its potential customers. *Demographic research* is done to determine what location would best attract target customers. Computerized site-selection programs and marketing consultants provide data on area population forecasts, descriptions of households by income, median age of market-area residents, and information about the competition.

Store Design Store architects have to create an environment that is conducive to both retail operations and consumers' shopping needs. They consider the exterior design, major entrances, the relationship of the building to the mall or surrounding stores, interior layout, and space planning. Many stores are developing flexible interiors with movable panels instead of permanent walls. Interior aesthetics must enhance merchandise and be in keeping with the store image.

In addition, department relationships, aisle space, and traffic patterns are considered to make the departments and merchandise accessible and to help customers to find what they want easily. To comply with the Americans with Disabilities Act, aisles must be wide enough for easy wheelchair access. An environment is created to make the store easy for customers to shop.

Renovations Many retailers are renovating existing stores, sometimes to reflect the characteristics of local communities and to increase market share. Many luxury retailers have been renovating to attract younger customers with a less intimidating and more accessible atmosphere, but in doing so, have lost their individuality and Old World charm. Renovation is a way to reposition a store, generate new traffic, and broaden the customer base without the expense of building a new store.

A NEW LOUIS VUITTON STORE IN TOKYO, JAPAN, IS AN EXAMPLE OF MODERN "INDUSTRIAL" STORE DESIGN. *(COURTESY OF LOUIS VUITTON, PARIS)*

Interior Environment The store's interior design and atmosphere should appeal to target customers. For example, to create a lavish environment, Neiman Marcus employs a full-time art curator to oversee its expansive art collection. Attracting the mature customer to a store or department with quality merchandise requires the creation of a warm, comfortable atmosphere. This may be achieved with wood paneling, comfortable seating, paintings, and furniture, such as those found in an elegant home. To appeal to overwhelmed baby boomers, merchandise might be presented in a simple, orderly environment with neatly folded merchandise, such as that found at the Gap. To attract teens, retailers employ graphics, humor, and music. Macy's, for example, launched teen shops with concrete floors, exposed steel tubing, rotating laser lights, media walls, and music videos to create a club atmosphere.

Seasonal Visual Merchandising

Visual merchandising managers, along with marketing and merchandising executives, make up a *seasonal calendar* indicating the dates on which specific merchandise is to be featured and the number and location of windows and interior displays that are to show the merchandise. Seasonal merchandising themes are planned up to a year in advance in conjunction with the seasons, other store promotions, and arrivals of new merchandise. In some cases, the theme may involve a tie-in with a vendor to introduce a new collection or brand. Planning a theme gives a focus to visual merchandising and a consistent look throughout the store.

The visual merchandising plan also includes a budget covering the cost of new mannequins or refurbishing existing ones, lighting, signage, props, special effects, posters and other background art, and the cost of paying staff needed to create and maintain the windows and interior displays.

Windows

The visual statements made in downtown store windows or at mall store entrances are the customers' first encounter

H&M USES BOTH CUTOUT FIGURES AND CONTEMPORARY MANNEQUINS IN THE WINDOW OF ITS KNIGHTSBRIDGE STORE IN LONDON. *(PHOTO BY GINI STEPHENS FRINGS)*

with the store and must effectively and correctly convey the store's image and fashion focus and entice shoppers into the store. As marketing executive Virginia Meyer commented, "Store windows attract, compel, and persuade. . . . A good presentation can and should stop you, get your attention, and maybe even make you smile. In a very broad sense, visual presentation not only helps to sell the merchandise itself, but the store as well."[3] In addition, as Gilbert Vanderweide, a visual merchandising director, observed, "Windows tell you what's going on inside the store."[4]

A window is a total environment, a complete statement on its own. Windows are usually the most dramatic of the store's visual statements. They can be humorous or theatrical. To attract attention, windows may feature animation, posters, cutouts, video art, dramatic lighting, holograms, or other special effects. Some stores use look-through windows to make the windows part of the total store environment.

Window Themes
Special event windows tie in to events and store promotions or convey the spirit of a holiday season. They create excitement and interest in visiting the store.

Fashion message windows feature a designer collection or the newest fashion trends and suggest ways to coordinate accessories. These windows are created to attract attention and coax customers to buy a new garment and/or accessory.

Interior Presentations

Customers are further exposed to fashion and accessory purchase suggestions by interior presentations that may be located near the entrance to the store, at major focal points, at entrances to each floor, or in departments. In urban stores, the focus is on the main floor. However, stores in shopping malls, which may have few or no windows, must capitalize on the wide store entrance that gives the passing shopper a sweeping view of the selling area, giving entry area displays great impact.

AN INTERIOR PRESENTATION AT FENWICK, LONDON. *(COURTESY OF FENWICK, LTD., PHOTO BY GINI STEPHENS FRINGS)*

Presentation areas positioned in front of each department or shop guide customers to that area. Different levels of interest are created on ledges, shelves, counters, platforms, or even hanging from the ceiling. Merchandise presentations may take the form of groups of multiple mannequins or single items, shown on a form or stand. Sportswear is usually shown in groups, whereas eveningwear may be shown individually.

Environments or *lifestyle presentations* feature appropriately dressed mannequins posed in lifelike situations. The environment is enhanced with accessories, props, and furniture to complement the featured merchandise. Lifestyle environments help customers to identify with the apparel and accessories presented. Also, by showing total wardrobing concepts, including accessories, they help to educate and entice the customer.

423

MAXSTUDIO●COM

CONTEMPORARY STYLIZED MANNEQUINS AT MACY'S, DESIGNED BY MIRA KALMAN. *(PHOTO BY GINI STEPHENS FRINGS, COURTESY OF MACY'S)*

Elements of Visual Merchandising

Enhancements The elements used to show or enhance the clothes on display include mannequins and other forms, vitrines, fixtures, ladders, poles, columns, platforms, tables or other furniture, boxes, paintings and other wall decoration, fabrics, banners, graphics (posters, counter cards), lighting effects, accessories, and other props. Most of all, visual merchandisers try to enhance merchandise with other merchandise. Details are very important; every viewpoint has to be considered.

Technology Retailers are using an increasing amount of video technology to show merchandise. Windows and departments may feature video presentations of fashion shows to add excitement and interest.

Mannequins Mannequins change with fashion trends and are made in the image of the current ideal of beauty. For elegant fashion, perfectly coiffed, traditional lifelike mannequins are preferred. However, they are very expensive to buy and maintain. To save money, many stores have replaced them with stylized mannequins.

Visual Merchandising in Multi-Unit Stores

Standards Manuals The corporate office sets standards for consistent visual merchandising. Standards manuals list exact specifications for all forms, fixtures, and props and their placement. Quarterly addenda update the standards as new ideas are implemented. Visual merchandising designers set up the presentations, and then sales associates may be trained to maintain these standards in each department.

Presentation Packages The corporate or central visual merchandising office may also create presentation packages for branch stores so that the entire group or chain will have the same look. Large presentation packages, including floor sets or *plan-o-grams* and digital photographs, are prepared at the flagship store and sent to other units to show them how to merchandise visually. Each retailer wants to have a total vision. This is easier to achieve in a private-label chain, such as Banana Republic or Ann Taylor, which has identical apparel and accessories in each store. It becomes more difficult to create a cohesive look for a multibrand retailer. They can set guidelines, but they have to be more flexible and allow customizing of packages for differences in various regions.

Telecommunications   Many stores are using teleconferencing to show actual visual presentations to other stores in their chain so that local visual artists will be able to replicate the presentations. They also use virtual computer mock-ups to share visual concepts with colleagues across the country via intranets.

Designer or Brand In-Store Shops

In the case of in-store designer or brand boutiques, the vendor has visual merchandising requirements for presenting its line of merchandise. Apparel designers want to make a unique statement or create an atmosphere to complement their clothing. In some cases, the manufacturer supplies the fixtures and/or other enhancements so that they are the same in every store. It is often difficult to reconcile the individuality of these shops with the store's own identity. Some are de-emphasizing in-store shops or eliminating them altogether. Still other stores try to merge the look of the designer boutique with the store's image.

■ A RICH, WARM, TRADITIONAL ENVIRONMENT CREATED IN BERGDORF GOODMAN'S MEN'S DEPARTMENT. *(COURTESY OF BERGDORF GOODMAN)*

Departments

Large stores are divided into departments and designer or brand shops by fashion category or lifestyle. Traditionally, the main selling area is reserved for cosmetics, jewelry, and accessories. The rest of the store is divided into groups of departments and shops that relate to one another by category or price range. Department location is considered, and some shops are given prime

CLOTHING FIXTURES
AT GIEVES &
HAWKES, SAVILE
ROW, LONDON.
*(COURTESY OF
GIEVES & HAWKES)*

location to attract attention. Destination departments, containing merchandise such as swimsuits, lingerie, or coats that customers seek because they are needed, can be in secondary locations. Retailers make an effort to drive foot traffic to the back merchandise walls of the store to prevent "dead zones."

Successful visual merchandising invites customers into a department. Visual merchandising must draw the customer to the department most suited to his or her lifestyle. There is no sign that says, "If you are age 38 to 50, live in the suburbs, and wear an average size 10, go to the Miss Macy department." Yet each department is merchandised with certain lifestyle statistics in mind. Visual environments, informational signing, and/or large lifestyle photographs on the walls help customers to find the department best suited to their size and tastes.

Stock is arranged in an orderly, attractive manner to contribute to the visual effect of the department and to help customers quickly find what they want. As popular apparel or accessories are sold, the department manager and sales staff need to rearrange the merchandise. Visual designers teach department staff members how to layer clothes on hangers, how to display folded merchandise, and how to arrange merchandise by color groups.

Fixtures In apparel departments, clothing is hung on fixtures that are arranged, usually in a grid pattern, to give access and a clear view of the department from every angle. Assortments may be displayed on *wall racks, rounders* (circular racks), *four-way* or *star fixtures* (with four arms), *T-shaped stands* (with two arms), *I-beams* (straight bars), or *collection fixtures* (with folded merchandise on shelves on one side and hanging clothes on the other). Assortment displays must permit customers to see an entire range of colors or styles in each size. To avoid visual monotony, the fixtures are usually mixed. Although wall fixtures utilize space well and rounders show off a color story, they are not the most desirable means of display because the customer is confronted with nothing but sleeves. On frontal projection fixtures, such as the four-way or the T-stand, the garments face outward so that the customer can see the fronts. The first hanger on a sportswear T-stand is usually an H-shaped hanger showing a coordinated outfit so that the customer can see how the various pieces work together. Fixtures are becoming more sophisticated, and many stores are also creating their own unique custom fixtures to fit in better with overall store design.

Folding and Stacking   Stores such as the Gap have made simple folding and stacking a popular and space-saving way to display merchandise. Store standards dictate placement of shelves or tables and how the merchandise should be folded and grouped. Many retailers have found that merchandise on tables is more accessible.

Accessories   Much more attention is being paid to visual merchandising of accessories. Traditionally located in the main selling area, some accessories are now available on apparel floors, too, so that customers can quickly accessorize their clothing purchases. Accessories can be shown in *vitrines* (glass cases), on shelves or tables, or on wall display racks. Stores must balance the salability of accessible, "open-sell" merchandise with the security and exclusivity of glass-case display.

Fashion Advertising

The advertising director, creative director, art director, writers, and layout artists work together to create retail advertising. They are often assisted by advertising agencies, especially in the area of broadcast.

The largest portion of the marketing budget in a retail store is normally allocated to advertising. *Advertising* involves the planning, writing, designing, and scheduling of paid announcements designed to attract customers' attention to a fashion product or event. Advertising uses wit, shock, elegance, celebrities, and other creative approaches to get attention.

Advertising is designed to reach specific target customers or potential customers. Therefore, advertising style must be altered to reach various types of consumers. To the contemporary customer, trendy clothes are sold with sex and sizzle; to the upwardly mobile professional, merchandise is presented in enhanced status images; to the family-oriented consumer, fashion is presented as a blend of fashion and value.

Kinds of Advertising

Stores use four basic types of advertising: image, special event, item, and promotional.

Image Advertising

Image advertising focuses on fashion image, event, fashion leadership, community goodwill, or a new or remodeled store. While it may show merchandise, the product is of secondary importance. The goal is to communicate the store image as a brand to build consumer confidence, promote community goodwill, create a mood, or create excitement about a new store. A variety of strategies, such as shock, controversy, humor, and celebrity models, are used to create a lasting impression. Even mass merchants try to create an image of great merchandise for less money.

Special Event Advertising

Special event advertising is a call to come to the store at a particular time for an event such as a personal appearance. Retailers are able to quantify the response to these ads by counting the people who attend and checking *point-of-sale* (POS) data during that time.

Item Advertising

Item advertising is created to sell merchandise. The goal of item advertising is sales as a direct result of an ad, but the results are difficult to track due to the combination of media used in one campaign. This type of advertising may be done as a cooperative arrangement between manufacturers and retailers.

Promotional Advertising

Promotional advertising is price directed. It might proclaim that a store has special values, or it might announce storewide sales or clearances. Some stores, such as Macy's, Old Navy, and Mervyn's, are more promotional than others and, therefore, do more promotional advertising. Most stores advertise promotional events, such as sales, customer appreciation weeks, and special buys.

Direct Response

To promote instant sales, retailers provide the means for direct response in all types of advertising. E-mail addresses and 800 numbers are provided in many advertisements to encourage immediate sales without a visit to the store.

Cooperative Advertising

Fiber producers, fabric producers, and apparel manufacturers often cooperate with retailers to pay for advertisements that feature their merchandise. Co-op allocations are based on a percentage of net sales to the retailer and may provide a large percentage of media and/or production costs. This additional money enables retailers to make ads larger or to run them more frequently. The resulting increased advertising volume may also help the retailer to qualify for a lower media rate. Many retailers would not be able to advertise merchandise without co-op money from vendors and producers.

Scheduling and Planning

An *advertising plan* is a guide for a specific period (such as a week, a quarter of the year, or a season) and for the amount of advertising that a store intends to do in that period. The advertising plan is based on past experience, present conditions, and future expectations. Ads are most often scheduled up to a year ahead of the selling season, whereas the actual content may be planned closer to the selling season to allow for immediate flexibility.

A *budget* is prepared, indicating the allocation of funds for advertising production and media. Advertising space in newspapers or time on radio or television must be contracted. A *production schedule*, or timetable, is developed detailing how and by whom the ad production is to be carried out in order to meet media deadlines and other requirements.

Media

In advertising, *media* is a general term used to cover all methods of transmitting a sales message. The media include newspapers, newspaper inserts, magazines, radio, television, outdoor boards, bus sides, bus shelters, urban train stations and kiosks, the Internet, and direct mail. Fashion advertisers are faced with an overwhelming abundance of media choices that are rapidly changing. Advertising department or agency media buyers must choose the medium or combination of media that is right for both product and type of customer. Each consumer group has unique tastes, ideas, and interests and consequently responds to different media. Media buyers must choose which particular radio or television station, newspaper, magazine, or other vehicle will reach the appropriate customer for specific merchandise. Where the ad is placed and how often the ad appears are as important as the ad itself.

Several ads are usually placed in different media to support each other and strengthen the campaign. Peter Connolly, executive vice president of marketing for Tommy Hilfiger, said, "Not everyone just reads magazines, or just watches TV or just looks at outdoor advertising. And they do different things at different times of the day. You really need to have a mix of media."[5] To balance the spot radio commercial aimed at the car commuter, the store might also place an ad covering the same material in the newspaper for bus and train commuters to read. Repetition and consistency make the advertising message memorable. The same ad heard at the same time every day on the radio, or a fashion ad every week on the same page in the newspaper, makes people keenly aware of the store brand, as well as the fashion message.

Newspapers

Newspaper advertisements, or *run-of-press* (ROP), are popular among most fashion retailers for the following reasons:

- They provide visual as well as verbal means of telling consumers what merchandise the company has to offer.
- They may be offered daily.
- Layouts, art, and copy are relatively easy to produce.
- Media costs are comparatively low.
- They provide a turnaround time from idea to appearance in as little as 48 hours.

Space and Positioning   Media buyers buy space in newspapers that reach the store's potential customers. Day after day, readers in specific geographical areas or trade groups are exposed to the company's fashion message. The retailer can buy a certain desirable position in the paper, such as the back page of the front section, on a contractual basis.

Supplements   The use of preprinted advertising, especially in magazine format inserted into newspapers, is a successful form of advertising for retailers. Many stores are using the glossy magazine format because, like a catalog, it has a longer "coffee table life" and can be zoned for any area of the country.

Vendors who contribute money toward the cost of supplements like the huge circulation and relatively low cost per thousand. Inserts are particularly cost-effective when the retailer has many branch stores in an area served by just one newspaper. Circulation may be anywhere from a million copies to many millions for stores spread over many states.

Magazines   Stores advertise in magazines that have target markets similar to their own. National retailers such as Saks Fifth Avenue regularly advertise in fashion magazines such as *Vogue* because they can benefit from national circulation. These ads are often image ads that build the retail name as a brand. To attract attention, some retailers pay for impact units of multiple pages, which may also give them premium positions within the magazine. Some retailers also preprint their ads on heavier stock so that they stand out when inserted in the magazine.

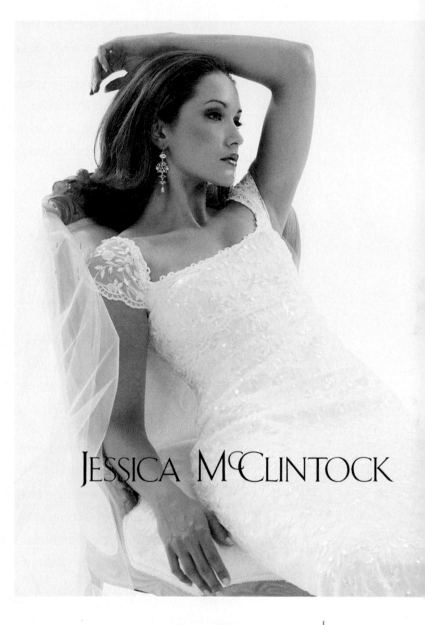

THIS JESSICA MCCLINTOCK BRIDAL AD APPEARED IN NATIONAL MAGAZINES. *(COURTESY OF JESSICA MCCLINTOCK)*

Some national magazines also have regional editions that carry pages of local store advertising. Retailers may also advertise in shelter or general-interest magazines to reach certain markets. Metro or regional magazines are used by stores to target customers in a specific area. There is a large proliferation of fashion, beauty and lifestyle titles to chose from, in addition to teen, general interest, and entertainment magazines.

To provide direct consumer response, some retailers insert pages of catalog-like advertisements into magazines. Frequently, inserts provide 800 numbers or information to facilitate online ordering. Other stores may use tear-out response cards inserted next to their ad in the magazine to pull traffic into the store and to track the success of the ad. Customers are requested to bring the cards to the store to exchange for a free gift or a gift with purchase.

T e l e v i s i o n   Television advertising is growing in popularity as the general public is watching more and reading less. The medium also offers the advantage of being able to show how clothing might fit into a real-life situation. However, advertising is hampered by consumers' opportunity to browse channels. Other major drawbacks to TV advertising are the costs of airtime and production.

Time Buys Purchased by media buyers, the cost of *airtime* is determined by the length of the commercial, the time of day and the day of the week it is to be shown, and the size of the audience. Prime time, the most expensive, is between 7:00 and 10:00 p.m. when the greatest number of adult viewers is watching. Airtime in a large city with a large viewing audience is much more expensive than airtime in a smaller city or town. Media selection is based on how successful stations are at reaching viewers as measured by subjective gross rating points.

Production A TV commercial might cost anywhere from $50,000 to $500,000 or more for a 30-second production. Commercials are usually contracted out to a broadcast agency. Production costs cover fees for the writer, producer, director, talent, and voice-over announcer; camera work; travel; location; editing; music; and expenses for wardrobe, props, lighting, film, and developing.

National Television   National television advertising is used by large national firms that sell and distribute apparel across the country and have large enough advertising budgets to pay for production and buy network television time. Sears, for example, used TV advertising in its "Softer Side of Sears" campaign to enhance its image. A network television show reaches millions of potential consumers throughout the country. Cable television shopping networks such as QVC and HSN provide an opportunity for direct sales response.

Retailers use actresses, actors, and music stars in their ads to appeal to the public and get attention. The Gap, for example, has used Madonna and Missy Elliott in its TV ads. Retailers also compete to dress the stars of TV shows to appeal to viewers.

R a d i o   Because viewers can see the fashion, television has an advantage over radio for apparel advertising. However, radio can make the listener aware of a store location, brand name, or timing of a particular sale. Peak radio listening hours, which cost more than other periods, are during drive time, the rush hours when commuters listen most to their car radios. Stations are selected for their target market appeal. Buyers might choose a rock station to reach teenagers versus an oldies, classical music, talk, or news-format station for baby boomers.

E-Commerce The multimedia capabilities of the Internet allow advertisers to combine graphics, text, sound, and moving images on banner ads, sold on a cost-per-click or click-through basis. However, retailers have to differentiate their ads because millions of Web sites are competing for attention. Retailers continually evaluate design elements of their Web sites, searching for the best presentation to engage consumer response. They use A/B and multivariate testing (showing alternative designs) and analytical software to measure each design's success.

When a consumer makes a purchase from an e-commerce site, the retailer obtains the customer's e-mail address. The retailer can then use that address for advertising, delivering messages about special promotions and products, and inviting the consumer to trunk shows, parties, and designer appearances. E-mail allows the retailer to be much more specific and tailor the message to the consumer's demographics and buying history.

Direct Mail Direct mail is an extremely popular and highly effective form of advertising because it is addressed to each individual customer. Direct mail has become especially important as retailers compete for market share. As discussed in Chapter 2, consumer profile databases, with information gleaned from purchases, can isolate specific groups of customers according to their

PAGES FROM AN ANN TAYLOR CATALOG. *(COURTESY OF ANN TAYLOR)*

433

buying habits, such as frequency of purchases, average dollar amount of purchases, and the exact departments where purchases were made. Stores are able to mail specific postcard ads to target audiences, such as mothers of small children, large-sized customers, or petite women. These cards advertise new merchandise, sales, and in-store events.

Statement enclosures are advertisements that are sent with monthly billings to charge customers, usually the retailer's best customers. They combine photographs, often provided by manufacturers, with order forms or 800 numbers.

Catalogs have become a tremendously popular form of advertising because of the shopping convenience they provide to working women, retirees, and those people living away from major metropolitan areas. Retailers may produce specialty catalogs, for shoes for example, in cooperation with vendors.

Store newsletters or magazines, such as Saks Fifth Avenue's *5* or Bloomingdale's *B*, are used by some retailers to give customers fashion trend information. These are not catalogs per se, but simply communicate a manufacturer's or store's merchandising image to customers. In addition, *look books* (image brochures), provided by manufacturers, are sometimes mailed or given out to customers in the store.

Outdoor Signing

Building-scapes, outdoor boards, train platforms, city or mall kiosks, buses, and bus shelters have been surprisingly successful vehicles for fashion advertising. Companies such as the Gap and Levi Strauss pioneered this method, which has grown into a very important medium. Some malls are trying out double-sided, moving triple-sided, and cylindrical kiosks that will carry large ads in the common areas of the malls and on the surrounding sidewalks.

The Advertising Department

Because they do so much advertising, some large retail stores have in-house advertising departments. The advertising director supervises three areas: art, copy, and production.

Art   The art department is responsible for *layouts*, the composition of all parts of the ad. Layouts can be made on computers using software programs such as QuarkXPress and Adobe Photoshop. Photographs are digitally scanned and incorporated into the layout with the copy, store name logo, and any other graphic art to complete the ad.

The use of photography is currently popular because its realistic qualities lend themselves to promotional or item advertising. Stylists assist the photographers by booking models, scouting for locations, acquiring or renting props, accessorizing, arranging for hair and makeup artists, and obtaining permits.

Copy   Copywriters produce the written description for advertisements. The good writer pictures the customer who is reading the ad and writes to him or her. Buyers give merchandise information, highlighting unique selling points, to the advertising department. Copy for fashion merchandise, which emphasizes an editorial fashion message, is quite different from sales copy, which stresses value or unique features.

Traffic   The traffic department is responsible for the flow of projects (graphics, illustrations, photographs, and copy) among the store, service bureaus (which output electronic files into proofs), engravers, printers, newspapers, and radio and television stations. The finished ad can be transmitted electronically via E-mail or satellite to newspapers or printers around the world or posted to an FTP site (file transfer protocol, a third-party Internet site) for downloading.

■ ADVERTISING DESIGNER ROB CORDER DISCUSSES AN AD PROOF WITH PEGGI DAVIS. *(PHOTO BY GINI STEPHENS FRINGS)*

Advertising Agencies

Many retailers, even those with their own in-house staffs, use outside advertising agencies to handle special projects and media buys or for concept development. Agencies also help when there is a heavy workload or for a special project, such as a magazine format insert. Stores also use agencies as a cost-effective way of producing timely advertising without having to retain an expensive in-house staff. Payment may be handled on a project fee basis or as an annual contract.

In large agencies, groups of people are assigned to particular accounts under the direction of an account executive, who acts as a liaison between the agency and the client. Agencies also use freelance copywriters, illustrators, and production artists to help them with heavy workloads and special projects. The drawback to using agencies is that it takes time for them to become acquainted with the store's point of view. On the other hand, an agency can offer objective ideas about how to project the store's image and broaden its customer base.

Publicity

Publicity is usually handled by the directors of fashion, special events, and/or public relations.

Publicity is the spreading of information about people, special events, or newsworthy topics through various communications media. There are no media costs for publicity, but for that very reason, it is difficult to obtain. It is also considered more meaningful than advertising because it is the result of an editor's choice, rather than a paid announcement. Media editors choose the material they use based on what information may highlight fashion trends or be of interest to the community. They also decide how, when, and where the message will be used. Publicity helps to promote the sale of fashion merchandise by making a style, manufacturer, retailer, trend, or other aspect of fashion better known to the public.

Publicity Campaigns

Retailers hope to bring their names to the public eye by calling attention to newsworthy developments in their stores. They may create events such as fashion shows or celebrity personal appearances to obtain publicity. Stores provide the media with information about such events or topics in the hope that the media will publicize them. A publicity campaign may be handled by the public relations office, the fashion office, or an agency.

As part of a publicity campaign, a *press package* consisting of a news release and photographs is prepared to send to media editors. A *news release* is a written statement of the important facts about a designer, fashion trends, or a coming event and is often accompanied by glossy photographs, which may be provided by vendors. These are usually sent by e-mail to the media.

To achieve maximum benefits from publicity, public relations or fashion office staff direct publicity to the media whose audience would be most interested in their message. News may be approached from various angles to ensure that each medium gets a unique story.

Newspaper fashion editors usually use the publicity releases and photos sent by retailers to write their articles. Paying advertisers are becoming more demanding of the media in their requests for publicity.

Word of Mouth Spreading information about a product or store to friends is the best kind of free publicity. If people have a great experience shopping, find what they want to buy, and have good customer service, they are keen to spread the word. It may not be the usual media outlet, but it is one of the most influential forms of publicity.

Special Events

Corporate directors of special events and/or public relations, regional managers, and store coordinators and their staffs need superb organizational skills to carry out a wide variety of special events.

Consumers are shopping more in stores that offer a special experience. *Special events* are designed to give customers a specific time and reason to come into a store or to create goodwill. They represent an attempt to replace or renew the personal customer contact that has been lost in many large stores. When well planned and executed, special events can enhance the store's identity, build customer loyalty, and create a sense of community spirit. The retail store as "theater" also caters to the many consumers who enjoy shopping as entertainment.

Most special events are planned and carried out by a special events director and, in the case of a fashion show, in cooperation with the fashion director. In a large flagship store, separate offices may handle each function: fashion, public relations, and special events. In a branch or smaller store, all three functions may be managed out of one office. The special events office must schedule events in conjunction with the advertising department to support store strategies. The special events office schedules designer guest appearances in the store and sends press releases and invitations for both in-store and community events.

Events may include the launch of a new brand or product, wardrobing clinics, fashion seminars, and/or fashion shows. Many events are tied in to conventions or community and charity events, such as charity fashion shows. Events may also be co-sponsored by vendors or magazines. Henri Bendel, for example, often partners with a fashion magazine for an in-store event. The magazine provides access to its database for invitations, the store pays for advertising, and the editor may make a personal appearance.[6] Retailers are constantly looking for new ways to make the shopping experience exciting.

Fashion Shows

Fashion shows are special events that communicate a fashion story. These are usually co-sponsored by a vendor. The selection and organization of the fashions and model bookings may be done by the fashion office, whereas invitations and other arrangements may be handled by the special events department. There are four possible ways to organize these presentations: as formal shows, department shows, designer trunk shows, or informal modeling.

Formal fashion shows take a great deal of advance planning involving booking models and fittings and arranging for a runway, scenery, lighting, microphones, music, seating, and assistants. Clothes are generally grouped according to styling, color, or other visual criteria. Models and music are selected to complement the clothes and set a mood. A designer-centered event can cost from $10,000 to $500,000. Because of their cost, these shows are usually reserved for charity events, and stores look for co-sponsors to share costs. For an Italian designer collection show, for example, costs could be split among the store, the designers, and the Italian Trade Commission.

Designer trunk shows are done in cooperation with a single vendor and are a popular way to sell expensive collections. Invitations are sent to the best customers according to customer profile databases. The designer or a representative travels from store to store with the collection, which is usually shown on models in the designer collections department. Customers get to see the entire collection unedited by a buyer and may order from the samples in their size. Some designers and retailers do 50 percent of their total business through trunk shows.

Department fashion shows, on a much smaller scale, are produced in-store to generate immediate sales. Usually, a platform is set up directly in the department that carries the clothes.

Informal fashion shows are the easiest to produce. A few models walk through the store showing the fashions they are wearing to customers who are shopping or having lunch in the store's restaurant. The models can take their time, and customers enjoy asking them questions. This is often done in conjunction with a trunk show.

Marketing Evaluation

All the people involved in marketing—directors, managers, coordinators, artists, writers, designers, and buyers—evaluate the effectiveness of their efforts to plan for the future.

At the end of an event or advertising campaign, sales are analyzed and the campaign's effectiveness is evaluated. Advertising can be evaluated by sales volume, but it is very difficult to analyze sales results in relation to visual merchandising or special events. For example, unless a fashion show actually takes place in a department and people stay afterward to make purchases, how can the value of the event be measured? Some retailers are experimenting with electronic systems that track people window shopping and entering and exiting the store. Management usually evaluates the effectiveness of a campaign as a whole and makes recommendations for the next year.

SUMMARY

RETAIL FASHION MARKETING ENCOMPASSES ALL THE ACTIVITIES NEEDED TO SELL MER-
CHANDISE, PARTICULARLY VISUAL MERCHANDISING, ADVERTISING, PUBLICITY, AND
SPECIAL EVENTS. RETAILERS USE MARKET RESEARCH TO DEFINE TARGET CUSTOMERS
TO MATCH THEIR IMAGE AND ROLE IN FASHION LEADERSHIP. VISUAL MERCHANDISING
IS THE IN-STORE PRESENTATION OF A MERCHANDISING MESSAGE. ADVERTISING IS THE
USE OF PAID TIME OR SPACE IN MEDIA, SUCH AS TELEVISION, RADIO, NEWSPAPERS,
MAGAZINES, AND DIRECT MAIL. THERE ARE NO MEDIA COSTS FOR PUBLICITY, BUT ANY
MATERIAL USED IS THE CHOICE OF THE MEDIA EDITORS. SPECIAL EVENTS SUCH AS
FASHION SHOWS DRAW PEOPLE INTO THE STORE AND CREATE COMMUNITY GOOD-
WILL. MARKETING EFFORTS ARE COORDINATED WITH BUYERS IN EACH MERCHANDIS-
ING AREA. MARKETING HAS ITS LIMITS, HOWEVER; IT IS ULTIMATELY THE CONSUMER
WHO ACCEPTS OR REJECTS FASHION.

Terms and Concepts

Briefly define and discuss the following terms and concepts:

1. Marketing
2. Advertising
3. Publicity
4. Special events
5. Visual merchandising
6. Lifestyle displays
7. Image advertising
8. Merchandise or promotional advertising
9. Media
10. Radio and television spots
11. Direct-mail advertising
12. Cooperative advertising
13. Layouts
14. Copy
15. Ad production
16. Advertising agencies
17. Press release
18. Editorial credits
19. Inserts
20. Display packages
21. Standards manuals
22. Trunk shows

Questions for Review

1. What is the purpose of fashion marketing?
2. Explain the difference between advertising and publicity.
3. Discuss the types of media used in advertising and give examples of how each type reaches target groups.
4. Explain how cooperative advertising works.
5. Why is it essential for a buyer to be involved in marketing?
6. Why is visual merchandising important?
7. Explain how a store's fashion image is conveyed to consumer groups.

Projects for Additional Learning

1. Analyze the advertising campaign of a large chain store. Search through newspapers covering a one-month period and clip the store's advertisements. Are they always on the same page of the newspaper? Do they have a high-fashion image or popular appeal? Do they show the merchandise to good advantage? Do you think that the advertisements are effective? What other types of advertisement do they use? Magazines? Television? Billboards? Web sites?

2. Attend a special event at a local store. What is the purpose of the event? To draw people into the store? To create community goodwill? Describe the event and add your own photographs, if possible. Do you think the event was carried out successfully?

3. Visit a local department or specialty store and evaluate its visual merchandising. Do the displays carry out a theme throughout the store? Describe the decor and display techniques, both in windows and in interiors. Is lighting used effectively? Is merchandise attractively arranged? Do you feel that the total image of the store successfully relates to the merchandise offered?

Notes

1 As quoted in "Ferragamo Today," *Women's Wear Daily*, February 11, 1991, p. 7.

2 As quoted in "Lauren at 25," *Women's Wear Daily*, January 15, 1992, p. 7.

3 Virginia Meyer, vice president, marketing, Cato Corporation, interview, June 2, 2000.

4 Gilbert Vanderweide, interview, April 29, 2003.

5 Peter Connolly, executive vice president, marketing, Tommy Hilfiger, as quoted in "Media Maze," *Women's Wear Daily,* May 28, 1999, p. 6.

6 Teril Turner, marketing director, Henri Bendel, interview, April 28, 2003.

ROWS OF LACE AND SHEER RUFFLES REPEAT THROUGHOUT
THIS EXQUISITE GOWN BY OSCAR DE LA RENTA.
(COURTESY OF OSCAR DE LA RENTA, PHOTO BY DAN LECCA)

APPENDIX

Career Guidelines

How will you fit into the fashion business? Choosing a career—not just a job, but work that you will enjoy and build on for the future—is one of the most important decisions of your life. This book will help you to make that decision.

This appendix tries to give a realistic picture of fashion career possibilities. It surveys job opportunities in textiles, fashion design, marketing, production, retailing, and promotion. In planning for your career, you should first understand yourself, your talents, and your ambitions. You should then apply these abilities and interests to the field that offers you the best employment opportunities.

The Textile Industry

If you enjoy working with fabrics, you will find several possibilities for interesting employment in the textile industry. A wide variety of skilled and talented people is needed, including artists to create new designs, scientists to develop fibers and finishes, and marketing specialists to market fibers to mills and fabrics to manufacturers.

Fiber and Fabric Development

Research   Science and chemical engineering students may be interested in a career in the laboratories of the large chemical corporations that develop new fibers or at fabric companies or fiber associations that experiment with new treatments and finishes for fabrics.

Textile Design and Merchandising   Textile designers and stylists need a combination of specialized art and technical training. For print design, designers have to be able to apply their skills to two-dimensional design, yet with the understanding that the end use will be in a three-dimensional garment. Fabric stylists have to know the technical aspects of fiber and fabric production so that they are able to create interesting new blends of yarns, as well as new knit and woven constructions. Computer knowledge is also essential.

Marketing

For the outgoing person, marketing provides a variety of interesting careers, including product development, public relations, advertising, and sales. Marketers work with both manufacturing and retail customers. Entry-level junior sales representatives can advance to sales, account, and marketing manager positions.

Training and Advancement

Some marketing and styling positions are available in New York City and Los Angeles. Sales representatives may be located wherever there are manufacturing centers. Otherwise, textile production is done in the South, the Los Angeles area, or overseas. It is important to try to get some experience through a summer job or an internship before graduation. A skilled and experienced person can later advance to a management position.

Apparel Manufacturing

Career opportunities for young people entering the apparel industry vary widely. The most interesting aspect of manufacturing is its diversification. Each person within the company must know something about all areas so that the company operations run harmoniously. Each area of manufacturing, product development, sourcing, and marketing calls for different abilities.

Design and Merchandising

The prospective fashion designer must be artistically creative, yet understand the technical and marketing aspects of the business as well. Besides being responsible for the original ideas for garments, designers must have a thorough knowledge of fabrics and garment construction, be able to make patterns, have a thorough knowledge of CAD systems, and be enthusiastic.

Fashion designing is highly competitive. The better prepared aspiring designers are, the broader their opportunities will be. Graduation from a good design college is essential. Upon graduation, the budding designer might start as an assistant in the design or sample department. Any entry-level job will provide useful experience.

Merchandising offers the opportunity to mesh business acumen with a design sense. Retailing experience is very helpful as background training. The merchandiser works with the designer so that the line will fit into company financial and sales goals. The merchandiser usually starts as an assistant merchandiser.

If you are interested in fashion design or merchandising, take every opportunity to observe and analyze new trends at fashion shows, visit manufacturers, and learn to objectively critique apparel and accessories that you see in stores.

Patternmaking

Patternmakers have an important function in the production process: they translate the design idea into a pattern for the actual garment. A patternmaker must understand basic mathematics, have a good eye for proportion and line, and be able to achieve a perfect fit.

To prepare for a career as a patternmaker, you must learn how to drape a pattern on a dress form, draft perfect flat patterns, and create patterns by computer. Your first job may be as an assistant or as a sample cutter or pattern grader.

445

Sourcing

Sourcing managers must plan and monitor production to ensure that delivery dates are met. Therefore, a well-organized person is best suited for a career in fashion production. Besides technical knowledge, a sourcing manager needs to travel to the countries where factories are located.

Marketing

If you are outgoing and enjoy working with people, you may like marketing, a career field that involves working directly with customers. You might begin a career as a showroom assistant or junior sales representative in New York or Los Angeles. A college education in fashion merchandising or marketing and retailing experience are recommended.

Training and Advancement

For the most part, fashion manufacturers are located in large cities. Students interested in design positions must be prepared, in most cases, to relocate to New York, Los Angeles, or wherever there is an opening.

As most manufacturers do not have training programs, you may try to arrange an unpaid internship with a manufacturer on your own. Your ingenuity will be appreciated. Initially, it is a good idea to get experience in a small company where you can observe the entire operation. Later, opportunities for advancement are better in large companies that promote from within. Designer Karl Lagerfeld said, "If you are good at what you do, you will be noticed."[1]

Retailing

Approximately one of every eight employed persons in the United States works in retailing in some capacity. It is absolutely necessary to get retail selling experience while getting a college education. Also, knowledge of computer information and financial systems is essential. Unless a person has dealt with customers and heard their comments, questions, and complaints, he or she cannot understand the basis of retailing. Retailers also look for graduates with leadership ability. Working part-time as a salesperson at a store near your school or during the holidays, in the summer, on Saturdays, or after school may provide your initial opportunity and experience.

A few large stores offer summer internship programs for college students, which are excellent opportunities for experience. An internship gives the college student a better chance at employment after graduation. Because most stores do not offer this program, you may need to ask permission to work as an intern without pay. Creating this kind of situation for yourself demonstrates your motivation and initiative. Use this time to ask questions and learn as much as you can about all aspects of running the store; think of it as free education.

A college degree or junior college diploma is necessary for a retail management career. Retailers like the creative thinking of the merchandising majors as well as the business skills of the retailing majors. Many students are also getting MBA degrees to round out their education and give them an edge in the job market.

Training

After college graduation, a fortunate few are able to get into a retail management training program at large stores such as Macy's. A typical program consists of work experience in a variety of departments and formal classes conducted by senior executives and training department personnel, some via computer conferencing. Training programs are followed by the opportunity to become an executive.

Large stores usually have two main tracks to management: through the buying line (merchandising) or through the store line (operations). Most department stores' training programs combine both tracks, providing a well-rounded experience. Every store has its unique organization structure and job opportunities.

Buying–Line or Merchandising Track   After a training program, the first executive position is that of assistant buyer, who spends much of his or her time maintaining sales and inventory records.

With experience, the assistant may become an associate or single-vendor buyer and, later, a buyer or a planner-distributor. A buyer might advance to the position of group buyer, divisional merchandise manager, or general merchandise manager. The general merchandise manager is part of senior management and sets merchandising policies for the entire store.

Store–Line Track The second career track in retailing is in store-line operations. The department manager is responsible for having the goods on the selling floor, keeping current records of stock, and, in a branch store, ordering replenishments of stock from the main store. This person needs a background in sales and management training. The department manager is the role model for sales staff and the liaison among sales associates, customers, and buyers.

The department manager may advance to section manager, floor manager, assistant store manager, operations manager, or manager of a branch store. The operations manager oversees building maintenance, overhead, receiving, and the movement of goods within the store. The store manager is responsible for merchandising, sales, employees, and the general success of the store.

Alternate Training Most stores now offer flexible career paths from the merchandising track to the operations track and back again. For example, a trainee may begin work as a sales associate, then as an assistant department manager, assistant buyer, department manager, associate buyer, and so on. Able performers from both merchandising and operations might successfully work their way up to senior management. Senior management is responsible for the administration and organization of the store, establishing store policies and controlling operations. These managers need a solid background in the ranks of lower management as support.

Marketing

Fashion marketing is another creative career. Fashion marketers communicate a fashion message to the public to boost sales.

Copywriters

Copywriters work on advertising and publicity for all levels of the industry. They may work directly for producers, manufacturers, and retailers or for agencies. Fashion writers and editors also work for trade and consumer fashion publications. The job requires a college journalism major and some experience, perhaps on a college newspaper.

Artists

Artists design advertising and catalog layouts and/or direct photo shoots. They might work for the in-house advertising department or for advertising agencies. Their artistic skills must be technically perfect. Naturally, advertising or graphic design training is necessary. Fluency with computer design programs is mandatory.

Visual Merchandising Designers

Visual merchandising designers decorate store windows and arrange interior presentations of merchandise to attract customers. Advancement opportunities include positions as store design managers and corporate design directors. A college art or merchandising major is a prerequisite.

Special Events Director

Imagination, ingenuity, and organizational skills are needed to create special events. A fashion merchandising degree and experience in staging shows or running school publicity events is a good background.

Finding a Job

Research

After determining how your interests and abilities fit into the fashion business, you should investigate the companies that could be prospective employers. There are many different types of companies, both large and small. The advantage of working for a large company is that there is usually opportunity for promotion. In a small company, you can more easily learn every phase of the business.

Read about companies that interest you. Many large corporations have Web sites. While most just offer shopping, some such as www.lizclaiborne.com and www.hm.com (H&M) give interesting corporate and career information. Fashion and business libraries have directories such as *Standard & Poor's Register of Corporations* that list addresses and information on national and international companies. You can also try Switchboard.com to find a company's address and phone number. You can write or call these companies to ask for annual reports or for other available information.

Meet professionals at lectures, fashion shows, Fashion Group meetings, and career seminars. Interview them at their offices for class projects. Continually read trade periodicals to keep abreast of industry news so that you will be able to answer questions intelligently at an interview. You should know as much about the company as your interviewer!

Preparations for an Interview

Graduating students often feel defeated before they start. However, it is necessary to be persistent and work at getting a job—prospective employers admire people with drive and enthusiasm. Tommy Hilfiger said, "Young people entering the business need both drive and persistence."[2]

Résumé   First, you need a *résumé* listing the appropriate highlights of your education, experience, and activities. List only the courses, experience, and activities that relate directly to your chosen career. Part-time or summer fashion retailing experience is very important.

Your résumé should be typed on a computer and printed. The professional look of your résumé should demonstrate your knowledge of visual presentation, as well as your familiarity with computers.

Each résumé must be accompanied by a *letter of introduction,* asking for an interview and stating where you can be reached by phone and e-mail, your job objective, and the reasons you want to work for the company.

You may need to send out as many as 100 résumés to land a job, but don't be discouraged; this is normal. If the company asks for *recommendation letters,* then you need to have a list of teachers and professionals who may be contacted.

Be sure to follow up the letter and résumé with phone calls, or your letters may be ignored. Try to get interviews even if there are no positions open with the excuse that you want to ask them some questions about their company. Most often, an applicant's enthusiasm and persistence can convince an employer that the applicant would be an asset to the company.

Portfolio   If you are seeking a creative position, you will need a portfolio in addition to a résumé. The portfolio should look professional, exhibiting only the best examples of your work. Include any projects that won awards or prizes. A design major might include sketches of new ideas (simple technical sketches on graph paper are fine) with fabric swatches and 8- by 10-inch photographs of completed garments worn by professional-looking models.

The Interview

When you finally have obtained an interview, make the most of it. Each interview is good practice for the next one. In the fashion industry, attitude is immensely important. You need to show a prospective employer that you have a true passion for the business.

A professional appearance is absolutely essential for a job interview in the fashion field. You are making a visual statement of what you know about fashion and about your own self-perception.

Your fashion and company research will be useful during the interview. Make sure you keep reading *Women's Wear Daily* or *Daily News Record (DNR)* so that you are acquainted with the latest news in the industry.

The interviewer may ask questions such as "Why do you want to become a buyer (designer, etc.)?" and "Why do you want to work for this company?" Obviously, without proper research, you could not specifically answer these questions. You should also be prepared to ask interesting questions that show your interest in the job or the company. The fashion industry looks for sharp, focused minds.

No matter what your training or college major, companies will be looking for the following:

- Good skills learned in college and on the job
- A well-developed résumé
- A professional-looking portfolio (in design or communications)
- A fashionable, professional appearance
- The ability to express oneself clearly (except possibly for technical positions)
- A pleasant personality and a positive attitude to demonstrate that you will get along with your colleagues
- Enthusiasm, self-motivation, and a high energy level
- Awareness and an eagerness to learn
- A willingness to take responsibility

The First Job

Your first job after school or college should be considered an *apprenticeship,* a period of learning on the job. If your employer has no training program, try to set up your own apprenticeship or internship so that you can move around and learn all aspects of the business. You may want to try to set up an unpaid internship during a summer vacation. Try to learn as much as possible. Think of your first job as a free education. Never stop learning and your career will always be rewarding. Odile Laugier, former vice president of design at Adrienne Vittadini, once said, "I've been here 13 years and I'm still learning."[3]

The important thing is to obtain experience. You should then demonstrate how efficient and talented you are by doing a good job. Companies are always looking for responsible people to promote to better positions. If you are not promoted, at least you have gained experience for moving on to something else. Contacts that you make on the job will be valuable later. For example, fabric sales representatives often hear of job openings with apparel manufacturers and spread the word.

Be flexible and pleasant with your coworkers. A little humor and diplomacy go a long way toward promoting positive working relationships. Changes in fashion make the business exciting, but the creative people involved make it even more interesting.

Students often talk of opening their own businesses after graduation, and it seems that working for oneself would be easy. However, most small-company failures are caused by lack of experience. Before opening your own business, get as much experience as possible, both in a large company and in a successful small one to see how they are run. Working for yourself is actually more difficult than working for someone else because you must be self-disciplined. There are rewards, of course, for those who have ambition and creativity and are willing to work long and hard.

If you want to move up in the fashion field, give your education, training, and work all the effort and enthusiasm you can. Make the most of each situation. You get out of life what you put into it. Best wishes for a successful and rewarding career.

Preparations for a Job Interview

1. Write your résumé. Include information on education, awards, experience, and interests that relate directly to your chosen field.

2. What fashion career do you think would bring you the greatest satisfaction? List the positive and negative aspects of this career in two columns on a sheet of paper.

Analyze why you think you will do well and be happy in this career. What positive attributes do you have that you could bring to the job? How is your education preparing you? How will you enter the field, and what are your advancement expectations?

3. If you are a design or communication major, outline what you plan to include in your portfolio. Ask your teachers to help you to select your best work. Develop an overall graphic theme for your portfolio.

4. Arrange to interview a professional in your chosen field (designer, retailer, sales representative, or other). Ask about all aspects of the job. What does he or she like and not like about it? What makes it interesting? How did he or she start out and advance? What valuable advice can this professional give you? College interviews and contacts often lead to jobs.

5. Research a company that interests you on the Web. Write to them for an annual report or other information that might be available. Also check the Web for articles about the company. Read the material and make notes of important information that you need to remember for an interview.

Notes

1 Karl Lagerfeld, quoted in "The Designer Fallout," *Women's Wear Daily,* July 1, 2002, p. 7.

2 Tommy Hilfiger, designer, interview September 1994.

3 Odile Laugier, former vice president of design at Adrienne Vittadini, interview, April 30,1992.

Fashion Industry Terminology

Learning the terminology of the fashion industry is an important part of a fashion education. By using correct terminology, you show that you are familiar with the business. Many fashion terms are from the French language because France has long been the capital of fashion innovation. For further clarification, check the index and refer to the text to see how the term was used.

accessories   Articles such as jewelry, scarves, hats, handbags, and shoes, worn or carried to complete a fashion look.

acetate   A man-made fiber of cellulose chains.

acrylic   A man-made fiber made of long-chain synthetic polymer.

advertising   Any paid message in the media used to increase sales.

advertising director   The person in charge of the personnel and activities of the advertising department.

alta moda   The Italian couture.

apparel   Clothing, not necessarily fashionable.

apparel industry   The manufacturers, jobbers, and contractors engaged in the manufacture of clothing (also called the garment business, the needle trades, the rag trade).

artisans   People who do skilled work with their hands.

atelier (ah-tel-yay')   The French term for designer workshop. Ateliers are classified as *flou* (for soft dressmaking) or *tailleur* (for tailoring suits and coats).

automatic replenishment   A store allows a manufacturer to restock basics without a purchase order; continuous open-to-buy.

balance   Visual weight in design.

balance of trade   The difference in value between a country's exports and imports.

base goods   The solid fabric used as the basis for a group of sportswear.

bespoke   The English term for made-to-measure men's suits.

bodies   Garment silhouettes.

book inventory   The dollar value of inventory, as stated in accounting records.

boutique (boo-teek')   The French word for a small shop with unusual clothing and atmosphere.

branch store   A store owned and operated by a parent store; generally located in a suburban area under the name of the parent store.

brand name   A trade name that identifies a certain product made by a particular producer

brand portfolio   A wide range of products under one brand

brick and click   An industry buzz word to describe retail stores that have Web sites.

bridge fashion   The style and price range between designer and better.

buyer   A merchandising executive responsible for planning, buying, and selling merchandise.

buying office   An independent or store-owned office that is located at a market center and buys for one chain or for many stores.

buying plan   A general description of the types and quantities of merchandise that a buyer expects to purchase for delivery within a specific period.

chain store organization   A group of stores that sell essentially the same merchandise and are centrally owned, operated, and merchandised.

classic   A fashion that is long-lasting.

classification   An assortment of related merchandise grouped together within a department of a store.

collection   A group of garments designed for a specific season.

commissionaire (ko-me-see-ohn-air')   A store representative in a foreign city.

commodity merchandise   Standard, basic merchandise.

computer-aided design (CAD)   An integrated computer system that aids in designing and patternmaking; used in both textile and apparel design.

computer-aided manufacturing (CAM)   Computerized patternmaking, grading, marker making, cutting, and sewing machines.

computer-integrated manufacturing (CIM)   A computer connection to integrate computer-aided design and manufacturing systems.

consumer   Someone who buys merchandise.

consumer demand   The effect consumers have on the marketplace.

consumer obsolescence   The rejection of merchandise in favor of something newer, even though the "old" still has utility.

contemporary styling   Sophisticated, updated styling; originally designed for the age group that grew out of juniors.

contractor   An independent producer who does the sewing (sometimes the cutting) for manufacturers; an outside shop.

converter   A textile producer that buys greige goods from mills and dyes, prints, and finishes it before selling it to a manufacturer.

cooperative advertising   Advertising costs shared by a textile producer, a manufacturer, and/or a retailer.

coordinated sportswear   Sportswear designed to mix and match interchangeably.

corporate selling   Selling management to management, without the use of sales representatives.

cotton   A vegetable fiber from the boll of the cotton plant; the world's major textile fiber.

couture (koo-tour')   The French word for dressmaking; applied to fashion businesses that make clothes to order.

croquis   Original paintings of textile designs.

custom-made   Apparel made to a customer's special order; cut and fitted to individual measurements; the opposite of ready-to-wear.

cutter   The person who cuts material during the manufacturing process.

cutting order   A company order to cut and produce a specific quantity of garments.

cut-to-order   A cutting order based on orders received.

cut-to-stock   A cutting order based on projected sales estimates.

database marketing   Using information about customers gathered from credit cards and other sources to plan marketing strategies.

demographics   Statistical studies of population characteristics such as birthrate, age distribution, or income.

department store   General merchandise store, including apparel, household goods, and furniture.

designer   A person employed to create ideas for garments or accessories in the fashion industry.

design resource   Any resource from which a designer obtains ideas; can be trade newspapers, design reports, fashion magazines, museums, historic-costume books, nature, theater, films, fabrics, and so on.

design services   Reports and ideas available by subscription to manufacturers and retailers; predictives.

direct-mail advertising   Any printed advertising distributed directly to specific prospects by mail.

discount retailing   Low-margin retailing; retailers able to offer inexpensive merchandise by buying in quantity and keeping operating costs low.

discretionary income   Income left after basic necessities have been paid for.

disposable income   Income minus taxes; a person's purchasing power.

divisional merchandise manager   A person in the middle management of a retail store; the executive responsible for the merchandising activities of a related group of departments; supervises buyers and assistants.

doors   Fashion industry jargon for the number of retail stores at which a particular product is sold.

draping   A method of making a pattern by draping fabric on a dress form.

electronic data interchange (EDI)   The exchange of business data between two parties by means of computers.

electronic retailing   Shop-by-computer retailing.

elements of design   Design ingredients: color, fabric, line, and shape.

ergonomics   The development of workplace equipment and standards designed to improve the safety, health, and efficiency of workers.

e-tailing   An industry buzzword signifying electronic retailing.

ethnic or folk costume   Traditional national or regional dress; often inspiration for fashion design.

fabrication   The selection of the appropriate fabric for a garment.

factory outlet stores   Stores that sell manufacturers' overruns directly to consumers.

fad   A short-lived fashion.

fashion   The prevailing style of any given time; implies change in style.

fashion cycle   Fashion change; refers to the introduction, acceptance, and decline of a fashion.

fashion director   The fashion expert of an organization who works with designers or buyers to form the fashion image of the company.

fashion editor   The head fashion reporter at a magazine or newspaper who analyzes the fashion scene and interprets it for readers.

fashion forecast   A prediction of fashion trends.

Fashion Group International   An international association of professional women in the fashion business; founded in 1931.

fashion merchandising   The planning required to have the right fashion merchandise available in the proper quantities and place at the right time and priced to meet consumer demand.

fashion press   Reporters of fashion news for magazines and newspapers.

fashion retailing   The business of buying fashion merchandise from a variety of resources and reselling it to ultimate consumers at a convenient location or via the Internet, television, or catalogs.

fashion trends   New directions in fashion styling.

Fédération Française de la Couture   French couture trade association composed of three main membership classifications (each called a Chambre Syndicale) and associated groups of manufacturers and artisans.

457

fibers   Natural or synthetic strands from which yarns are made.

filament   A continuous strand of fiber.

finishing   The last treatments given to fabrics; the final handwork or final touches done to a garment.

first pattern   The trial pattern made in the design department for the sample garment.

flagship store   The largest and most representative store in a chain organization.

flax   A natural fiber made from the stem of the flax plant and used to make linen.

flexible manufacturing   A combination of methods used to make manufacturing most effective.

floor-ready standards   A requirement by retailers that manufacturers have merchandise preticketed and on hangers, ready to be put on the selling floor.

franchising   The selling by a manufacturer of the rights to retail its merchandise.

full-fashioned knits   Knit garments with pieces shaped on the knitting machine.

furnishings   Men's clothing category, including shirts, accessories, and item sportswear.

garment packages   Apparel manufacturing done by textile producers.

generic name   The family name given to each type of fiber.

globalization   The trend for manufacturers and retailers (and all businesses) to expand throughout the world.

grading   The process of making a sample size pattern larger or smaller to make up a complete size range.

greige goods (gray goods)   Unbleached, unfinished fabrics bought by converters.

gross margin   The difference in dollars between net sales and the net cost of merchandise during a given period.

haute couture   Dressmaking houses in Paris that belong to the Chambre Syndicale of the Fédération Française de la Couture and meet the criteria to be on its Couture-Creation list (see Chapter 8).

imports   Goods made in a foreign country.

issue plan   Production schedule.

items   Garments sold on an individual basis.

Jacquard loom (jah-kard')   A loom invented by Joseph Jacquard in France in 1801 that weaves an elaborate pattern (such as damask, brocade, or tapestry) by controlling each warp thread separately.

jersey   The basic construction of all weft knits.

jobber   A middleman between the producer and the commercial consumer.

junior   A size range of female apparel; in odd numbers, 3 to 15.

knockoff   A copy of a higher-priced style.

leased department   Within a store, a department run by an outside company.

licensing   A manufacturer is given permission to use a designer's name or designs in return for a fee or a percentage of sales.

line   An apparel manufacturer's collection of styles; also, visual direction in a design caused by seams, details, or trimming.

line buying   Buying lines from reliable manufacturers.

linen   A vegetable fiber derived from the woody stalk of the flax plant.

loss leader   An item sold at less than the regular wholesale price for the purpose of attracting retail buyers to other merchandise.

lyocell   A new type of solvent-spun cellulosic fiber.

MAGIC   Men's Apparel Guild in California, the world's largest men's apparel trade show, held each February and August in Las Vegas.

man-made fibers   Fibers made from cellulose in plants or from chemicals derived from petroleum, gas, and coal.

markdown   The difference between the original retail price and a reduced price.

marker   A pattern layout put on top of the fabric for the cutter to follow.

market   A group of potential customers, or the place, area, or time at which buyers and sellers meet to transact business.

market driven   Responding to market or consumer needs.

marketing   The process of planning, promoting, and selling merchandise.

marketing chain   The flow of product development, production, and distribution from concept to consumer.

markup   The difference between cost price and selling price.

mass production   The production of merchandise in quantity.

media   Means of communication: newspapers, magazines, radio, TV, direct mail, and the web.

merchandise plan   A budget or projection of the sales goals of a merchandise classification, a department, or an entire store for a certain period, including the amount of stock required to achieve those sales.

merchandise representatives
Consultants trained by manufacturers to train sales associates in the stores.

misses   A size range in feminine apparel in even numbers, 6 to 16.

mixed-use shopping centers   Shopping centers that have retail stores, restaurants, residential units, and perhaps movie theaters and office space.

moda pronta   Italian ready-to-wear.

mode or **moda**   A synonym for fashion; used mainly in Europe.

modular manufacturing   A manufacturing method utilizing a small group of people who work together to produce a finished garment.

national brands   Manufacturers' brands that are available nationwide.

natural fibers   Fibers that nature provides, including cotton, wool, silk, flax, and ramie.

North American Free Trade Agreement (NAFTA)   A trade agreement, implemented in 1994, creating a free market between the United States, Canada, and Mexico.

nylon   A durable man-made fiber made of long-chain synthetic polymer.

off-price   A price lower than the original wholesale price or below the normal wholesale price; usually special purchases, closeouts, or overruns.

offshore assembly   Fabric purchased and cut in the United States, but sent to Mexico or the Caribbean countries for sewing.

open-to-buy   The amount of money a buyer can spend on merchandise to be delivered within a given period, minus the amount allocated to merchandise on order.

operations   Steps in production; activities of running a business.

overhead   The costs of operating a store or company.

overlock machine   A machine with needle and loopers that creates an edge finish while sewing a seam.

performance fabrics   High-tech durable and flexible fabrics that use interesting fiber blends and finishes.

physical inventory   A physical count of stock on hand.

piece goods   The trade term for fabrics.

piecework   The rate by which many factory workers are paid.

plant capacity   The quantity of garments that can be made in a factory at a certain time.

polyester   The most widely used man-made fiber, made of long-chain synthetic polymer.

Première Vision   French for "first look"; the name of the international fabric trade fair held each March and October in Paris.

prêt-à-porter   French for ready-to-wear; literally, "ready to carry."

preticketing   Ticketing of merchandise by the manufacturer so that the merchandise is ready for prompt distribution at the retail store.

price line   A specific price point at which an assortment of merchandise is offered for sale.

price range   The range between the lowest and highest price lines carried.

private label   A store's own brand.

product data management systems (PDM)   Computer software systems used to organize and edit a line.

production pattern   The final pattern made to company size standards.

progressive-bundle system   A manufacturing system requiring one operator to repeat one assembly task and grouping operators to follow the order of production; section work.

promotion   Products offered at special prices.

promotional stores   Stores that stress special sales, bargains, and price reductions.

proportion   The relation of one part of a design to another; an important principle of garment design.

psychographics   The use of psychological, sociological, and anthropological factors to construct market segments.

publicity   Messages about a company and its policies, personnel, activities, or services used without payment to the media.

quotas   A means of regulating exports and imports.

ramie   A natural vegetable fiber derived from the stem of a nettlelike shrub.

rayon   A man-made fiber made from rejuvenated cellulose.

ready-to-wear   Apparel that is mass-produced (opposite of custom-made).

receiving   The area of the store where packages are opened, checked, and marked.

repeat   The repetition of a print in fabric design.

resource   A term used by retailers for a manufacturer, wholesaler, vendor, or distributor; or a source for ideas or information.

retailing   The business of buying goods at wholesale markets or producing goods and selling them to the ultimate consumer.

retail price   The wholesale price plus a markup covering the retailer's operating costs and a profit.

sales per square foot   The amount sold per square foot of store floor space; a measure of productivity.

sample   The trial garment or prototype.

sample cut   A 3- to 10-yard length of fabric used by the design department to make up a trial sample garment.

Savile Row   A street in London famous for its men's tailors.

selected distribution   Limiting the number of stores that may buy merchandise to maintain exclusivity.

sell-through   The ability of a line to sell regularly and steadily at full price.

Seventh Avenue   The main street of New York City's garment district; the term is used to represent the whole district.

showroom   A place where sales representatives or management show a line of merchandise to potential buyers; called *salon de presentations* in France.

silhouette   The outline of a garment.

silk   The only natural fiber in filament form; obtained from the cocoons spun by silkworms.

soft goods   Fashion and textile merchandise.

sourcing   The worldwide search for the best available fabrics or garment production at the best price.

spandex   A man-made fiber of long-chain synthetic polymer comprised of stretchable segmented polyurethane; known best by the DuPont brand name of Lycra.

special events   Activities set up to attract customers to a selling place.

specialty store   A retail establishment that handles narrow categories of goods, such as men's apparel, women's apparel, or shoes.

spinning   The process of extruding and hardening man-made fibers; the process of drawing and twisting staple fibers together into yarn or thread.

standard allowed hours   The time it takes to complete each assembly operation or garment.

stock turnover   The number of times a store's merchandise stock is sold and replaced in a given period.

store image   The character or personality that a store presents to the public.

style   Certain characteristics that distinguish a garment from other garments; a particular look in fashion.

style ranges   Categories of styles that appeal to different consumers.

stylist   A fashion expert; generally selects colors, prints, or styles for presentation or prepares fashion merchandise for photographic presentation in an advertisement or catalog.

tanning   The process of transforming animal skins into leather.

target market   The group of consumers to whom a producer, manufacturer, or retailer aims products, services, and advertising.

textile fabrics   Cloth made from textile fibers by weaving, knitting, felting, crocheting, laminating, or bonding.

texture   The surface interest in a fabric.

texturing   The process of crimping or otherwise modifying continuous filament yarn to increase cover, abrasion resistance, warmth, resiliency, and moisture absorption or to provide a different surface texture.

toile (twahl)   The French word for a muslin sample garment.

trademark   A company's individual registered mark and name for a product.

trend buying   When retailers buy from new resources to obtain fashion newness.

trendsetter   A designer or fashion leader who sets a fashion direction that others follow.

trunk show   A show of designer clothes that moves from store to store, often accompanied by a personal appearance by the designer.

unit control   Systems for recording the number of units of merchandise bought, sold, in stock, or on order.

UNITE   Union of Needletrades, Industrial and Textile Employees.

unit production systems (UPS)   A production system using computer-guided conveyors to move garments automatically from one work station to the next; automatic progressive-bundle system.

universal product codes (UPC)   Standard codes that identify style, color, size, price, fabrication, and vendor on price tags and enable this information to be fed through an electronic data interchange system.

variants   Modifications of basic generic fiber compositions for special applications.

vendor   A seller, resource, manufacturer, or supplier.

vendor analysis   Statistical analysis of the profits made on merchandise from individual vendors.

vertical integration   The joining of companies at different levels of production and marketing, such as a fiber producer with a fabric mill.

virtual showrooms   Showing a manufacturer's line on the Internet.

visual merchandising   Making merchandise visually attractive to customers.

warp knitting   Knitting fabric in loops running vertically.

weaving   The process of forming fabric by interlacing yarns on looms.

weft knitting   Knitting fabric in loops horizontally or in a circle.

wholesale market   A market where commercial consumers buy from producers.

wholesale price   The price paid by commercial consumers for supplies and products.

Women's Wear Daily   Trade publication of the women's fashion industry.

wool   A natural fiber derived from animal fleece.

World Trade Organization (WTO)   The governing body for international trade, which replaced GATT.

yarn   A continuous thread produced by twisting or spinning fibers together.

Index